# VISIONS OF
# THE EAST

# VISIONS OF THE EAST

## Orientalism in Film

Edited by
Matthew Bernstein and Gaylyn Studlar

I.B.Tauris Publishers
LONDON • NEW YORK

Published in 1997 by
I.B.Tauris and Co Ltd
Victoria House
Bloomsbury Square
London WCIB 4DZ

ISBN 1 86064 304 3 Hardback
ISBN 1 86064 305 1 Paperback

Manufactured in the United States of America

To the memory of my grandparents:
Jean and Jack Polly
Julia and Samuel Bernstein

To Grace and Constance Goodwin

# Contents

viii   Contents

# Acknowledgments

This volume emerged from our shared research interests in the history of Orientalism in American film and from our discovery of an exciting body of work being carried on by our colleagues in film studies. We first thank the contributors for their fine work and their many kinds of cooperation in assembling this anthology. For additional help, we thank Professor Lester Friedman of Syracuse University, Professor Ivan Karp of Emory University, Mr. Jean-Marcel Humbert of the Musée du Louvre, and Priscilla Vail Caldwell of Martha Parrish and James Reinish, Inc., of New York. In addition, at Rutgers University Press we thank Victoria Haire for her expert copyediting; Marilyn Campbell for her eminently sensible guidance through the logistics of preparing this volume; and Leslie Mitchner for her constant and enthusiastic support and her extremely sage counsel, which helped to give this book its final shape.

Matthew Bernstein thanks Natalie, Justin, and Adam Bernstein for their unflagging support and high spirits. Gaylyn Studlar thanks her husband, Tommy Haslett, for his humor, his compassion, and his constant understanding.

# VISIONS OF
# THE EAST

Matthew Bernstein

# Introduction

Michael Rogin observed that every "transformative moment" in American film history, such as D. W. Griffith's *The Birth of a Nation* (1915), *The Jazz Singer* (1927), and *Gone With the Wind* (1939), used African-American characters "to stand for something besides themselves."[1] A similar claim could be made for the use of North African and Asian cultures in many of the American cinema's most popular or ideologically resonant films.

Consider: *The Sheik* (1921), which inaugurated the stardom of Rudolph Valentino, also initiated the most durable conventions for portraying the passionate and reckless actions a desert can inspire a westerner to take; *Shanghai Express* (1932), with its densely stylized re-creation of civil war China, fetishized star Marlene Dietrich as a disillusioned Western woman whose corruption thrived in the East; *Casablanca* (1942), often regarded as the quintessential Hollywood statement of individualism and community values, is set in a locale where "life is cheap";[2] the big-budget productions of *Cleopatra* (the 1963 version [Figure 1] the second most expensive film Hollywood has ever produced—Kevin Costner's 1995 *Waterworld* is first), which portray the East's most powerful female ruler; and *Raiders of the Lost Ark* (1981), which inaugurated the injection of theme-park-ride aesthetics into Hollywood filmmaking as its brave white hero fought the villains of North Africa.

This is obviously no coincidence, and three years before *Raiders of the Lost Ark*, Edward Said broached a concept that film critics could use to explain what the exotic settings and characters in these films

Figure 1. *Cleopatra* (1963). Photo courtesy of the Wisconsin Center for Film and Theater Research, Madison.

"stand for."[3] *Orientalism* describes a strand of colonialist discourse in the ideological arsenal of Western nations—most notably Great Britain, France, and the United States—for representing the colonies and cultures of North Africa and the "Middle East" (and eventually, those of Asia). It is a way of perceiving these areas that has been supported, justified, and reinforced by the West's colonialist and imperialist ventures. Most generally, Orientalism is a distinctive means of representing race, nationality, and Otherness.

In defining Orientalism, Said used the term *discourse* in Michel Foucault's sense, to refer to a body of texts that can construct social realities as individuals experience them. "The Orient," Said wrote, "was almost a European invention, and had been since antiquity a place of romance, exotic beings, haunting memories and landscapes, remarkable experiences."[4] Orientalism was an example of what Said called "imaginative geography," a social construct that coincides in many ways with the colonialist ideologies that prevailed in the 1800s, the peak of the British and French empires. But Orientalism is distinguished from colonialist discourse in part by its initial focus on North Africa and the eastern Mediterranean and more significantly by its basis in the historical threat that Islamic culture represented to western Europe. For the Ottoman Empire's very existence had cast Islam in Western eyes as a symbol of "terror, devastation, the demonic" wreaked by "hordes of hated barbarians";[5] Orientalism served to control and domesticate such a fearful yet fascinating prospect.

Since Said published *Orientalism*, cultural theorists and critics have pointed out that the regime of knowledge that Orientalism encompasses—structured around a basic dichotomy between East and West, and Other and Self—shares an ontological norm (white Western culture) with constructions of race, ethnicity, and sexual orientation in Western culture. And feminist critics have extended Said's model most dramatically and usefully by showing how Orientalism is imbricated with the construction of gender.[6] As Said summarized this work in 1985:

> We can now see that Orientalism is a praxis of the same sort, albeit in different territories, as male gender dominance, or patriarchy, in metropolitan societies: the Orient was routinely described as feminine, its riches as fertile, its main symbols the sensual woman, the harem and the despotic—but curiously attractive—ruler. Moreover, Orientals like Victorian housewives were confined to silence and to unlimited enriching production.[7]

Said's focus was primarily on academic writing, travel literature, and novels as embodiments of Western ideology.[8] But of course the imaginative geography of post-Enlightenment, scholarly Orientalism, and all its gender and racial correlaries were readily transformed into the materials of narrative and visual art: translations of the *Arabian Nights* (into French by Antoine Galland in 1703; into English most notably by Sir Richard Burton in the late 1800s); travel diaries by explorers and major European novelists; and French academic *Orientalist* painting.[9]

Western narrative and ethnographic cinemas of the late nineteenth and twentieth centuries inherited the narrative and visual traditions, as well as the cultural assumptions, on which Orientalism was based, and filmmakers discovered how popular Orientalism could be.[10] In Hollywood, for example, the representations of the East—typically titillating viewers with the thrills of unbridled passion, miscegenation, and wild adventure in a raw and natural setting—were by the teens conventional constructions. Every year between 1910 and 1920, film distributors handled between four and six romantic and action melodramas set in North Africa. During World War I, the producer of a diffuse war documentary found that the portion entitled *With Lawrence in Arabia* proved the most popular, and showed it for nine weeks in New York's Madison Square Garden.[11] In 1917 and 1918 Fox produced a writing/directing team's screen versions of *Aladdin and His Lamp* and *Ali Baba and the Forty Thieves*, both of which were acted by children.

The year 1920 saw the first screen adaptation of *Kismet*, starring stage actor Otis Skinner.

Most decisively of all for the cinema, Serge Diaghilev's Ballets Russes, with its staging of *Cléopatra*, *Thamar*, and *Schéhérazade*, which toured in the United States in the teens, contributed decisively to the mise-en-scène of Orientalist cinema. Douglas Fairbanks's 1924 *Thief of Bagdad* would consolidate many of the narrative and visual conventions that *Arabian Nights* films would follow, as *The Sheik* would do for romantic melodramas in exotic settings.[12]

By 1927, Paramount's *She's a Sheik* mounted an over-the-top parody of the studio-produced Orientalist film, showing half-Spanish, half-Arabian Bebe Daniels, herself the product of miscegenation, doggedly pursuing intermarriage with white, Christian, Foreign Legion captain Richard Arlen; outdueling Arab villain William Powell; and finally defeating Powell's marauders by having American itinerant moviemen project footage of an Arabian horde charging toward the camera (a literal illustration of Said's notion of Western projections of the East). By the year of *She's a Sheik*, even sturdy Western stars Tom Mix and Hoot Gibson had done their cowboy stuff in North Africa.[13] European feature films, after the travelogues of the Lumière Brothers and the Orientalist fictions of Georges Méliès, proved equally fascinated with the Orient: Jacques Feyder's *L'Atlantide* (1921) explored the lost world of Atlantis; Joe May's German serials exploited the exotic through their Indian settings; and Ernst Lubitsch specialized in epic tales of ancient empires and obsessions from *Eyes of the Mummy* (1916) through *The Loves of the Pharaoh* (1922). Orientalism would continue to infiltrate new genres and film series as the decades progressed, turning up in the exotic background to films noir like *The Maltese Falcon* (1941) and *Chinatown* (1974) and informing spy thrillers like the James Bond series.[14]

Yet Orientalism remains an equally pervasive term in the vocabulary of contemporary Western filmmaking. It is evidenced in the desert settings and Nazi-Arab villains of *Raiders of the Lost Ark*, the Chinatown mobsters of *The Year of the Dragon* (1985), the villains of *Jewel of the Nile* (1985), the street urchins of *Aladdin* (1992), the power-mad leader of the Crimson Jihad in *True Lies* (1994), the terrorists in *Executive Decision* (1996), and even the absurd scenarios of American cops beating up Arab dictators and terrorists in *The Naked Gun* (1988).

In *Orientalism*, Said expressed the hope that additional studies of other aspects of the phenomenon would follow his own,[15] and indeed cultural critics and theorists have taken up Orientalism as an intriguing and compelling paradigm for the representation of race, ethnicity, and gender in the media and particularly in film (as the select bibliography at the back of this book attests).

The essays collected in *Visions of the East* elaborate upon Said's initial frame work and insights from a variety of standpoints that incorporate more recent developments in the study of colonialist and postcolonialist cultures. The contributors to this volume draw upon feminist analysis, genre criticism, psychoanalytic interpretation, and political history; they see Orientalism in film as expressions of colonialist and imperialist cultures; as reworking time-honored genre conventions and psychoanalytic scenarios; as allegories of contemporary politics; as a means for subcultures to rework mainstream films; and as an ideological and aesthetic link between film, literature, theater, and dance. One point of divergence from Said's approach, it should be noted, is that most of the essays in this volume do not take the representation of Islam as an explicit point of departure; but Islam figures strongly in many of the analyses of particular films.

Ella Shohat's "Gender and Culture of Empire: Toward a Feminist Ethnography of the Cinema" is a detailed, suggestive, and comprehensive overview of the phenomenon of Orientalism in Western cinema. Building on her work in *Israeli Cinema: East/West and the Politics of Representation* (1989), Shohat in this essay persuasively shows how colonialist and patriarchal ideologies inform and mutually support each other in the genres and subgenres of the Orientalist, narrative film. Drawing on feminist perspectives, she outlines a variety of narrative conventions, rhetorical tropes, and iconography that inform the Orientalist film (such as the "Prospero complex" and the "dark continent" metaphor), all of which apotheosize the white Western explorer in "virginal" foreign landscapes. Shohat stresses how the social pressures that resulted in Hollywood's self-censorship compelled filmmakers to exoticize and eroticize the Third World (including Latin America) in a fantasy structure that evades proper Western courtship customs by offering visions of rape and polygamy. Shohat's insights are enhanced by her attention to the visual conventions of the Orientalist film and the counterexamples she adduces of Third World filmmaking that represent the East/West relationship differently.

Shohat's analysis applies to a broad range of films over a century of filmmaking, and many of the other essays in this volume draw upon her insights. Although the articles could be read in chronological order—insofar as they touch on nearly every decade in film history and blend a variety of analytical approaches—we have grouped them from two standpoints: the ways in which Orientalist texts relate to their historical moment and/or generic formulas; and the centrality of Orientalism to national cinemas, film styles, and film movements.

The five essays in the first half of *Visions of the East* stress the role of historical and generic contexts in specifying the logic and meanings of Orientalist texts from different periods. Robert Stam and Louise Spence noted that the advent of cinema occurred at the height of western European imperialism and colonialist ventures.[16] Antonia Lant's essay elaborates on this observation and undertakes in effect an archaeology of Orientalist film. She focuses not on the content of specific films but on a dense and rich nexus of associations in European culture between viewing projected images in darkened theaters and the experience of visiting ancient burial sites in Egypt. Such analogies in critical discourse were voluminous and varied: the cinematic creation and projection of images in times and persons past were likened to the preservation of dead kings and queens in underground tombs, and the cinema as a new form of writing was described as a form of hieroglyphics. Lant argues that Egypt held special resonance in Victorian culture as a gateway to the East, thus partaking of both Eastern and Western cultures, much in the way the theater marked a gateway from the concerns of industrial life to the fantasies of projected images. "Egypt," Lant writes, "and what it came to mean . . . provided a means of explaining, legitimating, but above all conceptualizing the new motion picture medium." In this light, she notes, André Bazin's celebrated discussion in the 1940s of the mummy complex recodified an already well established analogy.

Gaylyn Studlar's essay also contextualizes orientalism, but her focus is on American cinema of the teens and twenties, and the pertinent contexts in her discussion are dance performance and women's fan magazines. Studlar seeks to answer the question of why Hollywood's Orientalism had such a strong appeal to women viewers. She argues that prior analyses of individual films—finding masochistic pleasures for women in the fantasies of rape that appear in *The Sheik*, or stressing the consumerist indulgence in luxurious possessions of Cecil B. DeMille films—may be too reductive in seeing everywhere the repressive workings of patriarchal ideology. Instead, Studlar argues that modern dance—as evidenced in both the Ballets Russes and the performances of the Denishawn troupe—provided Hollywood with a powerful model for visualizing Orientalism (and gave the movies connotations of high-art respectability). Studlar further suggests that dance performers and performance styles in films—most apparently in the appearance of the vamps, the Cleopatras, and the Salomes—presented a self-assertive, exhibitionist "orientalized female" who temporarily blurred the boundaries of gender, ethnicity, and race.

Where Studlar discusses trends in modern dance and filmmaking cycles of the teens and twenties, Adrienne McLean focuses specifically on Hollywood gay choreographer Jack Cole. Like Studlar, McLean argues that dance styles provided choreographers and performers with the means and the space "to reorganize and reconceptualize standard binary gender roles," but here the liberating aspects of modern dance are extended to gay culture. Cole as a Western male was aligned with the oppressive strategies of Orientalism, but Cole as a gay male was at the same time a member of an oppressed and marginalized subculture. McLean illustrates the dynamic by which Cole choreographed Orientalist dance by first comparing Cole's work with that of his mentors, the prominent American dancers Ruth St. Denis and Ted Shawn, and the ways they approached the dance styles of other cultures. McLean then proceeds to analyze selected dance numbers choreographed by Cole from *Kismet* (1955), *On the Riveria* (1951), and the "Diamonds are a Girl's Best Friend" sequence in *Gentlemen Prefer Blondes* (1952). In addition to highlighting the singular contribution of one of Hollywood's most successful choreographers, McLean's essay broaches broader questions about the representation of foreign cultures, since the Orientalist elements of Cole's dance numbers were not necessarily performed within an Orientalist mise-en-scène.

McLean's essay, like Shohat's, demonstrates how Orientalism was incorporated into preexisting film genres such as the musical. Perhaps no other genre has proven so receptive to Orientalism as the melodrama. Where other critics have addressed miscegenation and the *romantic* melodrama,[17] Marina Heung focuses on race and gender relations in the familial variant of the genre, which she terms "the family romance of Orientalism." Heung shows how the narrative structure of the ever-popular *Madame Butterfly* story (which is the basis for the English musical hit *Miss Saigon*) reworks Freud's concept of the family romance, the child's fantasy of having other, more aristocratic parents. In *Madame Butterfly*, this scenario is transformed into the "ennobling" maternal melodrama of self-sacrificing Asian mothers who give up their children to "superior" Western couples.[18]

One benefit of stressing the generic context in an analysis such as Heung's is that it enables the critic to chart how the representation of subordinated cultures changes over time. Heung observes that the *Madame Butterfly* scenario has irresistible appeal because it soothes the cultural trauma that partly defines the postcolonial (and in the United States, the post–Vietnam War) period. She examines the 1992 winner of the Academy Award for Best Foreign Film, France's *Indochine*, in which the "classic" character configurations of the Orientalist family romance are inverted. Heung argues that in *Indochine* "a critique of colonialism is conveyed through the depiction of aberrant familial and sexual relationships." The aberrations orbit around the colonialist

heroine Eliane (Catherine Deneuve), and here the figure of woman becomes analogous to the position in which McLean locates Jack Cole—
oppressed within Western male culture and yet oppressing as a member
of that culture. In *Indochine*, Eliane's placement and characterization
allow the film's critical stance toward colonialism simultaneously to
uphold repressive gender and racial politics.[19]

Alan Nadel also charts the shifts over time in character configurations within a narrative formula. But he focuses specifically on the
Orientalist "Thief of Bagdad" and "Aladdin" variants. His intriguing
essay on Disney's *Aladdin*, the company's top-grossing film to 1992, situates the film in its most relevant political contexts. Nadel explores how
the constant shifts in identity and authority in the Disney film echo
U.S. foreign policy makers' shifting perceptions of different nations,
regimes, and leaders in the Muslim world.[20] Within this scheme, the
genie's omnipotence comes to represent the dual potential for good or
ill associated with nuclear power since the late 1940s. And the genie's
own transformative talents, powered by the improvisational pastiches
served up by Robin Williams, serve to cement the associations between
"A Whole New World," George Bush's "New World Order" that was alleged to follow the Gulf War against Iraq, and the Orientalist tourism
project that informs the logic of Disney's Epcot Center.

Disney's representations of entire cultures in theme parks and films
are an imperialist gesture, bespeaking the omniscience and omnipres-
ence of a great power. The essays on national cinemas in the second
half of *Visions of the East* stress the imperial foundation of Orientalism,
and follow broadly Said's methods of studying Orientalism: "as a dynamic exchange between individual authors and the large political concerns shaped by the three great empires—British, French, American—in
whose intellectual and imaginative territory the writing was produced."[21]

The first three essays demonstrate how central orientalism has been
to France's *cinéma colonial* of the 1930s. Charles O'Brien's overview
stresses the diversity of genres the cinéma colonial embraced, and the
ways in which strict binary oppositions between West and East are
undermined in several films. O'Brien draws on the work of Michel de
Certeau, who in his discussion of travel literature—one of the primary
objects of Said's original study—distinguished between the representation of a disembodied, abstracted "place" that can be mapped and conquered in service of an imperialist impulse on the one hand; and that
of an experienced, prerational "space" that cannot be so easily classified. O'Brien argues that cinéma colonial films manifested an analogous oscillation between "neutral" observation of—and engaged
participation in—an alien culture. O'Brien finds evidence of this dichotomy in portions of Julien Duvivier's *Pépé le Moko* (1936) and other

major films of the period, which often feature segments, actions, and shots that cannot be integrated smoothly into their overall classic style. The ideology of Orientalism, in France or any other Western nation, was, as O'Brien stresses, hardly confined to the fiction film; ethnographic films replicate Orientalism with all the prestige and authority that science can muster. Dudley Andrew explores the extremely popular, highly celebrated, and often neglected (in English) ethnographic films and docudramas of Léon Poirier in the 1920s and 1930s such as *La Croisière noire* (1926) and *L'Appel du silence* (1936). Andrew shows how these films appropriate the mysterious North African landscape in the service of a spiritual quest to reaffirm French national identity. To these works Andrew opposes in dialectical fashion the "documents" movement of the surrealists that Luis Buñuel represented in the 1920s and 1930s, which featured a predilection for "obtuse" facts—like the various shots and sequences O'Brien singles out in his essay—that refuse to surrender to an individual's projects and preconceptions. The most celebrated example of such facts for Andrew is the way in which the Hurdinos in Buñuel's *Las Hurdes* (1932) complicate any complacent definition of what it means to be human. But, Andrew argues, the antagonistic trends in filmmaking, represented by Poirier on the one hand and the surrealists on the other, share an attraction to the inexplicable and the sublime that often undergirds colonializing desire. This desire was articulated in the surrealists' fetishization of blood and suffering in the female body, and in Poirier's romanticization and femininization of the enigmatic, African "dark continent."

Sketching in the troubled and unstable tenor of French society in the 1930s, Janice Morgan provides an illuminating look at the gender, national, and class politics of *Pépé le Moko* (1936), undoubtedly the best-known product of the cinéma colonial in English-speaking countries. Morgan stresses how Jean Gabin's breakthrough role of Pépé, fetishized by adoring camerawork, is twice doubled in the film—with the Arab police officer Slimane, who like Pépé has dual affinities as a figure of exile; and with Gaby, the entrancing Parisian who grew up in Pépé's working-class district and reminds him of his irretrievably lost Parisian identity. Morgan places the Casbah as an integral element of the film's ideology. Labyrinthlike, it is an analogue to Pépé's unconscious desires that entrap him, and at the same time it is likened to the female body as an alluring and alien geography. Morgan further demonstrates how Pépé's existentialist crisis and failure to escape held a special resonance for French men in the 1930s. It would be interesting, in this regard, to trace out how the Hollywood remakes of *Pépé le Moko* (*Algiers* in 1938 and *Casbah* in 1948) modify these meanings; clearly, it was precisely such metaphors for the Casbah that postcolonial works such as Gilles Pontecorvo's *The Battle of Algiers* (1966) would reverse.[22]

Great Britain boasted an equally multifaceted Orientalist cinema, ranging from such films as the documentaries of the John Grierson unit in the 1930s to Michael Powell and Emeric Pressburger's *Black Narcissus* (1947) and various adaptations of the works of Rudyard Kipling and E. M. Forster. It is here represented by Gabriel Pascal's 1946 version of George Bernard Shaw's *Caesar and Cleopatra*, a film Mary Hamer notes was intended by its producers "as Britain's challenge to the United States for command of the postwar film audience." Hamer begins by noting that "Europeans have used Cleopatra as a way of contemplating what authority looks like when it is lodged in a woman's body and of containing the alarm engendered by that prospect, always presented at a distance." Situating *Caesar and Cleopatra* in relation to Shaw's personal biography (as a colonized Irishman who wrote the play shortly after agreeing to an unconsummated marriage), and to Great Britain's burgeoning rule over Egypt both when Shaw wrote the play and when the film was produced, Hamer analyzes the film's reproduction of psychoanalytic object relations as the rational, conquering Caesar comes face-to-face with the voiceless sphinx and the limits of his own masculinity. As in the cinéma colonial, we see here how a British Orientalist film of the classical era often undercuts the terms of its own colonialist ideology.

If *Caesar and Cleopatra* shows us the British adaptation of an Irish playwright's work under the guidance of a Hungarian émigré, the American 1940 adaptation of Somerset Maugham's short story "The Letter" provides us with a case of transatlantic adaptation that helps us identify the contours of classical Hollywood's Orientalism. Phebe Shih Chao's close analysis of *The Letter* studies how Jewish émigré director William Wyler, through subtle changes in the narrative and with carefully composed shot compositions, undercuts the absolute distinctions between white and Asian that the story's British protagonists—and author Maugham—seek to maintain. Like Hamer, Chao situates Orientalism as the ideological component of colonization. She specifically draws on and reworks Frantz Fanon's model of three progressive stages in the colonized's consciousness—from cooperation to disturbance to revolt—in response to the colonizer, and argues that Wyler reworks Maugham's story, which sympathizes only with the colonizers, to represent as well the hatred, resentment, and ultimate revenge of the colonized. Chao's close analysis provides us with a sense of the film's complex perspectives and the subtle manner in which the Asian characters triumph over the white aristocracy of Malaysia.

———

As these essays make clear, Orientalism in film represents what Said called "a marvelous instance of the interrelations between society, history, and textuality."[23] Yet, while Orientalism offers insights into films of the past century, it does not exhaust their meanings. Just as it is no longer satisfactory for academic critics to denote negative images of the peoples of North Africa and Asia, analysts of Orientalism recognize that simplifying films to a structured opposition between East and West cannot account for these films' specific articulation of power relations and even for their compelling appeal to audiences.[24] Moreover, the closer one looks at Orientalism in film, the more likely one is to find that such oppositions are blurred, complicated, and undone—perhaps momentarily, perhaps more substantially—by the operations of the texts themselves (for example, by the visual style as against the logic of the film's narrative). Like all representational texts, Orientalist films sustain a measure of ideological contradiction and incoherence.

At the same time, these essays should not suggest that the interpretations of Orientalist films they offer are the only ones that circulated when the films premiered or that prevail when they are watched today. These films were valued or dismissed for other qualities—their authorship and their generic affiliations, for example. In this light, one of the most interesting topics for further research would be the *reception* of Orientalist films among different audiences and even among creative talents. Adrienne McLean's essay on Jack Cole provides one instance of a subculture's reappropriation of Orientalist works,[25] while Ella Shohat's discussion of Abdel Salam's *The Mummy/The Night of Counting the Years* (1969) describes an Egyptian filmmaker's recasting of the "dark continent" metaphor that dominates films such as *The Mummy* (1932) and *Raiders of the Lost Ark*. Here, I can offer a brief extended example.

Universal's *Arabian Nights* (1942) is not a canonic film, but it grossed several million dollars during World War II (Figure 2). It inaugurated a string of low-budget, Technicolor fantasies starring Maria Montez, with scantily clad harem women and brutally nasty despots (*Ali Baba and the Forty Thieves* and *Cobra Woman*, both 1944, etc.). The formula was reproduced at other studios through the 1960s and upgraded in ancient and biblical wide-screen epics of the era (such as *Solomon and Sheba* [1959] and *Cleopatra*). Such films, particularly in their low-budget incarnations, would come to be known at the studios as "t and s" movies, which appealed, as one executive put it, to "morons who like this sort of thing."[26]

Who were the morons in question? Walter Wanger and Universal Pictures, the producers of *Arabian Nights*, discovered that in the midwar years, at least, this type of film appealed to American homefront

Figure 2. *Arabian Nights* (1942): the opening sequence.

audiences. Wanger felt these films attracted adolescent men in particular, whom he glibly speculated might be inspired to enlist for service in North Africa; he thus articulated the ways in which the films superimposed the conventions of imperialist ideology with the urgent antifascist fight. As it happened, *Arabian Nights* had its strongest showing in the Midwest: one first-run theater manager in Cincinnati reported that the film overcame threats of flooding to break opening-day records; another reported that audiences "just eat it up and I don't know where they all came from."[27] Was it similarly popular in larger cities, on the two coasts, or in the South? Were audiences responding to its fantasy, to its Technicolor, to its physical comedy, or to its peculiar combination of these elements?

Then, too, the Universal Technicolor Orientalist films had other meanings and appeals to other audiences. To some gay viewers of the postwar generation, like underground filmmaker Jack Smith, they would become camp classics. Smith published his celebrated essay "The Perfect Filmic Appositeness of Maria Montez" in *Film Culture* in the early 1960s, extolling the way Montez insisted on her beauty amid the low-budget trappings of the productions and their formulaic narratives (Figure 3).[28] In many ways, Smith structured his landmark film

Figure 3. Maria Montez in *Arabian Nights*.

*Flaming Creatures* (1963) around this representational dynamic. As Richard Dyer writes of Smith's film,

> It is as if Hollywood's successful attempts at beauty produce a rationalistic, controlling beauty, but all other attempts are bound to fail because of their marginality and cheapness, so that all that is left is the aspiration to beauty. This aspiration is bound to fail, just as drag queens will never be women.[29]

Thus *Arabian Nights* and the many films that followed came to have ironic meanings far removed from—or entirely opposed to—whatever rationales its producers could muster for them. The camp "take" on the films coexisted with vestiges of a "straight," romantic Orientalist allure, linked, however indirectly, to U.S. involvement in conflicts and nations overseas; and all these appeals allowed the genre to survive long after World War II.

Said observed that "Orientalism responded more to the culture that produced it than to its putative object, which was also produced by the West," and he used the example of Orientalism to demonstrate that no form of representation—scholarly, scientific, or artistic—is created apart from a political and social context. For Said, the urgency of this realization was rooted in his personal experience as a Palestinian educated by Western schools, living in the United States, and being aware of the strong anti-Arab and Anti-Islam bias that pervades Western society.[30] For scholars and students in film and media studies, of whatever background, the study of Orientalism and its consequent self-examination can contribute to a multiculturalist pedagogy, by compelling us to recognize how Western filmmaking has seductively and persuasively limited our perceptions and understanding of the many cultures it purports to represent.

We hope this anthology will fulfill many functions: to gather some of the best writing on Orientalism in film that has previously appeared, to bring insightful new research on the subject to light, and to provoke cultural and media critics and students to extend, amplify, and engage with the theoretical presuppositions and critical strategies that inform these writings.

## Notes

1. Michael Rogin, "Blackface, White Noise: The Jewish Jazz Singer Finds His Voice," *Critical Inquiry* 18, no. 3 (1992): 417–418.
2. See Robert Ray, *A Certain Tendency of the Hollywood Cinema, 1930–1980* (Princeton: Princeton University Press, 1985), 89–112, for an insightful analysis of *Casablanca's* politics and values.
3. Edward Said, *Orientalism* (New York: Vintage, 1979). The book was first published in 1978 by Pantheon.
4. Ibid., 1.
5. Ibid., 59–60. In fact, Said defines the field of his study as "the Anglo-French-American experience of the Arabs and Islam," taking the perceptions of Islam as a defining feature of the entire phenomenon (16–17), in particular Orientalism's attempt to characterize Islam as misguided Christianity (60–61) or as lacking an understanding of personal liberty (172).
6. See Lester Friedman's preface to *Unspeakable Images: Ethnicity and the American Cinema* (Urbana: University of Illinois Press, 1991), 1–9, for an extremely useful discussion of the history of academic film study of gender and ethnicity, a linkage suggested earlier in Robert Stam and Louise Spence, "Colonialism, Racism, and Cinematic Representation," reprinted in Bill Nichols, ed. *Movies and Methods, vol. 2* (Berkeley: University of California Press, 1985), 635.

    Critic Homi Bhabha developed Said's model through Lacanian psychoanalysis, positing that racial stereotyping is comparable to the sexual fetish (where the sexual fetish focuses on the penis and lack thereof, colonialist discourse focuses on the similarity and difference of skin color) in its psychic mechanisms and in the ambivalence that governs it. See "The Other Question—the Stereotype and Colonial Discourse," *Screen* 24, no. 6 (1983): 18–36. See Christine Anne Holmlund, "Displacing Limits of Difference: Gender, Race, and Colonialism in Edward Said and Homi Bhabha's

Theoretical Models and Marguerite Duras's Experimental Films," *Quarterly Review of Film and Video* 13, nos. 1–3 (1991): 1–22, for a clear presentation and compelling critique of Said and Bhabha's work relative to the experimental narratives of Marguerite Duras. See also, Reina Lewis, *Gendering Orientalism: Race, Femininity, and Representation* (New York: Routledge, 1996), for a recent critique of—and expansion of—the gender politics of Said's original formulation.

7. Edward Said, "Orientalism Reconsidered," *Cultural Critique* (fall 1985): 103.
8. Said does refer to film and the mass media in passing in *Orientalism*. He notes that the contemporary mass media have "intensified" the circulation of Orientalist stereotypes in popular culture (26); he also observes how "in the films and television the Arab is associated either with lechery or bloodthirsty dishonesty, . . . He leers suggestively as he speaks: this is a current debasement of Valentino's Sheik" (286–287).
9. See Mia I. Gerhardt, *The Art of the Story-Telling* (Leiden, the Netherlands: E. J. Brill, 1963) on the *Arabian Nights*; see Peter L. Caracciolo, "Introduction," in Caracciolo, ed., *The "Arabian Nights" in English Literature* (London: Macmillan, 1988), 3–31, for a survey of the meanings of the *Arabian Nights* for several centuries of British writers. Particularly striking are Caracciolo's observations on how the *Arabian Nights* generated new metaphors for nineteenth-century writers: John Ruskin associated Aladdin's genie in a bottle with the creative imagination itself, while Charles Darwin "used the *Nights* when voicing in tones of mingled wonder and recognition their first impressions of alien experiences." For an analysis of the Western translations in terms of Orientalism, see Rana Kabbani, *Europe's Myths of Orient* (Bloomington: Indiana University Press, 1986).

On the French Orientalists, see Linda Nochlin, "The Imaginary Orient," *Art in America* 71, no. 5 (1983): 118–131, 186–191. These painters treated the varieties of popular entertainment such as storytelling, snake charming, and dancing with a voyeuristic pleasure masked as an ethnographic, "dispassionate empiricism." Alternately, they used foreign settings and tales as "a stage for the playing out, from a suitable distance, of forbidden passions"—as when Eugène Delacroix rendered the death of Assyrian ruler Sardanapalus as a swirling spectacle of naked concubines totally subservient and helplessly murdered at the behest of their defeated and suicidal leader. Both approaches—the detached ethnographic record and the indulgence of fantasy—exemplify Orientalist paintings' affinity with the picturesque, which obscures its subjects' place in history. The particular history here involves the struggles of North Africa to resist French colonialism and of native cultures to survive the incursion of Western technology and governmental policies. The work of the Orientalists was part of the cultural nexus Antonia Lant explores in her essay in this volume.

10. See Ella Shohat and Robert Stam, *Unthinking Eurocentrism: Multiculturalism and the Media* (New York: Routledge, 1994), 100–114, for an illuminating discussion of how European and American cinemas functioned, from their earliest years, to reinforce a sense of national identity in their audiences.

11. These statistics derive from a survey of the *AFI Catalog: Feature Files, 1911–1920* (Berkeley: University of California Press, 1988).
12. See Lynn Garafola, *Diaghilev's Ballets Russes* (New York: Oxford University Press, 1989), for the most comprehensive account of the Ballets Russes. For a discussion of the Ballets Russes' place in modern art, see Peter Wollen, "Fashion/Orientalism/The Body," *New Formations* 6 (spring 1987): 15–17.

    For specific discussions of the Ballets Russes' relationship to and influence on American filmmaking, see Sumiko Higashi, *Cecil B. DeMille and American Culture: The Silent Era* (Berkeley: University of California Press, 1994), 166–176, on the work of Paul Poiret and Paul Iribe in De Mille's *The Affairs of Anatole*; Gaylyn Studlar, "Douglas Fairbanks, Thief of the Ballets Russes," in Ellen Goellner and Jacqueline Shea Murphy, eds., *Bodies of the Text: Dance as Theory, Literature as Dance* (New Brunswick: Rutgers University Press, 1995), 107–124, on that film's debts to the Ballets Russes; and Matthew Bernstein, *Walter Wanger, Hollywood Independent* (Berkeley: University of California Press, 1994), 15, 44–46, 136–191, 347–348, on one producer's importation of Ballets Russes–style Orientalism into Hollywood cinema from the 1920s through the 1960s.
13. Shohat and Stam, *Unthinking Eurocentrism*, 114–121, discuss the centrality of the Western to Orientalist and colonialist adventure films.
14. See "Narrative and Ideology in the Imperialist Spy Thriller," in Tony Bennett and Janet Woollacott, *Bond and Beyond: The Political Career of a Popular Hero* (London: Macmillan Education, 1987), 95–99.
15. Said, *Orientalism*, 24.
16. Stam and Spence, "Colonialism, Racism, and Cinematic Representation," 637. See also Shohat and Stam, *Unthinking Eurocentrism*, 100–125.
17. See, for example, Gina Marchetti, *Romance and the "Yellow Peril"* (Berkeley: University of California Press, 1993).
18. Alan Parker, who directed *Come See the Paradise* (1990), a melodrama about the internment of Japanese-American citizens during World War II, had an inspiration for his film similar to that for *Miss Saigon*. In the "Press Information" brochure printed for the premiere, he writes:

    > For many years I have had a haunting photograph by Dorothea Lange pinned to my wall. The picture shows a Japanese man sitting with his two grandchildren in San Francisco in 1941 awaiting deportation and internment. The old man's dignity and self-respect stare right out at you from the photograph, as does the bemused ingenuousness of his two grandsons. As with all great photographs, the story behind the stares demands to be told. (13)

19. For two other illuminating discussions of the ambivalent position of women in a popular colonialist/Orientalist text, see Caren Kaplan, "'Getting to Know You': Travel, Gender, and the Politics of Representation in *Anna and the King of Siam* and *The King and I*," in Roman De La Campa and E. Ann Kaplan, eds., *Late Imperial Culture* (London: Verso, 1995), 33–52; and Laura Donaldson, "*The King and I* in Uncle Tom's Cabin, or on the Border of the Women's Room," *Cinema Journal* 29, no. 3 (1990): 53–68.

20. Cf. Said's comments on the challenge of the contemporary Orient to Orientalism in *Orientalism*, 104–105.

Disney altered the lyrics to the opening song in *Aladdin* in response to protests by the American Arab Anti-Discrimination Committee. The original lyrics read:

> Oh, I come from a land
> From a faraway place
> Where the caravan camels roam.
> Where they cut off your ear
> If they don't like your face
> It's barbaric, but hey, it's home.

The final three lines were changed to:

> Where it's flat and immense
> And the heat is intense
> It's barbaric, but hey, it's home.

See John Evanfrook, " 'Aladdin' Lyrics Altered," *Variety*, 12 July 1993. With *Pocahontas*, the studio's next animated feature focusing on a nonwhite culture, Disney publicized the fact that it consulted with members of the Native American community. My thanks to film critic Eleanor Ringel of the *Atlanta Journal* and *Constitution*, who shared her clippings and press materials on recent Orientalist films.

21. Said, *Orientalism*, 14–15.

22. See Stam and Spence, "Colonialism, Racism, and Cinematic Representation," 642–644, for a discussion of how Pontecorvo's film reverses conventional colonialist and racist representations of Algerian culture.

23. Said, *Orientalism*, 24.

24. Discussions of negative images of Arabs and Asians do pervade the press, however. For some recent examples, see *The Arab in American Cinema: A Century of Otherness* (Washington, D.C.: American Arab Anti-Discrimination Committee, 1989), a supplement to *Cineaste* 17, no. 1; Laurence Michalak, *Cruel and Unusual: Negative Images of Arabs in American Popular Culture* (Washington, D.C.: American Arab Anti-Discrimination Committee, n.d.), which has some excellent quantitative information about the depiction of Arabs through the century; and Arthur Pais, "Arabs Angry from 'The Sheik' to 'Santa Barbara,'" *Variety*, 31 December 1990.

25. For other examples, see Michael Moon, "Flaming Closets," *October* 51 (winter 1989): 19–54.

26. Al Lichtman, letter to Walter F. Wanger, 8 January 1953, Box 96, File 7, Walter F. Wanger Collection, Wisconsin Center for Film and Theater Research, State Historical Society, Madison, Wisconsin. The phrase "t and s" was short for "tits and sand."

27. Bernstein, *Walter Wanger, Hollywood Independent*, 187.

28. Jack Smith, "The Perfect Filmic Appositeness of Maria Montez," *Film Culture* 27 (1962–1963): 28–32.

29.  Richard Dyer, *Now You See It: Studies on Lesbian and Gay Film* (New York: Routledge, 1990), 147–149. In a similar vein, see Sean Griffin, "The Illusion of Identity": Gender and Racial Representation in *Aladdin*," *Animation Journal* 3, no. 1 (1994): 64–73.
30.  Said, *Orientalism*, 22; and 10, 14.

Ella Shohat

# Gender and Culture of Empire: Toward a Feminist Ethnography of the Cinema

Although recent feminist film theory has acknowledged the issue of differences among women, there has been little attempt to explore and problematize the implications of these differences for the representation of gender relations within racially and culturally nonhomogeneous textual environments.[1] While implicitly universalizing "womanhood," and without questioning the undergirding racial and national boundaries of its discourse, feminist film theory, for the most part, has not articulated its generally insightful analyses vis-à-vis the contradictions and asymmetries provoked by (post)colonial arrangements of power. This elision is especially striking since the beginnings of cinema coincided with the heights of imperialism between the late nineteenth century and World War I. Western cinema not only inherited and disseminated colonial discourse, but also created a system of domination through monopolistic control of film distribution and exhibition in much of Asia, Africa, and Latin America. The critique of colonialism within cinema studies, meanwhile, has tended to downplay the significance of gender issues, thus eliding the fact that (post)colonial discourse has impinged differently on the representation of men and women. It is between these two major theoretical frameworks that my essay is

This essay was first published in *Quarterly Review of Film and Video* 13, nos. 1–3 (1991); 45–84, ed. Hamid Naficy and Teshome H. Gabriel. It appears here with the permission of Harwood Academic Publishers GmbH. Copyright © 1991 Harwood Academic Publishers GmbH.

situated, attempting to synthesize feminist and post/colonial cultural critiques.

In this essay I explore Western cinema's geographical and historical constructs as symptomatic of the colonialist imaginary generally but also more specifically as a product of a gendered Western gaze, an imbrication reflective of the symbiotic relations between patriarchal and colonial articulations of difference. I emphasize the role of sexual difference in the construction of a number of superimposed oppositions— West/East, North/South—not only on a narratological level but also on the level of the implicit structuring metaphors undergirding colonial discourse. While referring to some resistant counternarratives, I also examine the structural analogies in the colonialist positioning of different regions, particularly in sexual terms, showing the extent to which Western representation of otherized territories serves diacritically to define the "West" itself.

## Gendered Metaphors
### Virgins, Adams, and the Prospero Complex

An examination of colonial discourse reveals the crucial role of gendered metaphors in constructing the colonial "subaltern." Europe's "civilizing mission" in the Third World is projected as interweaving opposed yet linked narratives of Western penetration of inviting virginal landscapes *and* of resisting libidinal nature.[2] The early exaltation of the New World paradise, suggested, for example, by Sir Walter Raleigh's report— "a country that hath yet her mayden head, never sakt, turned, nor wrought"[3]—and by Crèvecoeur's letters—"Here nature opens her broad lap to receive the perpetual accession of new comers, and to supply them with food"[4]—gradually centered on the idealized figure of the pioneer. Linked to nineteenth-century westward expansionism, the garden symbol embraced metaphors related to growth, increase, cultivation, and blissful agricultural labor.[5] At the same time, the discourse of Empire suggests that "primitive" landscapes (deserts, jungles) are tamed; "shrew" peoples (Native Americans, Africans, Arabs) are domesticated; and the desert is made to bloom, all thanks to the infusion of Western dynamism and enlightenment. Within this Promethean master-narrative, subliminally gendered tropes such as "conquering the desolation" and "fecundating the wilderness" acquire heroic resonances of Western fertilization of barren lands. The metaphoric portrayal of the (non-European) land as a "virgin" coyly awaiting the touch of the colonizer implied that whole continents—Africa, America, Asia, and Australia— could only benefit from the emanation of colonial praxis. The revivification of a wasted soil evokes a quasi-divine process of endowing life

Figure 1. *Adventures of Robinson Crusoe* (1954): The Promethean master-narrative. Courtesy of the Museum of Modern Art, New York.

and meaning ex nihilo, of bringing order from chaos, plenitude from lack. Indeed, the West's *"Prospero complex"* is premised on an East/South portrayed as a Prospero's isle, seen as the site of superimposed lacks calling for Western transformation of primeval matter. The engendering of "civilization," then, is clearly phallocentric, not unlike the mythical woman's birth from Adam's rib.[6]

The American hero, as R.W.B. Lewis points out, has been celebrated as prelapsarian Adam, as a New Man emancipated from history (i.e., European history) before whom all the world and time lay available.[7] The American Adam archetype implied not only his status as a kind of creator, blessed with the divine prerogative of naming the elements of the scene about him, but also his fundamental innocence. Here colonial and patriarchal discourses are clearly interwoven. The biblical narration of Genesis recounts the creation of the World; the creation of Adam from earth (*adama* in Hebrew) in order for man to rule over nature. The power of creation is inextricably linked to the power of naming—God lends his naming authority to Adam as mark of his rule, and the woman is "called Woman because she was taken out of man." The question of naming played an important role not only in gender mythology but also in colonial narratives in which the "discoverer" gave names as a mark of possession ("America" as celebrating Amerigo Vespucci) or as bearers of a European global perspective ("Middle East" "Far East"). "Peripheral" places and their inhabitants were often stripped of their "unpronounceable" indigenous names and outfitted with names marking them as the property of the colonizer. The colonial explorer as depicted in *Robinson Crusoe* creates, demiurgelike, a whole civilization and has the power of naming "his" islander "Friday," for he "saves" his life on that day; and Friday, we recall, is the day God created Adam, thus further strengthening the analogy between the "self-sufficient" Crusoe and God (Figure 1).

The notion of an American Adam elided a number of crucial facts, notably that there were other civilizations in the New World; that the settlers were not creating "being from nothingness"; and that the settlers had scarcely jettisoned all their Old World cultural baggage, their deeply ingrained attitudes and discourses. Here the notion of "virginity," present, for example, in the etymology of Virginia, must be seen in diacritical relation to the metaphor of the (European) "motherland." A "virgin" land is implicitly available for defloration and fecundation. Implied to lack owners, it therefore becomes the property of its "discoverers" and cultivators. The "purity" of the terminology masks the dispossession of the land and its resources. A land already fecund, already producing for the indigenous peoples, and thus a "mother," is metaphorically projected as virgin, "untouched nature," and therefore as available and awaiting a master. Colonial gendered metaphors are visibly rendered in Jan Van der Straet's pictorial representation of the discovery of America, focusing on the mythical figure of Amerigo Vespucci, shown as bearing Europe's emblems of meaning (cross, armor, compass).[8] Behind him we see the vessels that will bring back to the Occident the treasures of the New World paradise. In front of him we see a welcoming naked woman, the Indian American. If she is a harmonious extension of nature, he represents its scientific mastery.[9] Here the conqueror, as Michel de Certeau puts it, "will write the body of the other and inscribe upon it his own history."[10]

In Nelson Pereira dos Santos's *How Tasty Was My Frenchman (Como Era Gostoso Meu Françes*, 1970), the patriarchal discourse on the encounter between Europeans and Native Americans is subverted.[11] Partly based on a diary written by the German adventurer Hans Staden, the film concerns a Frenchman who is captured by the Tupinamba tribe and sentenced to death in response to previous massacres inflicted by Europeans upon them. Before his ritualized execution and cannibalization, however, he is given a wife, Sebiopepe (a widow of one of the Tupinamba massacred by the Europeans), and he is allowed to participate in the tribe's daily activities.[12] In the last shot, the camera zooms in on Sebiopepe's face as she is emotionlessly devouring her French-man, despite the fact that she has developed a close relationship with him. This final image is followed by a citation from a report on Native American genocide by Europeans, which undermines the possibly disturbing nature of the last shot.[13] If pictorial representations of the "discovery" tend to center on a nude Native American woman as meta-phorizing the welcoming "new-found-land," in *How Tasty Was My Frenchman* the Native American woman is far from being an object of European discourse. Presented as linked to her communal culture and history, she herself becomes part of history. Her nudity is not contrasted with the discoverer's heavy clothing; rather, she is part of an environ-ment where nudity is not a category. The fact that the film employs largely long shots in which characters appear nude in the performance of their banal daily activities undermines voyeurism and stands in contrast to the fetishistic Hollywood mode that tends to fragment the (female) body in close shots.[14] In her interaction with the Frenchman, Sebiopepe represents, above all, the voice of the native American counternarrative.[15] In one scene, for example, a myth of origins prefig-ures the symbolic revolt of the Tupinamba. Sebiopepe begins to nar-rate in Tupi a Tupinamba Promethean myth concerning the god, Mair, who brought them knowledge. The Frenchman, at one point, takes over the narration and, in French, further recounts the deeds of the god, while we see him performing the divine deeds. The whitening of the Tupinamba God on the image track evokes the Promethean colonial discourse concerning the redemption of the "natives," but here that discourse is relativized, especially since the Native American woman ends the myth in Tupi, recounting the rebellion of the people against the god, while the image track shows the destruction of the Frenchman's work. Her voice, then, recounts the tale of the people who revolted, undercutting the masculinist myth of availability, submissiveness, and redemption (Figure 2).

## Graphological Tropes

The inclination to project the non-Occident as feminine is seen even in the nineteenth-century Romantic depiction of the ancient Orient of Babylonia and Egypt, reproduced in films such as D. W. Griffith's *In-tolerance* (1916) and Cecil B. De Mille's *Cleopatra* (1934) (Figure 3). In *Intolerance* Babylon signifies sexual excess, building on the Book of Revelation as "Babylon, the Great, the Mother of Harlots and of the Abominations of the Earth." De Mille's *Cleopatra* explicitly expresses this view by having the sexually manipulative Cleopatra addressed as Egypt and by presenting the Orient as exclusively the scene of carnal delights.[16] The ultimate subordination of the woman Cleopatra and her

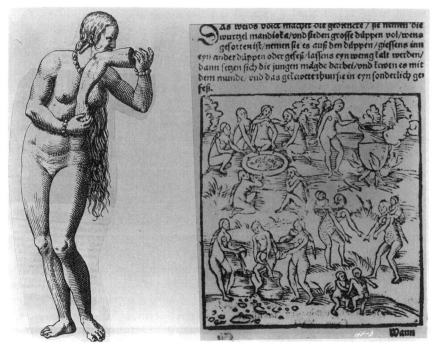

Figure 2. *How Tasty Was My Frenchman* (1970): Counternarrative to the "Discovery discourse." Courtesy of the Museum of Modern Art, Rio de Janeiro

country Egypt is not without contemporary colonial overtones, suggested, for example, in the Anglo-aristocratic "Roman" court where sarcastic jokes are made at the expense of a presumably black Cleopatra, asserting that Rome could never be turned into the Orient or ruled by an Egyptian. (The historically dark Cleopatra is turned by Hollywood conventions of beauty into a European-looking white woman, just as the iconography of Christ has gradually de-Semitized him.)[17] The visual infatuation with Babylon's and Egypt's material abundance, emphasized through a mise-en-scène of monumental architecture, domestic detail, and quasi-pornographic feasts, cannot be divorced from the intertext of colonial travel literature whose reports also obsessively recounted the details of oriental sensual excesses (Figure 4).

Cinema, in this sense, enacted a historiographical and anthropological role, writing (in light) the cultures of others. The early films' penchant for graphological signifiers such as hieroglyphs (in the different versions of *Cleopatra*), Hebrew script (*Intolerance*), and the image of an open book as in "The Book of Intolerance" and the marginal "notes" accompanying the intertitles (which pedagogically supply the specta-

Figure 3.
*Cleopatra*
(1934): The
iconography
of a feminized
Egypt. Cour-
tesy of the
Museum of
Modern Art,
New York.

tor with additional information) imply Hollywood as a kind of Western popular griot. By associating itself with writing, and particularly
with "original" writing, early cinema lent a pedagogical, historical, and
artistic aura to a medium still associated with circuslike entertainments.
(It is not a coincidence, perhaps, that Siegfried Kracauer, for example,
referred to films as "visible hieroglyphs.") And by linking a new ap-
prentice art to ancient times and "exotic" places, cinema celebrated its
ethnographic and quasi-archaeological powers to resuscitate forgotten
and distant civilizations, a celebration implicit in the construction of
pseudo-Egyptian movie palaces. The "birth" of cinema itself coincided
with the imperialist moment, when diverse colonized civilizations were
already shaping their conflicting identities vis-à-vis their colonizers.
These films about the ancient world suggest, perhaps, a Romantic

Figure 4. *Intolerance* (1916): Babylon and the pornographic intertext of travel literature. Courtesy of the Museum of Modern Art, New York.

nostalgia for a "pure" civilization prior to Western "contamination." They also represent a romantic search for the lost Eastern origins of Western civilizations, analogous to Schlieman's excavations in Troy. It is within this context that we can understand the "structuring absence"— in the representation of Egypt, Babylonia, and the (biblical) Holy Land— of the contemporary colonized Arab Orient and its nationalist struggles.[18] Through a historiographical gesture, the films define the Orient as ancient and mysterious, participating in what Jacques Derrida in another context calls the "hieroglyphist prejudice." The cinematic Orient, then, is best epitomized by an iconography of papyruses, sphinxes, and mummies, whose existence and revival depend on the "look" and "reading" of the Westerner. This rescue of the past, in other words, suppresses the voice of the present and thus legitimates by default the availability of the space of the Orient for the geopolitical maneuvers of the Western powers.

The filmic mummified zone of ancient civilizations, then, is dialectically linked to the representation of the historical role of the West in the imperial age. Reproducing Western historiography, First World cinema narrates European penetration into the Third World through the figure of the "discoverer."[19] In most Western films about the colonies (such as *Bird of Paradise* [1932], *Wee Willie Winkie* [1937], *Black Narcissus* [1947], *The King and I* [1956], *Lawrence of Arabia* [1962], and even Buñuel's *Adventures of Robinson Crusoe* [1954]), we accompany, quite literally, the explorer's perspective. A simple shift in focalization to that of the "natives," as occurs in the Australian-Aboriginal *Nice Coloured Girls* (1987),[20] or in the Brazilian *How Tasty Was My Frenchman*, where the camera is placed on land with the "natives" rather than on ship with the Europeans, reveals the illusory and intrusive nature of the "discovery." More usually, however, heroic status is attributed to the voyager (often a male scientist) come to master a new land and its treasures, the value of which the "primitive" residents had been unaware.[21] It is this construction of consciousness of "value" as pretext for (capitalist) ownership which legitimizes the colonizer's act of appropriation. The "discovery," furthermore, has gender overtones.[22] In this exploratory adventure, seen in such films as *Lawrence of Arabia* and the *Indiana Jones* series, the camera relays the hero's dynamic movement across a passive, static space, gradually stripping the land of its "enigma," as the spectator wins visual access to oriental treasures through the eyes of the explorer-protagonist. *Lawrence of Arabia* provides an example of Western historical representation whereby the individual Romantic "genius" leads the Arab national revolt, presumed to be a passive entity awaiting T. E. Lawrence's inspiration. (Arab sources obviously have challenged this historical account.)[23] The unveiling of the mysteries of an unknown space becomes a *rite de passage* allegorizing the Western achievement of virile heroic stature.

## Mapping Terra Incognita

The masculinist desire of mastering a new land is deeply linked to colonial history and even to its contemporary companion, philosophy, in which epistemology partially modeled itself on geography. The traditional discourse on nature as feminine—for example, Francis Bacon's idea that insofar as we learn the laws of nature through science, we become her master, as we are now in ignorance, "her thralls"[24]—gains, within the colonial context, clear geopolitical implications. Bacon's search for expanding scientific knowledge is inseparable from the contemporaneous European geographical expansion, clearly suggested by his language of analogies and metaphors: "[A]s the immense regions of the West Indies had never been discovered, if the use of the compass had not first been known, it is no wonder that the discovery and advancement of arts hath made no greater progress, when the art of inventing and discovering of the sciences remains hitherto unknown."[25] And Bacon finds it "disgraceful [that] while the regions of the material globe . . . have been in our times laid widely open and revealed, the intellectual globe should remain shut up within the narrow limits of old discoveries."[26] Traveling into the indefiniteness of the ocean, the Faustian overreacher's voyage beyond the Pillars of Hercules aims at the possibility of a *terra incognita* on the other side of the ocean. Studying topography, systematizing the paths, as Hans Blumenberg points out, guarantees that the accidents of things coming to light ultimately lead to a universal acquaintance with the world. "So much had remained concealed from the human spirit throughout many centuries and was discovered neither by philosophy nor by the faculty of reason but rather by accident and favorable opportunity, because it was all too different and distant from what was familiar, so that no preconception (*praenotio aliqua*) could lead one to it."[27] The logic of explorers from Robinson Crusoe to Indiana Jones is, in this sense, based on the hope that "nature" conceals in its "womb" still more, outside the familiar paths of the power of imagination (*extra vias phantasiae*). It is within this broader historical and intellectual context that we may understand the symptomatic image of penetration into a cave placed in a non-European land to discover that "Unknown," seen, for example, in the Rudyard Kipling–based *The Jungle Book* (1942), *Raiders of the Lost Ark* (1981), *Indiana Jones and the Temple of Doom* (1984), and the E. M. Forster–based *A Passage to India* (1984).

Colonial narratives legitimized the embarking upon treasure hunts by lending a scientific aura, encapsulated especially by images of maps and globes. Detailed descriptions of maps were probably inspired by the growing science of geography, which determined the significance of places through its power of inscription on the map, with the compass on top as the signature of scientific authority. Geography, then, was microcosmically reflected in the map-based adventures, which involved the drawing or deciphering of a map, and its authentication through the physical contact with the "new" land. Western cinema, from the earliest anthropological films through *Morocco* (1930) to the *Indiana Jones* series, has relied on map imagery for plotting the Empire, while simultaneously celebrating its own technological power—implicitly vis-à-vis the novel's reliance upon words or static drawings, and later still photographs—to illustrate vividly the topography. For example, venture-narrative films mark maps with moving arrows to signify the progress of the Westerner in his world-navigation, a practice characterizing even the recent *Raiders of the Lost Ark* and *Indiana Jones and the Temple of Doom*. By associating itself with the visual medium of maps, cinema represents itself scientifically, as being a twentieth-century continuation of the discipline of geography.

Films often superimposed illustrative maps on shots of landscapes, subliminally imposing the map's "claim" over the land, functioning as a legal document. *King Solomon's Mines* (1937, 1950, 1985), as Anne McClintock suggests in her discussion of the Rider Haggard work, explicitly genderizes the relation between the explorer and the topography.[28] Menahem Golan's version, for example, reveals in the second shot of the film a small nude female sculpture engraved with Canaanite signs, explained by the archaeologist to be a map leading to the twin mountains, the Breasts of Sheba, below which, in a cave, are hidden King Solomon's diamond mines. The camera voyeuristically tilts down on the female body/map, scrutinizing it from the excited perspective of the archaeologist and the antique dealer. The road to utopia involves the deciphering of the map, of comprehending the female body; the legendary twin mountains and the cave metaphorize the desired telos of the hero's mission of plunder. The geology and topography of the land, then, are explicitly sexualized to resemble the physiology of a woman.

The recurrent image of the spinning globe, similarly, entitles the scientist to possess the world, since the globe, as the world's representation, allegorizes the relationship between creator and creation. Cinema's penchant for spinning-globe logos serves to celebrate the medium's kinetic possibilities as well as its global ubiquity, allowing spectators a cheap voyage while remaining in the metropolitan "centers"—Lumières' location shootings of diverse Third World sites, such as India, Mexico, and Palestine being symptomatic of this visual national-geographics mania. The spinning globe virtually became the trademark of the British Korda brothers' productions, many of whose films, such as *Sanders of the River* (1935), *The Drum* (1938), *The Four Feathers* (1939), and *The Jungle Book*, concerned colonial themes.[29] The overarching global point of view sutures the spectator into a godlike cosmic perspective. Incorporating images of maps and globes, the Jules Verne–based film *Around the World in 80 Days* (1956), for example, begins by its omniscient narrator hailing the "shrinking of the world" as Verne was writing the book.[30] The "shrinking" relates the perspective of upper-class British men whose scientific confidence about circling the world in eighty days is materialized, thus linking the development of science to imperialist control: "Nothing is impossible. When science finally conquers the air it may be feasible to circle the globe in eighty hours," says the David Niven character (Figure 5).

Science, knowledge, and technology can also be read allegorically as linked to imperial expansionism in the film's citation of George Méliès's film *A Trip to the Moon (Le Voyage dans la lune* [1902] based on Verne's *From the Earth to the Moon* [1865]), in which the "last frontier"

Figure 5. *Around the World in 80 Days* (1956): Global ubiquity. Courtesy of the Museum of Modern Art, New York.

explored is seen first in the imagistic phallic penetration of the rounded moon (Figure 6).[31] This imagination of the "last frontier," in a period when most of the world was dominated by Europe, reproduces the historical discourse of the "first frontier." The narrative is structured similarly to the colonial captivity narrative where the skeleton creatures carrying spears burst from the moon's simulacrum of a jungle but are defeated by the male explorers' unbrellalike guns, which magically eliminate the savage creatures. Such a film, not in any obvious sense "about" colonialism, but one produced in a period when most of the world was dominated by Europe, can thus be read a an analogue of imperial ex-

Figure 6. *A Trip to the Moon* (1902): Penetrating the "last frontier." Courtesy of the British Film Institute.

pansion.[32] Similarly in recent films such as *Return of the Jedi* (1983), the conquest of outer space exists on a continuum with an imperial narrative in which the visualization of the planet provides the paradigm for the representation of Third World "underdevelopment" (deserts, jungles, and mountains). The Manichean relationship between the American hero and the new land and its natives involves exotic creatures, teddy-bear-like Ewoks whose language remains a mystery throughout the film, who worship the technologically well-equipped hero, and who defend him against evil, ugly creatures who have unclear motives. The American hero's physical and moral triumph legitimizes the destruction of the enemy, as does the paternal transformation of the friendly "elements" into servile objects, along with his assumed right to establish new outposts (and implicitly to hold on to old outposts, whether in Africa, Asia, or America).

## The Dark Continent

The colonial films claim to initiate the Western spectator into an unknown culture. This is valid even for films set in "exotic" lands and ancient times that do *not* employ Western characters (for example, *Intolerance*,[33] *The Ten Commandments* [1923, 1956], *The Thief of Bagdad* [1924], and *Kismet* [1944]), yet whose oriental heroes/heroines are played by Western stars. The spectator is subliminally invited on an ethnographic tour of a celluloid-"preserved" culture, which implicitly celebrates the chronotopic magical aptitude of cinema for panoramic spectacle and temporal voyeurism, evoking André Bazin's formulation of cinema as possessing a "mummy complex."[34] Often the spectator, identified with the gaze of the West (whether embodied by a Western male/female character or by a Western actor/actress masquerading as an Oriental), comes to master, in a remarkably telescoped period of time, the codes of a foreign culture shown, as Edward Said suggests, as simple, unself-conscious, and susceptible to facile apprehension. Any possibility of dialogic interaction and of a dialectical representation of the East/West relation is excluded from the outset. The films thus reproduce the colonialist mechanism by which the Orient, rendered as devoid of any active historical or narrative role, becomes the object of study and spectacle.[35]

The portrayal of a Third World region as undeveloped, in the same vein, is reinforced by a topographical reductionism, for example, the topographical reductionism of the Orient to desert, and metaphorically, to dreariness. The desert, a frequent reference in the dialogues and a visual motif throughout the Orientalist films, is presented as the essential unchanging decor of the history of the Orient. While the Arabs in such films as *Lawrence of Arabia*, *Exodus* (1960), and *Raiders of the Lost Ark* are associated with images of underdevelopment, the Westerner, as the antithesis of the oriental desert, is associated with productive, creative pioneering, a masculine redeemer of the wilderness. The films reflect a culturally overdetermined geographical-symbolic polarity; an East/West axis informs many films on the oriental theme. As if in a reversion to deterministic climate theories such as those of Madame de Staël or Hippolyte Taine, the films present the East as the locus of irrational primitivism and uncontrollable instincts. The exposed, barren land and the blazing sands, furthermore, metaphorize the exposed, unrepressed "hot" passion and uncensored emotions of the Orient, in short, as the world of the out-of-control id.

The Orient as a metaphor for sexuality is encapsulated by the recurrent figure of the veiled woman. The inaccessibility of the veiled woman, mirroring the mystery of the Orient itself, requires a process of Western unveiling for comprehension. Veiled women in Orientalist paintings, photographs, and films expose flesh, ironically, more than they conceal it.[36] It is this process of exposing the female Other, of literally denuding her, which comes to allegorize the Western masculinist power of possession, that she, as a metaphor for her land, becomes available for Western penetration and knowledge. This intersection of the epistemological and the sexual in colonial discourse echoes Freud's metaphor of the "dark continent." Freud speaks of female sexuality in metaphors of darkness and obscurity often drawn from the realms of archaeology and exploration—the metaphor of the "dark continent," for example, deriving from a book by the Victorian explorer Stanley.[37] Seeing himself as explorer and discoverer of new worlds, Freud in *Studies on Hysteria* compared the role of the psychoanalyst to that of the archaeologist "clearing away the pathogenic psychical material layer by layer," which is analogous "with the technique of excavating a buried city."[38] The analogy, made in the context of examining a woman patient, Fräulein Elisabeth Von R., calls attention to the role of the therapist in locating obscure trains of thought followed by penetration, as Freud puts it in the first person: "I would penetrate into deeper layers of her memories at these points carrying out an investigation under hypnosis or by the use of some similar technique."[39]

Speaking generally of "penetrating deeply" into the "neurosis of women" thanks to a science that can give a "deeper and more coherent" insight into feminity,[40] Freud is perhaps unaware of the political overtones of his optical metaphor. Penetration, as Toril Moi suggests, is very much on Freud's mind as he approaches femininity,[41] including, one might add, the "dark continent of female sexuality." The notion of the necessary unveiling of the unconscious requires an obscure object in order to sustain the very desire to explore, penetrate, and master. David Macey's suggestion that psychoanalysis posits femininity as being in excess of its rationalist discourse, and then complains that it cannot explain it,[42] is equally applicable to the positing of the Other in colonial discourse. Furthermore, Freud uses the language of force; for example, "we force our way into the internal strata, overcoming resistances at all times."[43] Looking at the Eastern roots of civilizations, Freud employs ancient myths and figures such as the Sphinx and Oedipus to draw parallels between the development of the civilization and that of the psyche. (Although Freud did not speculate at any great length on Egyptian mythology, over half of his private collection of antiquities reportedly consisted of ancient Egyptian sculptures and artifacts.)[44] The psychoanalyst who heals from the suppressed past (most of Freud's studies of hysteria were conducted in relation to women) resembles the archaeologist who recovers the hidden past of civilization (most of which was "found" in Third World lands). As in archaeology, Freud's epistemology assumes the (white) male as the bearer of knowledge, who can penetrate woman and text, while she, as a remote region, will let herself be explored till truth is uncovered.

Figure 7. *The Mummy* (1932): Western knowledge rescues the ancient Egyptian past from oblivion. Courtesy of the British Film Institute.

The interweaving of archaeology and psychoanalysis touches on a nineteenth-century motif in which the voyage into the origins of the Orient becomes a voyage into the interior colonies of the "self." ("Un voyage en Orient [était] comme un grand acte de ma vie intérieure," Lamartine wrote.)[45] The origins of archaeology, the search for the "roots of civilization" as a discipline are, we know, inextricably linked to imperial expansionism. In the cinema, the *Indiana Jones* series reproduces exactly this colonial vision in which Western "knowledge" of ancient civilizations "rescues" the past from oblivion. It is this masculinist rescue in *Raiders of the Lost Ark* that legitimizes denuding the Egyptians of their heritage, confining it within Western metropolitan museums—an ideology implicit as well in the Orientalist *Intolerance, Cleopatra,* and the *Mummy* series. (These films, not surprisingly, tend to be programmed in museums featuring Egyptological exhibitions; Figure 7.) *Raiders of the Lost Ark,* symptomatically, assumes a disjuncture between contemporary and ancient Egypt, since the space between the present and the past can "only" be bridged by the scientist. The full significance of the ancient archaeological objects within the Eurocentric vision of the Spielberg film is presumed to be understood only by the

Western scientists, relegating the Egyptian people to the role of ignorant Arabs who happen to be sitting on a land full of historical treasures—much as they happen to "sit" on oil. Set in the mid-1930s when
most of the world was still under colonial rule, the film regards the
colonial presence in Egypt, furthermore, as completely natural, eliding a history of Arab nationalist revolts against foreign domination.

The American hero—often cinematically portrayed as a cowboy—is
an archaeologist implicitly searching for the Eastern roots of Western
civilization. He liberates the ancient Hebrew ark from illegal Egyptian
possession, while also rescuing it from immoral Nazi control, subliminally reinforcing American and Jewish solidarity vis-à-vis the Nazis and
their Arab assistants.[46] The geopolitical alignments here are as clear as
in the inadvertent allegory of *The Ten Commandments*, where a WASPish
Charlton Heston is made to incarnate Hebrew Moses struggling against
the Egyptians, thus allegorizing in the context of the 1950s the contemporary struggle of the West (Israel and the U.S.) against Egyptians/
Arabs.[47] That at the end of *Raiders of the Lost Ark* it is the U.S. Army
that guards the "top secret" ark—with the active complicity of the ark
itself—strengthens this evocation of geopolitical alliances.[48] *Raiders of
the Lost Ark* significantly develops parallel linked plots in which the
female protagonist, Marion, and the ark become the twin objects of
the hero's search for harmony. The necklace that leads to the ark is
first associated with Marion, who becomes herself the object of com-
peting nationalist male desires. She is abducted by the Nazis and their
Arab assistants much as the ark is hijacked by them, followed by Dr.
Jones's rescue of Marion and the ark from the Nazis. The telos of the
voyage into unknown regions—whether mental or geographical—then,
is that the Westerner both knows the Orient (in the epistemological
and biblical senses) and at the same time brings it knowledge, rescuing it from its own obscurantism.

### Egyptology and *The Mummy*

A different perspective on these issues is suggested in the Egyptian film
*The Mummy/The Night of Counting the Years* (*Al Mumia*, 1969) directed
by Shadi Abdel Salam.[49] Based on the actual case of the discovery of
pharaonic tombs in the Valley of the Kings in 1881, a year before the
full British colonization of Egypt, the film opens with the French
Egyptologist Gaston Maspero informing his colleagues about the black-
market trade in antiquities coming from the reigns of pharaohs such
as Ahmose,[50] Thutmose III,[51] and Ramses II.[52] The government's archaeological commission, under Maspero, delegates an expedition,
headed by a young Egyptian archaeologist, to investigate the location
of the tombs in Thebes in order to end the thefts. In Thebes, meanwhile,

the headman of the Upper Egyptian Horobbat tribe, which had been living off extracting artifacts from the pharaonic tombs, has just died, and his brother must initiate his two nephews into the secret of the mountain. Still in grief over their father's death, the sons are repelled by the dissection of the mummy merely to get at a gold necklace depicting the sacred "Eye of Horus." The protesting brothers must choose between two betrayals, both of them grave: the vulturelike lootings of ancient kingdoms and the desecration of their mummies, or the betrayal of their father's secret with the consequence of cutting off their source of income and therefore their ability to feed hungry Horobbat mouths. Any revelation of the secret would mean ultimately destroying their family and tribe in the name of respect for "the dead" now viewed by the elders as nothing more than leathery mummies. The older brother is assassinated by the village elders when he refuses to sell the artifact on the black market, while the younger brother, Wannis, is torn between his guilt over owing his life to ancient Egyptian corpses ("How many bodies did my father violate in order to feed us?" he asks his mother) and the condemnation of his people. Wandering through the ruins of Thebes and Karnak—for him not simply a memento of an older civilization but the very living reminder of his childhood playground— the long-take swirling camera movements reflect his ethical and even epistemological vertigo, his conflicting internalized responsibility for his Egyptian heritage vis-à-vis his immediate responsibility for present-day lives. After being reassured that the "effendi archaeologists" are trying to understand Egypt's past and not plunder it, he reveals the secret knowledge to Maspero's assistant. The expedition, before the village can prevent it, empties the graves and carries out the mummy-coffins, destined for the museum (Figure 8).

*The Mummy/The Night of Counting the Years* is set in the late nineteenth century, at the height of imperial Egyptology. By the time Britain occupied Egypt in 1882, the country was bankrupt of its archaeological treasures, which were exhibited in London and Paris as testimony of Western scientific progress. In the heroic, almost sanctimonious, language of the Egyptological mission, archaeological reports on the 1881 discovery describe the rescue of the ancient East's powerful kings from Arab clans in a way that associates the Westerner with emperors and royal dynasties. The simplistic positing of a rupture between present and past Egypt conveniently empowers the Western claim over Egypt's past,[53] thus naturalizing the presence of the Rosetta Stone, for example, in the British Museum. Abdel Salam's film implicitly challenges the archaeological master-narrative by foregrounding the voices of those on the margins of Egyptological texts. If the film opens with an archaeological project and ends with its successful accomplishment, it

Figure 8. *The Mummy/The Night of Counting the Years* (1969): Amplifying the voices on the margins of the Egyptological texts. Courtesy of the British Film Institute.

also undermines that mission by focusing on the concrete dilemmas of living Egyptians. The nondiegetic musical motif based on Upper Egypt popular music ("Al Arian"), and the slow rhythm evocative of the regional atmosphere, furthermore, cinematically convey the cultural force of their environment.[54] The film does not end, significantly, with the narrative closure of safe placement of the artifacts in a museum, but rather with the slow vanishing of the boat carrying the Egyptologists and the mummies, all from the perspective of the devastated tribe. If *How Tasty Was My Frenchman* opens with the penetration of the Europeans seen from the perspective of the Native Americans, *The Mummy/ The Night of Counting the Years* ends with the emptiness left behind by the intrusion of Europe. Reportedly, the Egyptian women of the tribe mourned when the mummies were taken, yet Shadi Abdel Salam presents, in long shot and through depsychologized editing, a unified communal silent gaze where the whistling wind becomes a voice of protest. Their gaze, far from conveying the triumphant conclusion of the archaeological narrative, unveils the disastrous rupture in their very lives, thus subverting the self-celebratory Egyptological definitions of dispossession and theft.[55]

Archaeological reports often inadvertently display metaphors that suggest capitalist values attached to their own profession. In his account of the 1881 discovery, the archaeologist Howard Carter, who worked on the discovery of Tut-ankh-Amen's tomb, writes: "Incredible as it may seem, the secret was kept for six years, and the family, with a banking account of forty or more dead pharaohs to draw upon, grew rich."[56] Abdel Salam's *The Mummy/The Night of Counting the Years*, in contrast, emphasizes the ambivalent relationships between the tribe and the treasures, between the Egyptian people and their ancient heritage. The tribe lives on theft, yet its circumstances of hunger imply a critique of the imperial class system. The archaeological redemption, in other words, must be seen in its historical and cultural context, that is, taking the only power the tribe possesses without bringing anything in return. It would be simplistic, however, to view *The Mummy/The Night of Counting the Years* as a mere condemnation of Egyptology. The film illuminates class relations within a colonial dynamics in which the tribe, in order to survive, is obliged to deal with the "small" black-market dealers, for the "effendies" from Cairo will not even pay them and arrest them. Class formations of Egyptian society, particularly within imperial context, force the small village to regard the ancient artifacts as a means of survival, a system in which the only power of the tribe is their secret. The effendies are viewed from the perspective of the tribe as strangers, cut off, in other words, from the national reality. *The Mummy/The Night of Counting the Years*, in contrast with Western representations of Egypt, does not stress the grandeur of ancient Egypt at the expense of contemporary Arab lives; rather, it exposes the complex, multilayered dimensions of Egyptian identity.

An allegory on Egyptian identity, the film offers a meditation on the destiny of a national culture. To cite Shadi Abdel Salam: "We have a national culture but it lies buried at the bottom of the memory of the people who are not always aware of its great values."[57] Speaking in an improbably literary Arabic (rather than an existing dialect), the villagers represent the Arab culture heritage, while they are simultaneously presented as continuous with the ancient past, emphasized, for example, through the ancient Egyptian eye makeup worn by the actress Nadia Lutfi. In a symbolic, syncretic continuity of pharaonic and Arab Egypt, the film associates the ancient "Eye of Horus"—first shown in a close shot, as if looking at the brothers (directly at the spectator)—with the Arab sign of "hamsa," the hand extended against the evil eye, seen on the boat on which the older brother is murdered. Shots of a gigantic monumental fist similarly accompany a dialogue between Wannis and a migrant worker about a "hand holding a fate no one can read," and "what fate can you read in a stone hand?" suggesting the hazardous nature of reading fate at the hands of the monuments. The contemporary popular middle Eastern culture of reading fate in the hands, in sum, is implicitly contrasted with the immortal grandeur but also the lifelessness of mere monuments.[58] A kind of visual dialogue of Arab Egypt with its past, furthermore, is rendered through montage, for example, when the image of the agonizing Wannis, looking up at the gigantic monument, is juxtaposed with a high-angle shot of Wannis, this time presumably from the monument's point of view. The presentation of Egypt's national identity as an amalgam of histories and cultures evokes the formulations, for example, by the writers Taha Hussain and Tawfiq al-Hakim, of Egyptian identity as a synthesis of pharaonic past, Arabic language, and Islamic religion. The film's opening intertitle, drawn from *The Book of the Dead*, promising that the one who shall go shall also return, and the final intertitle calling for the dead to "wake up," must also be seen within the context in which *The Mummy/The Night of Counting the Years* was produced.[59] During the period following the 1967 war, after the defeat to Israel, the Gamal Abdel Nasser regime lost much of its allure, and the general mood of despair went hand in hand with a felt need for critical reassessments. In this sense, the ancient inscription of resurrection is also allegorically a call to Egypt of the late 1960s for national rebirth.

## Textual/Sexual Strategies

### The Colonial Gaze

Still playing a significant role in postcolonial geopolitics, the predominant trope of "rescue" in colonial discourse forms the crucial site of the battle over representation. Not only has the Western imaginary metaphorically rendered the colonized land as a female to be saved from her environ/mental disorder, it has also projected rather more literal narratives of rescue, specifically of Western and non-Western women—from African, Asian, Arab, or Native American men. The figure of the Arab assassin/rapist, like that of the African cannibal, helps produce the narrative and ideological role of the Western liberator as integral to the colonial rescue fantasy. This projection, whose imagistic avatars include the polygamous Arab, the libidinous black buck, and the macho Latino, provides an indirect apologia for domination. In the case of the Orient, it carries with it religious/theological overtones of the inferiority of the polygamous Islamic world to the Christian world as encapsulated by the monogamous couple. The justification of Western expansion, then, becomes linked to issues of sexuality.

The intersection of colonial and gender discourses involves a shifting, contradictory subject positioning, whereby Western woman can simultaneously constitute "center" and "periphery," identity and alterity. A Western woman, in these narratives, exists in a relation of subordination to Western man and in a relation of domination toward "non-Western" men and women. This textual relationality homologizes the historical positioning of colonial women who have played, albeit with a difference, an oppressive role toward colonized people (both men and women), at times actively perpetuating the legacy of Empire.[60] This problematic role is anatomized in Ousmane Sembène's *Black Girl (La Noire de . . .*, 1966) in the relationship between the Senegalese maid and her French employer, and to some extent by Mira Hamermesh's documentary on South Africa *Maids and Madams* (1985), in contrast to the white-woman's-burden ideology in films such as *The King and I* (1956), *Out of Africa* (1985), and *Gorillas in the Mist* (1989). In many films, colonial women become the instrument of the white male vision and are thus granted a gaze more powerful than that not only of non-Western women but also of non-Western men.

In the colonial context, given the shifting relational nature of power situations and representations, women can be granted an ephemeral "positional superiority" (Edward Said), a possibility exemplified in *The Sheik* (1921). Based on Edith Hull's novel, George Melford's *The Sheik* introduces the spectator to the Arab world first in the form of the "barbarous ritual" of the marriage market, depicted as a casino lottery ritual from which Arab men select women to "serve as chattel slaves." At the same time, the Western woman character, usually the object of the male gaze in Hollywood films, tends to be granted in the East an active (colonial) gaze, insofar as she now, temporarily within the narrative, becomes the sole delegate, as it were, of Western civilization. The "norms of the text" (Boris Uspensky) are represented by the Western male, but in the moments of His absence, the white woman becomes the civilizing center of the film.[61] These racial and sexual hierarchies in the text are also clearly exemplified in Michael Powell and Emeric Pressburger (*Black Narcissus*), where most of the narrative is focalized through the British nuns and their "civilizing mission" in India. But ultimately the "norms of the text" are embodied by the British man, whose initial "prophecy" that the wild mountains of India are not suitable for and are beyond the control of the Christian missionaries is confirmed by the end of the narrative, with the virtual punishment of the nuns as catastrophes and mental chaos penetrate their order. Yet in relation to the "Natives" (both Indian men and women), the British women are privileged and form the "filter" and "center of consciousness" (Gérard Genette) of the film.

The discourse on gender within a colonial context, in sum, suggests that Western women can occupy a relatively powerful position on the surface of the text, as the vehicles less for a sexual gaze than a colonial gaze. In these friction-producing moments between sexual and national hierarchies, particularly as encapsulated through the relationship between Third World men and First World women, national identity (associated with the white female character) is relatively privileged over sexual identity (associated with the dark male character). At the same time, the same ambivalence operates in relation to Third World men, whose punishment for interracial desire is simultaneously accompanied by spectatorial gratification for a male sexual gaze as ephemerally relayed by a darker man. These contradictions of national and sexual hierarchies, present in embryo in early cinema, are accentuated in the recent nostalgia-for-empire (liberal) films that foreground a female protagonist, presumably appealing to feminist codes, while reproducing colonialist narrative and cinematic power arrangements. The desexualization of the "good" African or Indian (servant) man in *Gorillas in the Mist*, *A Passage to India*, and *Out of Africa*, not unlike the desexualization of the female domestic servant as in *The Birth of a Nation* (1916) and *Gone With the Wind* (1939), is dialectically linked to the placement of the Western woman in the (white) "pater" paradigm vis-à-vis the "natives."

## Rape and Rescue Fantasy

The chromatic sexual hierarchy in colonialist narrative, typical of Eurocentric racial conventions, has white women/men occupy the center of the narrative, with the white woman as the desired object of the male protagonists and antagonists. Marginalized within the narrative, Third World women—when not inscribed as metaphors for their virgin land as in *Bird of Paradise*—appear largely as sexually hungry subalterns.[62] In one scene in *The Sheik*, Arab women—some of them black—fight quite literally over their Arab man. While the white woman has to be lured, made captive, and virtually raped to awaken her repressed desire, the Arab/black/Latin women are driven by a raging libido. Here one encounters some of the complementary contradictions in colonial discourse whereby a Third World land and its inhabitants are the object of the desire for chastity articulated in the virgin metaphors, while also manifesting Victorian repression of sexuality, particularly female sexuality, through unleashing its pornographic impulse.[63]

The positing of female sexual enslavement by polygamous Third World men becomes especially ironic when we recall the subjection of African-American women slaves on Southern plantations with the daily lived polygamy of white men slaveowners.[64] Images of black/Arab woman in "heat" versus "frigid" white woman also indirectly highlight the menacing figure of the black/Arab rapist and therefore mythically elide the history of subordination of Third World women by First World men. The hot/frigid dichotomy, then, implies three interdependent axioms within the sexual politics of colonialist discourse: (1) the sexual interaction of black/Arab men and white women can *only* involve rape (since white women, within this perspective, cannot possibly desire black men); (2) the sexual interaction of white men and black/Arab women cannot involve rape (since black/Arab women are in perpetual heat and desire their white master); and (3) the interaction of black/Arab men and black/Arab women also cannot involve rape, since both are in perpetual heat. It was this racist combinatoire that generated the (largely unspoken) rationale for the castration and lynching of African-American men and nonpunishment of white men for the rape of African-American women.

It is within this logic that *The Birth of a Nation* obsessively links sexual and racial phobias. The animalistic "black," Gus, attempts to rape the virginal Flora, much as the "mulatto" Lynch tries to force Elsie into marriage, and the "mulatta" Lydia accuses an innocent white man of sexual abuse, while manipulating the unaware politician Stoneman through sexuality. The threat of African-American political assertion is subliminally linked to black sexual potency. It is not surprising, therefore, that the only nonthreatening black figure, the "loyal" mammy, is portrayed as completely desexualized. The thematization of blacks' hypersexuality diacritically foils (white) masculinist acts of patriotism. It is the attempted rape of Flora that catalyzes the grand act of white "liberation" (Figure 9). The opening intertitle, which states that the very presence of the African in America "planted the first seed of disunion," and the portrayal of idealized harmony between North and South (and Masters and Slaves) before the abolition of slavery, suggest that libidinal blacks destroyed the nation. The rescue of Flora, of Elsie, and of the besieged Northerners and Southerners (who are now once again united "in common defense of their Aryan Birthright") operates as a didactic allegory whose telos is the Klansmen's vision of the "order of things." The closure of "mixed" marriage between North and South confirms national unity and establishes a certain sexual order in which the virginal desired white woman is available only to white man. The superimposition of the Christ figure over the celebrating family/nation provides a religious benediction on the "birth." This abstract, metaphysical Birth of the Nation masks a more concrete notion of birth—no less relevant to the conception of the American nation—that of children from raped black women, just as the naming of the mulatto as "Lynch" crudely blames the victims. Furthermore, the white man,

Figure 9. *The Birth of a Nation* (1915): The national (white) identity catalyzed by fantasies of rape and rescue. Courtesy of the Museum of Modern Art, New York.

who historically raped Third World women, manifests latent rapist desires toward innocent white women via a projected black man, here literally masked in blackface.

Even when not involving rape, the possibilities of erotic interaction in films prior to the 1960s were severely limited by apartheid-style ethnic/racial codes. The same Hollywood that at times could project mixed love stories between Anglo-Americans and Latins and Arabs (especially if incarnated by white American actors and actresses such as Valentino in *The Sheik*, Dorothy Lamour in *The Road to Morocco* [1942], or Maureen O'Hara in *They Met in Argentina* [1941]) was completely inhibited in relation to African, Asian, or Native American sexuality. This latent fear of blood tainting in such melodramas as *Call Her Savage* (1932) and *Pinky* (1949) necessitates narratives where the "half breed" ("Native American" in *Call Her Savage* and "black" in *Pinky*) female protagonists are prevented at the closure of the films from participating in mixed marriage, ironically despite the roles being played by "pure white" actresses. It is therefore the generic space of melodrama that

Figure 10. *The Road to Morocco* (1942): The imperial path to the constitution of the couple. Courtesy of the Museum of Modern Art, New York.

preoccupies itself with "interracial" romantic interaction. The trajectory of constituting the couple in the musical comedy, for example, could not allow for a racially "subaltern" protagonist (Figure 10).

The Production Code of the Motion Picture Producers and Directors of America, Inc., 1930–1934, an even stricter version of the Hays Office codes of the 1920s, explicitly states: "Miscegenation (sex relation between the white and black races) is forbidden."[65] The delegitimizing of the romantic union between "white" and "black" "races" is linked to a broader exclusion of Africans, Asians, and Native Americans from participation in social institutions. Translating the obsession with "pure blood" into legal language, Southern miscegenation laws, as pointed out by African-American feminists as early as the end of the last century,[66] were designed to maintain white (male) supremacy and to prevent a possible transfer of property to blacks in the postabolition era. "Race" as a biological category, as Hazel Carby formulates it, was subordinated to race as a political category.[67] It is within this context of an exclusionary ideology that we can understand the Production Code's universal censorship of sexual violence and brutality where the assumption is one of purely individual victimization, thus undermining a possible portrayal of the racially and sexually based violence toward African Americans and implicitly wiping out the memory of the rape, castration, and lynching from the American record.[68] The Production Code, in other words, eliminates a possible counter narrative by Third World people for whom sexual violence has often been at the kernel of their historical experience and identity.[69]

## The Spectacle of Difference

An analysis of the history of First World cinema in racial and colonial terms uncovers a tendency toward national "allegory," in Fredric Jameson's sense, of texts that even when narrating apparently private stories, manage to metaphorize the public sphere, where the micro-individual is doubled, as it were by the macronation, and the personal and the political, the private and the historical, are inextricably linked.[70] The national and racial hierarchies of the cinema allegorize, in other words, extradiscursive social intercourse. In the period of the Good Neighbor Policy, Hollywood attempted to enlist Latin America for hemispheric unity against the Axis. As European film markets were reducing their film consumption due to the outbreak of World War II, Hollywood, in the hopes for South American markets and pan-American political unity, flooded the screens with films featuring "Latin American" themes. Interestingly, the trope of "good neighbor" very rarely extended to winning family status through interracial or international marriage. Marginalized within the narrative, and often limited to roles as entertainers, the Latin American characters in *The Gang's All Here* (1943), *Too Many Girls* (1940), and *Weekend in Havana* (1941) at the finale tend to be at the exact point from which they began, in contrast with the teleologically evolving status of the North American protagonists. Displaying "exoticism," the musical numbers in these films provided the spectacle of difference, functioning narratively by uniting the North American couple vis-à-vis the South Americans.

Films such as *The Gang's All Here* demonstrate a generic division of labor, whereby the solid, "serious," or romantic numbers such as "A Journey to a Star" tend to be performed by the North American protagonists Alice Faye and James Ellison, while the Latin American characters perform "unserious," "excessive" numbers involving swaying hips, exaggerated facial expressions, caricaturally sexy costumes, and "think-big" style props embodied by Carmen Miranda. Her figure in the number "The Lady with the Tutti-Fruitti Hat" is dwarfed by gigantesque vegetative imagery in which the final image of her as a virtual fertility goddess links this idealized quality with the beginning of the number where goods are unloaded from the South; the North here celebrates the South as the feminine principle capable of giving birth to goods consumed by the North (Figure 11). The bananas in Miranda's number, furthermore, not only enact the agricultural reductionism of Latin America but also form phallic symbols, here raised by "voluptuous" Latinas over circular quasi-vaginal forms. (But the Latina, as the lyrics suggest, will take her hat off "only for Johnny Smith," such as the "oriental" woman in films such as *The Road to Morocco* would only remove her veil for the Anglo-American.) This construction of Latinness (or Orientalness) as the locus of exoticism is not subsumable by hegemonic North American cultural codes. The South American characters therefore do not form part of any narrative development, and their presence is "tolerable" only on the folkloric level. Character interaction, in this sense, allegorizes the larger relation between the North and South (or West and East) and reflects an ambivalence of attraction/repulsion toward those on the "margins" of the Western Empire.

The gender and colonial discursive intersection is revealed in the ways that Hollywood exploited the Orient, Africa, and Latin America as a pretext for eroticized images, especially from 1934 through the mid-1950s when the restrictive production code forbade depicting "scenes of passion" in all but the most puerile terms, and required that the sanctity of the institution of marriage be upheld at all times. Miscegenation, nudity, sexually suggestive dances or costumes, "excessive and lustful kissing" were prohibited, while adultery, illicit sex, seduction, or rape could never be more than suggested, and then only if absolutely essential to the plot and severely punished at the end. The

Figure 11. *The Gang's All Here* (1943): The fertility goddess consumed by Empire. Courtesy of the Museum of Modern Art, New York.

Western obsession with the harem, for example, was not simply crucial for Hollywood's visualization of the Orient but also authorized the proliferation of sexual images projected onto an otherized elsewhere, much as the Orient, Africa, and Latin America played a similar role for Victorian culture.

Exoticizing and eroticizing the Third World allowed the imperial imaginary to play out its own fantasies of sexual domination. Already in the silent era, films often included eroticized dances, featuring a rather improbable mélange of Spanish and Indian dances, plus a touch of belly dancing (*The Dance of Fatima* [ca. 1903], *The Sheik*, and *Son of the Sheik* [1926]). This filmic practice of mélange recalls the frequent superimposition in Orientalist paintings of the visual traces of civilizations as diverse as Arab, Persian, Chinese, and Indian into a single feature of the exotic Orient[71]—a colonialist process that Albert Memmi terms the "mark of the plural." An "oriental" setting (most of the films on the Orient, Africa, and Latin America were studio-shot) thus provided Hollywood filmmakers with a narrative license for exposing flesh without risking censorship; they could display the bare skin of Valentino,

Douglas Fairbanks, and Johnny Weissmuller as well as that of scores of women, from Myrna Loy, Maureen O'Sullivan, and Marlene Dietrich dancing with her legs painted gold to Dolores Grey moving her hips with the "realistic" excuse of other, less civilized cultures. (The code that turned Jane's two-piece outfit into one piece in later films, did not affect, for the most part, the nude breasts of African women at the background of the *Tarzan* series,[72] evoking *National Geographic*'s predilection for "native" nudity.) In the desert and the jungle, the traditional slow-paced process of courtship leading to marriage could be replaced with uninhibited fantasies of sexual domination and "freedom," and specifically with fantasies of polygamy and even rape of presumably repressed white women. The display of rape in a "natural" despotic context continues to the present, for example, in the several attempted rapes of Brooke Shields in *Sahara* (1983). The Orient, like Latin America and Africa, thus is posited as the locus of eroticism by a puritanical society, and a film industry, hemmed in by a moralistic code.

## The Imaginary of the Harem

As with voyeuristic anthropological studies and moralistic travel literature concerning nonnormative conceptions of sexuality, Western cinema diffused the anachronistic but still Victorian obsession with sexuality through the cinematic apparatus. The outlet for Western male heroic desire is clearly seen in *Harum Scarum* (1965), a reflexive film featuring a carnival-like Orient reminiscent of Las Vegas, itself placed in the burning sands of the American desert of Nevada, and offering haremlike nightclubs. The film opens with Elvis Presley—attired in an "oriental" head wrap and vest—arriving on horseback in the desert. Upon arrival, Presley leaps off his horse to free a woman from two evil Arabs who have tied her to a stake. The triumphant rescuer later sings:

> I'm gonna go where the dessert sun is; where the fun is; go where the harem girls dance; go where there's love and romance—out on the burning sands, in some caravan. I'll find adventure where I can. To say the least, go East, young man. You'll feel like the Sheik, so rich and grand, with dancing girls at your command. When paradise starts calling, into some tent I'm crawling. I'll make love the way I plan. Go East—and drink and feast—go East, young man. (Figure 12)

Material abundance in Orientalist discourse, tied to a history of imperial enterprises, here functions as part of the generic utopia of the musical, constituting itself, in Jamesonian terms, as a projected fulfillment of what is desired and absent within the sociopolitical status quo. Yet the "absence" is explicitly within the masculinist imaginative terrain. The images of harems offer an "open sesame" to an unknown, alluring, and tantalizingly forbidden world, posited as desirable to the in-

Figure 12. *Harum Scarum* (1965): Entering the inaccessible *harim*. Courtesy of the Museum of Modern Art, New York.

stinctual primitive presumably inhabiting all men. In *Kismet* (1955), for example, the harem master entertains himself with a panopticonlike device that allows him to watch his many women without their knowledge. Authorizing a voyeuristic entrance into an inaccessible private space, the harem dream reflects a masculinist utopia of sexual omnipotence.[73]

The topos of the harem in contemporary popular culture draws, of course, on a long history of Orientalist fantasies. Western voyagers had no conceivable means of access to harems—indeed, the Arabic etymology of the word *harem, harim*, refers to something "forbidden." Yet Western texts delineate life in the harems with great assurance and apparent exactitude, rather like European Orientalist studio paintings, for example, the *Turkish Bath* (1862) which was painted without Ingres ever visiting the Orient. The excursions to the Orient, and on-location paintings by painters such as Ferdinand-Victor-Eugène Delacroix, similarly, served largely to authenticate an a priori vision. Inspired by the Arab popular tradition of fantastic tales, the travelers recounted the Orient to fellow Westerners according to the paradigms furnished by European translations of *A Thousand and One Nights* (*Alf Laila wa Laila*), tales which were often translated quite loosely in order to satisfy the European taste for a passionately, violent Orient.[74] This Orient was perhaps best encapsulated in the figure of Salome, whose Semitic origins were highlighted by the nineteenth-century Orientalist ethnographic vogue (e.g., Hugo von Habermann, Otto Friedrich).

The historical harem—which was largely an upper-class phenomenon—was in fact most striking in its domesticity. Memoirs written by Egyptian and Turkish women depict the complex familial life and a strong network of female communality horizontally and vertically across class lines.[75] The isolated but relatively powerful harem women depended on working-class women, who were freer to move, and therefore became an important connection to the outside world.[76] Despite their subordination, harem women, as Leila Ahmed points out, often owned and ran their property, and could at times display crucial political power, thus revealing the harem as a site of contradictions.[77] Whereas Western discourse on the harem defined it simply as a male-dominated space, the accounts of the harem by Middle Eastern women testify to a system whereby a man's female relatives also shared the living space, allowing women access to other women, providing a protected space for the exchange of information and ideas safe from the eyes and the ears of men. (Contemporary Middle Eastern vestiges of this tradition are found in regular all-female gatherings, whereby women, as in the harems, carnivalize male power through jokes, stories, singing, and dancing.) In other words, the "harem," though patriarchal in nature, has been subjected to an ahistorical discourse whose Eurocentric assumptions left unquestioned the sexual oppression of the West. The Middle Eastern system of communal seclusion, then, must also be compared to the Western system of domestic "solitary confinement" for upper-middle-class women.[78]

European women constituted an enthusiastic audience for much of the nineteenth-century Orientalist poetry written by Beckford, Byron, and Moore, anticipating the spectatorial enthusiasm for exoticist films. As travelers, however, their discourse on the harems oscillates between Orientalist narratives and more dialogical testimonies. Western women participated in the Western colonial gaze; their writings often voyeuristically dwell on "oriental" clothes, postures, and gestures, exoticizing the female Other.[79] If male narrators were intrigued by the harem as the locus of lesbian sexuality, female travelers, who as women had more access to female spaces, undermined the pornographic imagination of the harem. Interestingly, the detailed descriptions of Turkish female bodies in Lady Mary Wortley Montagu's letters, particularly drawn from her visit to the *hammam* (baths), points to a subliminal erotic fascination with the female Other, a fascination masquerading, at times, as a male gaze:

> I perceiv'd that the Ladys with the finest skins and most delicate shapes had the greatest share of my admiration, th'o their faces were sometimes less beautiful than those of their companions. To tell you the truth, I had the wickedness enough to wish secretly that Mr. Gervase had been there invisible. I fancy it would have very much improv'd his art to see so many fine Women naked in different postures.[80]

Female travelers, furthermore, were compelled to situate their own oppression vis-à-vis that of "oriental" women. Lady Mary Wortley Montagu often measures the freedom endowed to English vis-à-vis Turkish women, suggesting the paradoxes of harems and veils:

> 'Tis very easy to see that they have more liberty than we have, no woman of what rank soever being permitted to go in the streets without two muslins, one that covers her face all but her eyes and another that hides the whole dress. . . . You may guess how effectually this disguises them, that there is no distinguishing the great lady from her slave, and 'tis impossible for the most jealous husband to know his wife when he meets her, and no man dare either touch or follow a women in the streets. . . . The perpetual masquerade gives them entire liberty of following their inclinations without danger of discovery.[81]

In fact, Lady Mary Wortley Montagu implicitly suggests an awareness, on the part of Turkish women, not simply of their oppression but also of that of European women. Recounting the day she was undressed in the *hamman* by the lady of the house, who was struck at the sight of the stays, she quoted the lady's remark that "the Husbands in England were much worse than in the East; for they ty'd up their wives in boxes, of the shape of their bodies."[82]

The popular image-making of the Orient internalized, in other words, the codes of male-oriented travel narratives. The continuities between the representation of the native body and the female body are obvious when we compare Hollywood's ethnography with Hollywood's pornography. Ironically, we find a latent inscription of harems and despots even in texts not set in the Orient. *Harem structures*, in fact, permeate Western mass-mediated culture. Busby Berkeley's musical numbers, for example, project a haremlike structure reminiscent of Hollywood's mythical Orient. Like the harem, his musical numbers involve a multitude of women who, as Lucy Fischer suggests, serve as signifiers of male power over infinitely substitutable females.[83] The mise-en-scène of both harem scenes and musical numbers is structured around the scopic privilege of the master and his limitless pleasure in an exclusive place inaccessible to other men. Berkeley's panopticonlike camera links visual pleasure with a kind of surveillance of manipulated female movement. The camera's omnipresent and mobile gaze, its magic-carpet-like airborne prowling along confined females embodies the overarching look of the absent/present master—that is, of both the director/producer and vicariously of the spectator. The production numbers tend to exclude the male presence but allow for the fantasies of the spectator, positioning his/her gaze as that of a despot entertained by a plurality of females. Rendered virtually identical, the women in Berkeley's numbers evoke the analogy between the musical show and the harem not only as a textual construct but also as a studio practice whose patriarchal structure of casting is conceived as a kind of beauty contest (a "judgment of Paris"). Speaking of his casting methods, Berkeley himself recounted a day in which he interviewed 723 women in order to select only three: "My sixteen regular girls were sitting on the side waiting; so after I picked the three girls I put them next to my special sixteen and they matched just like pearls."[84]

## The Desert Odyssey

The exoticist films allow for subliminally transexual tropes. The phantasm of the Orient gives an outlet for a carnivalesque play with national and at times gender identities. Isabelle Adjani in *Ishtar* is disguised as an Arab male-rebel and Brooke Shields as an American male racer in the Sahara desert, while Rudolph Valentino (*The Sheik* and *Son of the Sheik*), Douglas Fairbanks (*The Thief of Bagdad*), Elvis Presley (*Harum Scarum*), Peter O'Toole (*Lawrence of Arabia*), Warren Beatty and Dustin Hoffman (*Ishtar*) wear Arab disguise. Masquerading manifests a latent desire to transgress fixed national and gender identities. In *The Sheik*, the Agnes Ayres character, assisted by Arab women, wears an Arab female dress in order to penetrate the oriental "marriage market," assuming the "inferior" position of the Arab women in order, paradoxically, to empower herself with a gaze on oriental despotism. The change of gender identities of female characters in more recent films such as *Sahara* and *Ishtar* allows as well for harmless transgressions of the coded "feminine" body language. In counternarratives such as *The Battle of Algiers* (*La Battaglia di Algeri*, 1966), however, gender and national disguises take on different signification.[85] FLN Algerian women wear Western "modern" dress, dye their hair blond, and even act coquettishly with French soldiers.[86] Here it is the Third World

Figure 13. *Lawrence of Arabia* (1962): Interracial homoerotic subtext. Courtesy of the British Film Institute.

that masquerades as the West, not as an act of self-effacing mimicry but as a way of sabotaging the colonial regime of assimilation.

Since clothing over the last few centuries, as a result of what J. C. Flugel calls "the Great Masculine Renunciation,"[87] has been limited to austere, uncolorful, and unplayful costumes, the projection to the phantasmic locus of the Orient allows the imagination to go exuberantly "native." Historically, the widely disseminated popular image in newspapers and newsreels of T. E. Lawrence in flowing Arab costume have partially inspired films such as *The Sheik* and *Son of The Sheik*, whose bisexual appeal can be located in the closet construction of Western man as "feminine."[88] The coded "feminine" look, therefore, is played out within the safe space of the Orient, through the "realistic" embodiment of the Other. David Lean's Lawrence, despite his classical association with norms of heroic manliness, is also portrayed in a homoerotic light. When he is accepted by the Arab tribe he is dressed all in white, and at one point set on a horse, moving delicately, virtually captured like bride. Drawing a sword from his sheath, the Peter O'Toole character shifts the gendered signification of the phallic symbol by using it as a mirror to look at his own newly acquired "feminine" "oriental" image. More generally, the relationship between Lawrence and the Omar Sharif character gradually changes from initial male rivalry to an implied erotic attraction in which Sharif is associated with female imagery, best encapsulated in the scene where Sharif is seen in close-up with wet eyes, identifying with the tormented Lawrence. (Figure 13). The interracial homoerotic subtext in *Lawrence of Arabia* forms part of a long tradition of colonial narratives from novels such as *Robinson Crusoe* (Crusoe and Friday) and *The Adventures of*

*Huckleberry Finn* (Huck and Jim) to filmic adaptations such as *Around the World in 80 Days* (Phileas Fogg and his dark servant Passepartout).[89] Most texts about the Empire, from the Western genre to recent nostalgia-for-Empire films such as *Mountains of the Moon* (1989), however, are pervaded by white homoeroticism in which male explorers, deprived of women, are "forced" into physical closeness, weaving bonds of affection and desire, in the course of their plights in an unknown, hostile land.

Homoeroticism, then, can simultaneously permeate homophobic colonialist texts. Within this symptomatic dialectic we may also understand the textual (dis)placement of the heterosexual African/Arab/Latino man, as playing the id to the Western masculinist superego. In *The Sheik*, for example, Valentino, as long as he is known to the spectator only as Arab, acts as the id, but when he is revealed to be the son of Europeans, he is transformed into a superego figure who nobly risks his life to rescue the Englishwoman from "real" Arab rapists.[90] And the Englishwoman overcomes her sexual repression only in the desert, after being sexually provoked repeatedly by the sheik. Valentino, the "Latin lover," is here projected into another "exotic" space where he can act out sexual fantasies that would have been unthinkable in a contemporaneous American or European setting. The desert, in this sense, functions narratively as an isolating element, as sexually and morally separate imaginary territory (Figure 14). The Orientalist films tend to begin in the city—where European civilization has already tamed the East—but the real dramatic conflicts take place in the desert where women are defenseless, and a white woman could easily become the captive of a romantic sheik or evil Arab. The positioning of a rapeable white woman by a lustful male in an isolated desert locale gives voice to a masculinist fantasy of complete control over the Western woman, the woman "close to home," without any intervening protective code of morality. Puritanical Hollywood thus claims to censure female adventurousness and the male tyranny of harems and rapes—but only, paradoxically, as a way of gratifying Western interracial sexual desires.

In the more recent reworking of *The Sheik* and *Son of the Sheik*, in Menahem Golan's *Sahara*, the male rescue fantasy and the punishment of female rebellion undergird the film. In *Sahara* the central figure, Dale (Brooke Shields), feisty race-car driver and only daughter of a 1920s car manufacturer, is presented as reckless, daring, and assertive for entering the male domain of the oriental desert and for entering the "men only" race. She also literally disguises herself as a man and adopts His profession and His mastery of the desert land through technology. Captured by desert tribesmen, she becomes a commodity fought over within the tribe and between tribes; the camera's fetishization of

Figure 14. *The Sheik* (1921): The desert as the site of the sexual imaginary.
Courtesy of the Museum of Modern Art, New York.

her body, however, is the ironic reminder of the Western projection of
stars' bodies as commodity. Scenes of Brooke Shields wrestling with
her captors not only suture the Western spectator to a national rescue
operation but also invite the implied spectator into an orgiastic voyeurism. The desire for the Western woman and the fear of losing control over her are manifested in her punishment through several
attempted rapes by Arabs. But at the end the courageous winner of the
race decides "on her own" to return to the noble light-skinned sheik
who had rescued her from cruel Arabs at the risk of his own life. The
woman, who could have won independence, still "voluntarily" prefers
the ancient ways of gender hierarchies (Figure 15).

At times, it is implied that women, while offended by Arab and Muslim rapists, actually *prefer* masterful men like Valentino.[91] Following
the screening of *The Sheik*, newspaper columnists were asking, "Do
women like masterful men?" To which Valentino replied: "Yes. All
women like a little cave-man stuff. No matter whether they are feminists, suffragettes or so-called new women, they like to have a masterful

Figure 15. Brooke Shields in *Sahara* (1982): Gender transgressions in the oriental desert. Courtesy of the Museum of Modern Art, New York.

man who makes them do things he asserts."[92] Edith Hull expressed similar opinions. "There can be only one head in a house. Despite modern desire for equality of sexes I still believe that physically and morally it is better that the head should be the man."[93] Edith Hull's novel and Monic Katterjohn's adaptation gratify, to some extent, a projected Western female desire for an "exotic" lover, for a romantic, sensual, passionate, but nonlethal, play with the *Liebestod*, a release of the id for the (segregated) upper-middle-class occidental women.[94] (The author of the source novel claimed to have written the book for relaxation when her husband was in the war and she was alone in India. She decided to visit in Algeria, where she was impressed with the fine work the French government was doing.) In this sense the phantasm of the Orient can be incorporated by Western women, forming part of the broader colonial discourse on the "exotic," while constituting an imaginary locus for suppressed sexual desires.

The rescue fantasy, when literalized through the rescue of a woman from a lascivious Arab, has to be seen not only as an allegory of saving the Orient from its libidinal, instinctual destructiveness but also as a didactic *Bildungsroman* addressed to women at home, perpetuating by contrast the myth of the sexual egalitarianism of the West. The exoticist films delegitimize Third World national identities and give voice to antifeminist backlash, responding to the threat to institutionalized patriarchal power presented by the woman's suffrage movements and the nascent feminist struggle. In this sense the narrative of Western women in the Third World can be read as a projected didactic allegory insinuating the dangerous nature of the "uncivilized man" and by implication lauding the freedom presumably enjoyed by Western women. In *The Sheik* and *Sahara* the Western woman directly rebels against the "civilized tradition" of marriage at the beginning of the film, calling it "captivity," only to later become literally captive of lusting Dark men. Transgressing male space (penetrating the marriage market by masquerading as an Arab woman in *The Sheik*, and participating in a male race by masquerading as a young man in *Sahara*), the female protagonist begins with a hubris vis-à-vis her Western male protectors (against the Arabians from the desert), and then goes through the "pedagogical" experience of attempted rapes. The telos, or quite literally, "homecoming" of this desert odyssey is the disciplinary punishment of female desire for liberation and renewed spectatorial appreciation for the existing sexual, racial, and national order.

---

My discussion of colonial constructions of gender has aimed at analyzing the crucial role of sexual difference for the culture of Empire. Western popular culture, in this sense, has operated on the same Eurocentric discursive continuum as such disciplines as philosophy, Egyptology, anthropology, historiography, and geography. From the erotic projections of *The Sheik* to the spectacular historiography of *Lawrence of Arabia*, or from the fantastic tale *The Mummy* (1932) to the Egyptological mission of *Raiders of the Lost Ark*, my reading has tried to suggest that despite some differences, having to do with the periods in which the films were produced, hegemonic Western representation has been locked into a series of Eurocentric articulations of power. Although a feminist reading of (post)colonial discourse must take into account the national and historical specificities of that discourse, it is equally important also to chart the broader structural analogies in the representation of diverse Third World cultures. Postcolonial narratives, as we have seen, serve to define the "West" through metaphors of rape, fantasies of rescue, and eroticized geographies. The popular culture of Empire has tended to rely on a structurally similar genderized discourse within different national and historical moments, a discourse challenged by resistant counternarratives such as *How Tasty Was My Frenchman, Nice Coloured Girls* (1987), and *The Mummy/The Night of Counting the Years*.

## Notes

1. Different sections of this essay were presented at several conferences: Third World Film Institute, New York University (1984); The Middle East Studies Association, University of California, Los Angeles (1988); Humanities Council Faculty Seminar on Race and Gender, New York University (1988); The Society for Cinema Studies, Iowa University (1989); The Conference on "Gender and Colonialism," University of California, Berkeley (1989); The Conference on "Rewriting the (Post)Modern: (Post)Colonialism/Feminism/Late Capitalism," The University of Utah, Humanities Center (1990).

2. Here some of my discussion is indebted to Edward Said's notion of the "femininization" of the Orient, in *Orientalism* (New York: Vintage, 1979). See also Francis Barker et al., eds. *Europe and Its Others*, Vols. 1 and 2 (Colchester: University of Essex, 1985), especially Peter Hulme, "Polytropic Man: Tropes of Sexuality and Mobility in Early Colonial Discourse" (vol. 2); Jose Rabasa, "Allegories of the Atlas" (vol. 2). Some of my discussion here on gendered metaphors appears in Ella Shohat, "Imagining Terra Incognita: The Disciplinary Gaze of Empire," *Public Culture* 3, no. 2 (1991): 41–70.

3. Sir Walter Raleigh, "Discovery of Guiana." Cited in Susan Griffin, *Woman and Nature: The Roaring Inside Her* (New York: Harper Row, 1978), 47.

4. St. John de Crèvecoeur, *Letters from an American Farmer, 1782*. Cited in Henry Nash Smith, *Virgin Land: The American West as Symbol and Myth* (Cambridge, Mass.: Harvard University Press, 1950), 121.

5. See Smith, *Virgin Land*. For nineteenth-century North American expansionist ideology, see Richard Slotkin, *The Fatal Environment: The Myth of the Frontier in the Age of Industrialization, 1880–1890.* (Middletown, Conn.: Wesleyan University Press, 1985).

6. For an examination of the representation of the American frontiers and gender issues, see Annette Kolodny, *The Lay of the Land: Metaphors as Experience and History in American Life and Letters* (Chapel Hill: University of North Carolina Press, 1975); and *The Land Before Her: Fantasy and Experience of the American Frontiers, 1630–1860* (Chapel Hill: University of North Carolina Press, 1984).

7. R.W.B. Lewis, *The American Adam: Innocence, Tragedy, and Tradition in the Nineteenth Century* (Chicago: University of Chicago Press, 1959). Hans Blumenberg, interestingly points out in relation to Francis Bacon that the resituation of paradise, as the goal of history, was supposed to promise magical facility. The knowledge of nature for him is connected to his definition of the paradisiac condition as mastery by means of the word. (*The Legitimacy of the Modern Age*, trans. Robert Wallace [Cambridge, Mass.: MIT Press, 1983].)

8. Jan Van der Straet's representation of America has been cited by several scholars: Michel de Certeau, "Avant propos," in *L'Ecriture de l'histoire* (Paris: Gallimard, 1975); Olivier Richon, "Representation, the Despot, and the Harem: Some Questions around an Academic Orientalist Painting by Lecomte-du-Nouy" (1885) in *Europe and Its Others* (vol. 1).

9. The gendering of colonial encounters between a "feminine" nature and "masculine" scientist draws on a preexisting discourse that has genderized the encounter between "Man and Nature" in the West itself. For a full discussion, see, for example, Griffin, *Woman and Nature.*

10. de Certeau, "Avant propos."

11. The film was distributed in the United States as *How Tasty Was My Little Frenchman.*

12. For a close analysis of *How Tasty Was My Frenchman* see Richard Peña, "How Tasty Was My Little Frenchman," in Randal Johnson and Robert Stam, eds., *Brazilian Cinema* (East Brunswick, N.J.: Associated University Presses, 1982; reprint, Austin: University of Texas Press, 1985).

13. The report concerns another tribe, the Tupiniquim, who were massacred by their "allies," the Portuguese, confirming the Native American stance, mediated in the film through the Tupinamba tribe, that despite tactical alliances, the Europeans, whether French or Portuguese, have similar desires in relation to the Native American land.

14. The film, which was shot in Parati (Brazil), has the actors and actresses mimic Native American attitudes toward nudity by living nude throughout the duration of the shooting. This production method is, of course, different from the industrial approach to shooting scenes of nudity. *How Tasty Was My Frenchman* can also be seen as part of a counterculture of the late 1960s, and its general interest in non-Western societies as alternative possibilities.

15. *How Tasty Was My Frenchman* does not criticize patriarchal structures within Native American societies.

16. Although Cleopatra was addressed as Egypt in the *Antony and Cleopatra* play, Shakespeare here and in *The Tempest* offers a complex dialectics between the West and "its Others."

17. Colonialist representations have their roots in what Martin Bernal calls the "Aryan model," a model which projects a presumably clear and monolithic historical trajectory leading from classical Greece (constructed as "pure," "Western," and "democratic") to imperial Rome and then to the metropolitan capitals of Europe and the United States. See *Black Athena: The Afroasiatic Roots of Classical Civilization*, vol. 1, *The Fabrication of Ancient Greece, 1785–1985* (New Brunswick, N.J.: Rutgers University Press, 1987). "History" is made to seem synonymous with a linear notion of European "progress." This Eurocentric view is premised on crucial exclusions of internal and external "others": the African and Semitic cultures that strongly inflected the culture of classical Greece; the Islamic and Arabic-Sephardi culture that played an invaluable cultural role during the so-called Dark and Middle Ages; and the diverse indigenous peoples, whose land and natural resources were violently appropriated and whose cultures were constructed as "savage" and "irrational."

18. Egyptology's mania for a mere ancient Egypt, for example, is ironic in an Arab context where Egypt is often perceived as *the* model of an Arab country.

19. This is true even for those films produced after the great wave of national liberation movements in the Third World.

20. Tracey Moffatt's *Nice Coloured Girls* (1987) explores the relocations established between white settlers and Aboriginal women over the last two hundred years, juxtaposing the "first encounter" with present-day urban encounters. Conveying the perspective of Aboriginal women, the film situates their oppression within a historical context in which voices and images from the past play a crucial role.

21. Female voyagers occupy very rarely the center of the narrative (*The King and I, Black Narcissus*). In contrast to scientist heroes, they tend to occupy the "feminine" actantial slot: educators and nurses.

22. The passive/active division is, of course, based on stereotypically sexist imagery.

23. See, for example, Suleiman Mousa, *T. E. Lawrence: An Arab View*, trans. Albert Butros (New York: Oxford University Press, 1966).

24. See Francis Bacon, *Advancement of Learning* and *Novum Organum* (New York: Colonial Press, 1899).

25. Ibid., 135.

26. Francis Bacon, *Novum Organum*, in *The Works of Francis Bacon*, James Spedding, et al., eds., (London: Longmans, 1870), 82.

27. Blumenberg, *The Legitimacy of the Modern Age*, 389.

28. For a illuminating reading of Haggard's *King Solomon's Mines*, see Anne McClintock, "Maidens, Maps, and Mines: the Reinvention of Patriarchy in Colonial South Africa," *South Atlantic Quarterly* 87, no. 1 (1988).

29. Television has incorporated this penchant for spinning-globe logos especially in news programs, displaying its authority over the world.

30. *Around the World in 80 Days* feminizes national maps by placing images of "native" women on the backs of maps of specific countries. The balloon used by the protagonist is referred to as "she" and called "La Coquette."

31. The feminine designation of "the moon" in French, *la lune*, is reproduced by the "feminine" iconography of the moon.

32. George Mèliés's filmography includes a relatively great number of films related to colonial explorations and Orientalist fantasies such as *Le Fakir-Mystère Indien* (1896), *Vente d'esclaves au Harem* (1897), *Cleopatre* (1899), *La Vengeance de Bouddah* (1901), *Les Aventures de Robinson Crusoe* (1902), *Le Palais des milles et une nuits* (1905). Interestingly, Mèliés's early fascination with spectacles dates back to his visits to the Egyptian Hall shows, directed by Maskelyne and Cooke and devoted to fantastic spectacles.

33. I am here referring especially to the Babylon section.

34. Bazin's Malraux-inspired statement in the opening of "The Ontology of the Photographic Image" suggests that "at the origin of painting and sculpture there lies a mummy complex." (*What Is Cinema*, trans. Hugh Gray [Berkeley: University of California Press, 1967], 9.) The ritual of cinema, in this sense, is not unlike the Egyptian religious rituals, which provided "a defence [sic] against the passage of time," thus satisfying "a basic psychological need in man, for death is but the victory of time." In this interesting analogy Bazin, it seems to me, offers an existentialist interpretation

of the mummy, which, at the same time, undermines Egyptian religion itself, since the ancient Egyptians, above all, axiomatically assumed the reality of life after death—toward which the mummy was no more than a means.

35. In this essay, I refer to some of the various subgenres of the Hollywood Orientalist film of which I have identified seven: (1) stories concerning contemporary Westerners in the Orient (*The Sheik* [1921], *The Road to Morocco* [1942], *Casablanca* [1942], *The Man Who Knew Too Much* [1956], *Raiders of the Lost Ark* [1981], *Sahara* [1983], *Ishtar* [1987]; (2) films concerning "Orientals" in the First World (*Black Sunday* [1977], *Back to the Future* [1985]); (3) films based on ancient history such as the diverse versions of *Cleopatra*; (4) films based on contemporary history (*Exodus* [1960], *Lawrence of Arabia* [1962]; (5) films based on the Bible (*Judith of Bethulia* [1913], *Samson and Delilah* [1949], *The Ten Commandments* [1956]); (6) films based on *The Arabian Nights* (*The Thief of Bagdad* [1924], *Oriental Dream* [1944], *Kismet* [1955]); (7) films in which ancient Egypt and its mythologized enigmas serve as pretext for contemporary horror-mystery and romance (the *Mummy* series). I view these films partially in the light of Edward Said's indispensable contribution to anticolonial discourse, that is, his genealogical critique of Orientalism as the discursive formation by which European culture was able to manage—and even produce—the Orient during the post-Enlightenment period.

36. Mallek Alloula examines this issue in French postcards of Algeria. See *The Colonial Harem*, trans. Myrna Godzich and Wlad Godzich (Minneapolis: University of Minnesota Press, 1986).

37. Freud associates Africa and femininity in *The Interpretation of Dreams* when he speaks of Haggard's *She* as "a strange book, but full of hidden meaning, . . . the eternal feminine . . . *She* describes an adventurous road that had scarcely even been trodden before, leading into an undiscovered region." James Strachey, ed., *The Standard Edition of the Complete Psychological Works of Sigmund Freud* (London: Hogarth Press, 1953–1974), SE IV-V, 453–454.

38. Joseph Breuer and Sigmund Freud, *Studies in Hysteria*, trans. James Strachey in collaboration with Anna Freud (New York: Basic Books, 1957), 139.

39. Ibid., 193.

40. Sigmund Freud, "On Transformations of Instinct as Exemplified in Anal Erotism," in *The Standard Edition of the Complete Psychological Works of Sigmund Freud*, SE XVII, 129, 135.

41. Toril Moi, "Representation of Patriarchy: Sexuality and Epistemology in Freud's Dora," in Charles Brenheimer and Claire Kahane, eds., *In Dora's Case: Freud, Hysteria, Feminism* (London: Virago, 1985), 198.

42. David Macey, *Lacan in Contexts* (London and New York: Verso, 1988), 178–180.

43. Breuer and Freud, *Studies on Hysteria*, 292.

44. Stephan Salisbury, "In Dr. Freud's Collection, Objects of Desire," *New York Times*, 3 September 1989.

45. "My voyage to the Orient was like a grand act of my interior life."
46. Linking Jews to the history, politics, and culture of the West must be seen as continuous with Zionist discourse, which has elided the largely Third World Arab history and culture of Middle Eastern Sephardic Jews. For a full discussion of the problematics generated by Zionist discourse, see Ella Shohat, "Sephardim in Israel: Zionism from the Standpoint of Its Jewish Victims," *Social Text* 19/20 (fall 1988). This debate was partially continued in *Critical Inquiry* 15, no 3 (1989) in the section "An Exchange on Edward Said and Difference." See especially Edward Said, "Response," 634–646.
47. *The Ten Commandments*, partially shot on location in Egypt, was banned by the Egyptian government.
48. On another level we might discern a hidden Jewish substratum undergirding the film. In the ancient past Egypt dispossessed the Hebrews of their ark, and in the present (the 1930s) it is the Nazis; but in a time tunnel Harrison Ford is sent to fight the Nazis in the name of a Jewish shrine (the word "Jewish" is of course never mentioned in the film), and in the course of events the rescuer is rescued by the rescuee. A fantasy of liberation from a history of victimization is played out by Steven Spielberg, using biblical myths of wonders worked against ancient Egyptians this time redeployed against the Nazis—miracles absent during the Holocaust. The Hebrew ark itself performs miracles and dissolves the Nazis, saving Dr. Jones and his girlfriend, Marion, from the Germans, who, unlike the Americans, do not respect the divine law of never looking at the Holy of Holies. The Jewish religious prohibition of looking at God's image and the prohibition of graven images (with the consequent cultural deemphasis on visual arts) is triumphant over the Christian predilection for religious visualization. The film, in the typical paradox of cinematic voyeurism, punishes the hubris of the "Christian" who looks at divine beauty, at the same time nourishing the spectator's visual pleasure.
49. *Al Mumia* (*The Mummy*) was exhibited in the United States under the title *The Night of Counting the Years*.
50. Ahmose freed Egypt from the Hyksos invaders and ushered in the "New Empire" period of ancient Egyptian history.
51. Thutmose III, Egypt's greatest warrior pharaoh, conquered Palestine and Syria.
52. Ramses II is the reputed pharaoh of the Exodus.
53. Howard Carter and A. C. Mace's narrative of their predecessor's 1881 discovery, for example, links the Egyptologists' rescue of mummies to the ancient Egyptian priests' protection of their kings: "There, huddled together in a shallow, ill-cut grave, lay the most powerful monarchs of the ancient East, kings whose names were familiar to the whole world, whom no one in his wildest moments had ever dreamed of seeing. There they had remained, where the priests in secrecy had hurriedly brought them that dark night three thousand years ago; and on their coffins and mummies, neatly docketed, were the records of their journeyings from one hiding place to another. Some had been wrapped, and two or three in the course of their many wanderings had been moved to other coffins. In forty-eight hours—

we don't do things quite so hastily nowadays—the tomb was cleared; the kings were embarked upon the museum barge." (Shirley Glubok, ed., *Discovering Tut-ankh-Amen's Tomb* [abridged and adapted from Howard Carter and A. C. Mace, *The Tomb of Tut-ankh-Amen*] [New York: Macmillan, 1968], 15.)

54. In a relatively recent interview following the screening of *The Mummy* on Egyptian television, Shadi Abdel Salam was slightly criticized for relying on a Western musician when Egypt has its own musicians. Abdel Salam insisted that the Italian musician was chosen for his technical knowledge, and that his role was basically to arrange a preexisting popular Egyptian music. Khassan Aawara, *"Al Mumia," Al Anba*, 30 October 1983 (Arabic).

55. In addition to Edward Said's pioneering critical writings on Orientalist discourse and specifically on Egypt, see Timothy Mitchell, *Colonising Egypt* (Cambridge: Cambridge University Press, 1988).

56. Glubok, *Discovering Tut-ankh-Amen's Tomb*, 15.

57. Guy Hennebelle, "Chadi Abdel Salam Prix Georges Sadoul 1970: La momie est une reflexion sur le destin d'une culture nationale," *Les Lettres Françaises* 1366 (30 December 1977): 17.

58. "They were the mightiest Pharaohs. What became of them?"—a meditation in the film reminiscent in some ways of Shelly's "Ozymandias."

59. See, E. A. Wallis Budge, ed., *The Book of the Dead* (London: Arkana, 1989).

60. See, for example, Cynthia Enloe, *Bananas, Beaches, and Bases: Making Feminist Sense of International Politics* (Berkeley: University of California Press, 1989), 19–41.

61. See Boris Uspensky, *A Poetics of Composition* (Berkeley: University of California Press, 1973).

62. For a critical discussion of the representation of black female sexuality in the cinema, see Jane Gaines, "White Privilege and Looking Relations—Race and Gender in Feminist Film Theory," *Screen* 29, no. 4 (1988). On black spectatorship and reception of dominant films, see, for example, Jacqueline Bobo, *The Color Purple*: Black Women as Cultural Readers," in Diedre Pridram, ed., *Female Spectators: Looking at Films and Television* (New York, Verso, 1988); Manthia Diawara, "Black Spectatorship: Problems of Identification and Resistance," *Screen* 29, no 4 (1988).

63. The mystery in the *Mummy* films, which often involves a kind of *Liebestod*, or haunting heterosexual attraction—for example, *The Mummy* (1932), *The Mummy's Curse* (1944), *The Mummy's Hand* (1940)—can be seen in this sense as allegorizing the mysteries of sexuality itself.

64. In her striking autobiography, Harriet Jacobs, for example, recounts the history of her family, focusing especially on the degradation of slavery and the sexual oppression she suffered as a slave woman. Her daily struggle against racial/sexual abuse is well illustrated in the cases of her master, who was determined to turn her into his concubine, his jealous wife, who added her own versions of harassments, and the future congressman, who, after fathering her children, did not keep his promise to set them free. Fagan Yellin, ed., (*Incidents in the Life of a Slave Girl Written by Herself* [Cambridge, Mass.: Harvard University Press, 1987].)

65. Citations from the Production Code of the Motion Picture Producers and Directors of America, Inc., 1930–1934 are taken from Garth Jowett, *Film: The Democratic Art* (Boston: Little Brown, 1976).

66. Here I am especially thinking of Anna Julia Cooper and Ida B. Wells.

67. Hazel V. Carby, "Lynching, Empire, and Sexuality," *Critical Inquiry* 12, no. 1 (1985).

68. For discussion of rape and racial violence, see, for example, Jacquelyn Dowd Hall, "'The Mind that Burns in Each Body': Women, Rape, and Racial Violence," in Ann Snitow et al., eds., *Powers of Desire* (New York: Monthly Review Press, 1983).

69. Haile Gerima's *Bush Mama* anatomizes contemporary American power structure in which rape performed by a white policeman is subjectivized through the helpless young black woman.

70. Fredric Jameson, "Third World Literature in the Era of Multinational Capitalism," *Social Text* 15 (fall 1986). Although Jameson speaks of allegory in a Third World context, I found the category germane for the First World, increasingly characterized by "Othernesses" and "differences" within itself.

71. For example, Ferdinand-Victor-Eugène Delacoix, as Lawrence Michalak points out, borrowed Indian clothing from a set designer for his models, threw in some "Assyrian" motifs from travel books and Persian miniatures, and invented the rest of the Maghreb from his imagination. ("Popular French Perspectives on the Maghreb: Orientalist Painting of the Late 19th and Early 20th Centuries," in Jean-Claude Vatin, ed., *Connaissances du Maghreb: sciences sociales et colonisation* [Paris: Editions du Centre National de la Recherche Scientifique, 1984].)

72. Images of nude breasts of African women in the *Tarzan* series relied on travelogues. Trinh T. Minh-ha in *Reassemblage* (1982) attempts to question the focus on breasts in ethnological cinema. For her broader critique of anthropology, see *Women, Native, Other* (Bloomington: Indiana University Press, 1989), 47–76.

73. Fellini's $8^{1}/2$, meanwhile, self-mockingly exposes this pornographic imagination of the King Solomon-style harem as merely amplifying the protagonist's actual lived polygamy.

74. For the Orientalist ideology undergirding the translations of *A Thousand and One Nights* to European languages, see Rana Kabbani, *Europe's Myths of Orient* (Bloomington: Indiana University Press, 1986).

75. See, for example, Huda Shaarawi, *Harem Years: The Memoirs of an Egyptian Feminist (1879–1924)*, trans. Margot Badran (New York: Feminist Press at City University of New York, 1987).

76. See Lois Beck and Nikki Keddie, eds., *Women in the Muslim World* (Cambridge, Mass.: Harvard University Press, 1978); Mervat Hatem, "The Politics of Sexuality and Gender in Segregated Patriarchal Systems: The Case of the Eighteenth- and Nineteenth-Century Egypt," *Feminist Studies* 12, no. 2 (1986).

77. For a critique of Eurocentric representation of the harem, see Leila Ahmed,

"Western Ethnocentrism and Perceptions of the Harem," *Feminist Studies* 8, no. 3 (1982).

78. The artistic representation of the solitary confinement of upper-middle-class Western women within the household is fascinatingly researched and analyzed by Bram Dijkstra, *Idols of Perversity* (New York: Oxford University Press, 1986).

79. Protofeminist Western women such as Hubertine Auclert, Françoise Correze, Mathea Gaudry, and Germaine Tillion, as Marnia Lazreg suggests, reproduced Orientalist discourse in their writings. For a critique of Western feminism and colonial discourse, see, for example, Marnia Lazreg, "Feminism and Difference: The Perils of Writing as a Woman on Women in Algeria," *Feminist Studies* 14, no. 3 (1988); Chandra Talpade Mohanty, "Under Western Eyes: Feminist Scholarship and Colonial Discourses," *Boundary* 2: no. 12 (1984); Gayatri Chakravorty Spivak, "French Feminism in an International Frame," *Yale French Studies* 62 (1981); *In Other Worlds: Essays in Cultural Politics*, chap. 3, "Entering the Third World" (New York and London: Methuen, 1987).

80. Robert Halsband, ed., *The Complete Letters of Lady Mary Wortley Montagu*, vol. 1 (London: Oxford University Press, 1965), 314.

81. Robert Halsband, ed., *The Selected Letters of Lady Mary Wortley Montagu* (New York: St. Martin's Press, 1970), 96–97.

82. Halsband, *The Complete Letters of Lady Mary Wortley Montagu*, vol. 1, 314–315.

83. For an analysis of the "mechanical reproduction" of women in Busby Berkeley's films, see Lucy Fischer, "The Image of Woman as Image: The Optical Politics of *Dames*," in Patricia Erens, ed., *Sexual Stratagems: The World of Women in Film* (New York: Horizon Press, 1979).

84. Quoted in Fischer, "The Image of Woman as Image," 44.

85. For a detailed analysis of *The Battle of Algiers*, see Robert Stam, "Three Women, Three Bombs: *The Battle of Algiers* Notes and Analysis," *Film Study Extract* (New York: Macmillan, 1975). See also Barbara Harlow's introduction to Alloula, *The Colonial Harem*, ix-xxii.

86. In *Battle of Algiers* FLN Algerian men at one point wear Arab female dress—a disguise whose ultimate goal is to assert Algerian national identity. This ephemeral change of gender identities within anticolonial texts requires a more elaborate analysis of the Third World masculine rescue operation of Third World women from the violation of First World men. Such feminist criticism directed at the works of Frantz Fanon and Malek Alloula within the Algerian/French context has been addressed, in the black/white North American context, at Malcolm X and the Black Panthers.

87. See J. C. Flugel, *The Psychology of Clothes* (London: Hogarth Press, 1930). For an extended discussion of Flugel's writing on fashion, see Kaja Silverman, "The Fragments of a Fashionable Discourse," in Tania Modleski, ed., *Studies in Entertainment: Critical Approaches to Mass Culture* (Bloomington: Indiana University Press, 1986); Also Silverman, *The Acoustic Mirror: The Female Voice in Psychoanalysis and Cinema* (Bloomington: Indiana University Press, 1988), 24–27.

88. The American journalist Lowell Thomas was instrumental in the popularization of T. E. Lawrence in the West; his show, which consisted of lecture and footage he shot from the Middle East front, was, after a short time, moved to Madison Square Garden. See John E. Mack, *A Prince of Our Disorder: The Life of T. E. Lawrence* (Boston: Little Brown, 1976).

89. Leslie Fiedler argues that homoerotic friendship between white men and black or indigenous men is at the core of the classical American novel. See *Love and Death in the American Novel* (New York: Criterion Books, 1960).

90. Interestingly, Leslie Fiedler's *The Inadvertent Epic* comments on another white woman novelist, Margaret Mitchell, whose *Gone With the Wind* is structured according to scenarios of interethnic rapes.

91. For an analysis of Valentino and female spectatorship, see Miriam Hansen, "Pleasure, Ambivalence, Identification: Valentino and Female Spectatorship." *Cinema Journal* 25, no. 4 (1986).

92. *Movie Weekly*, 19 November 1921.

93. Ibid.

94. Denis de Rougemont partially traces the Liebestod motif to Arabic poetry. See *Love in the Western World*, trans. Montgomery Belgion (New York: Harper Row, 1974).

# PART ONE

# HISTORICAL AND
# GENERIC CONTEXTS

Antonia Lant

# The Curse of the Pharaoh, or How Cinema Contracted Egyptomania

When, in 1945, André Bazin asked himself "What is Cinema?" he proposed in reply that at the origin of all the plastic arts might be a "mummy complex," a fundamental psychical human need to reverse the finality of death.[1] Egyptian embalmment, he argued, was merely the earliest instance of an essential human drive to preserve life by the presentation of life, a drive producing statues, paintings, prints, and photographs, and satisfied most recently, and most thoroughly, through the new medium of the cinema. Through his identification of such a transhistorical plight for humanity, under which these widely divergent representational practices could be grouped, and through his own religious convictions, which endowed reality with God-given meaning, Bazin would come to find it incumbent upon cinema to strive for the greatest possible evocation of reality through analogical representation even while recognizing the inevitable failure of the medium ultimately to achieve its goal. Cinematic representation, he argued, would approach reality only asymptotically, never merging with it. The art of cinema would thus inevitably thrive on a "fundamental contradiction which [was] at once unacceptable and necessary": the contradiction between aspiring to become identical with reality but expiring—ceasing to exist as cinema—at the point of its success.[2]

This essay first appeared in *October* 59 (Winter 1992): 87–112. It is reprinted with the permission of the MIT Press. Copyright © 1992 Massachusetts Institute of Technology and October Magazine, Ltd.

Bazin came to champion those film stylists whose work demonstrated a "faith in reality" over a "faith in the image"; he deplored German Expressionism, which did "every kind of violence to the plastics of the image," and he also rejected Soviet montage, since it "added" to reality, creating a meaning "not objectively contained in the images themselves but derived exclusively from their juxtaposition," hence imposing an "interpretation of an event on the spectator."[3] He favored instead the work of Jean Renoir, William Wyler, Robert Flaherty, and others whose cinematic language and, especially, whose use of the long take and the shot-in-depth was best able to approximate the nature of reality in its combination of perceptible ambiguities within a spatially and temporally unified whole. Above all, Bazin praised the Italian neorealists and singled out Roberto Rossellini and Vittorio de Sica for their efforts to "transfer to the screen the *continuum* of reality," for their "wonderfully sensitive antennae" and "cinematographic tact."[4]

Bazin's answer to the ontological question, and his consequent arguments for a realist film style, have since been at the heart of debates about the political and aesthetic nature of cinema—debates raging virtually since his death in 1958. The limits of a prescriptive criticism such as Bazin's, which impugns the validity of metaphorical meaning and consequently calls into question such practices as surrealist and abstract cinema as well as Soviet montage, have been forcefully pointed out.[5] Several essays appearing in *Screen* magazine during the 1970s—the peak period of Bazin-bashing—criticized Bazin's analysis of the cinema for its naïveté and its teleological form, and rejected his apparent proposal that the projected image simply transmits reality's meaning transparently, an idea stridently at odds with the structural and psychoanalytical understanding of the film text and its spectator that was being developed within the pages of the journal.[6] But for this Manichaean opposition to have been erected, as John Belton has pointed out, it was necessary to flatten out Bazin's far more complex investigation into representation and subjectivity.[7] It required the suppression of Bazin's insight into the fundamental contradiction that is cinema, to which Christian Metz had readily proclaimed himself indebted; for Metz's formulation in "The Impression of Reality in the Cinema" that "the secret of film is that it is able to leave a high degree of reality *in its images*, which are, nevertheless, still perceived as images," harkens back to Bazin.[8]

Bazin's work has survived the vicissitudes of disputation and praise to find a central place in film theory and history. Perhaps the most recent evidence of this is the issue of *Wide Angle* commemorating the thirtieth anniversary of Bazin's death, an issue comprising five new essays that both rehabilitate and expand the Bazinian base.[9] There Philip Rosen reads Bazin's ideas as symptomatic of their intellectual and historical moment, arguing that while Bazin may have stressed the importance of spatial continuity in cinematic representation, temporal continuity is as significant, if not more so, if we are to understand the direction of and pressures on his writing.[10] Even the indexical quality of the cinematographic image, Rosen argues, and Bazin's explication of the process of image making as being equivalent to forming a death mask, a mold, a decal, has a fundamentally temporal character, inevitably implying a pastness, a past lost despite the presence of the image. The apparently eternal human obsession with overcoming death, the mummy complex, is also then, paradoxically, a temporal or, rather, historical product, a product of the nineteenth century, with its growing industrial challenges to previous perceptions and classifications of time.

I also return to Bazin's most famous trope, the mummy complex, but to a different end, for no one has yet discussed the fact that Bazin's explanation of cinema's origins and power in terms of a relation to Egypt (and particularly the ancient civilization) is not unique. We may, in fact, trace the descent of his essay from a plethora of earlier printed, painted, architectural, and filmic texts that infuse the cinema with a pharaonic past or that associate it with an exotic though distant Arabian present. The alliance between optically novel and illusory forms of representation and ideas about Egypt precedes even the invention of cinema. It is detectable at least since the French Revolution and persists throughout the nineteen century—across lantern shows, panoramas, dioramas, photographs, and photographic criticism, and on into the emerging sphere of cinema itself. Further, the intersection between Egyptianate material and prefilmic and filmic culture has both a physical and conceptual component: projected moving images and traces of Egypt can and do inhabit the same tangible architectural space; but there is also a magnetism between conceptual accounts of the nature of entertainment by projected light and Egypt—an imaginative association pulling together the ancient culture and modern spectacular invention.

While the historical material accumulated in this essay could be seen to be arranged and acting teleologically, one representation handing on the Egyptophilic baton to the next until it infects the cinema and, ultimately, Bazin, this would be to underestimate the density and complexity of the objects and concepts at hand. There was an association between the blackened enclosure of silent cinema and that of the Egyptian tomb, both in theoretical texts and in the use of Egyptianate architectural style for auditoriums: a perception of cinema as a necropolis, its projections mysterious and cursed, issuing a warning to spectators;[11] an understanding of cinema as a silent world that speaks through a pictorial language, as hieroglyphics revealed by light, and a consequent ennobling of the newest visual medium through alignment with some of the oldest word-images; a noted parallel between mummification as preservation for a life beyond life and the ghostliness of cinematic images, whose production and arrangement also manifest a power over the ordering and representation of time; a link between the chemistry of mummification and that of film development and printing; an alliance between modern sexuality, particularly female screen sexuality, and myths surrounding the Sphinx and its silent unreadability; and lastly, an uncanny parallel between archaeologists' descriptions of their discoveries of tombs and the effects and conditions of film projection. In these accounts Egypt parallels cinema in serving as a portal to the revelation of mystery and the fantastic. Howard Carter inevitably (and obstetrically) invokes the onset of cinema when he writes of puncturing the entrance to Tut-ankh-Amen's tomb with "a hole large enough to insert an electric torch" and of "its light reveal[ing] an astonishing sight."[12] He dramatizes the moment when, the wall pierced, a beam of light penetrates the darkness, falling directly onto the dazzling object—in his case "what to all appearances was a solid wall of gold."[13]

The sheer extent of the evidence of overlap between Victorian visions of Egypt and early motion picture culture impels us to ask what function the aura of Egypt served in cinema's beginnings that it took root there with such tenacity. What did it enable contemporaries to grasp? For in all the ways I have sketched above, it seems that Egypt, and what it came to mean in the century between Champollion's unlocking of the Rosetta Stone in 1822 and the coming of sound to cinema in the late 1920s, provided a means of explaining, legitimating, but above all conceptualizing the new motion picture medium. It became central to debates over the nature of cinema itself, and it was this legacy to which Bazin, inevitably, referred.

To begin to make the case that Western notions of Egypt shared an intellectual and physical arena with cinema, we could do worse than to reexamine Etienne Gaspard Robertson's *Fantasmagorie*, that ghoulish and popular entertainment of immediately postrevolutionary France. Painter, teacher of physics, and pioneer balloonist, Robertson staged his illusions in pitch blackness in a disused chapel (replete with crumbling tombs) in the vicinity of an old Parisian Capuchin monastery.[14] By the light of concealed magic lanterns, Robertson shone glass slides painted with images onto columns of smoke or cambric screens, moving the slides forward and back in relation to the receiving surfaces so as to vary the scales of the projected shapes. On the far side of the screen (or smoke) his audiences saw visages of the recently deceased Robespierre, Marat, and Danton (among others) materialize in the dust. Contemporary accounts record audiences shuddering and cowering before the phantasms, whose ethereality was intensified by Robertson's blackening of the majority of the slide in order to preclude any projection of its straight edges.[15] His shows centered on satanic and macabre topics, topics of haunting, loss, and the past. Occasionally they evoked the context of Egyptological archaeology, as in one scenario about "A Grave Digger" who, "with a lantern, searches for treasure in an abandoned temple; he opens a tomb, and finds a skeleton, whose head is still ornamented with a jewel; at the moment when he attempts to remove this, the corpse makes a movement and opens its mouth; the grave digger falls dead with terror. A rat was lodged in its skull."[16] Other dramas prefigured the subject matter of early trick films, as in "A Mad Woman" who is "little by little illuminated from behind, and ends by being metamorphosed into a skeleton"; such crossings of the boundary between death and life were to be staged again and again in Méliès's films and in *The Haunted Curiosity Shop*, an R. W. Paul trick film discussed later in this essay.[17]

In his *Mémoires*, published in 1830, Robertson remembered the necromancy in Simmelesque terms—the *Fantasmagorie* as a haven from crowded Paris, a passage into the hush and deathliness of the mausoleum. He recalled that he compelled patrons to pass through "several detours appropriate to eliminate impressions still lingering from the profane noise of a great city" before permitting them to cross "the paved cloisters of the ancient convent, decorated with fantastic paintings" and to arrive "before a door of antique form, covered with hieroglyphics and seeming to announce the entrance to the mysteries of Isis." Inside was "a somber place, hung with black, weakly illuminated by a sepulchral lamp . . . whose purpose [was] announced only by some gloomy images: [the] profound calm, an absolute silence, a sudden isolation on coming from a bustling street, were like preludes of an ideal world."[18] For Robertson, the physical presence of the antique gate presages the onset of another world. The entering ceremony, passing down passages and across courtyards and ultimately through the pharaonic door, provides a spatial separation between the present of Paris and the past of ghostliness, the mysteries of Isis.[19] The spatiotemporal transition into an "ideal world" is amplified but also embodied in the conjunction of the entertainment with Egypt. Robertson understood the *Fantasmagorie*—a protocinematic experience in that it depended on projected, moving images—in terms of entering the architectural and cultural space of the Nile necropolis; the Capuchin setting of ancient tombs and the darkness of the interior, insulated from the Paris beyond, had an Egyptianizing effect on the performance enclosure, which was made concrete in the hieroglyphically embellished gate and enhanced through the quality of temporal revisitation that ghosts, mummies, and reproduced images all possess.

Versions of Robertson's show spread through Europe and the United

States, as Ted Barber has documented.[20] Its Egyptian associations were augmented when, in late 1801, the anglicized *Phantasmagoria* was transferred by the magician Paul de Philipsthal to London, where it ran for two years at the Lyceum on the Strand.[21] The poster advertising the show's "Optical Illusions and Mechanical Pieces of Art" promised to "introduce the Phantoms or Apparitions of the DEAD or ABSENT, in a way more illusive than has ever been offered to the Eye in a public Theatre," but this claim was also accompanied by a cautionary note: "To prevent mistakes, the public are required to notice, that the *Phantasmagoria* is on the left-hand, on the ground floor, and the *AEGYP-TIANA* on the right-hand, up stairs."[22] The imaginary and physical alliances with Egypt that Robertson made are here reinforced by the suggestion that two concurrently running shows may be confused— the *Aegyptiana* was a series of "eighteen scenic pictures" based on prints in Dominique Vivant Denon's brand-new book *Travels in Upper and Lower Egypt*, a prelude to his *Description of Egypt* (1809–1822).[23]

Robertson, Philipsthal, and other purveyors of magic lantern shows persistently associated the "ideal world" of projected images with death and bereavement, with the "dead or absent" of Philipsthal's poster. Far from encountering levity and happiness, an effect now commonly attributed to the cinema of Hollywood's studio era, Robertson likened the experience of *his* viewers to that of a woman who had lost her love and who "after a thousand detours" had arrived in the middle of the pyramids or catacombs. "There, surrounded by the inmates of death, along with the night and her imagination, she awaits the apparition of the object of her love."[24] He called his shows "séances," affirming again the rehearsal of or meeting with death offered to his spectators, a pleasure (or need) understood by both Gorky and Kracauer in their later accounts of the nature of cinema.[25] Here begins the affinity between ideas about ancient Egypt, with its elaborate culture of death, and an entertainment form produced out of the dark—dependent on it, its methods concealed, and its substance intangible, contained in a crypt entered through the gate of the "priests of Memphis."[26] The crepuscular world of the *Fantasmagorie*, both strangely removed from and linked to daily experience, could be explained by its contiguous existence with the structures, motifs, and names of the pharaohs.

The concatenation of Egypt with ancestral cinematic forms—panoramas, dioramas, and lantern shows—intensified in Britain with the opening of the overland trade route to India in the 1840s, which crossed over Egyptian soil. The "first feature-length, British-made panoramic river trip" was a transparent panorama of the Nile, opening in London at the appropriately named Egyptian Hall on 16 July 1849 (Figure 1).[27] This panorama had two halves, one the journey upstream of the west bank, the other downstream of the east—and a tableau of the torchlit

Figure 1.  Engraving of the Egyptian Hall, Piccadilly, London, ca. 1821.
Courtesy of the British Museum.

interior of Abu Simbel was projected at the halfway point. A second
panorama, the "Overland Route to India," began at the Gallery of Illustration, Regent Street, in April 1850 and drew a quarter of a million
customers before it closed. It consisted of a moving middle section for
the overland part of the route, but still images of Gibraltar and Malta
at the outset and Ceylon and Calcutta at the end; a traveling painted
scene was unwound to illustrate the journey from Cairo to Suez.[28]

This central part of the route—Alexandria, Cairo, Suez—rapidly became the most popular subject of the new *touring* panoramas. "The
Overland Mail," also of 1850, was enhanced by the presence of its designer, Albert Smith, as an expert commentator and by musical accompaniment (Figure 2).[29] Smith did not use projected slides, but lighting
effects were included in the show by deploying cutouts and illumina-
tion by candles. After opening at the Egyptian Hall, it visited forty-eight
English municipal centers in two months during the fall of 1851 before closing. Three years later, when the Crystal Palace was moved to
Sydenham from Hyde Park (after the Great Exhibition of 1851), one of
the main displays incorporated full-scale plaster casts of two figures
from the temple of Ramses at Abu Simbel, with a Sphinx avenue extending before them (Figure 3). The casts were melted to twisted fragments in the Crystal Palace fire in 1938, but their likenesses survive in

MR. ALBERT SMITH'S ENTERTAINMENT—"THE OVERLAND MAIL," AT WILLIS'S ROOMS.

Figure 2. "The Overland Mail" panorama, with Mr. Albert Smith comment-ing. *The Illustrated London News*, 8 June 1850. Courtesy of the Olin Library, Cornell University.

Delamotte's beautiful photographs.[30] Here, the apogee of Victorian ar-chitectural achievements—the highly modern glass-and-iron conserva-tory—encases reproductions of some of the world's oldest and largest sculptures. They are fully integrated into the Victorian exhibition space, with British greenhouse technology surrounding the statues with a lush tropical vegetation that the Upper Nile habitat lacks.

Clearly the burgeoning of images of Egypt is part of the colonialist project that involved mapping and photographing, claiming both terri-tory and subjects by reproducing them in visual form—Delamotte's photographs incorporate Egypt and the tropics into urban Britain. These are habits well noted as defining characteristics of nineteenth-century European politics and culture, spurred by imperialism and ac-companied by the rise of the classifying disciplines of anthropology, geography, archaeology, ethnography, and so on.[31] The linkages between Egyptology and the origins of cinema, which are part and parcel of

Figure 3. Philip Delamotte's 1854 photograph of the plaster Colossi of Abu Simbel, installed at the Crystal Palace, Sydenham.

these imperialist obsessions, are expressed through the very existence of the photographic image and through the writings of early filmmakers and critics, who themselves perceived (and celebrated) the colonizing powers of cinema. Photographic images taken (an operative word) outside Europe and exhibited within Europe functioned as symbols for taking possession and could thereby assuage the "irresistible desire for spaces to conquer."[32] An article from 1906 entitled "The Grand Tour" described the reaching of far-off lands via cinema as a contracted and willfully rearranged geography: "You can have them [other places] in the moving pictures, by which, literally, distance is annihilated and, in the words of Puck in Shakespeare's *A Midsummer Night's Dream* you may 'put a girdle round the earth' in 40 minutes."[33] The members of the Kalem Company, dubbing themselves "The International Producers" on the strength of their far-flung location shoots—in Ireland, Egypt, and the Holy Land—encapsulated the aggrandizing thrust of their work through a promotional image of a globe on which their company literally shone. The advertisement was accompanied by the caption: "The Kalem lens is turned upon all parts of the world" (Figure 4).[34]

Figure 4.
Advertisement
in the *Kalem
Kalendar*, 15
June 1912.
Courtesy of
the Academy
of Motion Pic-
ture Arts and
Sciences.

**The International Producers**

THE Kalem lens is turned upon all parts of the world and the resultant feature films represent the highest achievement in photographic and dramatic art.

But even viewed from this broader, colonialist perspective, Egypt still carries a particular signifying weight. It is not simply any old place for which any number of other Others—oriental, non-Western countries—could have been substituted. While the intersection of "things Egyptian" with cinema is certainly part of the larger Western effort to girdle the earth, it demands a more careful and flexible explanation than that allowed for by a simple binary formulation of the East as the Other, which would buttress the West's understanding of itself. This could not explain why it was Egypt—both Arabic and ancient—rather than India or China, for instance, that had a special affiliation with spectacle, with the moving panoramic image, and ultimately with the cinema in the Victorian psyche. It could not explain why it was the overland section, the one on Egyptian soil, that moved in the panorama of the "Overland Route to India" of 1850, or why the sequence along the Suez Canal in *A Policeman's Tour of the World* (Pathé, 1906) is the most cinematically adventurous of the entire film because of its inclusion of several inter-cut traveling shots and binocular mask shots (the only moving and masked shots in the film) and its resultant instantiating of the specta-tor as "master tourist."[35] Further, in Kalem's globe advertisement, why is it Egypt that takes the closest and most privileged position in rela-tion to the company's sun/lens, represented there by a Shakespearean-looking sphinx, a pyramid, and a camel, and presiding over five other locations at which Kalem had studios or had shot films: New York, the Rocky Mountains, the Western Plains, Jerusalem, and Jacksonville, Florida?

I have already suggested that cinema's overlap with Egypt is bound to discourses on death, on preservation, on silence, and on light pro-jection, all resonant with pharaonic import via recent Victorian exca-vation and exhibition. But the two fields are also bound through the contemporary politics and economics of Egypt, particularly as they pertained to imperial ambition and questions of national and racial identity. Egypt was not only an idea but a place—and the tension be-tween these two aspects had its own repercussions for the cinema. Egypt could not be held in place simply as an Other, for it served as the *entry point* to the East, the "Gateway to India" for Europe, and particularly for Britain; it signified a foothold, a staging point. The use of Egypt-ianate elements in cinema design may thus be feeding precisely on this transitional aura, on this power to signify a passage to a new scene, a promise of changing experience. (Here, in part, is the significance of *The Policeman's* elaborate Suez Canal shots.) That Egypt was both a Christian and Muslim country, with a history of pharaonic religions as well, contributed to its status as a point of interchange between Eu-rope and Africa, the Middle East, and beyond. Richard White writes of this "ambiguity" of Egypt along similar lies, noting that while it was "indisputable part of the Orient, the Orient being less a place in the East than part of a discourse in the West," it was not easily placed within Africa or Asia, or within the East or the West.[36] This quality of undecidability about Egypt (for the West) also had explanatory power for cinema, for it could nourish expressions of uncertainty about the nature of the new motion picture medium itself. But in order to sup-port this claim, we must first lay out in a more concrete way how, and then why, cinema "contracted" Egyptomania.

———

The Egyptian Hall was erected in Piccadilly in 1812, several decades before the overland panoramas showed there. Lessee and showman William Bullock titled it "The London Museum of Natural history" for exhibiting "curiosities" of all kinds—including the spoils of Egyptology.[37] (Indeed, one of the biggest attractions of 1804, when Bullock's museum was still in Liverpool, had been the display of an Egyptian mummy that had been brought from Egypt by Napoleon's fleet and then captured by an English Privateer. Perhaps the pull of this object, a trophy of Anglo-French rivalry over Egypt, encouraged Bullock to encase his entire entertainment in the Egyptianate style when he moved to London.)[38] Colossal figures of Isis and Osiris decorated the building's entrance. Bullock's personal passion was stuffing birds, and in 1817 he published a book, *Concise and Easy Method of Preserving Objects of Natural History*, effectively modernizing, or perhaps disguising, mummification as taxidermy.[39] In 1821, under his auspices, the Egyptian Hall came to house Giovanni Battista Belzoni's vast array of Egyptian antique booty; the mummies, papyri, and statues he had amassed from his Nile sojourns attracted a crowd so huge that nineteen hundred people paid half a crown each to visit the hall on the first day, and it stayed open for a year.[40]

The hall changed ownership several times through the nineteenth century but continued to present a wide assortment of public entertainments, from Laplanders with live reindeer to Tom Thumb, Géricault's *Raft of the Medusa*, Napoleon's captured carriage, stuffed animals in a jungle setting, Siamese twins, and, in 1865, ventriloquist Colonel Stodare's speaking head, called "The Sphinx."[41] Albert Smith reported finding Egyptian mummies and other "accumulated rubbish" in the hall's cellars when working there in the early 1850s;[42] in the 1860s and 1870s several conjurers (Hermann, Dr. Lynn, and the Fakir of Ooloo) entertained with Egyptian magic, and a poster campaign for Professor Pepper's performances boasted: "The New and the Wonderful! Always at the Egyptian Hall" (Figure 5).[43] By the turn of the century, when the hall was operated by magician Nevil Maskelyne, with David Devant as a partner, visitors (including filmmakers Georges Méliès and Emile Cohl) still flocked to curiosity and magic shows, but they were also attracted by another spectacle: The Egyptian Hall had become a cinema on 19 March 1986, when it began presenting Edison and R. W. Paul films—only the third venue (by ten days) for films in England.[44] By now a billboard affixed to the outside of the building promoted "Improved Animated Photographs" and dubbed the hall "England's Home of Mystery" (Figure 6).

By the mid-1890s, then, popularized Egyptology and the infant cinema were rubbing shoulders under the same roof, and through both

Figure 5. Advertisement for Professor Pepper's show at the Egyptian Hall, London, ca. 1865. Courtesy of the Hulton Picture Library, London.

the rhetoric of advertisement and their physical juxtaposition, Egyptology's version of Egypt was being fed into the understanding of the cinematic experience. The cinema's dark world of projected, mute images, realized in a newly invented social space—disjunct from reality, but part of it—was given meaning through its contiguity with the silent relics of ancient Egypt, sometimes actually present, but always permanently invoked by the building's imposing facade. The cohabitation of mummies and cinema was realized.

But Egypt played midwife to film's birth in a further sense: as subject matter. It was present in fictional scenes, including stagings of both modern and historical events, in trick films, and as actuality footage, shot on location.[45] At least four film companies sent crews to Egypt before the First World War; the Lumière Brothers, Edison Company, Pathé, and Kalem Film Company.[46] Five versions of *Cleopatra* were filmed between 1908 and 1918 alone, in 1908, 1909, 1913, 1917, and 1918, well before the more famous sound versions by De Mille and Mankiewicz in 1934 and 1963, respectively. Filmed Bible stories with Egyptian settings included *La Vie de Moise* (Pathé, 1906), *The Prodigal Son* (Pathé, 1909), *The Life of Moses* (Vitagraph, 1909–1910), and *I Maccabei* (Itala, 1911). "The Flight into Egypt," a core element of Christ's life story, was signified by the sphinx against which Mary and child rest in *La Vie et la Passion du Christ* (Pathé, 1902–1905). With its very large but human features, the sphinx was obviously a painted flat, but by Kalem's *From the Manger to the Cross* (1912) and *La Vie et la Passion de Notre Seigneur Jésus-Christ* (Pathé, 1913) location shooting had secured a more realistic image of those very monuments old enough to have witnessed the flight itself. The sphinx and pyramids, as disseminated by photography, had become bearers of the authenticity of the story on account of their age.

Figure 6.  Photograph of the Egyptian Hall, Piccadilly, London, ca. 1898. Courtesy of the Hulton Picture Library, London.

Tales of Egypt also boosted exploration of cinema's particular capacity to reproduce an object "freed from the conditions of time and space that govern it," in Bazin's words.[47] Tales of awakening mummies and magical amulets facilitated, even gave form to, cinema's power to rearrange time and space, as well as providing resonances with death. It is partly for these reasons that mummy films proliferated in the United States: there were two of *The Egyptian Mummy* (1913 and 1914); two of just *The Mummy* (1911 and 1914); *The Egyptian Mystery* (1909); *An Egyptian Princess* (1914); *The Mummy and the Cowpunchers* (1912); *The Mummy and the Hummingbird* (1915); and so on. *The Egyptian Mystery* (Edison, 1909) told the story of a pendant found in an ancient Egyptian tomb that would cause anything its wearer's hands rested upon to disappear.[48] After a series of vanishings, accomplished with ease through cinematography, resolution comes when an iceman, the last owner of the charm, touches his reflection, and he, the reflection, and the pendant all vanish together, literally blacking out the fiction, with Egypt providing the logic for cinema's magic. In *The Mummy* (Thanhouser, 1911), contact with a live household electric wire brings a mummy accidentally to life. The resulting "visitor from the distant past," a dancing Egyptian princess, eventually marries her owner—a New York science professor and amateur Egyptologist—"in spite of the fact that there is a difference of several thousand years in their ages."[49] Here again the power of the modern inventions of electricity and cinema can be expressed through Egypt, which also furnishes the titillating story of a younger man's love for an older woman. *The Dust of Egypt* (Vitagraph, 1915) starts in the past, on the banks of the Nile, where a princess drinks a potion and wakes up in present-day Manhattan by hatching from a mummy case.[50] The film, and its publicity, dramatize the contrast between twentieth-century and ancient ways, but to the former's advantage: "Imagine the wondrous and peculiar actions of an individual who has lived three thousand years ago, planted in the heart of New York in the present era." It promises comedy produced out of the princess's use of "telephone, matches, cigars, and other conveniences of modern times"[51] (Figure 7).

One of the first of the mummy series may be *The Haunted Curiosity Shop*, directed by the British magician Walter Booth in 1901, and produced by R. W. Paul, who had provided the projectors, his second Theatrographs, for the Egyptian Hall shows in 1896.[52] *The Haunted Curiosity Shop* is a one-scene trick film with a single, frontal, static camera position. The setting is an interior, with a pedestal, cupboard doors, and a painted backcloth decorated with a mummy case, statues, canopic jars, plinths, busts, and figurines—a veritable Victorian fantasy of the Egyptian burial chamber. An old curio dealer, leafing

Figure 7. Publicity artwork for *The Dust of Egypt* (1915). Courtesy of the New York Public Library.

through his catalog, is startled by the sudden appearance of a disembodied hand with a wand (or sword), and then of a skull wearing an Egyptian headdress. Cupboard doors fly open, and the skull floats off the table and leftward to a shelf, where it turns into a woman's upper body and head. While the shopkeeper closes the cupboard, the woman's lower body enters from left and attaches itself to her waiting upper half. The woman dances, and as she turns she becomes a black woman—or rather, a white woman in blackface—with black gloves. Horrified, the dealer shuts her in the cupboard, but as he closes it she turns white again, and she then appears as a ghost outside the cupboard. He opens the cupboard again to discover a mummy, which changes into a man in ancient Egyptian tunic and headdress. He in turn becomes a skeleton, which prods the dealer and disappears. That is the last we see of the performing mummy, although the immobile painted mummy remains on the backcloth throughout the rest of the film, which continues with the transformation of an armored man into three gnomes and of the gnomes into a fleeting image of a man's face, wreathed in smoke. This face, bearded and triangular in shape, may be that of producer Paul, and is also reminiscent of Robert's fuliginous masks (Figures 8–10).

This very short film of 140 feet narrates several bizarre metamorphoses: sexual (from male to female to male, via the closet), racial (white to blackface to white), and corporeal, both in the sense of fragmentation and regeneration and in the sense of a life cycle that extends from preserved life as the mummy to flesh, to skeleton, and to ghost—themes developed to the hilt in Karl Freund's *The Mummy* and its offspring, *Charlie Chan in Egypt, The Mummy's Hand*, and so on. Why did Egypt become embedded in the cinema in this way, even developing its own subgenre, the mummy film? On one level, Egyptology and the cinema have utterly separate lineages: they would seem to share the same century purely by chance. As Egyptology's triumphs were drawing to a close, the cinema was just emerging. The final great discovery of Tut-ankh-Amen's tomb in 1922 marked the hundredth anniversary of Champollion's discovery, and only coincidentally the flourishing of the narrative motion picture in a more standardized form, which itself celebrated Egyptology's riches in a film, *Tut-ankh-Amen's Eighth Wife* (1923). But at another level, we should not be surprised that Egyptology had a legacy for the cinema, that Egypt became a mode of expressing the new experience of film, a way of embodying it, of placing it, of giving it a concrete referent. Even before the arrival of cinema, writers on Egypt associated that culture with magic, preservation, and silent, visual power—all qualities that anticipate the character of cinema.

Florence Nightingale, who began her travels in Egypt in 1849, in almost the same month as Flaubert, wrote home of the country that "there is not a corner [of it] which is not a picture."[53] She described statues as "gigantic phantoms . . . of a dead past," and her description of the Nile after leaving Cairo for a five-month voyage reads like an account of film spectatorship: "The strange effect of the atmosphere makes the figures on the shore appear gigantic. You lose all feeling of distance. You seem to lose all feeling of identity too, and everything

Figures 8–10. *The Haunted Curiosity Shop* (1901). Courtesy of the National Film Archive.

becomes supernatural."[54] Her seeing of the Egyptian world as moving scenes and tableaux, as if the objects were changed through her vision of them, can be understood as another symptom of the habits of imperialism, of the need to conceive and grasp the rest of the world "as though it were an exhibition" for Western delectation and use.[55]

Oscar Wilde matched Egypt to the photographic in his short story "The Sphinx Without a Secret," a tale of a man besotted with a society woman whose photo is the last trace he has of her. Consoling him, the man's friend describes her as "a woman with a mania for mystery. . . . She had a passion for secrecy, but she herself was merely a sphinx without a secret."[56] "Do you think so?" asks the doting man as he stares at her photograph. The inability of the woman's photograph to answer, to have a voice, is expressed by Wilde through the metaphoric link to the silence of ancient Egypt, an association continued in the images of Bara as sphinx, Garbo as sphinx, and reexamined in Laura Mulvey and Peter Wollen's *Riddles of the Sphinx* (Figure 11).[57]

Egyptology and the cinema are pulled together through the needs and obsessions of the nineteenth-century imagination. At its crudest, this need can be described as a question of self-identity. The Victorian psyche celebrates the massive cultural upheavals of industrialization even as it seeks reassurance through them. It aspires to the imperial grandeur of past kingdoms while confronting again and again in this

Figure 11. Advertisement for *Cleopatra*, *Motion Picture News*, 10 November 1917. Courtesy of the International Museum of Photography at the George Eastman House.

desire earlier demises and losses. Cinema can be understood to express and partially satisfy these desires. This seems at least to be the hope of *The Bioscope*'s text on Kalem's 1912 Egyptian films, which it found to "re-people ruined cities . . . revivify vanished civilizations, [and] make the grave give up its dead . . . for the cinematograph interprets dead facts into the language of life."[58] This ability of cinema to breathe life into the dust of Egypt continues the function of the cult of the ruin, updating it, even surpassing it.

By the late nineteenth century the Roman and Greek empires within Europe were to a large extent already claimed, but bringing home an obelisk, as Napoleon did, could bestow on this society the status of ancient Egypt, the status of a founding civilization, eternally present through its magnificent monuments and mummified bodies. Georg Simmel theorized this consolation of the antique for his contemporaries in his essay *The Ruin* (1911): "The ruin creates the present form of a past life. . . . [In the apprehension of an antique] we command in spirit the entire span of time since its inception; the past with its destinies and transformations has been gathered into this instant of an aesthetically perceptible present."[59] Here we understand the tie of the fascination of the ancient Egyptian ruin (some of the oldest and certainly largest ruins) to the cinema, for both promise to condense the past in an instant. In this drive to assert mastery over space and time, the Victorian imagination mapped the content of Egyptology over the form and, ultimately, over the content of silent cinema; at the same time Egyptian architecture sometimes came to encase the entire experience of film spectatorship in the building of new Egyptianate cinemas, of which the Grauman's Egyptian, Los Angeles, built in 1922, is only the most famous.[60]

The nineteenth century packaged the pharaonic past to represent timelessness and the conquest of death (Belzoni described Thebes as "a city whose antiquity reaches far beyond historical notice"), and these are capabilities that the new medium of cinema could also be understood to inherit.[61] Cinema controlled time and space, objectifying it, rearranging it at will. As Vitagraph boasted of *Dust of Egypt*: "In one tenth of a second you are transported from our present day world back to the Egypt of three thousand years ago."[62] The new language of cinema would be termed hieroglyphic by theorists of the medium, and Vachel Lindsay would write in 1915 that the cinema auditorium is "an Egyptian tomb" in which "we realize our unconscious memories when we see the new hieroglyphs."[63] Sergei Eisenstein used the metaphor of the hieroglyph (as well as others, admittedly) to characterize film as visual writing, while Terry Ramsaye explained that cinema's genesis was derived from the pictorial alphabet in his 1926 book of film history, *A Million and One Nights*.[64] It became almost a commonplace for cinema's early historians to explain the newest art in terms of the oldest, to attribute to it a hieroglyphic structure and thus to describe it not only as a universal language but as an originating language that had been derived from a dead language renewed by the Victorians.[65] By lashing the histories of cinema and Egypt together, dignity, legitimacy, and a heritage were bestowed both on the newest Victorian technology of narrative and spectacle and on its inventors.

However, meanings of ancient Egypt were not quite so singular and stable. Far from the conquest of death, as I have already discussed, the arrival of cinema seemed to invite an encounter with death. Its appeal lay precisely in the practice of death it offered its audience, and the association with Egypt enabled this deathliness of the preserved image to be conceived and expressed. The legacy of the ancient Egyptians also became tainted (from the point of view of European scholars) by its association with the mysterious and supernatural, the questionable and disreputable.[66] There was a persistent, dubious link of Egypt to magic, current throughout the nineteenth century; the official publication of the Society of American Magicians was named "The Sphinx," and to pick another example from many, Houdini staged a spectacle of escapology at the pyramids. A certain prurient pleasure accompanied the unwrapping of a mummy before the Prince of Wales in 1862, the first x-raying of a mummy in 1898, and Belzoni's description of excavating tombs with their "strong smell of mummies."[67] He writes in sensationalist, macabre style of falling into piles of them: "It is scarcely possible by description to convey an adequate idea of these subterranean abodes, or of the strange and horrible figures with which they are filled." "What a place of rest! [Being] surrounded by bodies, by heaps of mummies on every side . . . filled me with horror."[68]

In addition, the dynastic dramas of ancient Egypt, elaborated after the decoding of the Rosetta stone, provided a rich seam of possibilities for narratives incorporating nonnormative notions of sexuality. These stories were quite outside the bourgeois worldview, and yet they were undeniably recognizable because of the welter of domestic detail that accompanied them on the tomb walls, as well as through the objects that survived. Florence Nightingale drew light projection together with Egypt again when she wrote that "the curious part of these painted grottoes [the tombs] is the literal matter-of-fact delineation of all the details of everyday life—their dressing, eating, working, walking, writing, doctoring, talking, dancing, their sickness and their health, their indoors and their outdoors, their business and their play . . . a magic lantern glimpse into the domestic economy of 4,000 years ago."[69] The consuming Victorian preoccupation with sexuality, particularly female sexuality, could be thematized through this newly available imagery of powerful queens, androgynous kings, and bewildering sphinxes, all made vivid through their combination with the everyday. Thus Egypt, as processed during the nineteenth century, offered the cinema both legitimation and the allure of the exotic. The configuring of Egypt with the cinema expressed cinema's twin realist and fantastic character. By mining the pharaonic archive, the disturbing potential of the cinema to produce pornography through extremely realistic representations of the human body could be diffused, safely channeled, into a distant yet compelling culture, claimed through the imperialism of Egyptology. Roman Egypt, contemporary Arabian Egypt, and ideas about the harem, the sheik, Arabian nights, and the vamp could then ride into the cinema on the back of pharaonic Egypt, as it were.

It is another, related topic, and one beyond the scope of this essay, to document the complex intersection between definitions of the vamp—the modern woman of the teens and twenties who drained men of their wills and ultimately their blood—and Orientalist discourse, including that about ancient Egypt. The vamp's quintessential lair was, after all, her rug-draped couch, while her pose was that of the odalisque.[70] Theda Bara, initiator of the vamp role, was wreathed in Orientalist publicity. Her name was purportedly an anagram of "arab death" (more or less), and she wore "many odd ornaments," including an emerald ring given to her by a blind sheik in whose family it had been passed down for "more than 2,000 years." The gift was made on condition that any male children of Bara's would inherit it and be taught Arabic.[71] Two years before the release of *Cleopatra*, a *Photoplay* article described Bara as "daughter of the Sphinx . . . born under the shadow of the Sphinx and in physical texture . . . as bizarre a woof of bloods as she is cosmopolitan in mentality. . . . Theda . . . opened her destructive eyes on an oasis in the Sahara."[72] The Fox publicity bureau then published a hieroglyphic text to coincide with the release of *Cleopatra*, apparently sent as a homage by a fan who was convinced that "Miss Bara was the reincarnation of the most famous vampire of history."[73] Bara's modern face was superimposed on the Egyptian sphinx to clinch the connection.

We find another piece of evidence in Alexander ("Sasha") Kolowrat's biblical genre production, *Sodom and Gomorrha: The Legend of Sin and Punishment*, directed by Michael Kertesz (later Curtiz) in 1922 as Austria-Hungary's answer to *Intolerance* (1916). The central female character, Miss Mary Conway (played by Lucy Doraine, who also at times plays Lot's wife and the queen of Syria), is introduced as "'the modern girl' equipped with all the refinements of a decadent epoch, a sphinx with mystical eyes, a girl who evokes one's wildest desires and craves sacrifice, so that an honest man, robbed of his wits, is driven to commit deeds beyond his better judgment."[74] The sphinxness of modern women is surely a defense, a way of figuring her desires as a series of riddles, illegible for modern culture, that reiterate Freud's question. This conjunction also consolidates the notion of an eternal feminine, again through the link to a most ancient civilization and its women: women have always been the same, this iconography insists, or at least vamps have.

Through the sets of relations I have described we can say that Bazin's notion of the mummy complex emerges not out of the blue in 1945, but from a specific constellation of geographical, political, and ideological factors that shaped the aesthetic experience of early cinema through its relation to the history of Egyptology: the two passions shared

Figure 12. Reginald Marsh, *A Paramount Picture*, 1934, tempera on panel, 36 inches by 30 inches. Collection of Merrill C. Berman.

150 years of conjugality, though at different stages in their evolution. While at one level Egypt and the cinema had entirely separate histories, at the turn of the century they could both be understood to offer an irresistible darkened and silent world in which mystery, exoticism, and melodrama combined through the means of a new language—hieroglyphics and cinematography—theretofore unknown. Nineteenth-century histories of the Egyptian past had a central importance in the crystallization of Western cinema: they were part of its material formation, of how it could be explained.

But Bazin's formulation can also be seen as the last flowering of this relation, for the symbiotic association of cinema and Egyptiana was ending. With the coming of synchronized sound, the power of the silent Egyptian past over the cinema disintegrated (or at least went underground)—as Reginald Marsh recorded in *A Paramount Picture*, his painting of 1934 showing a melancholy, Depression-era filmgoer leaning obliviously against a gigantic, glamorized portrait of Claudette Colbert in De Mille's *Cleopatra* (Figure 12). This was also the moment when Egypt began to make cinema for itself and for distribution in the West. To adapt Said's terminology, the Orient began to speak, and through cinema.[75] This modernization and encounter changed the range of Egyptianate meanings available to Western cinema, and its theories, and although the fascination with Egypt continued, and still does, the Egyptianizing discourse gradually weakened as theorists began to ask new questions of the cinema and as its status as a medium of entertainment became more evident and fixed. The realist cinema came to the fore, while the cinema of mystery was channeled into the mummy genre and into the avant-garde.[76] To put it hyperbolically, it was a coup in which cinemas called Alhambra and Oriental were replaced by Greek-sounding Odeons, and we eventually began to talk about a classical cinema and a classical style.

## Notes

In writing this essay, I benefited from discussions with Annette Michelson, Tom Gunning, Richard Allen, and Andrew Brower. I would also like to acknowledge the contributions of two audiences to whom I delivered parts of this essay, at the Society for Cinema Studies Annual Conference, Washington, D.C., 1990, and at the First Annual Screen Studies Conference, Glasgow, 1991, and especially the comments of Richard Abel, Geoffrey Nowell-Smith, and Peter Wollen. The research for this essay was assisted by a Presidential Fellowship from New York University, and by Ava Rose and David Lugowski. The development of this work into a book-length study has been supported by the J. Paul Getty Program. I published three related essays on Egyptomania and cinema subsequently: "Beams from the East: Egypt in Early Cinema," in Roland Cosandey and Francois Albera, eds., *Cinéma sans frontiéres, 1896–1918/Images across Borders* (Editions Payot/Nuit Blanche Editeur, Lausanne and Quebec: 1995), 73–94; "Haptical Cinema," *October* 74 (fall 1995): 45–73; "Pourquoi filmé les pharaons?" in Jean-Marcel Humbert, ed., *L'Egyptomanie à l'épreuve de l'archéologie* (Paris: Réunion des Musées Nationaux, 1995), in press.

1. André Bazin, *What Is Cinema?* vol. 1, trans. Hugh Gray (Los Angeles: University of California Press, 1967), 9.
2. André Bazin, *What Is Cinema?* vol. 2, trans. Hugh Gray (Los Angeles: University of California Press, 1967), 26.
3. Bazin, *What Is Cinema?* vol. 1, 24, 25, 26.
4. Ibid., 37, and Bazin, *What Is Cinema?* vol. 2, 32.

5. Annette Michelson, "Review of *What Is Cinema?*" *Artforum* (summer 1968): 67–71.

6. See, for example, Colin McCabe, "Theory and Film: Principles of Realism and Pleasure," *Screen* 17, no. 3 (1976): 7–27. "Bazin-bashing" is Philip Rosen's phrase, from his essay "History of Image. Image of History: Subject and Ontology in Bazin," *Wide Angle*, 9, no. 4 (1987): 7–34.

7. John Belton, "Bazin Is Dead! Long Live Bazin!" *Wide Angle* 9, no. 4 (1987): 74–81.

8. Christian Metz, *Film Language*, trans. Michael Taylor (New York: Oxford University Press, 1974), 14.

9. *Wide Angle*, 9, no. 4 (1987).

10. Rosen, "History of Image, Image of History."

11. Maxim Gorky, "A Review of the Lumière Program at Nizhni-Novgorod" (1896), reprinted in translation in Jay Leyda, *Kino: A History of the Russian and Soviet Film* (London: Allen and Unwin, 1960).

12. Howard Carter, quoted in Shirley Glubok, *Discovering Tut-ankh-Amen's Tomb*, abridged and adapted from Howard Carter and A. C. Mace, *The Tomb of Tut-ankh-Amen* (New York: Macmillan, 1968), 71.

13. Ibid.

14. Erik Barnouw, *The Magician and the Cinema* (New York: Oxford University Press, 1981), 19. There is some dispute as to when Robertson's *Fantasmagorie* began, but all agree that it was certainly under way by 1799. See X. Theodore Barber, "Phantasmagorical Wonders: The Magic Lantern Show in Nineteenth Century America." *Film History* 3, no. 2 (1989): 85n.

15. Barber, "Phantasmagorical Wonders," 76.

16. Etienne Gaspard Robertson, *Mémoires récréatifs, Scientifiques et anecdotiques d'un physicienaéronaute*, published in 1830, republished by Langres: Café-Clima Editeurs, 1985, and quoted in David Robinson, "Robinson on Robertson," *New Magic Lantern Journal*, 4, nos. 1–3 (1986): 10. Translated by Robinson.

17. Ibid., 9.

18. Ibid., 6.

19. It is worth noting here than Cecil B. DeMille's *Cleopatra* of 1934, set mostly in Egypt, opens and closes with the visual motif of entering and leaving a granite tomb. The film's first image is of two stones parting to reveal the action beyond. The end of the film mirrors this movement, with the stones rejoining and shutting out the spectacle.

20. Barber, "Phantasmagorical Wonders."

21. Barnouw, *The Magician and the Cinema*, 21.

22. Ibid., 23. A Boston showing of the *Phantasmagoria* in 1804 included an Egyptian Pygmy Idol in the show, which changed into a human skull. See Barber, "Phantasmagorical Wonders."

23. Richard D. Altick, *The Shows of London* (Cambridge, Mass.: Harvard University Press, 1978), 199.

24. Robinson, "Robinson on Robertson," 6.

25. A recurring motif of Kracauer's post-1940, post-Holocaust notebooks, as presented by Miriam Hansen in her paper "Kracauer's 'Kermesse Funèbre':

*Theory of Film*, Marseilles, 1940," given for the Columbia Seminar, Museum of Modern Art, 28 March 1990. Gorky, "A Review of the Lumière Program."

26. Robinson, "Robinson on Robertson," 8.

27. Altick, *The Shows of London*, 205. The Egyptian Hall is illustrated in Brian M. Fagan, *The Rape of the Nile: Tomb Robbers, Tourists, and Archaeologists in Egypt* (New York: Charles Scribner's Sons, 1975), 239.

28. Patrick Conner, ed., *The Inspiration of Egypt: The Influence on British Artists, Travellers, and Designers, 1700–1900* (Brighton: Brighton Borough Council, 1983), 147.

29. Ibid. Albert Smith's entertainment is illustrated on 146.

30. One of Philip Delamotte's photographs of the Colossi of Abu Simbel, 1854, published in the *Sale Catalogue of the Crystal Palace*, 28 November 1911, is cited and illustrated in Conner, *The Inspiration of Egypt*, 92–93.

31. See, for example Jean-Louis Comolli, "Machines of the Visible," in Theresa de Lauretis and Stephen Heath, eds., *The Cinematic Apparatus* (New York: St. Martin's Press, 1980), 121–142, and the writings of Michel Foucault, especially *Discipline and Punish: The Birth of the Prison*, trans. Alan Sheridan (New York: Vintage, 1979).

32. Riciotto Canudo, "The Birth of a Sixth Art" (1911), in Richard Abel, *French Film Theory and Criticism: A History/Anthology, Volume 1, 1907–1929* (Princeton: Princeton University Press, 1988), 60.

33. "The Grand Tour," *Views and Films Index* (*Film Index/Films Publishing Co.* after 19 September 1908), no. 2 (5 May 1906), 6.

34. *Kalem Kalendar*, 15 June 1912, 8.

35. Philip Rosen, "Disjunction and Ideology in a Preclassical Film: A *Policeman's Tour of the World*," *Wide Angle* 12, no. 3 (1990): 24.

36. Richard White, "Sun, Sand, and Syphilis: Australian Soldiers and the Orient, Egypt 1914," *Australian Cultural History* 9 (1990): 50. I thank Ian Craven for drawing my attention to this article.

37. William Bullock, *A Companion to the London Museum and Pantherion, containing a brief description of upward of 1500 natural and foreign curiosities, antiquities, and productions of the fine arts, now open for public inspection in the Egyptian Temple* (1813), 1. Catalog consulted at the National Art Library, London.

38. Ibid., 104.

39. Bullock had the dubious honor of owning the last great auk shot in England, a flightless bird now extinct. One should remember this Victorian passion for wax museums and glass cases of stuffed birds in the context of the origins of cinema.

40. Altick, *The Shows of London*, 245, and Fagan, *The Rape of the Nile*, 240.

41. Exhibition references from Egyptian Hall Catalog Index, National Art Library, London. Bullock sold his interest in the Egyptian Hall in 1826–1827.

42. *The Times*, 18 September 1854, quoted in Altick, *The Shows of London*, 250.

43. Illustrated in Fagan, *The Rape of the Nile*, 241.

44. John Barnes, *The Beginnings of the Cinema in England* (New York: Barnes

and Noble, 1976), 117. Photograph of the Egyptian Hall is illustrated in Fagan, *The Rape of the Nile*, 341. The Egyptian Hall was demolished in 1904 when Piccadilly was widened. A new building named the Egyptian Hall replaced the previous one, but it is quite unlike it in design. It is, however, marked by a commemorative plaque to Maskelyne and Devant, installed by the Magic Circle, London. I am grateful to Donald Crafton for the information that Cohl visited the Egyptian Hall, which he noted as "L'Egyptien" in his unpublished diaries.

45. Actuality films included Pathé's *Boat on the Nile* (1905), *From Cairo to the Pyramids* (1905), *A Corner of Ancient Egypt* (1910), and Urban's *Lord Kitchener in Egypt* (Urban Movie Chats, 1911–1914).

46. In 1903, cameraman A. C. Abadie, working for the Edison Company, traveled to the Middle East and Europe for three months, completing many films in Egypt, including: *Egyptian Fakir with a Dancing Monkey*; *Panoramic View of an Egyptian Cattle Market*; *Primitive Irrigation in Egypt*; *Going to Market, Luxor, Egypt*: *Excavating Scene at the Pyramids of Sakarrah*; and *Tourists on Donkeys at the Pyramids of Sakarrah*. The Kalem films included: *A Prisoner of the Harem*; *Egyptian Sports*; *Egypt the Mysterious*; *Captured by Bedouins*; *An Arabian Tragedy*; *Ancient Temples in Egypt*; *Egypt, as It Was in the Time of Moses*; *A Tragedy of the Desert*; *Winning a Widow*; and *How Photoplays Are Made in Egypt* (released as *Making Photoplays in Egypt*) See Robert S. Birchard, "Kalem Company, Manufacturers of Moving Picture Films," *American Cinematographer* 65 (August/September 1984): 34–38.

47. Bazin, *What Is Cinema?* vol. 1, 14.

48. The film is described in *Moving Picture World*, 10 July 1909, 61.

49. *The Mummy* is reviewed in *Motion Picture World*, 11 March 1911, 546.

50. *Vitagraph Bulletin*, 1915, 42.

51. Publicity material, *Dust of Egypt* clippings file, Lincoln Center Library for the Performing Arts. I thank Bruce Brasell for drawing my attention to the film.

52. John Barnes, *Pioneers of the British Film: The Beginnings of the Cinema in England*, vol. 3, *1898: The Rise of the Photoplay* (London: Bishopsgate Press, n.d.) 8. Paul was probably the first British film entrepreneur to build a studio in Britain specifically for filmmaking. He too had made a film called *Cleopatra*, in 1898, described in his catalog as a panorama again, though this was a "panoramic picture of the Thames embankment from Cleopatra's Needle to Waterloo Bridge." Catalog of R. W. Paul films, consulted at National Film Archive, London.

53. Florence Nightingale, *Letters from Egypt: A Journey on the Nile, 1849–1850*, selected by Anthony Sattin (New York: Weidenfeld and Nicolson, 1987), 39.

54. Ibid., 48 and 72.

55. Timothy Mitchell, *Colonising Egypt* (Cambridge: Cambridge University Press, 1988), 6 and 13. Mitchell includes a chapter entitled "Egypt at the Exhibition" and takes Heidegger's phrase "the fundamental event of the modern age is the conquest of the world as a picture" as his epigraph. Mitchell's entire book is germane to this discussion.

56. Oscar Wilde, "The Sphinx without a Secret," in *The Complete Works of Oscar Wilde* (Leicester: Galley Press, 1987), 218.
57. I thank Ben Singer for drawing my attention to the advertisement for *Cleopatra* in *Motion Picture News*, 10 November 1916, that shows Bara as the sphinx.
58. "Some Egyptian Pictures," *The Bioscope*, 27 June 1912, 937.
59. Kurt H. Wolff, ed., *Georg Simmel, 1858–1918: A Collection of Essays with Translations and Bibliography* (Columbus: Ohio State University Press, 1959), 265 and 266.
60. See Stephen Kern, *The Culture of Time and Space, 1880–1918* (Cambridge, Mass.: Harvard University Press, 1983). For a discussion of oriental style in cinema auditoriums, see David Naylor, *American Picture Palaces: The Architecture of Fantasy* (New York: Von Nostrand Reinhold, 1981), 82–108. The Portland Oriental, decorated mainly with Far Eastern motifs—including dragons, elephants, and other elements borrowed from Angkor Wat—was crowned with a circle of Egyptian mummies arranged end-to-end in a ring on the ceiling dome.
61. Giovanni Battista Belzoni, *Description of the Egyptian Tomb Discovered by G. Belzoni* (London: Murray, 1821), 5.
62. Publicity material, *Dust of Egypt* clippings file, Lincoln Center Library for the Performing Arts.
63. Vachel Lindsay, *The Art of the Moving Picture* (1915; rpt. New York: Liveright, 1970), 282.
64. Terry Ramsaye, *A Million and One Nights: A History of the Motion Picture* (New York: Simon and Schuster, 1926), lx and elsewhere. Sergei Eistenstein, "The Cinematographic Principle and the Ideogram," *Film Form*, trans. and ed. Jay Leyda (San Diego: Harcourt Brace Jovanovich, 1949), 28–44.
65. This topic is discussed by many writers, but most relevant for this essay is Miriam Hansen's "The Hieroglyph and the Whore: D. W. Griffith's *Intolerance*," *South Atlantic Quarterly* 88 (spring 1989): 361–392.
66. In his massive study, *Black Athena*, Martin Bernal argues that the value of Egypt as a founding culture for Europe was eroded during the nineteen century (and displaced by the civilization of Ancient Greece) because the geographical placement of Egypt with Africa was perceived as an indelible blemish in the context of mounting Aryanism and what Bernal terms "the explosion of Northern European racism"; questions of ancient Egyptian racial identity are strangely literalized in *The Haunted Curiosity Shop*. See Martin Bernal, *Black Athena: The Afroasiatic Roots of Classical Civilization*, vol. 1 (New Brunswick: Rutgers University Press, 1987), xv.
67. Belzoni, *Description of the Egyptian Tomb*, 6. On x-raying mummies, see Rosalie David and Eddie Tapp, ed., *Evidence Embalmed: Modern Medicine and the Mummies of Ancient Egypt* (Manchester: Manchester University Press, 1984).
68. Ibid.
69. Nightingale, *Letters from Egypt*, 55.
70. Zeynep Çelik and Leila Kinney discuss the "epistemological status" that the Ingresque odalisque had attained by the end of the nineteenth century

in "Ethnography and Exhibitionism at the Expositions Universelles," *Assemblage* 13 (December 1990); 41, especially.

71. *Toledo News*, 7 April 1916.
72. Wallace Franklin, *Photoplay*, September 1915, 69.
73. Theda Bara clipping file, Lincoln Center Library for the Performing Arts.
74. Quoted from an intertitle of the restored film, as translated into English in the *Sodom and Gomorrha* brochure of the Austrian Film Archive, Vienna. I thank Helmut Pflügl of the archive for drawing the film to my attention.
75. Edward Said, *Orientalism* (New York: Vintage, 1979).
76. Egypt and the Orient have been significant in such avant-garde films as Jean Marie Straub and Danièle Huillet's *Too Early/Too Late* (1980–1981), Laura Mulvey and Peter Wollen's *Riddles of the Sphinx* (1976), Leslie Thornton's *There was an Unseen Cloud Moving* (1987), and Harry Smith's *The Magic Feature* (or *Heaven and Earth Magic*, ca. 1958).

Gaylyn Studlar

# "Out-Salomeing Salome": Dance, the New Woman, and Fan Magazine Orientalism

"The feminine instinct within Salome to command and
rule that which she loved persists in the race
from the legend of Eve to the newest divorce story."[1]
—Alla Nazimova

Virtually from its beginnings, the cinema has been drawn to Orientalism, a phenomenon defined by Edward Said as "a Western style for
dominating, restructuring, and having authority over the Orient."[2] Hollywood's creation of an imaginary East, represented archetypally as mysterious and sensuous, would seem to be an especially significant and
rich arena for film studies. Certainly, it would appear relevant to any
historical inquiry into film's representation of gender and sexuality in
relation to formations of race and ethnicity. Said suggests that the West's
creation of an imaginary East originally was rooted in a comingling of
fear and fascination that grew out of contact with Islamic culture and
a fear of the Ottoman Empire; the West's gradual empire-building in
the East came to be justified through an Orientalist discourse that served
as a rhetorical means of controlling the Near East as an alien place
associated first, and foremost, with chaos.[3]

Even the most cursory glance at Hollywood film indicates a wide
range of narrative formulas for Orientalism, from biblical films to historical biopics with Middle or Far Eastern settings, from Foreign Legion films to Arabian Nights adventures. As might be expected, the
popularity of Orientalist films has varied over time, with periods in
which they flourished counterpointing others in which their popularity waned. One of the periods of greatest popularity of Hollywood

This is a revised version of an essay that was first published in the *Michigan Quarterly
Review* 34, no. 4 (1995): 486–510. It appears here with the permission of the *Michigan
Quarterly Review*.

Orientalism was simultaneous with the broadly registered influence of Orientalism evident in American culture at large. For the purposes of this essay, I am setting off these years as 1916–1926. In 1916, the year before the United States entered World War I, two important Orientalist events occurred: the appearance of D. W. Griffith's *Intolerance* and the Ballets Russes' debut in the United States. The year 1926 was the last one in which Hollywood engaged in the exclusive production of silent features before talkies emerged as a "realistic" counterforce to the heady romanticism of many Orientalist silent films. It was also the year of Rudolph Valentino's death and of the posthumous release of his last film, *The Son of the Sheik*.

Valentino's last film, and the film that brought him to stardom, *The Sheik* (1921), were not anomalies but part of a well-established Orientalist trend in filmmaking that included allusions to the Orient through prologues, flashbacks, and dance interludes, through set and costume design. Films also often included isolated characters marked as oriental or were full-fledged Orientalist narratives. The latter included *Cleopatra* (1917) and *Salome* (1918) (both starring Theda Bara), imported German films such as Ernst Lubitsch's *One Arabian Night* (1920), adaptations of popular stage plays such as *Kismet* (1920) and *The Morals of Marcus* (1915), parodies of these such as *The Slim Princess* (1915), as well as the first of three film versions of *The Garden of Allah* (1916), and precursors to *The Sheik*, other Englishman-turned-sheik films such as *The Man Who Turned White* (1919).[4]

While there are many avenues for exploring Hollywood Orientalism during these years, emergent film scholarship often takes one of two approaches. Either it focuses on analyzing the representation of interracial sexual relationships in individual films, or it links consumerism and Orientalism, especially as they relate to film's appeal to women. Operating within the first category, film scholars have set about analyzing the narrative and visual strategies of a limited number of silent film miscegenation dramas such as Cecil B. DeMille's *The Cheat* (1915) and Griffith's *Broken Blossoms* (1919).[5] These films are said to suggest the erotic and ideological implications of Hollywood's reliance on a "fantasy of the violation of the white woman by a man of color."[6]

Paramount's blockbuster hit of 1921, *The Sheik* remains the 1920s archetypal example of an Orientalist miscegenation drama in this vein (Figure 1). In the final reel, the sheik is revealed to be the son of an English lord, but to hint of such a violation resonates with the much discussed topic of "racial suicide," which was discussed in the 1920s in the context of women's newly emergent sexual desires, waves of immigrants from eastern and southern Europe, and eugenicists' concerns with ethnic mixing in the United States.

Figure 1. In *The Sheik* (1921), the costume of a dancing girl hides a defiant woman with a gun. Production still courtesy of the Museum of Modern Art/ Film Stills Archive.

"Shriek for the Sheik!" became a tagline for studio exploitation of its hit film.[7] Those expected to shriek were the thousands of female movie patrons who had already made the film's source, Edith M. Hull's much maligned novel of the same name, into an international best-seller. Hull's book was dismissed in the strongest terms by reviewers as a "cheap brand of fiction shocker for flappers" and a "salacious" fantasy formulated to titillate the "New Woman" and satisfy her prurient tastes in literature.[8]

Advertisements reassured audiences that *The Sheik* was "IN THE FULL TORRENT OF ORIENTAL TRADITION," even though the film toned down the story of the high-spirited "New Woman" captured by a North African desert chieftain by eliminating the book's infamous rape scenes. In response to the censorship, some female reviewers predicted box-office disaster, but the film was still astoundingly successful and was instrumental in elevating dancer-turned-actor Rudolph Valentino into a cult figure (Figure 2).[9] The film spawned a cycle of sheik films

Figure 2.
Elevating
dancer-
turned-actor
Rudolph
Valentino into
a cult figure.
Courtesy of
Cinema Col-
lectors, Los
Angeles.

and was credited (or blamed) with bringing orientalist terms into popular sexual discourse: flappers became *shebas* and their boyfriends,
*sheiks*.

Reviewers of the time assumed *The Sheik*'s primary "machinery of
excitation . . . [was] that delicious masochistic appeal of the fair girl in
the strong hands of the ruthless desert tyrant."[10] Contemporary film
scholars offer amazingly convergent explanations. Ella Shohat suggests
that the film is another product of "the (Western) male gaze."[11] Acting
"as the Id," the hero allows the heroine to overcome "her sexual repression," but the real purpose of the narrative is to permit the male
viewer to project his "unthinkable" sexual fantasies into an exotic imaginary space "where women are defenseless, playing off the masculine
fantasy of complete control over the Western woman without any intervening code of morality."[12] With implied reference to women viewers, Gina Marchetti suggests that *The Cheat* and *The Sheik* are "rape

fantasies" that reveal "the internalization of a patriarchal ideology that insists on female passivity and submission to male domination, as an expression of some deep-rooted masochistic desire, and as a way in which society toys with forbidden sexuality to make it acceptable as 'punishment' rather than as 'pleasure.'"[13]

If *The Sheik* serves as a powerful reminder of the role of the historical female audience in the star-making process, it also suggests the methodological problems entailed by any attempt to theorize and historicize the relationship of Orientalism to female spectatorship through single film texts. This is because we generally do not know, with rare exceptions like *The Sheik*, which films were the most successful with women. While studies of single films can certainly be useful, they do not seem prepared to answer intriguing questions raised by Hollywood's reliance on Orientalism during these years and its relationship to female spectators.

*The Sheik* may suggest a fascination with sexual violation as a transgression of racial boundaries that absolves the white woman of any responsibility for seeking a sexual liberation beyond the boundaries of mundane American norms. However, does reference to female masochism fully explain Orientalism in relation to women during this era? If not, why did Hollywood Orientalism of these years assert such a strong appeal to women? What forms did this appeal take—and why?

To assume that *The Sheik* and its narrative of miscegenation serve as the litmus test of Orientalism's appeal to female spectators is to ignore a whole field of cinematic signifiers and cultural intertexts that targeted *female* consumers of film in the 1910s and 1920s through a visual language of Orientalism well established in fashion, design, and the arts. One cultural intertext that has been used to explain silent film Orientalism's particular connection to women's fantasies is consumerism. The stylistic convergence of Orientalist iconography with consumer trends has been well documented as part of late-nineteenth- and early twentieth-century marketing in department store displays and consumer packaging design that served as an exotic appeal to the fantasies of women and as a means of selling middle-class consumer goods.[14] Orientalism is also seen as functioning during the early period of the twentieth century as an aesthetic counter to vulgar materialism so that the changing middle class might be reassured that they still retained traditional genteel values (Figure 3).

Working within this argument, Sumiko Higashi argues that the consumer role of American women in the 1910s and 1920s was one in which they were linked "to a sinful world of luxury associated with the demimondaine"; as a result, she claims, they became "the embodiment of commodification in theatrical spectacles designed to stimulate

WHO can account for the whims of Fashion? Women don't attempt to. They simply accept them. And how quickly are those whims sensed and felt to be inevitable?

So the vogue of Florient Talc comes very naturally as an outcome of the present mode. The art of the Orient enriches every phase of Fashion's fancies. Oriental colorings and designs in costume call for "Flowers of the Orient" in the boudoir.

Florient Talc best carries out the feeling of this art. Its perfume seems a very part of these costly fabrics.

The color too, is different, a warm Oriental tone, just off the white.

And again one senses another vogue — a new use of Florient Talc. For while it is fulfilling the duty of an after-the-bath powder, Florient Talc imparts a delicate fragrance which lingers exquisitely about the woman who uses it — as a *powdered perfume.*

For trial box of Florient Talc send 4c to
COLGATE & CO. Dept. 14 . 199 Fulton Street, New York
In Canada : 137 McGill Street, Montreal

*Florient Talc*
*Flowers of the Orient*

Sold at your favorite store—Florient Talc, Face Powder, Extract, Toilet Water, and Soap

Figure 3. Orientalism as an aesthetic counter to vulgar materialism. Advertisement for Florient talc, ca. 1920.

acquisitive behavior," and so "occupied center stage but played a perverse role in the enactment of Orientalist fantasies."[15] Certain the connections between consumerism and the figure of the vamp are worth discussing, but Higashi makes the analogy between consumerism and Orientalist fantasy an extreme one: "The impassioned relationship between buyers and commodities, in short, is one of temptation, seduction, and finally rape" (104).

Orientalist fantasies associated with the attainment of momentary luxury were linked to the New Woman's culturally encouraged acquisition of consumer goods. Nevertheless, the reason for the marketplace's, especially the cinematic marketplace's, successful exploitation of Orientalia and oriental designs seems to exceed Higashi's explanation through a theory of the female consumer's desire for acquisition. We know that the relationship of women to Orientalism was a culturally pervasive one, both long-standing and complex. To define the New Woman solely as a consumer in her relationship to Orientalism is to ignore the consolidation of Orientalism in other mediums directly and distinctly aimed at women that were neither exclusively consumeristic nor inevitably masochistic.

It is within the consideration of one of these other mediums that I wish to suggest another way of answering the question of how Hollywood addressed women's fantasies within the governing iconography of Orientalism. During the silent years, the U.S. film industry engaged in a broad assimilation of Orientalist influences, but dance played a crucial role in Hollywood's visualization of an imaginary Orient identified with unleashed sexual desires and women's fantasies. The movie industry showed an unbridled enthusiasm for the visual styles associated with dance, for dance-inspired costumes, poses, and decor, for the stars and themes of dance.

In many ways, dance was the easiest form from which to borrow. Its spectacle, like that of film, was dependent on motion and was also pantomime set to music; unlike the movies, dance was art, both respectable and seductive, and its presold appeal to women, a growing part of the middle-class film audience, was indisputable. Indisputable too was dance's association with Orientalism. Aesthetic dancing was almost inseparable from Orientalism, an impression cemented by the Ballets Russes when they made their eagerly anticipated tour of the United States in 1916. But was the fantastic and fantasy-provoking iconography of dance Orientalism aimed at women and shaped through their imaginations? Or was it, merely, as Ella Shohat suggests, another venue for men's colonialist imagination played out through the "male gaze"?[16]

Dance, I will argue, was associated in the early twentieth century on a number of cultural fronts—including film—with a feminine desire to

escape bourgeois domesticity's constraints and to create other, transformative identities that were convergent with those qualities of the
New Woman that disturbed social conservatives. Thus, dance played
on the imaginary Orient's symbolic value to Westerners as a place where
personal identity is liminal, where identities are lost, transmuted, re-
covered.[17] Certainly, that liminality of identity might have appealed to
women in the 1920s, an era in which women's newfound possibilities
for sexual and social freedom were much discussed and derided.

In a 1920 editorial, *The Ladies' Home Journal* observed that men were
dismissing the young American "girl" as "impossibly bold, brazen, independent, mannerless, [and] immodest"; modern women were accused
of "becoming mannish, indifferent to home and children, egotistical,
avid of power, irreligious, iconoclastic, and altogether a most distress-
ing problem to solve!" The editorial dismissed such talk as "pure rot"
and responded to the most common criticisms of female behavior:
"Dancing is but the exuberance of youth and of youthful age and bobbed
hair makes a Bolshevist no more than pink tea makes a social lion."[18]

The stereotypical qualities attributed to the New Woman to condemn
her are similar to those that dance scholar Elizabeth Kendall uses to
praise those women who were instrumental in founding American artistic dance: "These new dancers . . . were ballet girls possessed of those
'unballetic' qualities of the new American woman—her 'great fund of
life,' her self-absorption, her fearlessness, her unbounded imagination,
and her often monstrous daring."[19] The New Woman's desires for freedom were strongly felt in American concert dance, which became one
place where the emblematic value of the Orient as a locus of release
from repression could be safely acted out with pagan abandon (Figure
4). In dance, those qualities of the New Woman often at odds with cultural norms of traditional femininity became attached to sensual ritualized movement and to the spectacle of orientalized identities
associated with ambiguous feminine power.

Women's newly realized social and sexual freedoms were crystallized
in dance in the figure of Salome. Richard Strauss's opera *Salomé*, was
scheduled to run at the Metropolitan Opera in 1907 but was quickly
withdrawn. Reviewers compared Salome's "transports of rage or gross
sensuality" to the "red-light heroines of the contemporary stage" and
accused the opera of sickening "the public stomach."[20] But women did
not seem to be turned off by the character or her perverse desire to
kiss the dead lips of John the Baptist. Not long after the appearance of
Strauss's opera, President Theodore Roosevelt was asked to intervene
should an outbreak of "Salomania" occur in the United States, as it
had in Britain, where middle-class women held all-female private the-

atricals to imitate Maud Allen's version of Salome's dance of the seven
veils.[21] Allen's dance was outdated by the time a flurry of Salomes swept
vaudeville stages in the United States. The Met's prima ballerina, Bianca
Froelich, took her seven veils from her opera appearance into popular
theater. In spite of the competition, dancer-entrepreneur Gertrude
Hoffman dominated the field until Ruth St. Denis returned home from
Europe to start "Out-Salomeing all the Salomes."[22]

In the period from 1900 through the 1920s orientalism infused aesthetic dancing, an extremely popular form of entertainment with
women. Early-twentieth-century trends in concert dance demonstrate
the creation of what Said describes as an imaginary Orient of "romance,
exotic beings, haunting memories and landscapes, remarkable experiences."[23] Women frequented performances of classic dancers such as
St. Denis and Roshanara who danced with bare feet and uncorseted
bodies à la Orientale. St. Denis's influential repertoire was heavily dependent on borrowings from or imaginings of Eastern dance (Figure
5). Her *Radha*, *The Cobras*, *Incense*, and *East Indian Suite* were followed by *Egypta*, *O-Mika*, and numerous other exotic numbers that

Figure 4. Denishawn dancers in an imaginative rendering of Indian dance.
By permission of the Dance Collection, New York Public Library for the Performing Arts, Astor, Lenox, and Tilden Foundations.

Figure 5.
Ruth St.
Denis in a Far
Eastern
mode, ca.
1920. By per-
mission of the
Dance Collec-
tion, New
York Public
Library for
the Perform-
ing Arts,
Astor, Lenox,
and Tilden
Foundations.

inspired a generation of women to become dancers.[24] Thus, Orientalism
in the United States emerged through modest and easily overlooked
avenues, shaped at least in part, by women as well as through the
masculinist venues of academic painting, monumentalist architecture,
and the political domination of colonial cultures.

One arena where dance's Orientalism was strongly articulated as
being aimed at women was in a cinematic extratextual form very clearly
and specifically addressed to women—the fan magazine. Beyond the
consideration of film texts, there is a need to contextualize film's iconography of the Orient and its appeal to women in the 1910s and 1920s.
Dance was an important vehicle for silent film Orientalism that was
emphasized to a great degree in the extratextual mechanism of the fan
magazine.

As I have argued elsewhere, the fan magazine addressed its readers
as female in its articles, interviews, advertisements, fiction, and contests, and its address was similar to other forms of female-centered

culture, including women's magazines and dance magazines.[25] Orientalism's connection to female consumerism of the period was inescapable and is particularly evident in the fan magazine, targeted so obviously to women as consumers of cinema and of film stars. Yet, what makes fan magazines of this period so interesting is that they tended to construct their female readers not as passive, overinvolved consumer-spectators who uncritically believed everything Hollywood set before them. Women readers were addressed as active insiders, savvy to and critical of the industry's machinations, and, paradoxically, as appreciative fans with a wealth of knowledge about their assumed focus of interest: stars. One scholar has suggested that female fan-readers of these years were thought by conservative social commentators to be too independent and too obsessive in their interests as well as "contemptuous of traditional social rules about woman's ambitions and pleasure."[26]

In their complex and sometimes ironic treatment of Hollywood's construction of Orientalism aimed at women, fan magazines suggest the value of reaching beyond the examination of single film texts to explore a phenomenon assumed to be loaded predictably with sexist as well as racist connotations. As to be expected, fan magazines varied their format for the presentation of Orientalist discourse. By the late 1910s, they included narrative versions of films, such as *The Victoria Cross* (1917), which featured a renegade English hero disguised in seminude indigenous costume and a heroine who (imitating Ruth St. Denis) chooses to "don the dress of a Nautch-girl," in this instance, to escape India's "fires of revolution."[27] Fan magazines also featured stories in serial form, such as one in *Photoplay* that places Peggy Roche, a "saleslady," into a series of Pearl White-like adventures in the Mideast. In one episode Peggy prefigures Lady Diana's bold desert journey in *The Sheik* to assume "the full attire of a Turkish Hanoum" as she passes unchallenged through a Pasha's palace (Figure 6).[28] Within the context of fan magazine narratives, heroines could be, like Lady Diana in *The Sheik*, adventurous and daring, while the stars who were featured in its pages were also daring, if only in matters of fashion and occupation.

Fan magazine Orientalism was also promoted through varied and sometimes subtle means linked to dance. Having the same gender-specific audience known to fill dance matinees, fan magazines often featured photo layouts and articles with exclusive emphasis on dance. Many of these, such as "Figures of the Dance," "Flavored with Tartar," "Two Pierrots," "Outstripping Salome," "The Spirit of the East," and "Desha of Stamboul," featured "dance personalities" from film, concert dance, vaudeville, the ballet corps of the Capitol Theater of New York City, and other venues.[29] Often these dancers, male and female, were

*Peggy, in the full attire of a Turkish Hanoum was passing unchallenged between the two sentries at the gate of Yussouf Pasha's official residence.*

The thin man with the lined face was George Siefert, of Chicago, representing a saddlery and leather goods concern. The stout little man in the white helmet was George Drummond, of Kansas City, interested in rifles and munitions. The man with the bald head was George Hagan, of Jersey City, and his talk ran mainly to wool.

Each of the three had his feet cocked up on the verandah railing, each was regarding the scene with a sort of absorbed introspection, and each had an iced drink upon the little table in front of them. As Peggy appeared, the three heads turned simultaneously in her direction.

Figure 6. The Orient (and the fan magazine) as a site for daring female adventure. Peggy Roche, "saleslady," assuming the attire of a Turkish anoum, *Photoplay*, 1917.

Figure 7.
Highly
charged roles
broke down
gendered and
ethnic
binarisms.
Ballet's Anna
Pavlova and
Hubert
Stowitts, as
photographed
for
*Shadowland.*

pictured in oriental costuming that rendered their sexuality ambiguous and their appearance androgynous. This collapse of conventional gender codification in some fan magazine iconography followed trends in concert dance, especially in the Ballets Russes' ambiguous inscription of sexual difference. Not only is the polarization between genders subverted, but there is also sometimes an alluring and nonconformist play with the oriental that suggests the subversion of the absolute polarity of Western and Eastern subjectivities (Figure 7).

Peter Wollen suggests that Ballets Russes' designer Léon Bakst, couturier Paul Poiret, and Henri Matisse "created a scenography of the Orient that enabled them to redefine the image of the body, especially, but not exclusively, the female body."[30] These artists, who were "the last orientalists and the first modernists,"[31] were influenced by performative femininity: decorative, sensual, and often vigorously dramatic. Dance redefined the female body, not only through the revolutionary influence of the Ballets Russes, but also through Isadora Duncan (who directly inspired Poiret) and numerous others who drew on Delsarte and dress-reform ideals to fashion (literally) a new concept of the female body in movement that suggested sensuality, athleticism,

Figure 8.
Athletic and
androgynized:
female trans-
formation
through
dance.
"Cinema Star"
Edith Roberts
in *Shadow-
land,* Decem-
ber 1920.

and sometimes even androgyny or a sliding of gender identity (Figure 8).[32]

    As Elizabeth Kendall suggests, Hollywood in the late 1910s exploited
theatrical dance to the extent of making it "a presence, a mood, instead of a choreographic art with rules."[33] The fan magazine extended
this trend to translate dance into a "presence, a mood" virtually inseparable from Orientalism. The link between female stars and contemporary forms of dance, especially those in the Orientalist mode,
was enthusiastically promoted in fan magazines such as *Motion Picture Magazine, Photoplay, Motion Picture Classic,* and *Shadowland.* The
presence of dance in the U.S. film capital was extremely strong, with
Theodore Kosloff, Ernest Belcher, Ruth St. Denis, and her husband,
Ted Shawn, all opening dance schools that were approved of by the
industry as one of the few formal means of preparation for movie careers that did not endanger the morals of young women.[34]

Echoing dancer-turned-film-star Irene Castle in her numerous pro-
nouncements on the value of dance in building health, "What Chance
Has the Plain Girl in the Movies?" advised that "a girl must give time
and attention to the business of acquiring grace since the body is the
instrument on which soul music is played." The fan article's emphasis
on the best preparation as "good health" does not seem to point to dance
training, but it is accompanied by a picture of a barefoot dancer in-
triguingly draped in lamè; she wears an Egyptian headpiece modeled
after the one worn by Violet Romer, the principal dancer in the stage
version of *Kismet* (1912), and she is posed in a modified arabesque position.[35] Such a visual emphasis on dance, often lacking verbal explanation, seems to assume that dance in the oriental mode had a strong
connection to film that audiences/readers would immediately recognize.

Certainly, fan magazines were eager to establish the movies' connection to the dance world. Actresses frequently were claimed to come
from dance backgrounds; the roster of successful actresses that were
actually Denishawn-trained talent was long and included Louise Brooks,
Carmel Myers, Margaret Loomis, Carol Dempster, and Blanche Sweet.
The "New Woman" of concert dance did not seem as dangerous as some
other cultural manifestations of the phenomenon. She may have been
employed and in a field that involved public exhibitionism, but dance
iconography provided reassurance of her continuation of more respectable female artistic preoccupations of the past.

Dance as a "classic" art stood as an ideal symbolic merger between
traditional middle-class female gentility and contemporary ideals of
feminine freedom from bodily and imaginative restraints. In similar
fashion as dance, fan magazines, like other "women's" magazines, attempted to chart a course between affirming the need to embrace the
modern while simultaneously upholding traditional sexual and familial values.[36] It followed that fan magazines's strategies for depicting actresses rarely made use of costumes and sexually suggestive poses
evoking the harem dance girl and her presumed function for the male
gaze. If the gentility of dance as high art served an important purpose
in removing the stigma of the movies and, more specifically, of
seminudity from female film performers, then such blatant masculine-
aimed appeals might threaten to undermine the fan magazine's creation
of female display meant for the specular consumption of women fans.

In this context, the fan magazine's sympathetic reliance on dance
iconography as a cultural production traditionally associated with
female performers, and more recently associated with female audiences,
reminds us of an important fact sometimes overlooked, that women's
spectatorship during these years worked primarily to sustain female
stars.[37] Male matinee idols on the order of Valentino and Wallace Reid
were relatively rare in comparison with the many successful female

stars. A number of them, including Madame Petrova, Clara Kimball Young, Alla Nazimova, and Norma Talmadge, had their own production companies to create pictures around their star presence.

Fan magazines offered portraits of Denishawn graduates and other female stars in highly stylized, dance-derived poses. Photographs of actresses often featured oriental mode costumes that were striking in their resemblance to the dance costume designs of St. Denis and Bakst, and to the fashion and theatrical costume creations of courturier Paul Poiret. Dance-inspired oriental costuming drew from fantastical Bakst-influenced lamé halter tops and Turkish harem pants as well as Poiret high fashion. The influence of the latter is evident in a *Photoplay* layout of 1917, where Mae Marsh's "At Home" ensemble takes its cue from Poiret's velvet-and-silk ensemble "Melodie."[38] There were also many literal interpretations of Japanese kimonos and Chinese robes (Figure 9). Often actresses (such as Bessie Love, Helen Eddy, Mae Marsh, and Margaret Loomis) were featured in such costumes for film exploitation, that is, when they were starring in film productions based on oriental themes or co-starring the industry's premier Asian leading man, Sessue Hayakawa.[39] At other times, actresses orientalized for no obvious reason were posed contemplating a statue of Buddha (Leatrice Joy) or other artwork identified as generically oriental (Petrova) or sharing space with a five-foot high oriental vase (Norma Talmadge).[40]

By 1920, orientalized costuming became the dominant trend in fan magazine camera studies of stars. In *Vogue* in 1921, the Far Eastern influence was declared the rage in American fashion.[41] The consumerism of the New Woman linked her to new, daring styles. These styles had their roots in dress reform that encouraged female athleticism and in the Orientalist-inspired designs of key figures such as Poiret whose blurring of fashion with stage costume was significant in bringing the world of performance (and the imaginary Orient) into the realm of the everyday. His designs for the theatrical productions of *Le Minaret* (1913) and *Aphrodite* (1914) formed the basis of high-fashion gowns. Poiret's fashion wear, while stereotyped as excessive with Orientalist ornamentation (tassels, embroidery, feathered turbans, and faux jewels), developed over the years from his notoriously restrictive hobble skirt to an emphasis on classical draping, on simplicity and freedom in design, and on Orientalist costume fantasy literally made material. Designer Jean Worth dismisses Poiret's dresses in terms that suggest the latter's evocation of an imaginary East: "They are hideous, barbaric. They are really only suitable for the women of uncivilized tribes. If we adopt them, let us ride on camels and ostriches."[42] There was also strong moral resistance to Poiret's work in the United States. Anticipating the designer's arrival in New York in 1913, a Catholic cardinal warned that

Figure 9.
Dance-derived
star study
for motion
pictures,
*Shadowland*,
1920.

the designs from Paris were "a social as well as moral danger to the Christian community for the licentious nature of its creations."[43] In spite of such responses, Poiret's "licentious" influence on American fashion was inevitable.

The condemnation of Poiret's designs for their barbarism and their provocative revelation of the female body set the stage for Hollywood's most highly stylized figuration of sexualized femininity in the "vampire" or "vamp." Emerging in the early 1910s, the movie archetype of the vamp reflected the convergence of modernity and the Oriental that was already widespread in fashion through the influence of Poiret and Bakst. Even at its most extreme, the iconography attached to film's "antique" vamp was filtered through dance and operatic icons of Salome and Cleopatra. Dance "high art" incarnations of Cleopatra and Salome became the representational foundation for Hollywood's proliferation of vamps in the late 1910s and 1920s. Vamp costuming was drawn from various sources, including Bakst's ballet designs for *Clêopatra* and *Schéhérazade*, Poiret's pantaloon gowns, otherwise known as "harem skirts," and the latter's theatrical designs adapted to fashion.[44]

The moral disorder of the East was attached to the vamp as a woman who perverted the proper gender-alignment of power and sexual passion.[45] This figure had been a staple of high-art dance in the early twentieth century. As Peter Wollen suggests, the Ballets Russes unsettled gender norms and solidified a cultural fantasy revolving around the Orient as the locus of decadent passion. The ballets company's were often characterized by a gender inversion of sexual power in which the phallicized woman is desiring and the feminized man is desired. Radical in implication, the Ballets Russes' inversion of sexual power was accomplished in large measure through visual presentation, such as in *Clêopatra*, where Ida Rubinstein's towering presence was dramatically contrasted with Nijinsky's feline "Golden Slave."

In the Ballets Russes and other dance formats, brutal sensuality began to be associated with a female figure. That figure was translated into film as the orientalized vamp who came to represent the "New Woman."[46] Associating the moral disorder of the East with female power was resonant with cultural fears that men were on the verge of capitulating to the sexual and social demands of women. To many conservatives, modern women were the metaphorical daughters of Salome because they were increasingly destructive and dominating in their sexuality. In 1922, William J. Robinson declared in a popular marriage manual that the "frigid" woman was "becoming rare," but the greatest contemporary danger was the "menace" of the woman of "excessive sensuality or the Woman Vampire." She threatened "the health and even life of her husband." Robinson concluded that a "hypersensual woman . . . with an excessive sexuality" deserved "the name vampire . . . in its literal sense" because "out of ignorance" (excessive demands) or "intentionally" (to kill her husband for his money), she demanded too much, sexually, from her mate.[47] Hollywood's favorite metaphor for the vamp's sexuality was one of a spider who entrapped and destroyed the hapless male.[48] Visually and symbolically, there was a popular conflation of ballet's ubiquitous orientalized phallic woman and film's representation of aggressive feminine sexuality associated with modern sexual mores. The result, in film, was the vamp, whose seductive sexuality, archetypally represented by Salome, was aimed at dominating the male in "unnatural" ways.

Hollywood's orientalized modern vamp conflated the New Woman's supposed perversion of gendered power with the sexual chaos long attributed to the Orient and more recently crystallized in Ballets Russes productions. That conflation was conventionalized in the figure of the screen vamp in films like *A Fool There Was* (1915).[49] The film's star, Theda Bara, was regarded as the most extreme example of the type, so extreme, in fact, that from the beginning of her short-lived popularity as the ultimate orientalized vamp, the actress was quickly dismissed as a constructed caricature of femininity in articles such as "Does Theda Bara Believe Her Own Press Agent?" (Figure 10).[50]

Nevertheless, the stereotype of the vamp persisted into the 1920s and was presented straight as the orientalized, fashionable woman in films such as Cecil B. DeMille's *The Ten Commandments* (1923), and in *Blood and Sand* (1922). In the latter, Nita Naldi plays Doña Sol to Valentino's doomed bullfighter, Juan Gallardo. Naldi's dominating vamp is immediately typed by her Poiret-derived fashions, her oriental tastes in home decorating, and by the cowering male servant who appears in turban and lamé trunks to serve her guests. The servant's presence symbolically anticipates the hero's ultimate sexual subservience to Doña Sol. Later, in a humiliating confrontation, Gallardo's mother and wife are forced to watch as, on his lover's disdainful command, he stoops to pick up her glove. Doña Sol is triumphant in her power over Gallardo, who will die in the bullring after his cruel lover publicly rejects him. Thus, the figure of the phallic orientalized woman suggests a displacement: the despotism traditionally attributed to the oriental male is combined with stereotypical feminine allure coded as mysterious and sensuous. In *Blood and Sand* as well as *A Fool There Was*, the orientalized vamp escapes punishment, and the restoration of the Anglo-Saxon patriarchal order is little more than implied.

The Orientalist influence on the representation of women is striking in its visual saturation of the movies and of fan magazine discourse, but it is at its most complex in the fan magazine's treatment of the "vamp." While the fan magazine sometimes assumed an ironic and undermining tone toward star construction, this tone was especially evident in its response to the movie industry's on-screen, textual conflation of the modern sexualized woman with oriental archetypes of the vamp, such as Cleopatra and Salome, associated with "cobra and incense"— and dance.

One example of this attitude occurs in *Picture Play*'s introduction of dancer and featured-film player Doraldina. The magazine declares: "there are moments when my faith in the wickedness of Salome and Cleopatra is sorely tried. It is my experience in motion pictures which has caused me to disbelieve everything that is written." After recounting how Theda Bara was exposed to be "the dutiful daughter of Ma and Pa Goodman, and a regular attendant at the synagogue, the article

We . . .  ¹Gladys Hall and
        ⁽Adele Whitely Fletcher

Theda Bara . . . . . . Herself

*toward the car and comes forward. A. W. F. pinches G. H. with dexterity and force, thus signifying to that martyred matron that it is Theda Bara. Miss Bara reaches the door of the car. She is young and slight and dark. She has something other than youth . . . She wears a beaded frock of rose canton crêpe, a rose hat with drooping poppies, a grey fox scarf and white kid slippers. She greets the chroniclers affably and gets into the car.)*

A. W. F. (*with her knack of making all parties concerned feel perfectly comfortable and at home*) : Miss Hall insisted that you weren't you. I think she expected you to imitate a snake in your exit from the doorway.

THEDA BARA (*laughing*) : You would have been inspirations to my erstwhile press-agents. But even if my previous rôles were realities, it isn't likely I'd look like them. I've known women who were really vampires——

G. H. (*hopefully*) : You've known vampires? Oh, when, where, how . . . ?

T. B.: Not here. America is an alien land to the vampire. They dont know how to "do it" over here. No, I meant

Photograph by
O. M. Hinm

Photograph by Witzel, L. A.

Theda Bara is conversant with books, authors, poets and painters. She has lunched with the poetic Drinkwater, and dined with the fascinating W. L. George. She has been received in the salons abroad, both of the Great and the Demi-Great. There is no topic from psycho-analysis to horoscopes that she does not know about and cannot discuss

in France. And they have not been of the lurid type. Rather, they were immaculately groomed, very well thought of, very widely received and quite unabashed.

A. W. F. (*looking at G. H. and speaking slowly*) : There aren't so many as there used to be, I understand, in any country . . . ?

T. B.: No. In Paris there is only one, really. And that is a natural outcome, after all, of the economic independence of woman. Most women today have some way of earning a livelihood. There's infinitely less cause for their adopting parasitic existences.

It's the New Women, the Modern Woman, you know, whom I want to portray in my picture for Mr. Selznick. Perhaps a characterization a trifle broader than the average modern woman. And I shall give the interpretation, whatever it may be, a touch of the exotic. People love it. I love it myself. And if you play the warm, colorful type of woman you've created a Lorelei in spite of yourself—without the benefits of leopard

21
PAGE

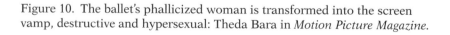

Figure 10. The ballet's phallicized woman is transformed into the screen vamp, destructive and hypersexual: Theda Bara in *Motion Picture Magazine*.

proceeds to demystify Doraldina as an exotic attraction. When she stops dancing, the article suggests, "the parson could call her Sister Saunders without exciting any comment."[51]

Fan magazines take an ambivalent stance toward the orientalized vamp. On the one hand, they often endorse the iconographic style and power of the star. While sometimes aligning the female star with the vamp's independence, narcissism, and sexual power, they also frequently draw attention to the constructed nature of the stereotypical screen vamp and disavow her danger. For example, a *Motion Picture Magazine* feature on Nita Naldi, published in 1922, declares that she "looks like a vamp and talks like a girl on the front porch of a summer hotel . . . God gave her the Orientalest-looking eyes . . . She'd be a knock-out in Turkey. I'd be her bookie in any harem." While photographs confirm Naldi's status as a sexy orientalized vamp, the star dismisses her casting as unrealistic because "the real vampire is the little baby doll with the liquid eye." At the same time, her affirmation of the proto-feminist attitudes of modern women is established: Naldi asserts that "a man is scared to death of a woman who looks as if she might have a couple of thoughts" (Figure 11).[52]

In the next year, *Motion Picture Magazine* described the "old-time vamp" as a "mythical creation":

She gazed hypnotically upon her victim from under ultramarine lids, her chin couched on the back of flexed and bejewelled fingers. Her movements were very slow and cat-like; and her Delsartean elegance was too exquisite for words. . . . [She] always kept a small Buddha on the tabouret beside her. She never sat down, but reclined languidly on a chaise-lounge; and she lived in a flat that resembled the harem scene in a comic opera.[53]

As late as 1927, *Motion Picture Classic* dismissed the "exotic vampire type de luxe" as a fiction, "a sort of little effigy of feminine evil . . . allowed to remain the same exaggerated, trite and hopelessly standardized type that she was ten years ago."[54]

While the screen "vampire type de luxe" was dismissed as a fiction, she continued to be constructed by Hollywood discourse. The conflation of the Modern Woman with the orientalized vamp found its most potent representative in Natacha Rambova, the dancer-designer responsible for the production and costume design of the most radical of the era's many film versions of *Salome*.[55] She was also Valentino's second wife. In that role, Rambova came to symbolize the New Woman as dangerously destructive to men and to the proper order of gender relations. In the popular press, she became the ultimate High-Art Dance Vamp (Figure 12).

Like so many other dancing American women, Natacha Rambova

"*Be nice to a man and he's as good as gone. Cater to him, run after him, spill a few tears over him at the breakfast table, and he will fall into the arms of the first vamp who throws him a red rose . . .*"

be opened by a little glycerine. Valentino taught me differently. Well, let me see . . . He and his wife are in love, if that'll help. She waited for him at the studio and went to see all the 'rushes' with him and things like that. And he's awfully obliging. He'd imitate the Sheik any time he was asked . . . I'm glad he's made good because he did it without any backing or pull. He's some lover!"

At this juncture, just when you want to know more, let us analyze before we proceed. Nita looks like a vamp and talks like a girl on the front porch of a summer hotel. Only more so. God gave her the Orientalest-looking eyes I've seen without benefit of make-up. She has the approved voluptuous figure and a red mouth and wicked-looking teeth. She'd be a knock-out in Turkey. I'd be her bookie in any harem. And she has extraordinarily beautiful hands. And exquisite nails. They could scratch a couple of dozen wives without a struggle.

Fred Niblo, when they began on "Blood and Sand," told her that he was going to take some close-ups of those hands if he didn't do another thing. "One woman in a thousand," he said, "has beautiful hands. You're that one."

"On the vamp matter," said Nita, "I just dont happen to look like an ingénue and that's why they cast me for the vampire, which is wrong again, because the real vampire is the

Photograph by Edward Thayer Monroe

Nita looks like a vamp and talks like a girl on the veranda of a summer hotel. God gave her the Orientalest-looking eyes I've ever seen. She has the approved voluptuous figure and a red mouth

little baby doll with the liquid eye. Every time. A man is scared to death of a woman who looks as if she might have a couple of thoughts. He wants to know it all. That's Men. The girl with the curls is the real vampire. I found that out when I was in the chorus. It was the blonde cutie that did all the damage to the front row.

"You take the vampire, especially as she is shown on the screen, and all she amounts to is a shimmie and a clinch behind the neck. Any woman can compete with those tricks. There's nothing to it. It's when there dont seem to be any tricks that the red flag is waving.

"As for my being a vamp and dressing like one and all that—what chance have I got? Looks is looks and I dont do anything about them one way or the other. If someone hands me a pair of

(Continued on page 89)

37
PAGE

Figure 11. The fan magazine model of the orientalized vampire: Nita Naldi "talks like a girl on the front porch of a summer hotel" in *Motion Picture Magazine*, ca. 1922.

Figure 12. Natacha Rambova, the ultimate High-Art Dance Vamp, as photo-graphed for *Photoplay.*

made herself over into her own exotic creation. She was a Utah heiress who became a ballet protégé of Theodore Kosloff and then a designer. Rambova was fond of Poiret gowns, was rarely photographed without one of her trademark turbans, and was associated with Egyptian spiritualism. Her most serious affrontery to public sensibilities was her apparent refusal to conform to established gender relations.

When Rambova presented Valentino with a "slave bracelet" to wear, that gesture came to be represented in public discourse (especially U.S. newspaper coverage) as the ultimate epiphany of the perverted Orientalist force of modern women who were shaping a woman-made masculinity destructive of American norms. The *Brooklyn Citizen* snidely suggested: "'A Slave? Not I,' said Rudy. 'At least I'm no woman's slave,' continued the ace of sheiks as he exhibited a cute little slave chain bracelet on his wrist."[56] Rambova's despotic influence over Valentino's productions brought a public outcry and caused her to be contractually barred from his film productions; after the actor's death, Adela Rogers St. Johns characterized Rambova as "dominating, artistic, fascinating," and suggested that not only had Valentino "adored" Rambova, but he had "allowed her to run his life, his business, his career, his finances." Their story echoed *A Fool There Was* and numerous other films; it was the tale of a vamp who wantonly destroyed a man, for Rambova's marriage to the actor "is generally conceded to have greatly injured Rudy's career. . . . And she left him, in the end."[57]

Yet, in keeping with fan magazine's ideologically complicated position toward modernity and the New Woman, Rambova was the subject of commentary that characterized her as being unfairly victimized by the press.[58] Although *Camille* and *Salome* were both generally dismissed as "bizarre," there was recognition in the fan magazines that Rambova's collaboration with Alla Nazimova created two of the most visually avant-garde films brought before American film audiences in the 1920s.[59]

A Russian émigré and former Stanislavski student, Nazimova was catapulted to fame on Broadway in *Hedda Gabler* in 1906 and hailed as a great actress. In Hollywood in films such as *Eye for Eye* (1918) and *The Red Lantern* (1919), the actress-dancer perfected a screen persona of an exotic woman of the world, sometimes overtly oriental, but always thoughtful and passionate. To sustain her popularity as a dramatic actress, Nazimova turned to making "artistic" pictures through her own independent production company. She hired Rambova to design the costumes for her production of *Aphrodite*, adapted from a controversial Pierre Louys's novel written in 1896. The dance heritage of the project was clear: the recent Broadway stage version had borrowed both Bakst and Michel Fokine from the Ballets Russes for design and choreography. Fearful of censorship and negative publicity, the film was aborted by Nazimova's home studio, Metro Pictures.[60] Nazimova began production of *Camille*. Rambova's designs for this film were startling for their combination of modernism and visual metaphor, but they would be eclipsed in their daring by her work for *Salome* (1923).

Rambova's costume and set designs for *Salome* were imitative of Aubrey Beardsley's drawings for Oscar Wilde's *Salomé* (but also influenced by Poiret). They were ridiculed by reviewers for the very qualities of visual presentation that dance had cultivated: the mixing of modernity with an imaginary Orient associated with the fantastic, both visually and sexually. Like Bakst's designs for the Ballets Russes, Rambova's at times strongly suggested the possibility of sliding gender identity and the reversal of traditional patriarchal power relations.[61] Maureen Turim observes that *Camille's* costume design "hints at a strategy . . . in which the spectacle of female seductive power becomes a celebration of modernity."[62] In both films, modernity was conceived in terms of dance and its figuration of the seductive power of Orientalism. Also, it could be argued, this vision of femininity was aimed primarily at a female audience.

To suggest such a reading acknowledges the formative role of dance in the era's figuration of powerful, seductive female sexuality (on-screen and off), but also follows the line of thinking suggested by Michael Moon. In his analysis of the dancing of Ida Rubinstein, Moon reacts to Bram Dijkstra's suggestion that, in the context of the many turn-of-the-century representations of feminine evil, Rubinstein, who danced Zobeida in *Schéhérazade* as well as Salome and Saint Sebastian, served merely as "an ambulant fetish expressive of the ideologically manipu-lated desires of [her] society."[63]

Moon's response to Dijkstra applies also to a consideration of the cinema's dance-influenced presentations of female subjectivity and fe-male spectators during the period under consideration. Moon believes that Dijsktra "fails to consider. . . [Rubinstein's] position as a powerful emblem for some of her lesbian admirers . . . of a will to exhaust the entire repertory of binary roles through which femininity was con-ceived."[64] We do not know if the lesbian sexuality of other female per-formers (including Nazimova or dancer Loie Fuller) played such an emblematic role for their audiences. But it is possible that the fan maga-zine narcissistically celebrated the female as a fetish object, not for the consumption/possession by the male (either on-screen or in the audi-ence), but self-consciously constructed for the female spectator.

In this respect, the fan magazine may have encouraged female-iden-tified fantasies centered on Orientalism in fashion and the visual arts as sexualized iconography virtually inseparable from dance. As the ob-ject of such projected fantasies, the orientalized female was a subject whose exhibitionism was not just passive but was associated with dance's construction of self-assertive, highly charged identities that tem-porarily broke down the binary roles through which not only feminin-ity but ethnicity and race were conceived. Dance Orientalism was associated with a process incorporating female identities at once wild and classically decorative, sensual and also athletically androgynous. The implications of these liminal, performative identities wordlessly moved beyond the more obvious dichotomies (sadism/masochism, "black"/white, colonizer/colonized, male/female) that were reasserted through the narrative strategies of so many of Hollywood's Orientalist film texts of the period, including *The Sheik*.

We might conclude that, within the context of modern dance's cultivation of a spectacle of physical freedom combined with emotional intensity, women's fascination with the Orient should be viewed not just in terms of the appeal of luxurious consumables but as part of a search for intensified experience. That desire has been associated with modern culture's search for personal meaning, whether provided to women during these years by the theater, film, and dance, or to men by secularized religiosity, colonialist adventure, or war.[65] According to Edward Said, as "a Western style for dominating, restructuring, and having authority over the Orient," Orientalism "depends for its strategy on this flexible positional superiority, which puts the Westerner in a whole series of possible relationships with the Orient without ever losing him the relative upper hand."[66]

While not completely overriding the inherent racist and colonialist power relations assumed in Orientalism as a practice, fan magazine Orientalism of the period may lead us to conclude that Orientalism played much more varied functions for women in relation to gender and racial difference than the satisfaction of masochistic rape fantasies or the desire for a simple consumeristic visual appropriation of luxury. The fan magazine suggests a dance-influenced discourse that complicates the phenomenon of Orientalism in relation to women's desires.

By drawing on forms closely associated with female-aimed culture, the fan magazine points to a female appropriation of Orientalism with more varied meanings and more interesting implications than films of the same time that required narrative recuperation of the New Woman's physical and sexual freedoms. Fan magazine Orientalism, like film Orientalism in general, was the product of a number of cultural intertexts. Nevertheless, its foregrounding of dance-influenced Orientalism modified the fan magazine's expected assertion of conservative gender, sexual, and racial boundaries to women's cultural identity.

While the fan magazine fed into stereotyped notions of women as consumers of the film experience par excellence, it also mediated the marketing of movies and the movie industry with a different perspective on Orientalism and the vampish New Woman for its female readers than that often offered by films. According to this perspective, female sexuality, even in the vampish oriental mode, was regarded as more playfully performative than truly destructive, or as one fan magazine article asserted on behalf of certain actresses, "We could vamp and make 'em like it."[67] However, this begs the question: who in the film audience was really "liking it"—men or women?

If women of the late 1910s and 1920s were unsure of their equality, the retreat to Orientalism as a site of intensified sensual experience and symbolic Otherness might have permitted them the temporary assumption of an exotic, performative identity within a textual economy of libidinal excess. The mysterious East identified with the release of sexuality and experiential (orgiastic) intensity seemed to have had a particular appeal to women both for its aesthetic and emotional intensity as well as for its comfortable distanciation from everyday reality.

Perhaps the symbolic mapping of the New Woman's desires for physical and sexual independence demanded the imaginary topography of the East, where the shift to the spectacle of the visible was not just luxurious (and consumable) but also austere and fantastic. That aesthetic topography held the promise of a different feminine identity—preposterous and improbable—but also destructive of the claims of prevailing ideology and, therefore, "evil." In such a world of oriental chaos, women might imagine themselves to be more than harem dancing girls. They might become "the Eternal Salome" acting out "all the forbidden adjectives" associated with antique exoticism, but also with the New Woman in her search for meaningful transformation in the modern world.[68]

## Notes

1. Quoted in Michael Morris, *Madame Valentino* (New York: Abbeville Press, 1991), p. 90.
2. Edward Said, *Orientalism* (New York, Vintage, 1979), 3.
3. Ibid., 111.
4. Prologues and dream sequences set in Egypt seem to have become particularly popular after the discovery of King Tut's tomb in 1992. See Pola Negri's *Bella Donna* (1923) and Nita Naldi's *Lawful Larceny* (1923).
5. Gina Marchetti, *Romance and the "Yellow Peril"* (Berkeley: University of California Press, 1993),17; Sumiko Higashi, *Cecil B. DeMille and American Culture: The Silent Era* (Berkeley: University of California Press, 1994),108; See also Miriam Hansen,"Pleasure, Ambivalence, Identification: Valentino and Female Spectatorship," *Cinema Journal* 25, no. 4 (1986): 24. Hansen assumed that the underlying fantasy does not have its origins in Western relations with Eastern cultures and nations, but is a projection and displacement of the fantasies and fears of American men regarding the sexuality of women and the racial/ethnic male Other defined by black/white racial relations in the United States.
6. Gina Marchetti, *Romance and the "Yellow Peril,"* 16.
7. *"The Sheik"* (advertisement), *Los Angeles Record*, 29 October 1921.
8. See, for example, *The New York Times*, 1 May 1921; and *Literary Review of the New York Evening Post*, 5 March 1921. Reviews were united in their criticisms: "tawdry, shoddy stuff. The ideals it inspires are cheap ideals,

the motives it develops are base ones. Rudolph Valentino suggests a sopho-more on his way to a masquerade." (Review in the *Globe*, ca. November 1921, clipping in the New York Public Library, Theater Arts Collection, hereafter cited as NYPL.) Similarly, *Motion Picture Classic* asserted that Valentino "fails lamentably." (Untitled clipping, *Motion Picture Classic*, January 1922, NYPL.)

Advertisements for the film capitalized on the book: "They can't print the book fast enough for the demand. It's the big controversational [sic] topic of the year. Everyone has read it or heard of it or wanted to borrow it or discussed it or wanted to read it or hid it or wondered when it would be made into a picture. And now it is *a* picture!" (Advertisement for *The Sheik*, *Denver Post*, 29 November 1922, NYPL.)

9. Adele Whiteley Fletcher, "Across the Silversheet," *Motion Picture Magazine*, November 1921, 108. Gertrude Chase, review in the *Telegraph*, 13 November 1921, clipping in NYPL. Chase states that "Valentino makes the Sheik a charming gallant whose brutalities are left entirely to the imagination."

10. "Has the Great Lover Become Just a Celebrity?" *Motion Picture Classic*, May 1926, 78. Gina Marchetti, *Romance and the "Yellow Peril*," 78.

11. Ella Shohat, "Gender in Hollywood's Orient," *Mid East Report* (January-February 1990): 40, 42.

12. Ibid., 42.

13. Gina Marchetti, *Romance and the "Yellow Peril*," 21.

14. Higashi, *Cecil B. DeMille and American Culture*, p. 90.

15. Ibid., 98 and 104.

16. Shohat, "Gender in Hollywood's Orient," 40.

17. Matthew Bernstein, *Walter Wanger, Hollywood Independent* (Berkeley: University of California Press, 1994), 45. This function for Orientalism, especially in relation to male subjectivity, is especially evident in Foreign Legion films and bears resemblance to notions surrounding the frontier West that were especially prevalent at the turn of the century. For an extended discussion of Valentino and the construction of the hero in *The Sheik* in relation to female fantasy, see Gaylyn Studlar, *This Mad Masquerade: Stardom and Masculinity in the Jazz Age* (New York: Columbia University Press, 1996), 150–198.

18. "What do we mean by 'Nice'?" (editorial), *The Ladies Home Journal*, November 1920, 1.

19. Elizabeth Kendall, *Where She Danced* (New York: Knopf, 1979), 10.

20. Review in *The Theatre*, quoted in Ibid., 74.

21. *New York Times*, 16 August 1908, cited in Judith Lynne Hanna, *Dance, Sex, and Gender* (Chicago: University of Chicago Press, 1988), 88.

22. Kendall, *Where She Danced*, 77. Hoffman moved on to other ventures and was especially successful in imitating the Ballets Russes with her own show entitled Saisons des Ballets Russes.

23. Said, *Orientalism*, 1.

24. In arguing for the gender-bending use of oriental dance in Jack Cole's Hollywood choreography, Adrienne McLean emphasizes how "classical" oriental dance, especially that of Ruth St. Denis, was often "rigidly gendered" and emphasized the spiritual rather than the sexual. See McLean's essay in this volume. The work of St. Denis often did demonstrate qualities that

could be interpreted this way, but it would be wrong to assume that Orientalist dance of the period I am discussing did not participate in breaking down conventional gender alignments and power relations. Even the casting of female dancers in the role of what McLean calls "unmarked transvestites" can be found in dance of this period, as in Desha's "The Rose of Stamboul," featured in *Shadowland*, June 1922, 12–13.

25. Gaylyn Studlar, "The Perils of Pleasure? Fan Magazine Discourse as Women's Commodified Culture in the 1920s," *Wide Angle* 13, no.1 (1991): 6–33. The format of *Dance Magazine* was very similar to that of fan magazines and included short stories as well as feature stories on dance stars.

26. Kathryn Helgesen Fuller, "Shadowland: American Audiences and the Moviegoing Experience in the Silent Film Era" (Ph.D. diss., Johns Hopkins University, 1993), 229. Fuller does not cite her source for this observation.

27. "The Victoria Cross," *Photoplay*, December 1916, 98–104, 116–119.

28. Victor Rousseau, "Peggy Roche: Saleslady; The Adventure of The Three Georges," *Photoplay*, March 1917, 128, 140–148.

29. "Figures of the Dance," *Motion Picture Classic*, February 1923, 50–51; Truman B. Handy, "Flavored with Tartar," *Motion Picture Magazine*, May 1922, 50–51, 96; "Two Pierrots," *Motion Picture Classic*, November 1924, 22; Herbert Howe, "Outstripping Salome," *Picture Play*, November 1917, 44–48; "The Spirit of the East: Posed by Alexander Oumansky and Doris Niles," *Shadowland*, March 1922, 30; "Desha of Stamboul," *Shadowland*, June 1922, 12–13;

30. Peter Wollen, "Fashion/Orientalism/The Body," *New Formations* (spring 1987): 5.

31. Ibid., 8.

32. Ibid., 10. See also Kendall, *Where She Danced*, 60–69 and Palmer White, *Poiret* (New York: Clarkson N. Potter, 1973). Poiret's gowns were strenuously criticized in the press, with one commentary in *l'Illustration* declaring: "To think of it! Under those straight gowns we could sense their bodies!" (Quoted in White, *Poiret* 41.)

33. Kendall, *Where She Danced*, 136.

34. For a discussion of Denishawn's role in Hollywood, see Ibid., 116–149. See also *Naima Prevots, Dancing in the Sun: Hollywood Choreographers, 1915–1937* (Ann Arbor, Mich.: UMI Research Press, 1987) for the influence of Belcher, Kosloff, Serge Oukrainsky, and Adolph Bolm, among others, on Hollywood as an early "dance mecca."

35. Gordon Gassaway, "What Chance Has the Plain Girl in the Movies?" *Picture Play* December 1921, 19. See also "Dance Assisted Her," *Los Angeles Examiner*, 29 October 1916, clipping in NYPL, Castle Scrapbooks, Robinson Locke Collection, series 2, no. 37.

36. See Studlar, "The Perils of Pleasure," 28–33.

37. William K. Everson, *American Film* (New York: Oxford University Press, 1978), 78.

38. Randolph Bartlett, "There Were Two Little Girls Named Mary," *Photoplay*, March 1917, 36.

39. "Margaret Loomis," *Picture Play*, November 1920, n.p.; "Helen Eddy" (pho-

tograph), *Motion Picture Magazine* March 1920, 8; Kenneth Curley, "The Idealist Speaks" on Bessie Love, *Motion Picture Magazine*, May 1922, 70.

40. "Leatrice Joy" (photograph), *Motion Picture Magazine*, July 1922, 11; Frederick James Smith, "Petrova and Her Philosophy of Life," *Motion Picture Classic*, September 1918. 18–19. "Popular Photoplayers" (Talmadge photograph), *Photoplay*, December 1922, n.p.
41. "Far Eastern Influence on Clothes" (photograph of Irene Castle), *Vogue*, January 1921, n.p., clipping in NYPL, Castle Scrapbooks, Robinson Locke Collection, series 2, no. 37.
42. Jean Worth (interviewed), *Vogue* (ca. 1908), quoted in White, *Poiret*, 43.
43. Cardinal Farley, letter printed in *New York Herald* (ca. September 1913), quoted in White, *Poiret*, 73. Poiret's influence meant that he was inevitably hired, however fleetingly, to design costumes for the movies, as were his assistants, Paul Iribe and Erté. "Ruth Clifford Wears Poiret Gown in *The Dangerous Age*," *Screen News*, 26 August 1922, 23. See Paul Iribe, "The Elimination of Geographical Lines," *Screen News*, 12 July 1924, 8; and "Erté: Greatest Fashion Genius Now in Pictures," *Photoplay*, May 1925, 78.
44. What Anne Hollander labels the "Basic Exotic Vamp Suit" she attributes to Hollywood invention and the appearance of Theda Bara in *Cleopatra* (1917). See Hollander, "Movie Clothes: More Real Than Life," *New York Times Magazine*, 1 December 1974, 68.
45. Janet Staiger declares her interest in "the specific cultural meanings" of the vampire in a short chapter in her book, *Bad Women*, but she does little in the way of tracing the iconography of the dark, hypnotic woman, and her discussion remains focused on a single film, *A Fool There Was* (1915), in light of social discourse on female power and the family. See Staiger, *Bad Women: Regulating Sexuality in Early American Cinema* (Minneapolis: University of Minnesota Press, 1995), 147–162.
46. The potentate's despotic control of women's bodies through "white slavery" and the harem continued to be a stereotyped depiction of Eastern sexual domination played upon in films including *The Sheik*, *Her Purchase Price* (1919), and *The Morals of Marcus* (1915).
47. William J. Robinson, *Married Life and Happiness*, 4th ed. (New York: Eugenics, 1922), 89, 93.
48. In an odd prefiguring of this, Gertrude Hoffman is depicted on the cover of *The Theatre* in 1912. She is costumed in a Ballets Russes–like firebird costume as she looks up at a huge spider web. "Gertrude Hoffman" (cover photograph), *The Theatre*, September 1912, n.p.
49. This was not the first "vampire" film, and at least two earlier films on the subject, *The Vampire* (Kalem, 1910) and *The Vampire* (Selig, 1913) were directly inspired by the "Vampire Dance" popularized in the early teens by Alice Eis and Bert French. See Staiger, *Bad Women*, 151.
50. Delight Evans, "Does Theda Bara Believe Her Own Press Agent?" *Photoplay*, April 1918, 62–63, 107.
51. Gladys Hall, "Viewpoints of a Vampire," *Motion Picture Magazine*, November 1922, 37.
52. Herbert Howe, "Outstripping Salome," *Picture Play*, November 1920, 44–45.

53. Frederick van Vranken, "The Vampire and the Flapper," *Motion Picture Magazine*, April 1923, 90.
54. Carter Greene, "We Could Vamp and Make-Em Like It: If They'd Only Make Us Real," *Motion Picture Classic*, June 1927, 48–49.
55. Theda Bara starred in a version in 1918 for Fox. *A Modern Salome* (1920) contained a Salome sequence. In the 1920s, in addition to the Nazimova version, there was a 1923 version starring Diana Allen.
56. "No Slave to a Wife" (caption to Valentino's photograph), *Brooklyn Citizen*, 11 November 1925, clipping in NYPL.
57. Adela Rogers St. Johns, "Why Do Great Lovers Fail as Husbands?" *Photoplay*, July 1927, 29.
58. Editorial in *Photoplay*, February 1926, 27.
59. One review announced "Bobbed and bizarre Dumas reigns at the Rivoli." Alan Dale, "Bobbed, Bizarre Is the Nazimova Film 'Camille,'" *American*, 22 October 1921. For an interesting discussion of the film's production and reception, see Morris, *Madame Valentino*, 69–74.
60. See Morris, *Madame Valentino*, 67–69.
61. The fact that Rambova clothed star Alla Nazimova in an imitation of a Denishawn soaring suit escaped attention at the time, as does the general dance influence on the film to current scholars.
62. Maureen Turim, "Seduction and Elegance: The New Woman of Fashion in Silent Cinema," in Shari Benstock and Suzanne Ferris, eds., *On Fashion* (New Brunswick: Rutgers University Press, 1993), 140–158.
63. Bram Dijkstra, *Idols of Perversity: Fantasies of Feminine Evil in Fin-de-Siècle Culture* (New York: Oxford University Press, 1988), 53.
64. Michael Moon, "Flaming Closets," *October* 51 (winter 1989): 23.
65. T. Jackson Lears, *No Place of Grace: Antimodernism and the Transformation of American Culture, 1880–1920* (New York: Pantheon, 1981), 120–123.
66. Said, *Orientalism*, 3, 7.
67. Greene, "We Could Vamp and Make-Em Like It," 48–49, 66.
68. "The Eternal Salome" (photograph of Marie Prevost), *Motion Picture Classic*, May 1922, 48. The caption states: "The personification of Salome seems to be irresistible to most actresses. Sooner or later they all try it—even ethereal blondes. Marie Prevost is the latest one to try 'to look that way'— you know—all the forbidden adjectives. We defy anyone to do it better than Marie does."

Adrienne L. McLean

# The Thousand Ways There Are to Move: Camp and Oriental Dance in the Hollywood Musicals of Jack Cole

Jack Cole (1911–1974) is often called "the father of American jazz dance."[1] He developed his dance style while working as a choreographer and dancer in Hollywood in the 1940s and 1950s, and "Cole technique" has strongly influenced both film dance and American theatrical dance generally. While he is probably equally famous today as a coach and mentor to female stars such as Betty Grable, Rita Hayworth, and, particularly, Marilyn Monroe, Cole's most important innovation in dance terms, the one that made his work so influential, was his coupling of "accurately observed" oriental, Indian, and African-American dance movements to jazz music.[2] If Cole's name is not currently well known among film scholars, it is partly because his films do not demonstrate what Jerome Delamater calls the "stylistic unity" of those canonical musicals where the choreographer (e.g., Busby Berkeley, Fred Astaire, Gene Kelly) functions as *auteur*, or where dance is the "controlling feature" of the mise-en-scène (as it is in the musicals of Vincente Minnelli).[3] Nevertheless, in his heyday Cole was one of the most powerful choreographers working in Hollywood, with contractual control over the movement design, camerawork, costuming, lighting, and editing of his dance numbers (Figure 1).[4]

   Another reason that Cole's importance may have been downplayed over the years is that he was gay, a fact well known by his coworkers but not, predictably, alluded to publicly outside of his creative environ-

Figure 1. Betty Grable, Jack Cole, and Jack Lemmon rehearsing the male harem dream sequence from *Three for the Show* (1955). Courtesy of the Museum of Modern Art/Film Stills Archive.

ment. Yet, Cole's status as an invisible gay man (to use Moe Meyer's term) is crucial to more than an understanding of the satiric, parodic, or misogynistic—"Camp"—elements of Cole's film work.[5] It is also a necessary precondition for his particular mode of deployment of oriental dance as a practice. Here, I examine the interaction between the irony, aestheticism, theatricality, and humor of Cole's discourse of Camp and the Orientalist dance practice he used in his musical numbers.[6] Meyer defines *Camp discourse* as "the total body of performative practices and strategies used to enact a queer identity, with enactment defined as the production of social visibility" of erased or displaced (closeted) homosexual identity.[7] Visibility, or invisibility, is the term that links Cole's Orientalist dance practice and his use of Camp discourse; for Cole's Orientalism, like his gayness, was often "invisible" as such. That is, because he worked within a dominant, patriarchal, and compulsorily heterosexual system of representation—classical Hollywood cinema— Cole's gay signifying system, like the Camp discourse of other gay performers and choreographers, became a "hidden transcript" within the "heterosexual frame" of his films.[8] What made Cole unique among his colleagues, however, was that his hidden transcript *was*, I suggest, oriental dance technique, which he manipulated precisely to reorganize and reconceptualize standard binary gender roles.

Cole did choreograph or direct the movement of several films with ostensibly oriental subject matter—including the two sound versions of *Kismet* (William Dieterle, 1944; Vincente Minnelli, 1955)—which employed conventionalized costumes, names, musical styles, and desert locales to ensure that audiences would "read" the subject as "exotic" and "foreign." But Cole's use of oriental dance was otherwise seldom recognizable through costume or music alone. Unlike his erstwhile mentors Ruth St. Denis (1877–1968) and Ted Shawn (1891–1972), for example, Cole relatively rarely created what film audiences would understand in visual terms to be "oriental dance." Instead, the dynamics of Cole's movement styles, his use of the body and the impulses that drive its expressive motions, were the loci of oriental influence on Cole's work, and the source of power supporting his hidden transcript.

The question is not whether Cole, or any other American, depicts non-Western cultures "authentically" or uses them to more "positive" ends. But, as Eve Kosofsky Sedgwick notes, forms of oppression are not all congruent; "the person who is disabled through one set of oppressions may *by the same positioning* be enabled through others."[9] More important, the supposition that one is *either* oppressed *or* an oppressor, or that "if one happens to be both, the two are not likely to have much to do with each other," is, according to Sedgwick, usually wrongheaded.[10] Orientalism and homophobia are often linked, for example; Orientalism is not only racist but homophobic.[11] Camp historically is also a direct consequence of homophobia; it is a "subterranean" discursive practice that results from living in a world of compulsory heterosexuality. Cole's Orientalist dance practice, because it was also a *Camp* practice, helped to undermine the homophobia of conventional "Hollywood Orientalism."

In her essay "Male Bonding, Hollywood Orientalism, and the Repression of the Feminine in Kubrick's *Full Metal Jacket*," Susan White uses the term *Hollywood Orientalism* to refer to Hollywood's tendency "to conflate Eastern culture with corrupt sexuality, a degraded or treacherous femininity and male homoeroticism."[12] Certainly many Hollywood films of many different genres—war films, biblical epics, adventure films, comedies, and musicals—routinely reproduce visually and thematically what Edward Said calls the "imaginative geography" of Orientalism, according to which the Orient is described as feminine and fertile, its main symbols being "the sensual woman, the harem, and the despotic—but curiously attractive—ruler."[13] Nick Browne also details the invidious and reprehensible ways in which American "dominant popular Orientalism" in early films, film theory, and theater design coexisted with and screened out institutionalized and violent racial repression of Orientals themselves.[14] I do not intend here to downplay the paranoid racism of Orientalism as a category of thought or expertise or as a liminal dreamscape on which to project displaced Western erotic and political desires. Rather, I argue that *because* Orientalism has, as Said tells us, "less to do with the Orient than it does with 'our' world,"[15] who chooses to practice it, and when, and why, demands further analysis. In other words, studying the basis of American Orientalism as it occurs in specific places and times will tell us nothing about the Orient but may teach us, as Browne's work so clearly shows, much about American culture itself.

Said, for example, claims that any American "comes up against the Orient" immured in and defined by "the main circumstances of *his* [sic] actuality"—that being American comes before being an individual, as it were.[16] Yet, even as we bear in mind the power differentials between the "unequal halves" of Occident and Orient,[17] the term *American* is obviously as overarching and imprecise as *oriental* itself. Orientalist practice in the field of American dance was constructed not by culturally dominant groups but by its structurally more marginalized or "outsider" members, in this case women and gay men.[18] In fact, Cole's approach is best understood against the backdrop of the type of Orientalism that pervaded U.S. popular culture during his years of dance training in the early 1930s, specifically the training he received from Ted Shawn and Ruth St. Denis. So before continuing this analysis of Cole's film work as an Orientalist and a Camp discourse, I will present a rather detailed introduction to Orientalism in American dance and film.

As is well known, from its earliest days the American motion picture was what Margaret Farrand Thorpe calls a "vampire art," for the film industry often drew from or exploited preexisting art and entertainment forms.[19] Since the motion picture's distinguishing feature was its ability to record movement, dance, as an art of movement, was an immediately attractive source of subject matter. By the middle teens, the iconography of eroticism and exoticism produced by "dominant popular Orientalism" in theatrical dance—not only burlesque and vaudeville but Serge Diaghilev's Ballets Russes and its numerous imitators as well—made dance even more appealing to Hollywood.[20] The lure of lucrative careers and instant fame turned Hollywood into a mecca of sorts for dancers and choreographers, and many well-known dance artists opened schools in Los Angeles. The introduction of sound, of course, only heightened what many perceived to be the "natural affinity" of dance and film;[21] by the mid-1930s, the musical was one of Hollywood's major genres, and remained so through the end of the 1950s.[22]

Perhaps the best known and most influential dance school founded in Los Angeles was Denishawn, which opened in 1915. Ruth St. Denis and Ted Shawn were, through the audiences they attracted and the students they trained (e.g., Martha Graham, Doris Humphrey, Charles Weidman, as well as Cole), the vanguard of what would eventually become American modern dance. Married in 1914, Shawn and St. Denis became famous for the "oriental" dances they created and performed, dances with titles like *Incense, The Cobras, Nautch, Yogi, Radha*—to list but one of Ruth St. Denis's early programs. Shawn and St. Denis often mixed works from one or another of their oriental "Suites"— Ancient Greek, Japanese, East Indian, Persian, Siamese, Chinese, and Egyptian, for example—so that, in the same evening, an audience of the 1920s might see *Sappho, Japanese Spear Dance, The Beloved and the Sufi, Kwan Yin, The Abduction of Sita*, and *Isis and Osiris*. Through the early 1930s, Denishawn supplied dancers and dance pieces for numerous Hollywood movies, including Griffith's *Intolerance* and several DeMille films; film performers also studied movement and dance at the school.[23] The fashionable Orientalism of Denishawn was never, for the most part, based on much more than extant popular imagery (St. Denis's initial, revelatory source of dance inspiration was the image of Isis on a poster advertising "Egyptian Dieties" cigarettes—"No better Turkish cigarette can be made").[24] Even after Denishawn toured the Orient and North Africa in 1925–1926—the first American company to do so—its dances continued to rely more on conventions of costume and setting than on faithfully adapted movement for their effectiveness (Figure 2).

Shawn's observations about the dances and dancers he encountered on the oriental tour are collected in a 1929 book entitled *Gods Who Dance* and other of his abundant dance writings; reading *Gods Who Dance*, one is struck both by its rampant racism toward what he calls "primitive people" and by the often amazingly "interlocutory" sense with which Shawn and St. Denis engaged and learned from their non-Western Others.[25] As difficult as it may be to comprehend, there seems to be no doubt that the spurious oriental dances of Shawn and St. Denis ac-

Figure 2. Ruth St. Denis and Ted Shawn in costume. By permission of the Dance Collection, New York Public Library for the Performing Arts, Astor, Lenox and Tilden Foundations.

tually inspired dance revivals in India and Japan; that the performances of Denishawn, like those of ballet dancer Anna Pavlova in 1922–1923, sparked a renewed interest in indigenous dance forms. Books in classical Sanskrit, for example, report on St. Denis's impact on the ancient dance forms of India.[26]

Here, one comes face-to-face with the ideology of Orientalism itself, as a "fact of [Western] human production" and a projection of Said's "imaginative geography." That is, to describe what Shawn, St. Denis, and Cole "learned from" the Orient, one must in some sense *become* an Orientalist, with all the dismaying chauvinisms and inequities of power that this entails. Certainly Shawn "found" the Orient he expected to find, that he wanted to find; huge areas were therefore blocked from his field of vision (e.g., "In Algiers and Tunis . . . I found almost no dancing worthy of the name").[27] Yet neither Shawn nor St. Denis ever really claimed that their oriental dance was anything more than pastiche, adaptation, a picking and choosing of the most dazzling theatrical effects.[28] As in the harem dances of nineteenth-century ballet or the frenzied voluptuousness of the Ballets Russes, which embody what Deborah Jowitt calls the pessimistic and secular strain of Orientalism,[29] authenticity was not, *could* not be, the point. The Denishawn strain of Orientalism differed only, but remarkably, in that it was less erotic than optimistic, spiritual, chaste, and, above all, respectable.[30]

Even though St. Denis learned to be a goddess by copying an advertisement for cigarettes, and Shawn became "Shiva" by making himself up into a living replica of a bronze statue, their dance had a quasi-religious and genuinely exhortatory impulse (Shawn had actually started off in divinity school). Shawn and St. Denis believed that they stood for enlightenment, and created imaginary idealized "other selves" that were meant, as gods and goddesses were, to be beyond human desire.[31] Their oriental personas were, as Jowitt writes, a "distillation of values both temporal and spiritual," their Orient a "storehouse of guises."[32] This aura of transformative power was both the source of the appeal of oriental dance to early feminists as well as its link to more patriarchal values of masculine dominance over sexualized and sometimes passive females.[33] On the one hand, the notion of idealizing the self through physical activity—of dance "as a vehicle for showing change," as Jowitt puts it—could be seized upon by eager American students who wanted to move, literally, beyond the status quo. On the other hand, the storehouse of guises that Shawn and St. Denis chose to draw upon, especially in the dances they performed together, were often rigidly gendered and conveyed, in Judith Lynne Hanna's words, "messages of male freedom and dominance counterposed to female subjugation and deference."[34]

Of course, despite marriage to St. Denis, despite a vigorous public display of heterosexuality, the fact remains that Ted Shawn was himself a closeted gay man for most of his life and also participated in an "invisible" Camp discourse, whether he (or indeed Cole) would have called it that or not. Accounts of the flamboyance and "tastelessness" of Shawn's dances and dance persona, in particular, bear no small resemblance to Margaret Thompson Drewal's more recent descriptions of Liberace and his "unmarked transvestism."[35] Unmarked transvestism is not technically cross-dressing; neither Shawn nor Liberace disguised themselves as women. Nevertheless, because it often takes the form of "outrageous display," unmarked transvestism has, according to Drewel, "a feminizing effect insofar as it makes the male performer into a glitzy object of the gaze."[36] Shawn biographer Walter Terry mentions the "dilemma" presented to otherwise "sympathetic" music and dance critics when faced with a typical Ted Shawn dance piece:

> [Critics] would groan when a primitive dance of fire found the men in silken capes walking along the stage and suddenly pulling open the capes to reveal

scarlet linings and bodies bare except for silver jockstraps. Shawn would justify his whole approach with a battery of explanations, sometimes ethnic, sometimes otherwise, but the truth was that he was, and always had been, guilty of bad taste, especially in matters of costume.[37]

If one looks at Shawn's "bad taste" as a Camp discourse, as a hidden transcript that, intentionally or otherwise, certainly confounds binary gender codes in a visual sense, it is not difficult to see why Moe Meyer says that Camp can, on the one hand, offer a "transgressive vehicle yet, on the other, simultaneously [invoke] the specter of dominant ideology within its practice, appearing, in many instances, to actually reinforce the dominant order."[38] Unmarked as transvestites, Liberace and Ted Shawn "evade[d] disclosure," notes Drewal, and maintained an "overt sexual anonymity" that was not threatening to a heterosexual audience: at the same time, however, it was *through* unmarked transvestism that Liberace and Shawn insinuated "their own voices, albeit in masked form, into official public discourse."[39] Camp, in short, exploits what Meyer calls the most predictable "blind spot" of bourgeois culture: "it *always* appropriates. And it appropriates whatever the agent of Camp chooses to place in its path."[40]

One of the most important things that Ted Shawn placed in the path of American bourgeois culture was the country's first professional all-men's dance group, of which Cole was a founding member. Established a couple of years after Ruth St. Denis left Shawn in 1931, "Ted Shawn's Men Dancers" was part of Shawn's mission to prove that dance was not only a religious activity but a "one-hundred-percent male" one.[41] From most accounts, Shawn's mission "worked"; that is, he and his dancers were accepted as "real" men—virile, rugged, athletic, powerful, *masculine*. Walter Terry finds irony in the effort and time that the Men Dancers put into proving that they were not what Shawn and other members of the company actually "were." Yet the point is that Shawn's hidden transcript succeeded; he "proved" that masculinity and gay identity are hardly antithetical terms. Shawn *was* one-hundred-percent male, and he was also gay.

In the context of American homophobia, of course, particularly during the years when Shawn and his group performed, public reticence is understandable; so is Jack Cole's in Hollywood of the 1940s and 1950s. The marginalization of dancing as a career for "real men" was something both worked within, and yet something which both men used their respective "strains" of Orientalism to counteract. Although Edward Said equates the *object* of Orientalism with the *subject* of "male gender dominance, or patriarchy, in metropolitan cultures," to identify with the Orient as Shawn and Cole did, even if the relation was one of *pseudo-mutuality*—to use Eve Sedgwick's term—was to risk *overtly* identifying themselves as feminine or feminized.[42] Yet the Orient is the fantasy location of the despot in addition to the harem, and Shawn and Cole both emphasized the despotic side of their masculinity in public discourse.[43]

The public personas of Shawn and Cole differed markedly, however. Where Shawn's masculinity offstage was fatherly (his nickname was Papa Shawn) or brotherly, patriarchal in a literal sense,[44] Cole fostered an aggressive, tough, and sexually dominating "outlaw" image.[45] The "exaggerated" public masculinities of Shawn and Cole functioned as a defensive mechanism against their homosexuality, representing what Chris Holmlund, adapting Joan Riviere's work on the meaning of femininity, calls the male masquerade.[46] Yet, as with Liberace, Camp enabled Shawn and Cole to have their cake and eat it too, to participate in a wickedly intelligent and perverse dialectic that alluded to their homosexual identity even as it apparently disavowed it.[47] Cole himself described his "savage manner" to one writer explicitly *as* "a defense": "Male dancers, [Cole] said, already had several strikes against them. Those who wore jewelry and a skirt—or *dhoti*—as Cole did in his Indian dances, were asking to have tomatoes thrown at them."[48] Cole's multiple masquerades were, then, in the end defenses against what was for Cole the biggest masquerade of all: *heterosexual* identity. Here, his roles as oppressor and oppressed interacted; the jewelry and the *dhoti*, in some instances, or the conspicuous lack thereof in others, signified in Cole's film dances both as Orientalist and as Camp practices.

Jack Cole did not remain with Ted Shawn's Men Dancers long, and the group itself was disbanded before World War II. Yet Shawn and St. Denis had obvious and profound effects on Cole's career. Although Cole said his oriental dances were always reacting against what he called the "inauthenticity" of Shawn's and St. Denis's creations (whose primary motif, as he put it, was "goosing angels"),[49] Cole's dances may or may not have been "absolutely authentic," as his student and protégée Gwen Verdon claims they were.[50] Cole had studied intensively with Indian dancer Uday Shankar and others; he had hung around the Savoy ballroom in Harlem when he was a boy, where he learned African-American dance styles. Cole made his dancers study with teachers like Shankar as well, and he also amassed one of the largest private collections of dance manuscripts, references, and artworks in the world.[51] Yet all of this could easily have resulted in nothing more than the oriental pastiches of Denishawn in its heyday. What distinguished Cole's work from St. Denis's and especially Shawn's was not its greater "authenticity," but Cole's determination to deploy and manipulate the strictly gendered *movements* of oriental dance as a form of unmarked transvestism. Cole displaced gender codes through dance movement itself, as well as through more conventional appurtenances of costume and makeup.

In 1941, "Jack Cole and Company" appeared as a specialty in their first movie, Walter Lang's musical *Moon Over Miami*, with Betty Grable. Among the twenty-seven films that followed were the Rita Hayworth films *Cover Girl* (Charles Vidor, 1944), *Tonight and Every Night* (Victor Saville, 1945), *Gilda* (Charles Vidor, 1946), and *Down to Earth* (Alexander Hall, 1947, in which Cole staged a satirical Denishawn-style "Greek Ballet"); *The Jolson Story* (Alfred E. Green, 1947); *On the Riviera* (Walter Lang, 1951); *David and Bathsheba* (Henry King, 1951); *The Merry Widow* (Curtis Bernhardt, 1952); *Three for the Show* (H. C. Potter, 1955, which featured a dream sequence about a male harem); the two *Kismets*; *Les Girls* (George Cukor, 1957); and the Marilyn Monroe films *Gentlemen Prefer Blondes* (Howard Hawks, 1953), *River of No Return* (Otto Preminger, 1954), *There's No Business Like Show Business* (Walter Lang, 1954), *Some Like It Hot* (Billy Wilder, 1959), and *Let's Make Love* (George Cukor, 1960). Even though he did not always receive screen credit, Cole was responsible for virtually all of Marilyn Monroe's film numbers; he worked closely with her on the nonmusical portions of her films as well. Cole himself appeared as a dancer in many of his films, and he had an acting and dancing role in Vincente Minnelli's *Designing Woman* (1957).[52]

Whether or not a Cole number had any apparent ethnic basis (e.g., Latin American, Spanish, oriental) in musical rhythm or dance style, Cole eschewed elaborate sets and extravagant costumes unless they were called for by either a film's narrative (e.g., the Denishawn parody "Greek Ballet" in *Down to Earth*, the "oriental splendor" of *Kismet*, the outré cabaret excesses of *Les Girls*) or features of a star's image (Grable, Hayworth, or Monroe dressed in skimpy, tight, or flamboyantly decorated dresses). Cole often used bare or sparsely decorated sets—a single tree branch, a couple of raised platforms, a draped curtain—in order to make dance itself the most visually interesting component of the mise-en-scène.

When the situation called for it, however, Cole could exceed or at least match Liberace in "outrageous display." In the "Greek Ballet" in *Down to Earth*,[53] for example, Cole spotlights the spectacular status of women, but he also insists on the spectacularity of men—in large and oiled numbers, either nearly naked or in jewelry and "skirts" (Figures 3 and 4). In the Latin American "You Excite Me" from *Tonight and Every Night*, the women wear fetishistic fur bras and hairpieces and split skirts, the men gigantic ruffled sleeves or cut-off T-shirts and tight pants. Marilyn Monroe's "Heat Wave" number from *There's No Business Like Show Business* surrounds her with near-naked sweat-drenched men in

Figures 3 and 4. Two frames from the "Greek Ballet" in *Down to Earth* (1947). (Digitized frame enlargements.)

tight Bermuda shorts. In Cole's works, then, there is what Eve Sedgwick calls a "coming to visibility of the normally implicit terms of a coercive double bind": namely, that being a "man's man is separated only by an invisible, carefully blurred, always-already-crossed line from being 'interested in men.'"[54] The "coercive double bind" Cole engages is that women *and* men are prisoners of gender roles. Unlike the dances of Shawn or St. Denis, Jack Cole's use the body's physical beauty to stand for more than spiritual power. Cole's dance combines the theatricality and spirituality of Denishawn, the voluptuousness and intensity of Diaghilev's Ballets Russes, and indigenous American as well as oriental and other ethnic dance styles. Most important, Cole's approach to dance and gender, like that of Ted Shawn and his Men Dancers, had profound effects on dominant or at least hegemonic dance culture. "Cole technique" became the basis of American jazz dance, and his influence can be seen even today in theater and film dance.[55]

In the last interview he gave, Cole described his affinity for ethnic and other forms of dance:

> I was interested in many things. I was interested in the Oriental theater, Japanese and Indian particularly. I was always interested in the culture of people and how they expressed themselves. I never wanted to *be*—people are always confusing why you are teaching them; they think you want to teach them to *be* an Indian dancer—but I was trying to expose them to a different attitude, to give them the excitement and the discovery of the thousand ways there are to move that are peculiar and different, totally different, that would never enter your head here. It opens up a new vocabulary of movement.[56]

Naturally, any claims about the hidden transcript of Cole's musical numbers would be best supported by a viewing of the numbers themselves. In lieu of that, I will discuss three numbers in detail: the dance to "Not since Ninevah" from the 1955 Arabian Nights musical *Kismet*, which combines visible "oriental" features such as costume and setting with oriental movement; the "Happy Ending" dance sequence from the conventional "show-within-a-show" musical *On the Riviera*, which is not explicitly oriental in costume or setting; and finally, Monroe's and Jane Russell's opening "Little Rock" number from the backstage musical *Gentlemen Prefer Blondes*.

"Not since Ninevah" is performed by the "three princesses of Ababu" (danced by Reiko Sato, Patricia Dunn, and Wonci Lui) who are joined by two tall male dancers (whose names I was unable to find). The number begins with the three princesses, who are tiny physically, dancing in a martial tempo to beating drums; they each have a sword and a shield. Their costumes are singularly unrevealing—baggy and opaque "harem pants," topped by long-sleeved bodices with high necks. All three of the dancers attack movement with gestures and steps that are precise and strong.

The two male dancers, who wear much more diaphanous "harem pants" and whose chests are oiled, hairless, and bare, begin dancing for the princesses to very syncopated and slow jazz music (one AND two AND three AND four). Their gestures, too, are deliberate and forceful, the movements of the hands and fingers as precisely choreographed as the larger motions of the legs and arms. The dance style as well as the costume signifies "Indian" or "Hindu"—the shapes the body makes in space, the relative importance given to the isolated expressive movements of the upper body over the locomotive powers of the lower, the spirals and curves of the head, torso, and arms counterpoised to the flat frontality of the positions of legs and feet. The princesses react to the men's dancing first by whistling and by making prizefight gestures among themselves (pushing up their sleeves, thumbing their noses); then they join the men and their dance, at which point the tempo of the music picks up (Figures 5 and 6).

According to Judith Hanna, classical Indian dance is "undergirded by many different religious belief systems and sectarian strands, each with doctrinal . . . and ritual peculiarities."[57] Despite the fact that specific countries and regions have their own characteristic styles and that the face alone, in the words of one oriental dancer and scholar, can have "a hundred delicate shadings not always obvious to the Western observer," spread knees, in which the legs are bent and opened to the side, are "invariably seen only in masculine types of dance."[58] Certain steps and positions, in other words, must be performed by male dancers, while others belong strictly to females. Jack Cole, however, rarely defines movements as "masculine" or "feminine" or restricts their performance to one or another gender. The three princesses of Ababu perform the same sorts of virtuosic movements as the men—including the knee bends—often in unison with them; they also ride the men like horses, and the dance ends with the men prostrate beneath the standing women (Figures 7 and 8).

Observing Cole's use of posture and gesture alone, then, one would have to conclude that physical power, competence, and complete ease with one's body are potentially, indeed demonstrably, feminine as well as masculine traits.[59] If the women's bodies are objectified, so are the men's—more so, in this case. Richard Dyer writes that images of the male body in popular culture are almost always of men "doing something"; they *must* be, in order to produce a "phallic mystique" of muscular potency and strength to counter the "passivity" so often associated with being looked at.[60] Cole instead reminds us continually that "being looked at" is not by definition a *passive activity*, and that images of women can be images of women "doing something" as well.[61]

Figures 5 and 6. Two frames from "Not since Ninevah" in *Kismet* (1955). Top frame, the three princesses of Ababu ogle two offscreen male dancers. Bottom frame, the male dancers with the princesses. (Digitized frame enlargements cropped from CinemaScope image.)

Figures 7 and 8. Frames from "Not since Ninevah." The final tableaux with princesses astride the male dancers. (Digitized frame enlargements cropped from CinemaScope image.)

In fact, "Not since Ninevah" foregrounds and complicates the very issue of "phallic mystique," through its unmarked transvestism not only of male but of female image. For "what happens to our understanding of the fetishization of the female body," Margaret Drewal asks, "when the signifier is a gay man? Fetishism or transvestism? Or both?"[62] In her discussion of the Rockettes, whose director and choreographer was Russell Markert (a gay man), Drewal suggests that the signified of the Rockettes is a [gay] "masked object of desire"—a phallic *woman*. The Rockettes are, in essence, cross-cross-dressing trans-transvestites, who stand for men who are masquerading as women in "perpetual displacements of sexual identity."[63] Drewal's description of the Rockettes applies equally well to the three Princesses of Ababu: they too are "women cast as men—complete with phalluses [swords] and military moves [the male movements of Oriental dance]—yet devoid of any personality in their veiled [trousered and armored] womanhood."[64] Since they are unmarked transvestites, they "evade disclosure"; but because they represent a gay signifying practice, a queer discourse that "piggy-backs" upon the dominant order, that order's monopoly is nevertheless contaminated and polluted.[65] Even as Camp is appropriated and turned into a "tamed expression of the American spirit," its trace lingers on.[66]

Given the otherworldliness, the fantasy elements, of a musical like *Kismet*, one could argue that the dancers have more leeway to alter the status quo simply because it is not a status quo that matters in any practical sense; that is, perhaps audiences do not attach the dance's messages to the dancers as *people*, but as fictional characters in an exotic dreamscape. Although I do not believe that this is the case, the issue does demand attention. That is one reason that I chose to examine the "Happy Ending" finale from *On the Riviera*, a modern-day backstage musical set on the French Riviera starring Danny Kaye (in a dual role) and Gene Tierney. (Another reason is that Cole himself happens to perform in the number, along with one of his most important and influential students and devotees, Gwen Verdon.)

"Happy Ending" predates "Not since Ninevah" and is performed on a bare split-level stage in modern dress, yet it exhibits many of the same movement concerns and characteristics as the more conventionally orientalized number. One of the ways in which "Happy Ending" borrows from oriental dance is that each performer's legs and lower body do not serve as the support for movements that radiate outward from the spine, as they do in classical ballet. In ballet, the body is taut but elevated, "pulled up," centered on a plumb line that begins in the crown of the head and extends in a straight line to the floor.[67] Even when the knees bend deeply, it is only to propel a movement upward; when the arms "droop" in the motions of a dying swan, for example, the chest remains lifted. Although in oriental dance there can be an equal emphasis on presenting beautiful shapes in space, and on reaching heavenward or extending the body fully, movements "into the ground" are also used. Cole uses the shifting dynamics of oriental dance in his knee drops and slides, in floor work alternated with jumps and extended poses, in the isolated movements of one part of the body against the total stillness of other parts. Again, what Cole does *not* use is the careful gender divisions of classical oriental dance. Here, too, in terms of movement and gesture quality, the women can be said to function as unmarked transvestites.

As in "Not since Ninevah," the female dancers in "Happy Ending" are physically as strong as the males. They do everything the men do; they are never supported by them. The controlled off-kilter stances and extremely stylized shapes—the line of the arms broken at the elbows, the wrists, the fingers; the legs and feet alternately pointed, flexed, turned in, turned out; the torso curved, hyperextended, flattened to the floor or lifted to the ceiling; the hips quiet, still, or gyrating in circles in isolation to the stillness of the upper body (or vice versa)—belong to all of the dancers. Costume alone (tube dresses for women, tuxedoes for men) separates "male" from "female" (Figures 9–12).

This is not to say that costume is not a very powerful signifier of gender and sexuality; indeed, when the nondancing female star (Corinne Calvet) of the musical's show-within-a-show appears at the end of the number, it is only to stand smiling in a skimpy feathered costume before a final clinch with one of the two Danny Kayes. And when we turn to the performance of Marilyn Monroe and Jane Russell in the opening "Little Rock" number of *Gentlemen Prefer Blondes*, clearly both costume and star image figure in extremely potent ways. Nevertheless, as in *Kismet*—as in most Cole musicals in fact—*Gentlemen Prefer Blondes* and *On the Riviera* exemplify the ways in which dance numbers can offer alternatives to the compulsory heterosexuality of the conventional boy-meets-girl narratives in which they are embedded.[68] Maureen Turim, Lucie Arbuthnot, and Gail Seneca also note in their otherwise very dissimilar essays on *Gentlemen Prefer Blondes* that the figures of Monroe and Russell in musical numbers signify something other than, something exceeding, their narrative and spectacular status as objects of the male gaze, however difficult the "fascination" of Monroe and Russell dancing is for these scholars to articulate.[69] Cole's contributions to "Little Rock" are obvious; his "stamp" is present in the precise and often complex arm and hand movements, the syncopation of the steps and body movements against the music, the general quirkiness and unexpected shifts of stage direction and figure placement. But surely it is too much to claim that Marilyn Monroe is, because of Cole's training, in any sense an "oriental dancer," much less a "trans-transvestite" or a "cross-cross-dresser" (Figures 13–16).

Figures 9–12. Sequence from "Happy Ending" in *On the Riviera* (1951). The female dancer in first three shots is Gwen Verdon. Jack Cole can be seen in the fourth shot, behind Danny Kaye's right shoulder; Corinne Calvet appears in the center of the screen. (Digitized enlargements.)

Figures 13–16. Sequence from the "Little Rock" number with Marilyn Monroe and Jane Russell, *Gentlemen Prefer Blondes* (1953). (Digitized frame enlargements.)

Of course Marilyn Monroe is not visually, recognizably, an oriental dancer, just as the dancers in *On the Riviera* are not. Yet I believe that, in Cole's hands, Orientalism was part of an often transformative and empowering Camp discourse; whether one calls her a phallic woman or not, what would Marilyn Monroe be *without* her musical performances, or the humor, ironic sense, confidence, and authority revealed by them? Even while Jack Cole was, as an Orientalist, as a man, as an American man, an "oppressor" in some senses, he also understood what it was, as a gay man, as an artist, as a dancer, to be oppressed. He had a great deal of sympathy for female stars such as Monroe and Rita Hayworth and the "ordeals" that their celebrity brought to them; this is why he was in such demand as a choreographer and coach by women stars.[70] Yet he could be brutal and demanding, and had a infamous and occasionally violent temper.[71] The scantily clad women tied to chandeliers in "Diamonds Are a Girl's Best Friend" in *Gentlemen Prefer Blondes*, for example, can also be read, like much appropriated Camp discourse, as "straight" misogyny.[72] In short, Cole's work is most interesting because of its different hidden transcripts and the way that, filtered through the dominant discourse that is classical Hollywood cinema, different forms of oppression intersect in it.

I also suggest that, even when performed by Marilyn Monroe or Jane Russell, American dance is profoundly marked by Cole's Orientalist practices, assumptions, and input, just as it is by African, Latin, Spanish, and other ethnic dance forms. In fact, film scholars may have taken only a limited interest in Jack Cole's work until now precisely *because* it looks so familiar, so similar to that of other choreographers who have acquired the status of film auteurs, such as Jerome Robbins and Bob Fosse.[73] But it was Cole's work, both through his films and, more crucially, through the dancers and choreographers who worked for him, that was the influential force. Over and over again dancers talk about how important Cole was: Barrie Chase believes that his "combining of modern, Oriental, and jazz movement, his way of digging into the ground, of breaking down dance steps and body movement, of exact counting of every part of every step" made Jack Cole "the innovator of the way we move now."[74] According to Barton Mumaw, Jack Cole "[changed] the shape of nightclub, film, and theater dance in his comparatively brief lifetime."[75] Agnes de Mille admits that other choreographers, including herself, Bob Fosse, and Jerome Robbins, "all stole from Jack Cole."[76] Although Jack Cole "was the first choreographer working in Hollywood to revolutionize dance in both technique and content," as a Fosse biographer writes, Cole remains unknown by all but the most "concerned" of scholars and fans (Figure 17).[77]

Musical numbers, even in Hollywood films, can permit, in ways we have only begun to think about, what Judith Hanna calls the

Figure 17.  Marilyn Monroe in *Gentlemen Prefer Blondes*. (Digitized frame enlargement.)

"exploration of dangerous challenges to the status quo without the penalties of the quotidian."[78] She goes on to say that any musical number *potentially* not only "reflects what is but also suggests what might be" in terms of sexual mores and gender roles.[79] In the end, *as* Orientalism, as a product of Said's "imaginative geography" and its racism and homophobia, Jack Cole's Orientalist dance practice *enabled* him in the context of Eurocentric domination of non-Western cultures, just as the fact that he was a male enabled him in the context of American patriarchy. Cole's Orientalist practice was *disabling* to him too, because through it he identified himself with qualities—femininity, passivity, homoeroticism—that both Orientalism as a department of thought and expertise *and* American culture itself insisted were incompatible with American masculinity. According to dance scholar Svea Becker, Cole's use of ethnic dance allowed him to observe and comment upon, as well as satirize, American society; but to do this, "he had to go outside of it."[80]

Cole's Orientalist dance practice introduces compelling issues into ongoing discussions of Orientalism—not only how American Orientalism "intertwines" with other forms of oppression but also, for example, the question of how we recognize Orientalism *as* a practice. That is, how do audiences "see" or comprehend oriental influence (as well as gay influence), unless it is conveyed by visible appurtenances of costume and narrative setting? If we are ever to understand other cultures, or to use aspects of our own inherited or chosen cultures, how do we integrate what we learn with what we already "know," without reproducing the expected, the already legible, the stereotypical?

In short, Jack Cole's Orientalist practice, like Camp discourse generally, demonstrates that sometimes very subtle analytical tools are needed to understand a given form of expression and that specific features of identity—such as gender and sexual identity as well as national identity—do affect how Orientalism is constructed at different times and places. Cole's Camp hidden transcript was facilitated and enabled by a hidden or unmarked Orientalism. Cole did not so much "go native," in what Susan White calls "explicitly masochistic and homosexual terms," à la T. E. Lawrence; he did not put off onto "Arabs, Asians and women, the 'natural' masochists of the world," a desire to "abase himself to the great white father."[81] Cole's Camp discourse instead confronted and satirized the hegemony of great white fathers by emphasizing the physical power and spiritual authority *of* Arabs, Asians, and women (before whom muscled white American men often abase themselves). While Cole's work was always an "articulation and mechanism" of what Eve Sedgwick calls "the enduring inequality of power between men and women,"[82] his Orientalist dance practice as a Camp discourse was also, according to Jack Babuscio, a "means of dealing with a hostile environment and, in the process, of defining a positive identity."[83] What emerges from this study, then, is how important it is, even in Hollywood films, to interrogate, and to untangle the threads of, what are always already multiple discourses not only of oppression but of expression as well.

## Notes

1. For complete biographical material on Jack Cole, see Glenn Loney, *Unsung Genius: The Passion of Dancer-Choreographer Jack Cole* (New York: Franklin Watts, 1984).
2. Shirada Narghis, for example, writing in 1945, called Jack Cole, "who performs authentic Indian dance techniques to swing tempo without loss of the general dignity of the art," an "exceptional" exponent of Indian dance. In Loney, *Unsung Genius*, 92.
3. Jerome Delamater, *Dance in the Hollywood Musical* (Ann Arbor: UMI Research Press, 1981), 117.

4. From 1944 to 1947, Cole had the only dance company in the history of Hollywood under permanent contract to a studio, in this case Columbia. He worked at Twentieth Century-Fox and M-G-M as well, where he also had control over most aspects of his numbers. See Philip K. Scheuer, "Dancing Isn't Decoration," *Dance Magazine*, May 1946, 28; Dorothy Spence, "Hollywood Dance Group," *Dance Magazine*, July 1946,16–19; Loney, *Unsung Genius*, chaps. 7–9; Kevin Boyd Grubb, *Razzle Dazzle: The Life and Work of Bob Fosse* (New York: St. Martin's Press, 1989), 30, 57–58; interviews with Cole in Delamater, *Dance in the Hollywood Musical*, 191–199, and in John Kobal, *People Will Talk* (New York: Knopf, 1985), 592–607.

5. Moe Meyer, "Reclaiming the Discourse of Camp," in Moe Meyer, ed., *The Politics and Poetics of Camp* (London: Routledge, 1994), 1–22.

6. For further discussion of the expressive components of camp, see Jack Babuscio's pioneering essay, "Camp and the Gay Sensibility," in Richard Dyer, ed., *Gays and Film* (London: British Film Institute, 1980), 40–57.

7. Meyer, "Reclaiming the Discourse of Camp," 5. Meyer defines *Camp* as "a specifically queer cultural critique"; *camp* (with a lowercase *c*) is what results when "Camp" is appropriated by the "un-queer" (1).

8. Margaret Thompson Drewal, "The Camp Trace in Corporate America: Liberace and the Rockettes at Radio City Music Hall," in Moe Meyer, ed., *The Politics and Poetics of Camp*, 177, 176.

9. Eve Kosofsky Sedgwick, *Epistemology of the Closet* (Berkeley: University of California Press, 1990), 32. Italics in original.

10. Ibid., 32.

11. See particularly Michael Moon's discussion of Orientalism in relation to homophobia in "Flaming Closets," *October* 51 (winter 1989): 19–54.

12. Susan White, "Male Bonding, Hollywood Orientalism, and the Repression of the Feminine in Kubrick's *Full Metal Jacket*," *Arizona Quarterly* 44 (autumn 1988): 132.

13. Edward Said, "Orientalism Reconsidered," *Cultural Critique* (fall 1985): 90, 103. See also Ella Shohat's essay in this volume.

14. Nick Browne, "American Film Theory in the Silent Period: Orientalism as an Ideological Form," *Wide Angle* 11, no. 4 (1989): 23–31.

15. Edward Said, *Orientalism* (New York: Vintage, 1979), 12.

16. Ibid., 11. Italics in original.

17. Ibid., 12.

18. For discussions of the importance of art and culture to gay identity, see Judith Lynne Hanna, *Dance, Sex, and Gender: Signs of Identity, Dominance, Defiance, and Desire* (Chicago: University of Chicago Press, 1988); Moon, "Flaming Closets"; Richard Dyer, "Getting Over the Rainbow: Identity and Pleasure in Gay Cultural Politics," in *Only Entertainment* (New York: Routledge, 1992), 159–172; Wayne Koestenbaum, *The Queen's Throat: Opera, Homosexuality, and the Mystery of Desire* (New York: Poseidon Press, 1993).

19. Margaret Farrand Thorpe, *America at the Movies* (New Haven: Yale University Press, 1939), chap. 8.

20. On the impact on art and popular culture of the Orientalism of Diaghilev and the Ballets Russes, see Peter Wollen, "Fashion/Orientalism/The Body," *New Formations* (spring 1987): 5–33; Moon, "Flaming Closets"; Gaylyn Studlar, "Douglas Fairbanks: Thief of the Ballets Russes," in Ellen W. Goellner and Jacqueline Shea Murphy, eds., *Bodies of the Text: Dance as Theory, Literature as Dance* (New Brunswick, N.J.: Rutgers University Press, 1995), 107–124; and Studlar's essay in the present volume.

21. John Martin, "Introduction to a Catalogue of Dance Films," *Dance Index* 4 (1945): 60. For another take on the "natural affinity," see Albert Lewin, "Dynamic Motion Pictures: Our Screen Actors and Directors Can Never Do Anything Significant with Their Art until They Realize that It Is Closer to the Dance than to the Drama," *Shadowland*, October 1923, 46, 75.

22. For early discussions of dance and film—in many of which, despite his relative obscurity today, Cole's name is prominently featured—see Arthur Knight, "Dancing in Films," *Dance Index* 6 (1947): 179–199; "Hollywood Dance Directors," in *Dance* 21 (February 1947): 9–15; Mary Jane Hungerford, "How to Get the Most from Screen Dancing," *Dance Magazine*, June 1948, 30–37; Arthur Todd, "From Chaplin to Kelly: The Dance on Film," *Theatre Arts* 35 (August 1951): 50–51, 88–90. See also Delamater, *Dance in the Hollywood Musical*; Rick Altman, *The American Film Musical* (Bloomington: Indiana University Press, 1987).

23. For an excellent discussion of dance in silent films, see "Dance in Film before 1930," in Delamater, *Dance in the Hollywood Musical*, 11–26. For more on Hollywood as an early dance center, see Naima Prevots, *Dancing in the Sun: Hollywood Choreographers, 1915–1937* (Ann Arbor, Mich.: UMI Research Press, 1987).

24. Deborah Jowitt, *Time and the Dancing Image* (Berkeley: University of California Press, 1988), 130. For more on the meaning and intensity of the lure of the "aura of Egypt" at this time, see Antonia Lant's essay in the present volume.

25. Ted Shawn, *Gods Who Dance* (New York: Dutton, 1929); see also *The American Ballet* (New York: Henry Holt, 1926); *Dance We Must*, 2nd ed. (n.p., 1950); *One Thousand and One Night Stands* (New York: Da Capo, 1979), which has chapter titles like "No Noh!" "Oriental Swing," and "Out of the East."

26. Walter Terry, *Ted Shawn: Father of American Dance* (New York: Dial Press, 1976), 47–48; Judith Lynne Hanna, "Classical Indian Dance and Women's Status," in Helen Thomas, ed., *Dance, Gender and Culture* (New York: St. Martin's Press, 1993), 126.

27. Shawn, *Gods Who Dance*, 178. Or, "In Delhi where still other dancers danced for us, my thoughts turned to Vanda Hoff, who made her debut in the Denishawn company and later starred in vaudeville in an act called 'The Dancing Girl of Delhi.' In loveliness, charm and real ability what infinite worlds above the real dancing girls of Delhi was our Vanda!" (99).

28. St. Denis's *Radha*, she later "happily admitted, was about a Hindu goddess dancing a Buddhist concept in a Jain temple" (in Terry, *Ted Shawn*, 47).

29. Jowitt, *Time and the Dancing Image*, 145.
30. Cole himself recounts his differences with the Orientalist practices of Denishawn in an anecdote involving Ruth St. Denis's reaction to a Cab Calloway record that Cole played at Denishawn in the early 1930s. St. Denis was "white with rage" when she heard the music and reprimanded Cole severely, telling him to "shut that damn thing off." Cole continues: "Later she went by and another boy and I were doing something, a bit of tap dancing and jazz dancing, and she let out a wail . . . and went up to her room. All of a sudden the gong rang in the school, which always meant to assemble in the big studio. We were all assembled, and Mr. Shawn came in (he always wore a Japanese kimono). We all sat down on the floor and, looking very serious, he says, 'The temple has been defiled.' They were always being very earnest about that kind of thing, but I had a sense of humor that got me into trouble around the school . . . I used to talk to Miss Ruth about jazz dance . . . and she'd say, 'But it's so sexual, dear.' She was a very dear, bright woman but in certain areas there were great Victorian blanks" (Delamater, *Dance in the Hollywood Musical*, 192–193).
31. Jowitt, *Time and the Dancing Image*, 137.
32. Ibid., 138, 147.
33. Ibid. (see especially "Sphinxes, Slaves, and Goddesses" and "The Veil of Isis"); Elizabeth Kendall, *Where She Danced* (New York: Knopf, 1979). See also Hanna, "Classical Indian Dance and Women's Status," 119–135; and Studlar's essay in this volume.
34. Hanna, "Classical Indian Dance and Women's Status," 129.
35. Drewal borrows the term from Marjorie Garber; in Drewal, "The Camp Trace in Corporate America," 173.
36. Drewal, "The Camp Trace in Corporate America," 173.
37. Terry, *Ted Shawn*, 75.
38. Meyer, "Reclaiming the Discourse of Camp," 11.
39. Drewal, "The Camp Trace in Corporate America," 177.
40. Meyer, "Reclaiming the Discourse of Camp," 17.
41. In Jane Sherman and Barton Mumaw, *Barton Mumaw, Dancer: From Denishawn to Jacob's Pillow and Beyond* (New York: Dance Horizons, 1986), 123. Mumaw was Shawn's longtime lover.
42. Said, "Orientalism Reconsidered," 103; Eve Kosofsky Sedgwick, *Between Men: English Literature and Male Homosocial Desire* (New York: Columbia University Press, 1985), 196.
43. Although, as Hanna points out in "Classical Indian Dance and Women's Status," female deference to male authority *is* strongly coded in both classical Indian dance and Indian culture.
44. See Gaylyn Studlar, "Valentino, 'Optic Intoxication,' and Dance Madness," in Steven Cohan and Ina Rae Hark, eds., *Screening the Male: Exploring Masculinities in Hollywood Cinema* (New York: Routledge, 1993), 23–45, for a discussion, drawn from Janice Radway's *Reading the Romance: Women, Patriarchy, and Popular Literature* (Chapel Hill: University of North Carolina, 1984), of the lure to women of dance as a "*safe* display" of masculinity, in which masculinity can be "enjoyed" as both brutal and gentle.

45. Here is how Cole, the "son of a New Brunswick [New Jersey] pharmacist," was described by a reviewer for the *Chicago Daily News* (27 March 1949): "He dances like a demon from the celestial frying pan of Baal, the sun god. His body wriggles amid almost superhuman strides. His eyes glare menacingly beneath rotating eyebrows from a bronzed hook-nosed face that reeks of brutality with a capital Biff!" ("Dancer-Choreographer Jack Cole," *UCLA Librarian* 38 [February 1985]: 9.)

46. In Chris Holmlund, "Masculinity as Multiple Masquerade: The 'Mature' Stallone and the Stallone Clone," in Cohan and Hark, *Screening the Male*, 216.

47. See Drewal, "The Camp Trace in Corporate America."

48. Loney, *Unsung Genius*, 89.

49. Ibid., 59. Other Denishawn dancers felt the same way, such as modern dance pioneer Doris Humphrey, for whom Cole also danced: "I just got tired of being Siamese, Burmese, Japanese and all the other 'eses.' I came from Oak Park, Illinois, and I wanted to find out as a dancer who I was, what Oak Park and I had to say in dance" (126).

50. In Loney, *Unsung Genius*, 59.

51. Ibid., 310.

52. In *Designing Woman*, the Cole character, a dancer, actually uses dance moves to win a one-sided fight with a gang of crooks. For a complete list of Cole's film work, credited and uncredited, see the appendix to Loney, *Unsung Genius*.

53. *Greek*, of course, was a popular synonym for *homosexual*. For further discussion of "Greek love," see Sedgwick, *Between Men*, 4–5.

54. Ibid., 89.

55. Loney, *Unsung Genius*, 353; see also Martin Gottfried, *All His Jazz: The Life and Death of Bob Fosse* (Bantam, 1991), 81, 89–94.

56. In Delamater, *Dance in the Hollywood Musical*, 193.

57. Hanna, "Classical Indian Dance and Women's Status," 121.

58. La Meri [Russell Meriwether Hughes], "Oriental Dance," in Anatole Chujoy and P. W. Manchester, eds., *The Dance Encyclopedia*, 2nd ed. (New York: Simon and Schuster, 1967), 689.

59. Hanna recounts how some Indian legends reproduce the inequality of power structures between male and female deities: "Variants of legends say Shiva and his counterpart the goddess Kali compete in dance contests in which Shiva wins. Shiva performed many dances that Kali was able to imitate perfectly. Out of frustration Shiva exploited [Kali's] sense of modesty and raised his right foot to the level of his crown and danced in that pose. Although Kali *could have emulated this pose*, feminine modesty led her to withdraw from the contest. *Kali lost not because she was an inferior dancer but because she was a woman and affirmed her subservience in this role*." ("Classical Indian Dance and Women's Status," 123; italics mine.) Cole obviously does not reproduce this inequality in his dances.

60. Richard Dyer, "Don't Look Now: The Instabilities of the Male Pin-up," in *Only Entertainment* (New York: Routledge, 1992), 103–119.

61. Steven Cohan makes a similar point in his "'Feminizing' the Song-and-

Dance Man: Fred Astaire and the Spectacle of Masculinity in the Holly-wood Musical," in Cohan and Hark, *Screening the Male*, 46–69.

62. Drewal, "The Camp Trace in Corporate America," 176.
63. Ibid., 176.
64. Ibid., 176.
65. Meyer, "Reclaiming the Discourse of Camp," 11; Drewal, "The Camp Trace in Corporate America," 177, 178.
66. Drewal, "The Camp Trace in Corporate America," 178.
67. For an interesting discussion of the "meaning" of the "taut" and "straight" line of ballet, see G. B. Strauss, "The Aesthetics of Dominance," *Journal of Aesthetics and Art Criticism* 37 (Fall 1978): 73–79.
68. For a more extensive discussion of musical numbers and classical Holly-wood narrative, see Adrienne L. McLean, "'It's Only that I Do What I Love and Love What I Do': *Film Noir* and the Musical Woman," *Cinema Journal* 33, no. 1 (fall 1993): 3–16.
69. Maureen Turim, "Gentlemen Consume Blondes," in Patricia Erens, ed., *Issues in Feminist Film Criticism* (Bloomington and Indianapolis: Indiana University Press, 1990), 101–111; Lucie Arbuthnot and Gail Seneca, "Pre-Text and Text in *Gentlemen Prefer Blondes*" (1982), in Erens, *Issues in Feminist Film Criticism*, 112–125. Neither essay mentions Cole at all, and they barely mention the musical numbers as performances or as choreography, as something other than costume and song lyrics.
70. Loney, *Unsung Genius*, 208.
71. Bob Fosse, who also had an infamous temper, said that Jack Cole was "the only guy I was ever afraid of" (in Gottfried, *All His Jazz*, 265).
72. Loney, *Unsung Genius*, 205. Dance scholar Svea Becker believes that "Diamonds Are a Girl's Best Friend" is "truly critical of American values" but that this went unnoticed at the time, and remains unnoticed today, be-cause "film critics didn't look to dance as a source for serious ideas" and "[today] audiences are too obsessed with the Marilyn Monroe Legend to think about choreography or satire." (Svea Becker, "Jack Cole in Holly-wood," in *Proceedings of the Twelfth Annual Conference of the Society of Dance History Scholars* [1989], 11.)
73. For information on Fosse's films, see Grubb, *Razzle Dazzle*, and Gottfried, *All His Jazz*. Besides Robbins's *West Side Story* (Robert Wise, 1959), see "The Small House of Uncle Thomas" in *The King and I* (Walter Lang, 1956), an Orientalist dance adaptation of Harriet Beecher Stowe's *Uncle Tom's Cabin*.
74. In Delamater, *Dance in the Hollywood Musical*, 115.
75. Sherman and Mumaw, *Barton Mumaw*, 151.
76. Gottfried, *All His Jazz*, 81.
77. Grubb, *Razzle Dazzle*, 57.
78. Hanna, "Classical Indian Dance and Women's Status," 120.
79. Ibid., 132.
80. Becker, "Jack Cole in Hollywood," 11.
81. Susan White, "Male Bonding," 137.
82. Sedgwick, *Between Men*, 5.

83. Babuscio, "Camp and the Gay Sensibility," 47; see also Chuck Kleinhans, "Taking Out the Trash: Camp and the Politics of Parody," in Meyer, *The Politics and Poetics of Camp*, 182–201. For a recent examination of gay labor in the Freed Unit at M-G-M, see Matthew Tinkcom's "Working Like a Homosexual: Camp, Visual Codes, and the Labor of Gay Subjects in the M-G-M Freed Unit," *Cinema Journal* 35, no. 2 (1996): 34–42.

Marina Heung

# The Family Romance of Orientalism: From *Madame Butterfly* to *Indochine*

## The Photograph That Started It All

On an October afternoon in Paris in 1985, Claude-Michel Schönberg, the composer of the successful musical *Les Misérables*, was thumbing through an issue of the magazine *France Soir*, when a photograph caught his attention. The photograph shows an Asian woman half-facing a young girl. Although a group of men are gathered closely around them, the woman and girl seem oblivious to everything but each other. The woman wears plain dark clothes and has her hair pulled back. Her furrowed brows and drawn mouth give her face a pained expression, and—although one has to look closely to see this—her downcast eyes are focused intently on the girl. The girl is wearing a T-shirt; her left hand is being held by someone in the crowd behind her. Her mouth is widened in a grimace, and she is sobbing.

This is the photograph that inspired Claude-Michel Schönberg and his collaborator, the librettist Alain Boublil, to write the hit musical *Miss Saigon*. Later, Richard Maltby, Jr., who contributed English lyrics, acknowledged, "the entire show was in that photo."[1] The woman in the photograph is a Vietnamese mother saying good-bye to her daugh-

This is a revised version of an essay that was first published in Carol Siegel and Ann Kibbey, eds., *Forming and Reforming Identities* (*Genders* #21) (New York: New York University Press, 1995), 222–256. It appears here with the permission of the New York University Press. The photo, copyright © 1985 by Kraipit, is reproduced courtesy of Sipa Press.

ter. As Schönberg explains: "The little Vietnamese girl was about to board a plane from Ho Chi Minh City Airport for the United States of America where her father, an ex-GI she had never seen, was waiting for her. Her mother was leaving her there and would never see her again."[2] For Schönberg and Boublil, the photograph resonated with the devastating pathos of the Vietnam War and its unexhausted legacy in human trauma: "The silence of this woman stunned by her grief was a shout of pain louder than any of the earth's laments. The child's tears were the final condemnation of all wars which shatter people who love each other."[3] Propelled by their reaction to this image, Schönberg and Boublil went on to write *Miss Saigon*. When the musical opened in New York City, the same photograph was featured prominently in the production *Playbill* and reproduced as the frontispiece in the souvenir program.

But for Schönberg and Boublil, the photograph had a further, decidedly more gendered, significance, one that centered on the figure of the mother. Referring to the nameless woman, Schönberg adds, "She knew, as only a mother could, that beyond this departure gate there was both a new life for her daughter and no life at all for her, and that she had willed it. . . . I was so appalled by the image of this deliberate ripping apart that I had to sit down and catch my breath."[4] By invoking the archetype of the self-sacrificing mother, Schönberg and Boublil were thus led to the inspirational intertext for *Miss Saigon*—Giacomo

Puccini's *Madame Butterfly*. In Puccini's opera, the geisha Cio-Cio-San (Madame Butterfly) gives birth to a son after Lieutenant B. F. Pinkerton, an American naval officer, has abandoned her following a brief "marriage." Three years later, when he returns to Japan with his new American wife, Cio-Cio-San agrees to give up her child to the couple and then commits *seppuku* (ritual suicide). For Schönberg and Boublil, the mother in the "Miss Saigon photograph" comes to incarnate the same awe-inspiring maternal selflessness: "Was that not the most moving, the most staggering example of 'The Ultimate Sacrifice,' as undergone by Cio-Cio-San in *Madame Butterfly*, giving her life for her child?"⁵ With "a heartbreaking photograph and a potential connection with a famous opera to start from,"⁶ Schönberg and Boublil began writing *Miss Saigon* as a contemporary musical, reframing the story of *Madame Butterfly* against the backdrop of Vietnam in 1975, when the U.S. military evacuated Saigon on the eve of the Communist takeover.

It comes as no surprise that *Madame Butterfly* should offer a ready-made reference point for the writers of *Miss Saigon*. Puccini's popular opera is in many ways a foundational narrative of East/West relations, having shaped the Western construction of "the Orient" as a sexualized, and sexually compliant, space that is ripe for conquest and rule. Many scholars have analyzed the ways in which race and gender are mutually imbricated within Orientalist discourse and practice, constituting a nexus along which racial and sexual domination operate reciprocally.⁷ Central to the Western Orientalist imaginary, the figure of the geisha (whose most well known incarnation is Cio-Cio-San/Madame Butterfly) epitomizes an exoticized and subservient femininity that is leavened with a tantalizing mix of passive refinement and sexual mystique. As a master-text of Orientalism, *Madame Butterfly* confirms the Asian woman's perpetual sexual availability for the Western male even as her convenient demise delimits such liaisons; in the end, Cio-Cio-San's suicide recapitulates the fate of the expendable Asian whose inevitable death confirms her marginality within dominant culture and history.⁸

At the same time, Schönberg and Boublil's conflation of an Orientalist myth with the flesh-and-blood realities of the Vietnam aftermath necessarily reflects the ideological exigencies of a specific cultural moment. Both the photograph and the musical it inspired are artifacts of the post-Vietnam era, and as such, their ideological effects should be understood in relation to the many literary works, autobiographical and documentary accounts, and mass media representations seeking to reenact, rationalize, and mythologize the experience of the war in order to install it within the collective memory. As many commentators have noted, mass media images of the Vietnam War perform the work of selective remembering and erasure, effecting what Michael Klein terms "historical amnesia."[9] Operating through "ideological condensation,"[10] these representations smooth over moral ambiguities and ideological contradictions by mythologizing history. Seeking to assuage the pain of military defeat through cathartic displays of spectacular excess and physical violence, these representations mask their ideological effects through what they conceal as well as what they contain.

In keeping with such strategies, the "Miss Saigon photograph" encodes an ideologically motivated subtext that displaces the familiar hypersexualized archetype of the Asian woman and instead installs her as a maternal icon within a familial discourse. As I will show, this elevation of the Vietnamese mother as a hypermaternalized icon participates in a restorative drama paradigmatic of the post-Vietnam era. For the United States, the end of the Vietnam War represented a profound trauma to the collective national psyche. In particular, anxieties about military and masculine prowess coincided with a pervasive societal insecurity about maleness and paternal legitimacy that in turn mobilized an insistent, even obsessive, revalorization of the patriarchal nuclear family. In this context, the dominant trope that I call the "family romance of Orientalism" allows for the "rebinding" of wounded masculinity by reenacting the saga of recovering lost fathers.[11] News reports on the plight of abandoned Amerasian children and stories of their adoption by American families, for instance, rehearse the story of Amerasian children yearning to come to the United States to find fathers that they have never seen, a quest that is usually underpinned by an unspoken deference to the superiority of American culture and the promise of material enjoyment. Most important of all, these tales prioritize the nexus between father and child, with scant attention to the mother.[12]

To return to the "Miss Saigon photograph," then, we recall its effect on Schönberg as a spectacle of maternal self-sacrifice. However, even as Schönberg projects a scenario foregrounding mother/child relations, he also imagines a future scene of reconciliation between daughter and father, as suggested in his remark: "The little Vietnamese girl was about to board a plane from Ho Chi Minh City Airport for the United States of America where her father, an ex-GI she had never seen, was waiting for her."[13] Thus, the Western male's reentry and his reattachment to the girl as her father provide narrative closure for a precipitating act of maternal sacrifice. With the male/paternal principle informing the "Miss Saigon photograph" as a structuring absence, the image's primal power clearly derives from not only its inscription of maternal nobility but also the circulation of the paternal at its edges. At this point, we begin to make further sense of the unexpected connection that Schönberg and Boublil draw between the photograph and *Madame Butterfly*. For what the photograph traces, albeit in strikingly oblique and harsh terms, is a nexus of relations involving an Asian mother, her child of mixed ancestry, and an European father, the father hovering at the edges as the obsessive object of desire. As this essay will show, the triadic "family romance" so constituted not only underpins the inaugural Orientalist myth of *Madame Butterfly* but also subtends contemporary representations of East/West relations, and is most notably distilled in the recent film *Indochine* (1992).

## *Madame Butterfly* as Maternal Melodrama: From Interracial Romance to Family Romance

In its original meaning as used by Sigmund Freud, the "family romance" refers to the (male) child's imagination that he has been adopted. In one version of the romance, the "foundling myth," the child imagines that, unlike the parents who have raised him, his "real" (biological) parents are from a socially elevated, aristocratic class. In a second version of the romance, the "bastard myth," the child imagines that he is the illegitimate son of his mother, who has conceived him through an extramarital affair. In this second version, the child imagines a biological father whom he has never met and now longs to identify.[14] In Freud's view, the "neurotic's family romance" expresses hostility toward fathers and is thus typically a male fantasy.[15] The "bastard" myth in particular speaks to the male experience of the Oedipal crisis, in that the child can, by disavowing the father that he knows, create the imaginary possibility that he can possess his mother in his father's place. Since the mother's identity is not in question, this scenario is teleologically oriented toward the recovery of paternity.

Both versions of Freud's family romance are recapitulated in post-Vietnam representation. Marthe Robert's paraphrase of the "bastard myth," in which a (boy-) child imagines a "royal, unknown father who is forever absent" and "relegat[ed] . . . to an imaginary kingdom beyond and above the family circle . . . but whose place cries out to be filled" —distills the essence of a narrative about the abandoned Amerasian child within the current phase of postcolonialist discourse.[16] Further, in the orientalized family romance, issues of class take on overtones of racial and cultural difference. As Richard de Cordova notes, because the child confers aristocratic status on his "lost" parents, there is a built-in class dimension in the "foundling myth" version of the family romance beyond its libidinal and psychic dimensions.[17] In the post-Vietnam narrative, this social dimension of the myth receives a cultural inflection as well, so that distinctions of proletarian/aristocratic are mapped onto an assumed polarity between East and West; as a result, the Amerasian child's search for a lost paternal figure incorporates an unspoken affirmation of the cultural superiority of the West.

To date, *Madame Butterfly* exists in the popular imagination as the quintessential interracial romance, one that depicts the collision of cultural differences within what Mary Louise Pratt calls the "contact zone."[18] However, an examination of the opera and of its literary and dramatic antecedents shows the extent to which the trope of the family romance is central to its mythic construction. Although Puccini's opera is by far the best known, multiple versions of the *Madame Butterfly* story exist, both in literary form and in staged and filmed versions.[19] Among these versions, only one—the opera—foregrounds the elements of the interracial romance. And even here, the romantic plot figures prominently only in the first half of the work, ending in Pinkerton's departure. In all the versions, there is no renewed contact between Butterfly and her lover/husband after he abandons her. Instead, Butterfly's discovery of Pinkerton's treachery takes place through her encounter with Pinkerton's American wife, who asks Butterfly to give up her son. In this way, Butterfly's dilemma is framed as her doomed struggle to sustain her own claims and desires against the forces ranged against her: the prerogatives of male paternal authority, Western cultural superiority, and a familialist ideology.[20] The familialist slant of the family romance operative in *Madame Butterfly* is revealed through Mrs. Pinkerton's appearance at the end of the John Luther Long, David Belasco, and Puccini versions. Once Mrs. Pinkerton appears as the "legitimate" spouse, it becomes a given that Butterfly's claims as wife and mother are immediately diminished, since she loses any rightful claim to a place in Pinkerton's family. At the end of each version of *Madame Butterfly*, dramatic tension revolves around contesting maternal and paternal claims on the child, which are then resolved through Butterfly's agreement to give him up and her ensuing suicide. By killing herself, Butterfly surrenders to paternal and familial prerogatives, and the extremity of her sacrifice seals her iconic destiny as the embodiment of fanatic excess and self-abnegation.

Butterfly's enduring mythic stature is earned, then, not only as the wronged woman of interracial romance but also as the sacrificial heroine of maternal melodrama. In the maternal melodrama, the woman as mother falls and then redeems herself, usually through a sacrificial act committed for the good of her child. Characterized by Christian Viviani as an "apologia for total renunciation, total sacrifice, total self-abnegation,"[21] the maternal melodrama ennobles the mother by chronicling how she "reconquer[s] her dignity while helping her child re-enter society thanks to her sacrifice."[22] The familialist and patriarchal tendencies shared by the family romance and the maternal melodrama have been duly noted. Geoffrey Nowell-Smith, for instance, notes that "melodrama enacts, often with uncanny literalness, the 'family romance' described by Freud."[23]

Like the classical family romance, the maternal melodrama allows a particularly male-orientated enactment of the Oedipal plot despite its ostensible focus on female protagonists. Thus, according to E. Ann Kaplan, the maternal melodrama is "arguably a *male* Oedipal drama," in which the "maternal sacrifice theme was addressed to male needs, desires and fantasies, as much (if not more than) to female desires."[24] Yet, despite the inherently male focus of the maternal melodrama plot, its activation in the *Madame Butterfly* myth creates an interesting tension between the patriarchal stereotype of the self-denying mother and the Orientalist portrayal of the Asian woman as a marginal presence without psychological dimension or moral agency.

Numerous writers have demonstrated how the textual invisibility and silence of the Third World woman provide the necessary conditions for the formation of First World female subjectivity.[25] In this context, *Madame Butterfly*'s invocation of the family romance and the maternal melodrama would seem to provide a departure from the schematic distinctions between First- and Third-World women evident in the typical colonialist text. No longer the faceless victim whose anonymity and victimization reflect the backwardness of an alien culture, Butterfly now emerges from the "subaltern shadow" to occupy center stage. At the same time, the cloak of Victorian domestic virtue falls on her shoulders, as she becomes the exemplar of the moral ideal of female self-sacrifice. In Gina Marchetti's words, Butterfly's role as a "patron saint of female submissiveness" is nevertheless underpinned by a fundamental irony: "Butterfly may be a fool, stigmatized by her racial difference, but she also rises to become a heroine, who is ironically destroyed by the Western values that elevated her to the status of martyr."[26]

In this light, the myth of *Madame Butterfly* appears as an exemplary text extolling the female virtues of domestic duty and self-sacrifice, except that these are now figured through the travails of an Asian woman. While this reveals, on the one hand, the pervasive reach of patriarchal definitions of femininity that apparently recognize no national or racial boundaries, one would still have to acknowledge that *Madame Butterfly* provides a rare instance in which the "other" woman is envisioned as possessing selfhood and agency, even if these qualities are at once diluted by their being subordinated to notions of women's place.

## The Drama of the "Other" Woman

In *Madame Butterfly*, as both the displaced wife/mistress and the non-European, Butterfly is of course doubly Other, and her rivalry with an

Anglo-American woman only underscores her marginality in relation to both family and culture. According to Christian Viviani, the theme of the "other" woman is a familiar subplot of the maternal melodrama.[27] Historically, this figure has functioned to signify female difference and all that is unassimilable and "other" about femininity. As Helena Michie notes, the other woman as mistress is "located outside the family as the not-wife, the locus of all that is troubling, problematic, unfamiliar about female sexuality and sexual difference."[28] Yet the very fact that the visible agent of Butterfly's defeat is another—Anglo-American— woman inevitably brings into focus issues of sexual and racial differ- ence forming the crux of patriarchal and Orientalist discourse.

Although it would be in keeping with the text's simplified politics to view the rivalry between Butterfly and Mrs. Pinkerton only in terms of East/West conflict, the relationship between First World and Third World women has ramifications irreducible to monolithic categories of difference and hierarchy. Thus, in considering the "problem" of the Western woman within colonial discourse, Laura E. Donaldson identi- fies "the Miranda complex" as symptomatic of the multivalent inter- sections of race and gender in relations between the First World and Third World. In analyzing Caliban's attempted rape of Miranda in *The Tempest*, Donaldson notes the contradictory distribution of power be- tween an enslaved male subject and his mistress, suggesting that the "peculiarities of Miranda's position emerge from her status as the sexual object of both the white European male and the native Other and as the loyal daughter/wife who ultimately aligns herself with the benefits and protection offered by the colonizing father and husband."[29] Donaldson's exploration of the differentials of race, gender, and power between the Western woman and the colonized male forms part of a growing body of work analyzing the ambiguous position of Western women in relation to imperialist politics and especially, to Third World women.[30] Extending Donaldson's analysis to the relationship between Western and non-Western women, then, we may conclude that this jux- taposition elicits a complex interplay of sameness and difference, since the counterpoint between them is based on a set of overlapping inter- relationships at once marking them as distinguishably different (based on race) and yet apparently the same (based on gender).

It is just such a contradictory interplay of sameness and difference that is activated through the entry of Kate Pinkerton into *Madame But- terfly*. First, as already noted, her entrance as "Mrs." Pinkerton brings into play a familialist discourse whereby legitimacy is judged in rela- tion to one's familial position. Yet, the very stroke of being cast in the role of the illegitimate wife/mother also sutures Butterfly into her he- roic apotheosis as noble mother. As I suggested above, this outcome presents an noteworthy instance within Orientalist discourse when the

Asian woman, despite her victimization by external forces, attains a degree of moral stature and agency by playing out the tragic role of the self-sacrificial woman. Upon further analysis, however, the play upon racial and gender sameness and difference activated by Kate Pinkerton's entry reveals itself as part of a strategy diluting and displacing this very agency that would otherwise serve to enshrine Butterfly as a paragon of Victorian domestic self-immolation. In other words, the paradigmatic narrative of *Madame Butterfly* mobilizes a strategically contradictory discourse of sameness and difference as an instance of what Jenny Sharpe calls the "textual displacements enacted through figures of re-semblance."[31] Therefore, notions of difference ultimately yield to an assertion of a commonality based on femininity and domestic mission. So, much in the same vein that colonial discourse often expediently engages antisexist rhetoric to foreclose a questioning of colonialism,[32] in *Madame Butterfly*, an assimilationist discourse subsuming difference and hierarchy is activated to neutralize the bad conscience of domination and expropriation.

Thus, for example, at the end of the opera, the fateful meeting between Butterfly and Kate Pinkerton ends with Butterfly's reassuring affirmation of the other woman's happy state: "Beneath the great bridge of Heaven / there's no happier woman than you / May you always be so . . . / don't be sad for me." At this juncture, a construction of racial and cultural difference collapses in favor of a gendered assertion of female mutual support. Along the same lines, Gina Marchetti notes how, in the 1915 Mary Pickford film based on *Madame Butterfly*, the dramatic tension elicited between the two women actually "helps to explain away many of the film's more disturbing contradictions," adding, "[Mrs. Pinkerton's] appearance . . . helps to quell any threat Pinkerton's racism or sexism might otherwise pose to white, male, American bourgeois hegemony."[33] Under this guise, the Pinkertons' expropriation of the child is "naturalized" away, its inherently imperialist stance softened and rationalized through the camaraderie created between mothers across national and racial boundaries. And insofar as Pinkerton is portrayed in every instance as a callous bounder,[34] his American wife becomes his good conscience and alibi who, through her benign identification with Butterfly, disarms attributions of plunder and expropriation forming the dark subtext of the orientalized family romance.

## Indochine as Post-Colonial Family Romance

In the late 1980s and early 1990s, three works—a play, a musical, and a film—achieved enormous popular success in the United States. In 1988, David Henry Hwang's *M. Butterfly* opened on Broadway and went on to win a Tony Award for Best Play for that year. In 1991, *Miss Saigon* began its current, very successful, New York run. Then, in 1993, *Indochine*, a French film directed by Régis Wargnier, won the Academy Award for Best Foreign Film of 1992. Despite their radically different contexts of production and authorship—a Broadway play written by an Asian American male, a musical written by two Frenchmen and an American, and a French "art" film—these productions shared critical and/or popular acclaim and at least one other similarity: their appropriation of the myth of *Madame Butterfly* as an explicit intertext or implicit subtext.

Among the three, the politics of representation are stretched to their polar opposites in *M. Butterfly* and *Miss Saigon*. Termed a "deconstructivist *Madame Butterfly*" by its author,[35] *M. Butterfly* uses the mythical framework of the Puccini opera self-reflexively to expose the shifting intersections of race and gender embedded in the Orientalist gaze.[36] On the other hand, *Miss Saigon* uncritically adapts the orientalizing assumptions of its operatic source to the "topical" setting of the Vietnam War, subsuming the material facts of politics and history to the demands of popular consumption and crass theatricality. But perhaps precisely because its historical vision is so shallow, *Miss Saigon* marks a critical juncture when the family romance within post-Vietnam representation begins to be foregrounded. This is signaled not only in the prominence given to the "Miss Saigon photograph" by the musical's producers but also in a notable dramaturgical moment in the staged production. The second act begins with a musical interlude that has no precedents in any previous version of *Madame Butterfly*. Here, the character John (an army friend of the male lead) stands facing the audience in front of a lectern on a dimly lit and bare stage. As he sings the number "Bui Doi" (dust of life), a collage of children's images is projected onto a screen suspended above the stage. John's song, presented as an address at an international conference, makes a plea for the Amerasian children who have been abandoned in Vietnam. When the number ends, titles flash onto the screen identifying the children as orphans looking for their fathers, ending with the appeal: "Please help us to help them." The political register of this interlude is all the more striking because it disrupts the representational codes of theatrical illusion operative in the production. However, in the context of a work that reduces both politics and history to theatricality and sentiment, its ultimate effect is that of an excrescence at best, and at worst, of tasteless opportunism.

Whereas *M. Butterfly* uses the myth of *Madame Butterfly* to expose the imbalance of power inherent in imperialist relations, *Miss Saigon* exploits history only as a pretext for theatrical excess and spectacle.

*Indochine*, however, is the only work of the three to deliberately engage the historical specificities of colonialist practice. An allegory of the end of empire, *Indochine* spans the late phase of French colonialism in Indochina, with the rise of a nationalist resistance movement in the 1930s and leading to the 1954 signing of the Geneva Agreement, which formally ended French involvement and, by partitioning Vietnam into north and south, set the stage for American intervention in the region. In this postcolonial allegory, the historical processes of colonial annexation and decolonization are enacted through a maternal melodrama doubly charged with the aura of colonial nostalgia and the mythic resonance of the orientalized family romance.

While at least one critic noted echoes of *Madame Butterfly* in *Indochine*,[37] the film's most striking departure is in sidelining colonialism as a male enterprise, so that the problematics of race, gender, and colonial disengagement are framed through the relationship between a white European woman and the "native" woman as colonial subject. In *Indochine*, individual histories and political relationships are configured as family romance, and a critique of colonialism is conveyed through the depiction of aberrant familial and sexual relationships. In an apparent corrective to the male bias of the Oedipal family romance, female-to-female relationships form the central focus. Although the film retains the basic structure of interracial romance, that relationship is devoid of racial or sexual conflict. Instead, tensions between East and West are played out as disturbances between a white European mother and an adopted Asian daughter, and the generic tensions inherent in the dramas of the "other" woman, the mother/daughter melodrama, and the classic stepmother tale provide the framework for rationalizing the essentialist schematics of gender, race, and colonial relations.[38]

From its first moments, *Indochine* is infused with the ambience of remembrance and loss that is the signature of postcolonial nostalgia. The credit sequence shows a river-borne funeral procession for a prince from Annam and his wife, who have been killed in an accident. Their orphaned daughter stands at the head of this procession, holding hands with Eliane Devries (Catherine Deneuve), a French colonial whose father owns one of the largest rubber plantations in Indochina. Eliane's voice-over relates that she has adopted the little girl as her daughter. Growing into a teenager, Camille (Linh Dan Pham) falls in love with Jean-Baptiste Le Guen (Vincent Perez), a French naval officer who is also her mother's ex-lover. To separate her from Jean-Baptiste, Eliane arranges to have him reassigned to the north, but Camille runs away to find him. They are reunited but start living as fugitives after she kills a French officer. Camille becomes pregnant and gives birth to a son; soon after, she is forced to flee alone after Jean-Baptiste and their son are captured. At the end of the film, Jean-Baptiste commits suicide, and Camille leaves to join the resistance fighters, turning her son over to Eliane. In the last scene, Eliane has left Indochina, and she is with her adopted (step)grandson, Etienne (Jean-Baptiste Huynh), in Geneva on the day of the signing of the Geneva Agreement.

*Indochine*, then, is "book-ended" by two adoptions across racial lines, both times with Eliane as the adoptive mother. Viewed historically, both adoptions have overtones of colonial expropriation, but their different circumstances parallel the historical process of colonial investiture and its unraveling: Eliane's first adoption confirms an unproblematized alliance between the French colonial and local ruling class, but her second "adoption" of her stepgrandson is a direct aftermath of anticolonialist resistance. The staple plot of the maternal melodrama, based on the disidentification between mother and daughter, foreshadows the political inevitability of Camille's alienation from Eliane, while the generics of the family romance and the narrative of the "other" woman are played out through a dizzying interlacing of multiple roles: Camille is the "other" woman (as Eliane's racial Other and sexual rival) and both the adopted child *and* the self-sacrificial Asian mother of the orientalized family romance.

Within the framework of maternal melodrama doubling as postcolonial critique, Eliane's characterization supplies the moral and psychological rationale for the demise of colonialism. Although Eliane's relationship with Camille is initially presented as intimate and warm (the first scene between them opens with the sound of their laughter), Eliane's will to possess and control, her sexual manipulativeness and emotional coldness, and her suppressed tendencies toward violence and cruelty cast her in the archetypal mold of the "phallic mother."[39] In one scene, she is shown whipping one of her workers who has tried to run away. Eliane then asks the man, "Do you think a mother likes beating her children?"—to which he replies, "You are my mother and my father." This episode unmasks not only the violence inherent in employer/ employee and colonizer/colonized relations, but also Eliane's conception of mothering as control through physical punishment. At the same time, the "male" flair with which she rules over her domain seems to derive from the authority abdicated by her father, who is mainly preoccupied with seducing local young women. She exhibits a pride and protectiveness over her subjects that is both paternalistic and maternal, as when her crew team, with all "native" members, beats another team powered by French rowers, or when she protects a child whose father is an opium smuggler. As she strides through her plantation, Jean-Baptiste reminds her that "it's men who do the commanding, you know," and she answers dismissively, "Men usually say that." When Jean-

Figure 1. Eliane (Catherine Deneuve) tangoes with Camille (Linh Dan Pham). Photo courtesy of Jerry Ohlinger.

Baptiste then points out how her workers are staring at her, her curt response is, "I'm their boss, that's all." At one point, Eliane confesses to Jean-Baptiste that she used to dream that she was a boy when she was young, and the film pointedly encodes her as "masculine" by having her wear trousers in contrast to Camille's bare-shouldered and "feminine" looks. Finally, in a bizarre extension of this gendered schematism, there is a scene during a Christmas party when Eliane does the tango with her daughter and, in a parody of heterosexual courtship, murmurs to Camille, "I'd like to be alone with you in a small mountain chalet—with a smoking chimney—like in a fairy tale" (Figure 1).

But the "phallic mother" of the maternal melodrama is eventually punished and denigrated for her excessive will to possess and control. In *Indochine*, Eliane receives retribution for her maternal fanaticism and her "phallic" domination, first through the humiliating outcome of her affair with Jean-Baptiste, and then through her daughter's competition with, and ultimate rejection of, her. In her brief affair with Jean-Baptiste, Eliane's veneer of confidence and self-control is unmasked as emotional obsessiveness and desperate dependency. Thus exposed, there is little in Eliane's behavior to disprove the charge hurled at Eliane by Yvette, the wife of Eliane's manager: "A lack of love is never good. It's the worst illness. The truth is no one here likes you. . . . Without love there's a smell. . . . You're beautiful, but your looks are deceiving." At one point Jean-Baptiste castigates Eliane, shouting: "A woman decides my fate. Is this how you run your colonies? . . . You won't let others live. You won't let them breathe. You treat people like trees. You buy them and drain them. You want to stifle them the way your father stifled you." With her misplaced fanaticism and suppressed hysteria, Eliane's portrayal in *Indochine* exemplifies the revisionist tactics of postcolonial representation in which colonial pathologies are allegorized through the figure of woman.[40] In *Indochine*, even Eliane's ostensibly sincere maternal devotion to Camille is tainted with hints of psychological aberration and moral blindness. In this light, her very closeness with Camille takes on the effect of an unhealthy symbiosis, one that is all the more "unnatural" since it is based on a nonbiological affiliation.

Most of all, Eliane's blindness, and by implication the pitfall of colonialism, are manifested as her failure to acknowledge the hierarchical relations inherent in colonialism—in other words, her inability to recognize difference. In the film's opening voice-over, Eliane acknowledges her former utopian dream of symbiotic merging by recalling her friendship with Camille's father: "Prince N'guyen and I had been inseparable. In our youth we had thought the world consisted of inseparable things: men and women, mountains and plains, gods and humans . . . Indochina and France." As this monologue suggests, Eliane's initial error—now recognized in retrospect—has been to deny the intransigence of political divisions ("Indochina and France") which form a continuum with other irreducible oppositions of gender, geography, and ontology ("men and women, mountains and plains, gods and humans"), and, by implication, of race and generation. Eliane's blindness to difference is further suggested in another scene, in which Camille asks Eliane about Frenchwomen: "Do all French girls have light skin like you?" Picking up a slice of mango, Eliane replies, "The difference between people isn't skin color—it's this [showing Camille the mango]." Disclaiming her own racial determination, she adds, "I'm an Asian" (Figure 2).

From Eliane's perspective, the story in *Indochine* is one in which her wish to erase difference is contested and finally shattered. Giving the lie to her fantasy of symbiosis and identification with Camille, the film suspends the two women between attributions of both sameness and difference. On the one hand, Eliane is a French colonial who was born in Indochina and has never seen France, and Camille is an Indochinese raised as French; thus, both possess equally marginalized and hybridized identities derived from their colonial milieu. On the other hand, the built-in polarizations of the maternal melodrama offer

a convenient framework to situate Eliane and Camille along the oppositional axis of mother/daughter, East/West, and colonizer/colonized.
Furthermore, contradicting Eliane's avowals that differences between
people are not based on skin color, stark visual contrasts in color coding and dress style suggest essential racial and generational differences
between mother and daughter. Thus, Eliane often wears black tunics
and loose-fitting trousers of a "native" cut, whereas Camille, the true
"native," consistently wears Western-style dresses in white or with a
floral design. In this way, Eliane is coded as "Asian," while Camille's
costuming style makes her seem more "Westernized" than her mother.
Although this sartorial coding superficially suggests the permeability
of racial and cultural categories, its basic schematism in the end only
confirms, through simple reversal, imputations of essentialized differences.

   Furthermore, while the film seems to posit a reciprocal exchange
of cultural valences between the women, these differences are valu-
ated hierarchically, so that the European protagonist is placed in a position of narrative authority, whereas the "other" woman occupies the
role of the visually subordinated and the silenced. Thus, the film's recasting of *Madame Butterfly* as a mother/daughter melodrama gives

Figure 2. Eliane tells Camille, "The difference between people isn't skin
color . . . " Photo courtesy of Photofest.

narrative centrality to the European woman whose original role is that of an interloper. This shift is crucial because it provides the stroke by which the imprimatur of tragic suffering is removed from the Asian woman and conferred on her European counterpart. Furthermore, in an unusual departure from orientalizing representational strategy, *Indochine* fetishizes the white European woman instead of the Asian, since it is Eliane who is sexualized, exoticized, and displayed as an object of the gaze. To an extent, of course, this effect derives from Deneuve's "star" status as a glamour icon. The result, in any case, is that Eliane, rather than Camille, enjoys the full range of feminine display, appearing alternatively in meticulously detailed renditions of high European period fashion or pastichized "oriental" couture, and so acquires the fetishized associations of the orientalized female body.

In this context, *Indochine* becomes another striking instance of Eurocentric discourse, which, according to Ella Shohat and Robert Stam, deploys European or European-American characters as mediating "bridges" to other cultures in order to "initiate" the spectator into otherized communities.[41] The narrative priority granted to Eliane is signaled in the credit sequence, where she appears dramatically clad in black mourning at the head of the funeral procession. This sequence—with its exotic locale, spectacular staging, and operatic musical background—at once engages the atmospherics of colonial nostalgia while also designating Eliane as the film's controlling consciousness. In this sequence, Eliane's voice-over narration (which is used throughout the film) provides the necessary exposition and marks the ensuing narrative as one to be known only through her "focalizing" perspective.[42]

The same cinematic mediations that endow Eliane with psychological complexity and visual fascination also encode Camille's subordinate status in distinctly monolithic and monochromatic registers. In the first half of the film, Camille wears exclusively pale or white Western-style clothing; in the second half—after she leaves Saigon—she is clad in generic "peasant" clothing of dark or neutral hue. In the credit sequence, the first close-up of her looking up at Eliane as a little girl already inscribes her as one who is spoken about, rather than one who speaks. In the second half of the film, after her departure for the north, the trajectory of her story departs from Eliane's, but even here, the mother's voice-over continues over the daughter's scenes, which thereby continue to be embedded within Eliane's authorizing perspective.

The film's erasure of Camille's subjectivity is especially evident in one short scene because it comes closest to allowing her to emerge as a "focalizing" presence. During her trip to the north, Camille and her traveling companions stop in a village to rest. The scene opens with Camille being served some rice and sitting down to eat, as all the others are doing. Suddenly, in a sustained close-up, she pauses and looks up with an expression of profound anguish. A series of point-of-view shots then reveal what she is looking at: a group of women and children whose faces reflect their personal trauma and, by extension, the devastation to which their homeland has been subjected. Though brief, this episode offers a wedge into Camille's subjectivity like no other in the film. In marking what we might interpret as the transformative moment of Camille's birth as a revolutionary, the scene has great dramatic force, yet this power is ultimately evacuated by its brevity as well as its rendering of Camille's subjectivity as inarticulate and mute. The film's progressive erasure of Camille is also illustrated in its last sequence, when we learn that Camille is part of the Vietnamese delegation that has arrived in Geneva to sign the peace accord. Here, what could have been a climactic scene confirming Camille's final incarnation as truly the "mother" of her country's liberation is instead elliptically rendered through an impersonal, extreme long shot of unidentified conference delegates on a hotel balcony. In the next scene, Etienne explains to Eliane how he avoided what would have been a reunion between himself and his biological mother in the hotel lobby. Since the refused encounter is recalled through Etienne's perspective, Camille's claims to being a visible presence and active agent are once again deflected.

By setting up Eliane and Camille as polar opposites—one masculine, Caucasian, and powerful, the other feminine, Asian, dependent, and "innocent"—*Indochine* reinstates the essentializing postures of patriarchal and Orientalist thinking. Given the mutual imbrication of Orientalist and patriarchal ideologies, it is not surprising that the film's schematic differentiations between East and West are projected onto the most fundamentally gendered themes—those of sexuality and reproduction. As we have seen, the family romance of the prototypical *Madame Butterfly* myth has operated in contradictory ways, simultaneously invoking and negating differences between the white European and the Asian woman. In the family romance of *Indochine*, the distribution of sexual, reproductive, and nurturant roles are likewise fraught with contradictions. On the one hand, the Asian woman is constructed in terms of both adolescent asexuality and mature fecundity. On the other hand, the white European woman displays a heightened and masculinized sexuality that is presented as fundamentally sterile and nonreproductive. In *Indochine*'s feminized recasting of the family romance and the maternal melodrama, therefore, there emerges a division of labor between First World and Third World women, whereby the former bears the taint of neurotic sexuality connotative of tragic suffering, while the latter—Asian women—are associated with the biological ("primitive") functions of the womb and the breast.

Earlier, we saw how Eliane's character is tainted with imputations of inappropriate phallic control and unfulfilled sexuality. At the same time, a heavy-handed symbolism associates her psychosexual masochism with sterility. After the failure of her affair with Jean-Baptiste and Camille's departure, her voice-over monologue—"Life continued as before—footsteps on dead leaves, sap oozing from wounded trees, and what I loved more than anything else, the smell of rubber"—is matched with shots of rubber being harvested on her plantation. Here, the sexual symbolism—with the rubber in its liquid form resembling both semen and milk—links Eliane's aspiration to masculine prowess with inescapable futility and lack of issue. These associations are later reinforced in a close-up of the oozing rubber when, before she leaves for France, Eliane goes out to her plantation for the last time, scrapes the latex from a tree, and allows it to run into a bowl.

In contrast, as the "other" woman and the native subject, Camille initially possesses an asexual innocence from which she then leapfrogs straight into pregnancy and maternity, with sexuality being almost totally elided in-between. If *Indochine* is to be read as an *ersatz Madame Butterfly*, with Camille as the stand-in for Butterfly, then what is truly remarkable is how her "romance" with Jean-Baptiste is completely voided of all romantic or sexual resonance. Indeed, only one scene in the film even approaches the semblance of a sexual or romantic encounter between Camille and Jean-Baptiste. This is the scene when they meet after he rescues her during a prisoners' escape attempt—and it takes place with Camille remaining unconscious practically all the way through. After Camille and Jean-Baptiste finally escape to a hidden valley in the north, their developing relationship continues to be depicted in a remarkably oblique manner. In fact, although this sequence represents the consummation of their romance, it is drastically condensed into three elliptical scenes. After they are led into the valley by a band of itinerant performers, there follows a brief dialogue when Camille tells Jean-Baptiste to leave without her. In the next scene, she wakes up in the morning thinking that he has left, only to find him crouched outside waiting for her. The next time we see her, she is already pregnant.

While *Indochine* engages the plot of interracial romance, this romance is neither truly romantic nor explicitly sexual. Instead, while Eliane bears the weight of the film's projection of neurotic sexuality, Camille is discursively confined to the biologically reproductive, on the one hand, and delimited to the familial and the nonsexual, on the other. Thus, in one of the only two scenes that depict a vaguely sexual intimacy between Camille and Jean-Baptiste, the two are making their escape from French authorities on a boat drifting in the labyrinthine waters of Ha-long Bay. Weathering storms and harsh weather, Jean-Baptiste takes the unconscious Camille and gives her water with a bottle; when the bottle runs dry, he drains the last meager drops from it and drips them from his mouth into hers. The use of the bottle, the maternal gesture of his oral feeding, and even the maternal pose that he strikes with Camille in his arms all suggest the ministering of a parent to a child rather than a man to a woman.

Throughout, Camille remains enmeshed in vocabularies and relationships relegating her to the familial roles of "daughter," and of a woman who undergoes both psychological and revolutionary rebirth. Thus, having separated from Eliane, she leaves for the north in search of Jean-Baptiste and immediately casts in her lot with another family consisting of three Vietnamese—a mother, father, and son. The whole saga of her northward journey, which ends with her capture and imprisonment, is articulated as a process of rebirth by which she casts off her positioning as colonial dependent to assume the role of a freedom fighter. In Eliane's description of Camille's journey, she uses language permeated with the rhetoric of sexual penetration and impregnation: "I often dreamed about her . . . I saw her walking through the open countryside. The scenery entered her body like blood. I thought—now she has Indochina inside her." Later, Camille and Jean-Baptiste seek refuge in a secret valley surrounded by mountains and entered only through a hidden entrance that is closed to the outside for part of the year. It is in this womblike enclosure that Camille's revolutionary incubation takes place and where she, literally, conceives her child. And, finally, the process of Camille's transformation from protected daughter and colonial subject to nationalist fighter inside the Poulo-Condor prison is described in explicitly reproductive terms. As Gus, Eliane's friend, exclaims in consternation at one point, Poulo-Condor is notorious as a "breeding ground" for Communists, and true to his word, Camille emerges from the prison in her new incarnation as the "red princess."

At once a biological mother and a daughter who undergoes rebirth, Camille is implicated in a nexus of reproductive relations that splits her into a biological mother and symbol of maternality functioning as an allegorical figure of national destiny. Yet as one who is mothered—literally by Eliane, figuratively by Jean-Baptiste—Camille herself cannot mother. A distinction must therefore be drawn between Camille's reproductive role as one who gives birth and her role as a mother who nurtures. In the same way that her pregnancy is presented without any foreshadowing, Camille's nurturing of her son after his birth is to all intents and purposes completely elided. In fact, after the birth scene, we see her with her son only once, in the scene when Jean-Baptiste comes to pick him up while she is sleeping next to her infant on a blanket. This one and only glimpse of mother and son is immediately followed by the scene when Jean-Baptiste is arrested with their son. After this, there is no further contact between Camille and her son, thus justifying Eliane's explanation to the grown-up Etienne that his mother "had no time to be attached to you—you had just been born [when you were separated]." The bond between Etienne and Camille is formally severed on the day of Camille's release from prison. Rejecting Eliane's offer to restore her "domain" to her, Camille tearfully turns her son over to Eliane, saying: "I don't want him to know how I've lived, how I suffered. I want him to be happy. Take him to France. Your Indochina is no more. It's dead."

A biological mother only in the most limited terms, Camille becomes the allegorical mother *and* daughter of her country's liberation. In an extension of this vision, the film sees Indochinese women in general as invisible, or else it writes the "native" female body as an undifferentiated signifier of an epic maternity. Thus, it turns out to be "Indochina," rather than Camille, who provides the nurturing milk for the infant Etienne. Eliane recalls for Etienne how one day, after he and his father have been captured by the French military, an anonymous Indochinese woman is called on to give him breast-milk. From this moment on, Eliane recounts, a nationalist legend about the "red princess" is born: "At every stop Indochinese women gave you milk. That's how the legend started. All the women claimed they'd fed you—even those who had been empty of milk for years, even those who had never seen you." Through a relay of signifiers, "the Asian woman" comes to signify "Indochina," at the same time that Asian femininity is overwritten as a signifier for a subjugated nurturing that does not discriminate as to whom it succors. Ironically, of course, this "Indochina," figured symbolically as a universally nourishing breast, most immediately "reproduces" Etienne, the son of mixed racial heritage whom his biological mother rejects and who is ultimately exiled from the land of his birth.

As it turns out, it is Eliane who raises Etienne, and so functions practically as his mother. We see her bringing him home to her plantation, taking him out for ice cream, and, most striking of all, standing over his crib when Jean-Baptiste returns to see his son. As Eliane tells the grown-up Etienne, "in my little domain, you were my little boy." In the last scene of the film, Eliane's assumption of a maternal role is confirmed. The two are in Geneva in 1954 on the day when the Geneva Agreement is signed. Although Etienne goes to the hotel where he knows Camille is staying, he leaves without seeing her. Explaining the incident to Eliane, he says that he couldn't imagine himself throwing himself at an Indochinese woman crying "Mother!" and adds, "You're my mother." The last shot in the film shows Eliane from behind, a black silhouette with outstretched arms looking over the waters of Lake Geneva. Earlier in this final scene, we have seen a white European woman standing with a "son" of troubled lineage. This ending, permeated with a palpable sense of loss, is, in equal measure, invested with a profound ambiguity. Eliane and Etienne are now in Switzerland and therefore still exiled from their homeland. And as Eliane looks into the distance, there is a certain monumental grandeur to her pose, as she seems to survey the history that she has witnessed and helped to create. However, it is suggested that this history, as it continues to unfold, has no place for her or Etienne, just as her affiliation with this "son" cannot ultimately provide solace for that other, greater, loss of a daughter.

At this moment, we recall that other image with which this essay began. As in the "Miss Saigon photograph," a shadow figure haunts the unseen space off-frame. Camille's absence from this concluding shot suggests that *Indochine*, the most explicit exposition of the orientalized family romance to date, cannot find the representational means to incorporate in its final frame both of the protagonists between whom the dialectics of its drama have been suspended. Having begun with the "Miss Saigon photograph" and ended with this closing image from *Indochine*, then, we have in fact traveled the distance between two refusals, two points of recalcitrance generated by Western discourse's refuge in the certitudes of patriarchy and racial hegemony, and by its enmeshment with the phantasms and blind spots of Orientalism. What this erasure foretells about the future vicissitudes of the romance—as postcolonial filiations continue to be transacted, negotiated, and reimagined—remains to be seen.

## Notes

1. Edward Behr and Mark Steyn, *The Story of Miss Saigon* (New York: Arcade, 1991), 176.
2. Claude-Michel Schönberg, "The Ultimate Sacrifice," in souvenir program for *Miss Saigon*, n.d., 4.
3. Ibid.
4. Ibid.
5. Ibid.
6. Alain Boublil, "From *Madame Chrysanthemum* to *Miss Saigon*," ibid., 5.
7. See Malek Alloula, *The Colonial Harem*, trans. Myrna Godzich and Wlad Godzich (Minneapolis: University of Minnesota Press, 1986); Sarah Graham-Brown, *Images of Women: The Portrayal of Women in Photography of the Middle East, 1860–1950* (New York: Columbia University Press, 1988); Rana Kabbani, *Europe's Myths of Orient* (Bloomington: Indiana University Press, 1986), 14–36; John McBratney, "Images of Indian Women in Rudyard Kipling: A Case of Doubling Discourse," *Inscriptions* nos. 3 & 4 (1988):

46–57; Edward Said, *Orientalism* (New York: Vintage, 1979), 188, 190, 207–8; Edward Said, "Orientalism Reconsidered," *Race and Class* 27, no. 2 (1985): 12; Ella Shohat's essay in this collection; David Spurr, *The Rhetoric of Empire: Colonial Discourse in Journalism, Travel Writing, and Imperial Administration* (Durham: Duke University Press, 1993),170–183; Anne McClintock, *Imperial Leather: Race, Gender, and Sexuality in the Colonial Context* (New York: Routledge, 1995).

8. See Renee E. Tajima, "Lotus Blossoms Don't Bleed: Images of Asian Women," in Asian Women United of California, eds., *Making Waves: An Anthology of Writings by and about Asian American Women* (Boston: Beacon Press, 1989), 311; James S. Moy, "The Death of Asia on the American Field of Representation," in Shirley Geok-lin Lim and Amy Ling, eds., *Reading the Literatures of Asian America* (Philadelphia: Temple University Press, 1992), 349–357.

9. Michael Klein, "Historical Memory, Film, and the Vietnam Era," in Linda Dittmar and Gene Michaud, eds., *From Hanoi to Hollywood: The Vietnam War in American Film* (New Brunswick: Rutgers University Press, 1990), 34.

10. Harry Haines, "'They Were Called and They Went': The Political Rehabilitation of the Vietnam Veteran," ibid., 82. See also Dittmar and Michaud's introductory essay, "America's Vietnam War Films: Marching Toward Denial," and Gaylyn Studlar and David Desser, "Never Having to Say You're Sorry: *Rambo*'s Rewriting of the Vietnam War," ibid., 1–15, 101–112.

11. In *Romance and the "Yellow Peril": Race, Sex, and Discursive Strategies in Hollywood Fiction* (Berkeley: University of California Press, 1993), 102–108, Gina Marchetti suggests that the American GI has surfaced in post-Vietnam made-for-TV movies as the "American 'white knight'" and that these narratives exemplify a "crisis of bourgeois patriarchy."

12. A typical treatment of the subject is illustrated by the statements included under the heading "Bui Doi: 'Dust of Life,'" in the souvenir program for *Miss Saigon*. These excerpts from Larry Engelman's book *Tears before the Rain: An Oral History of the Fall of South Vietnam* (New York: Oxford University Press, 1990) represent statements by Amerasian children in Vietnam, almost all of whom speak about their intense preoccupation with their lost fathers and their desire to locate them. The 1985 made-for-TV film *The Lady from Yesterday* recounts how a young Vietnamese woman comes to the United States with her son and finds the child's father, who is now married. In the 1990 film *Vietnam Texas*, a Vietnam vet goes to Little Saigon in Houston to find the woman he left behind in Vietnam, but the primary focus of the film is his reunion with the daughter born of this liaison. In the Lanford Wilson's play *Redwood Curtain* (New York: Hill and Wang, 1993), the leading role is that of a Vietnam vet in Oregon who encounters a young Amerasian orphan who has been adopted by Anglo-Americans and has built a fantasy world around finding the man who fathered her in Vietnam. (New York: Hill and Wang, 1993.) In *Romance and the "Yellow Peril,"* Marchetti discusses a number of film and made-for-TV movies focusing on the Amerasian child and provides a detailed analysis of

*The Lady from Yesterday*, 100, 103–108. See also Darrell T. Hamamoto's treatment of the same theme in *Monitored Peril: Asian Americans and the Politics of Representation* (Minneapolis: University of Minnesota Press, 1994), 100–102, 120–123.

13. See note 2.
14. James Strachey, ed., *The Standard Edition of the Complete Psychological Works of Sigmund Freud* (London: Hogarth Press, 1953–1974), vol. 9., 238–239.
15, Ibid., 238.
16. Marthe Robert, *Origins of the Novel*, trans. Sacha Rabinovitch (Bloomington: Indiana University Press, 1980), 26.
17. Richard de Cordova, "A Case of Mistaken Legitimacy: Class and Generational Difference in Three Family Melodramas," in Christine Gledhill, ed., *Home Is Where the Heart Is: Studies in Melodrama and the Woman's Film* (London: British Film Institute, 1987), 256.
18. Mary Louise Pratt, *Imperial Eyes: Travel Writing and Transculturation* (New York: Routledge, 1992), 4.
19. The story first appeared in the novella *Madame Chrysanthème* written in French by Pierre Loti. It was then rewritten in English as a short story entitled "Madame Butterfly" by the American writer John Luther Long. The popularity of the short story led the successful American playwright David Belasco to write and produce a one-act version for the New York stage. It was this play, which Puccini saw, that led the Italian composer to create *Madame Butterfly*. See John Luther Long, *Madame Butterfly, Purple Eyes, etc.* (New York: Garrett Press, 1968); David Belasco, *Six Plays* (Boston: Little Brown, 1929).

Aside from numerous filmed versions of opera productions of *Madame Butterfly*, Hollywood films based on the story include a 1915 film starring Mary Pickford, a 1922 version entitled *Toll of the Sea* starring Anna May Wong, and a 1933 film starring Cary Grant. An Italian dramatic film entitled *Dream of Butterfly* was produced in 1941.
20. As originally coined by Michèle Barrett and Mary McIntosh in *The Anti-Social Family* (London: Verso, 1982), the term familialism encapsulates the biological (and historically based) bias that elevates the notion of family defined in terms of blood kinship and paternal control. Within the colonial context, McClintock demonstrates in *Imperial Leather* how the family trope has historically been engaged to naturalize systems of domination, so that "filiation would take an increasingly imperial shape as the image of the evolutionary family was projected onto the imperial nation and colonial bureaucracies as their natural, legitimizing shape," and, since "the subordination of woman to man and child to adult were deemed natural facts, other forms of social hierarchy could be depicted in familial terms to guarantee social *difference* as a category of nature" (45).
21. Christian Viviani, "Who is without Sin? The Maternal Melodrama in American Film, 1930–39," trans. Dolores Burdick, *Wide Angle* 4, no. 2 (1980): 16.
22. Ibid., 14.

23. Geoffrey Nowell-Smith, "Minnelli and Melodrama," in *Home Is Where the Heart Is*, 73.
24. E. Ann Kaplan, "Mothering, Feminism and Representation: The Maternal in Melodrama and the Woman's Film 1910–40," ibid., 123–124. Both Kaplan and Marthe Robert note that the fall of the mother provides the condition for the idealization and fixation on the father. See E. Ann Kaplan, *Motherhood and Representation: The Mother in Popular Culture and Melodrama* (New York: Routledge, 1992), 91; Robert, *Origins of the Novel*, 28–29.
25. See Gayatri Chakravorty Spivak, "Three Women's Texts and a Critique of Imperialism," *Critical Inquiry* 12 (1985): 243–61; Chandra Talpade Mohanty, "Under Western Eyes: Feminist Scholarship and Colonial Discourses," in Chandra Talpade Mohanty et al., eds., *Third World Women and the Politics of Feminism*, (Bloomington: Indiana University Press, 1991), 51–80; Laura E. Donaldson, *Decolonizing Feminisms: Race, Gender, and Empire-Building* (Chapel Hill: University of North Carolina Press, 1992), 41. For instance, Jenny Sharpe acknowledges that the Indian woman appears in colonialist texts as an "absence," "negation," "screen," or "subaltern shadow" precisely because the conferral of authority and individualism upon the English woman depends on the "distancing of the English woman from her Eastern sisters. In a deployment of what Sharpe calls a "national and racial splitting of femininity," the perceived subjugation, victimization, and oppressed status of the third world woman accrues to the white European woman's attainment of individual self-definition and female agency. See Sharpe's *Allegories of Empire: The Figure of Woman in the Colonial Text* (Minneapolis: University of Minnesota Press, 1993), 12, 25, 47, 52. In her analysis, for instance, it is the exposure of the "barbaric" ritual of *sati* imposed on the Indian woman that confers on the Victorian mother/wife a degree of dignity and moral stature denied to her subaltern counterpart (102–109).
26. Marchetti, *Romance and the "Yellow Peril*," 81 and 88.
27. Viviani, "Who Is without Sin?" 11.
28. Helena Michie, *Sororophobia: Differences among Women in Literature and Culture* (New York: Oxford University Press, 1992), 3.
29. Donaldson, *Decolonizing Feminism*, 17. As Sharpe notes in *Allegories of Empire*, "The contradictions to white femininity are more evident in a colonial context where the middle-class English woman, oscillating between the dominant position of race and a subordinate one of gender, has a restricted access to colonial authority" (12).
30. See Nupur Chaudhuri and Margaret Strobel, eds., *Western Women and Imperialism: Complicity and Resistance* (Bloomington: Indiana University Press, 1992); Sharpe, *Allegories of Empire*; Vron Ware, *Beyond the Pale: White Women, Racism and History* (New York: Verso, 1992).
31. Sharpe, *Allegories of Empire*, 29.
32. Donaldson, *Decolonizing Feminisms*, 62.
33. Marchetti, *Romance and the "Yellow Peril*," 88.
34. See John Louis DiGaetani's chapter, "The American Presence in *Madame Butterfly*," in *Puccini the Thinker: the Composer's Intellectual and Dramatic*

*Development* (New York: Peter Lang, 1987), in which he analyzes Pinkerton's character as a imperialist.

35. David Henry Hwang, *M. Butterfly* (New York: Penguin, 1989), 95.
36. The play recounts the affair between a French diplomat, Rene Gallimard, and a Chinese opera singer, Song Liling, in Beijing in the 1960s. It is not until years later, after Gallimard has been arrested for passing on diplomatic secrets to Song, that he discovers that Song is really a man. Not only does Gallimard meet Song during her performance of an aria from *Madame Butterfly*, but the play continually invokes and reenacts moments from the opera to drive home its critique of Orientalism. The play suggests that Gallimard's grotesque and incredible ignorance of his lover's gender is only explicable as manifestation of the Western/male determination to view all Asians as subservient and sexually passive—in other words, as "feminine."

Hwang's play was, of course, based on real-life story. With the release of the filmed version of *M. Butterfly* in 1993, the saga of a French diplomat, Bernard Boursicot, and his Chinese lover, Shi Pei Pu, received renewed media coverage. On 15 August 1993, the *New York Times Magazine* featured a story, "The Spy Who Fell in Love with a Shadow," which was excerpted from Joyce Wadler's book on the affair, *Liaison* (New York: Bantam, 1993). On 8 October 1993, following the release of the film, the television program *20/20* produced a long segment on the story featuring interviews with the principals. All these accounts suggest fascinating ways in which the purportedly "real-life" details of the scandal followed the outlines of the orientalized family romance, albeit with bizarre variations. Keeping the paradigmatic narrative in mind, we might not be surprised that, despite the publicity given to the more sensationalistic aspects of the case, Wadler's account (which we are led to believe is based largely on Boursicot's revelations to her) explicitly describes how Boursicot's sexual interest in Shi faded fairly early in their relationship. In fact, we learn that he maintained an intense involvement with Shi only because of his desire to form a relationship with "their" son, who was born when Boursicot was away from China. Unlike his mythic counterpart Pinkerton, Boursicot was a doting father after he met his "son," and he worked fervently to bring his "family" with him to Paris. Boursicot, for instance, was quoted as saying that the "most wonderful day" of his life was the day when he met his "son" for the first time (Wadler, 123). Much of the succeeding narrative is then focused on Boursicot's continued loyalty to Shi as the "mother" of his son and on his efforts to bring his son to France. Shi and the son, Bernard, did come to Paris eventually. In an improbable echo of *Butterfly*, Shi and Bernard even moved in with Boursicot and his new consort, his homosexual lover. According to Wadler's account, however, there was no overt hostility between the two rivals.

37. Richard Corliss's review of the film is entitled "Mademoiselle Saigon"; in it he compares the role of the "handsome French officer" to "a kind of Lieut. Pinkerton in this *Mademoiselle Saigon*." *Time*, 21 December 1992, 72–73.

38. Regarding the classic stepmother tale, see Nan Bauer Maglin, "Reading Stepfamily Fiction," in Maglin and Naney Schniederwind, *Women and Stepfamilies: Voices of Anger and Love* (Philadelphia: Temple University Press, 1989), 255.

39. See Kaplan, "The Maternal Melodrama: The 'Phallic' Mother Paradigm," in *Motherhood and Representation*, 107–123.

40. Recent films include *Heat and Dust* (1983), *A Passage to India* (1984), *Out of Africa* (1985), *White Mischief* (1988), *Chocolat* (1988), *A World Apart* (1988), and *Outremer* (1990). In this vein, Laura Kipnis suggests that the postcolonial cinema places the female experience at its center as a way of acknowledging and assimilating the "historical wound of decolonization." In Kipnis's argument, "Post-colonial revision of history redeems the male expression of colonialism by coding colonialism as female. The filmic spectacle performs the work of disavowal by *gendering* colonialism, by displaying scandal onto the female. [As a result] colonialism itself is seen as a female enterprise—a 'female disease.'" Accordingly, postcolonial representations associate female mastery with diseased sexuality, and corrupted femininity is offered as a historical alibi for the political error of colonialism. Kipnis thus concludes that First World revisionist representations envision colonialism as a female pathological desire for control. See Laura Kipnis, "'The Phantom Twitchings of an Amputated Limb': Sexual Spectacle in the Post-Colonial Epic," *Wide Angle* 11, no. 4 (1989): 44, 50.

41. Ella Shohat and Robert Stam, *Unthinking Eurocentrism: Multiculturalism and the Media* (New York: Routledge, 1994), 205.

42. Shohat and Stam use Gerard Genette's notion of focalization to suggest that the "question of 'point-of-view' reaches beyond character perspective to the structuring of information within the story world through the cognitive-perceptual grid of its 'inhabitants.'" In Shohat and Stam's application of this notion, dialogue and mise-en-scène "construct . . . narrative dominance," allowing a viewer to know only what a character knows and aligning him/her with the character's ideological position. Ibid., 105–106.

Alan Nadel

# A Whole New (Disney) World Order: *Aladdin*, Atomic Power, and the Muslim Middle East

At one point in the film *Gunga Din* (1939), Victor McLaglen, playing a member of Her Majesty's Indian Regiment, is concerned about the health of his elephant. He attempts to take its temperature by putting one hand on the elephant's forehead and, for comparison, the other hand on his own. In its comic exaggeration, the scene foregrounds a motif that permeates the film and connects it to Kipling's poem by the same name: that the British soldier is the norm against which everything in the East—from elephants to water boys, manners to religion—is measured. The British regimental unit is merely the agency that proliferates the physical truths of the British thermal unit.

*Gunga Din*, however, is an American film, putting the East at a double remove from the source of its representation. For American audiences, the exotic Other is contained within the equally exotic norms of late nineteenth-century England. This type of exotic distancing, of course, typifies Orientalism, and I cite it here simply to provide a vivid paradigm for the treatment of the historically specific conditions that inform Walt Disney's *Aladdin* (1992), an animated film which draws heavily on U.S. representations of Iran and Iraq in recent decades, filtered through the lens of the U.S. State Department and intelligence community. Like *Gunga Din*'s India, Iran and Iraq have been represented in the United States public consciousness through a layer of remove in which the CIA substitutes for the British regiment, normalizing our understanding of the East through a recognizable western romance.[1]

This is the way, in general, that cultural narratives function. Repeated at sundry sites, in sundry forms, a group of narratives become cogent, such that their invocation at a specific moment represents credibility. The same narrative alluded to by political speeches, newspaper accounts, stand-up comics, television commercials, and even to some degree fashion magazines, by virtue of its repetition and ubiquity, acquires the familiarity and tacit veracity of a cliché. Vaguely recognizable and tacitly assumed, these narrative clichés comprise a set of loose "realities." At any given moment, they are the stories a culture tells itself, as though they were true. Commercial films, as I argue elsewhere,[2] are particularly revelatory of these narratives, because as large collaborative enterprises, they are the products of an extensive consensus about the ways to commodify the values and assumptions of a culture at a very specific historical moment. Thus *Aladdin* participates in a series of clichéd—often self-contradictory—narratives informing popular American assumptions about the Muslim Middle East, made recognizable though a form of western romance.

Although there isn't enough space here to give even the most concise comprehensive summary of the U.S. narratives constructed around Iraq and Iran in the post-World War II period,[3] in order to understand the moment of *Aladdin*'s production, we should recall some of the myriad ways in which the two countries have figured prominently in the national narratives of the United States. In the 1950s, the shah of Iran, who was more strongly supported by the CIA than he was by the Iranian people, rendered Iran the "good" Muslim country, as opposed to those "bad" Muslim countries favorable to the Soviets.[4] When "bad" Iranians deposed the shah to establish a fundamentalist state that shortly thereafter took Americans hostage,[5] Iran became "evil" and in the United States' eyes Iraq became "good" by virtue of its war with Iran. In the early 1980s, U.S. intelligence discovered a new set of "good" figures in Iran, the "moderates," who were "good" because they might become friends of the United States if it sold them weapons. After the sale, however, U.S. intelligence and the American public discovered that the "good" "moderates" were neither "good" nor "moderate," merely clever and out of ammunition. As James Piscatari notes, given Iran's intricate internal politics, which affect all its internal and external relations, "in which tactical shifts of alliance are common, it is not hard to see how inappropriate the Western search for a categorically defined 'Islamic foreign policy' or indeed, for 'moderates' within the regime has been."[6]

In contrast, the Iraqis looked even more "good" to U.S. intelligence, until they invaded Kuwait, when Iraq once more became "bad," with the Iraqi leader, Saddam Hussein, personifying evil. Then in a war waged primarily by air attack, "smart" bombs were able to succeed where U.S. intelligence had failed, by identifying the "bad" Iraqis. "The issue was raised to cosmic significance," as Noam Chomsky aptly puts it, "with visions of a New World Order of peace and justice that lies before us if only the new Hitler can be stopped before he conquers the world (after having just failed to overcome post-revolutionary Iran with its severely weakened military, even with the support of the U.S., USSR, Europe and the major Arab states)."[7]

If nothing else, this very cursory sampling of narratives that classified and evaluated Iraqis and Iranians, taken as a group, illustrates how vague and protean the Muslim Middle East is to Americans, even to those Americans in the intelligence community; with great facility, the same roles could be played by a secular Arab state or, equally and interchangeably, by a fundamentalist non-Arab state.[8] Foreboding, dark peoples on shifting sands, like characters out of *Aladdin*, play out the same story of "evil" in the guise of "good" in the guise of "evil" in the guise of "good," ad infinitum.

The answer to containing the evils of this protean Muslim world was, according to President George Bush, a "New World Order," an international coalition led by the United States and authorized by its military—especially its nuclear—supremacy. As Haim Bresheeth points out, in regard to the Gulf War, U.S. technological supremacy was crucial to the war's informing narrative: "While the U.S. has sold billions of dollars of armaments to the Gulf countries . . . the really efficient, lethal armaments, such as laserguided (surgical strike) bombs, were kept from the hordes, just in case. . . . This policy has paid dividends—the equation being: fewer Western casualties = fewer war casualties; high technology = surgical and accurate strikes; new technologies = Western civilization."[9]

In many ways, however, the New World Order was a throwback rhetorically to the earliest days of the Cold War, when the United States had a nuclear monopoly and policies were being formulated for the use of atomic power. As a 1948 State Department report asserted:

> Nuclear fuel has a dual nature. The processes for the production of atomic weapons and for development of atomic energy for peaceful purposes are, through most of their courses, identical and inseparable. Under a control plan which left individual nations free to do as they pleased with the atom, inspectors would have to look not only into the operations of the plant but also into the motives of the operators.[10]

Like the Muslim Middle East in the truncated narratives I cited, nuclear fuel itself was once represented as embodying good and evil, and that embodiment was connected to the invisible motives of individual nations. Under the world order hoped for at the end of World War II, therefore, those nations could not be left "free to do as they pleased with the atom," any more than they could be under the New World Order, which once again projected ambivalence about nuclear power onto a morality drama in which an Eastern world (in this case the Muslim Middle East rather than the Eastern Bloc of Communist countries), full of hidden motives and ambiguous identities, was disciplined by the West.

After the end of the Gulf War (March 1991)—which brings us to the cultural moment of *Aladdin*'s production—we find the "good" conquering forces (who had restored [un]democracy to Kuwait)[11] continuing to have trouble containing Iraq's "evil," trouble most vividly exemplified by a number of extensively reported, fruitless attempts to ferret out the particulars of Iraq's nuclear weapon capacity. In a feature article titled "Who Else Will Have the Bomb?" *Time* reporters, nine months after the end of the war, point out the fuzziness of Western knowledge about Iraq's nuclear program.[12] Acknowledging that Iraq may have been much closer to developing a bomb than Western experts thought, the essay's analysis becomes mired in uncertainties, qualifications, and hypotheticals: "US and International Atomic Energy Agency (IAEA) analysts *think* the war brought Saddam's program to a rude halt. *But inspectors are not at all certain* they have *yet* found all the equipment and material Iraq *may* have hidden away, and thus that they have eliminated the *chance* Baghdad *might* resume a bomb-building program *if* it can ever get out from intrusive international surveillance" (emphasis added).[13] The article goes on to say that "ironically, Iran's [nuclear arms] program resembles that of its archfoe, Saddam Hussein."[14] Eight months later, *Newsweek* recounts the latest in a succession of confrontations in the seventeen months since the end of the war over UN inspections to check Iraq's (suspected) nuclear weapons program. In a double layering of obscurity, the UN inspectors are described as seeking documents that were "*believed* to contain *clues* to Saddam's weapons plants" (emphasis added).[15]

As in the Cold War, in the era of the New World Order, the disciplining of "evil" proved incomplete, the evil Other hard to pin down. The need for additional measures thus continued to indicate the need for additional measures; increased security thus fomented insecurity.[16] *Aladdin* plays out these problems in a way that asserts the immense destructive potential of a nuclear-armed Muslim Middle East by connecting, in the film's mythical Arabia, the dissimulations of the Eastern Other to the dangers of atomic power. At the same time, the film resolves the conflicts in representation by reconfiguring the East, through a pastiche of Western myths and codes, as forms of performance within the spectacle of Western entertainment so that the good leader of the New World Order becomes the Master of Ceremonies in a theme park not unlike Disney World.

## The Duplicitous Arab World

In this light, the first thing we should note about *Aladdin* is the rampant dissimulation in the film, a characteristic that distinguishes *Aladdin* not only from the original story of Aladdin but also from the films that the Disney production draws most heavily upon for many of its events and images, the two versions of *The Thief of Bagdad*.[17] Although both versions of *The Thief*, like *Aladdin*, use the East as the exotic elsewhere that authorizes its text, each *Thief*, as the product of a different historical moment, instantiates a different cultural narrative. The Douglas Fairbanks version (1924), for example, develops the theme that happiness must be earned. Although it attributes this theme to the Koran, the thief seems more like an Horatio Alger character than an ancient Muslim rogue. The story shows how, with religious guidance, he is able to renounce the easy life of thievery, which provides material comfort, for the honest work of heroic trials, which allows for upward mobility. Although far less successful as a thief than the Fairbanks character, Aladdin forgoes his opportunity to become a prince. Whereas Aladdin is thus valorized as a commoner, the Fairbanks thief actually works his way up to prince.

The 1940 version of *The Thief*, on the other hand, is less about individual accomplishment than about political reform. The thief, Abu, is no longer the romantic lead but rather the street-smart youth who assists the true prince in reclaiming his throne from Jaffar, the fascistlike tyrant who usurped it. The usurpation was possible because the prince had lost touch with the common people, a problem remedied by his association with Abu. That union in the end allows the prince to lead a rebellion of the same peasants who at the outset had wished for his death. The film is thus a form of Empsonian "pastoral" in that it resuscitates a society by moving its principals through an exotic environment that reeducates them to traditional values. The agent of that reeducation must remain outside of the quotidian world that he (or she) helps to restore, a point emphasized in the 1940 *Thief* by the film's representation of Abu as a Huck Finn–like character, whose reward for saving the society is his permission to escape from it, to avoid tight clothing, proper education—or, as Huck would say, "sivilizing."

While *Aladdin* borrows many details from its predecessors—the images of the marketplace, the desirability of the princess, the names Abu and Jafar, the magic carpet, the rival suitors—these elements are organized in a very different relationship with one another. The 1924 *Thief*, for example, has a thief who becomes a prince, whereas the 1940 *Thief* separates the roles of prince and thief, and *Aladdin* has two thieves, Abu—now rendered as a monkey—and Aladdin, the worthy peasant. Unlike the 1924 thief, he is always worthy, and unlike the 1940 romantic hero, he is always a peasant.

The most striking difference between the films, however, is that in *Aladdin* virtually all of the characters, good or evil, have dual natures, and most of them assume at least one disguise or multiple personae. While at the beginning of the 1940 version of *The Thief of Bagdad*, the prince appears as blind beggar and Abu as his dog, the prince very quickly makes clear his true identity and we discover that his transformation was the result of Jaffar's magic, rather than the prince's deception. Only at the outset does the prince disguise himself, and that choice too is the result of Jaffar's trickery, not the prince's duplicity. Aladdin's multiple identities, however, like everyone else's, result from his own choices and actions. He is identified as street rat, diamond in the rough, and Prince Ali; his sidekick, the monkey Abu, who is a necessarily duplicitous thief, rogue, and pickpocket, also becomes a camel, a horse, and an elephant. The sultan's most trusted advisor, Jafar, is his most treasonous subversive; Jafar's henchman, Yago (a name alluding to quintessential duplicity), is a mindless parrot before the sultan and a crafty voice-mime behind his back. Even the earnest sultan assumes contrary views when under Jafar's hypnosis, and he is eventually changed into a humiliated puppet.[18]

The plot of the film, moreover, is an amalgam of conspiratorial plots, each of which involves deceit, employs disguise, and effects changes of character. This plot of plots within plots begins with a narrator explaining that this is a story of a young man who was more than what he seemed. It begins, the narrator tells us, at night in the desert, where "a dark man waits with a dark purpose." That dark man is Jafar, in disguise, who has found a way to make the blank desert surface reveal its secret identity as a monstrous leonine head with a cavernous throat opening to a cave of wonders. Although the throat opening appears to be a fiery abyss, it actually disguises a stairwell to treasures, or vice versa. Neither Jafar in disguise nor his henchmen, however, can enter the cave, the monstrous head informs him, only "one who is worthy." But this "worthy" person, just like his "unworthy" counterparts, must have a deceptive appearance; he must be "a diamond in the rough."

The iteration of the phrase "a diamond in the rough" accompanies a cut from the nighttime desert to a close-up in the daytime marketplace that clearly identifies Aladdin as that "diamond." He too is involved in plots and subterfuges, in his case focused on stealing food ("one jump ahead of the breadline") and avoiding arrest ("one jump ahead of the lawman"). He wishes not only to escape arrest but also to escape his identity as a "street rat." As he says in a song, "riff-raff, street rat— there's so much more to me."

Whereas Aladdin wishes to be more than a street rat, the sultan's daughter, Princess Jasmine, wants to be more (or at least other) than a princess, and therefore runs away from the palace and the prospect of an enforced marriage. New to the world of the street, she invokes the ire of a street vender when, penniless, she innocently gives a child one of his fruits. Aladdin saves her from the irate vender by pretending that she is his deranged sister. To demonstrate her insanity, she mistakes the monkey, Abu, for the sultan, a role that Abu then plays for the sake of her masquerade. The masquerade fails, however, when Abu cannot avoid lapsing into his other role as a compulsive thief. Their escape from the police for theft, however, is shortly followed by Aladdin's arrest by Jafar's orders because Jafar has (magically) learned that Aladdin is the diamond in the rough. The episode ends with Jasmine's revealing herself as the sultan's daughter to the arresting officers in a fruitless attempt to save Aladdin.

If nothing else, these opening episodes express extensive anxiety and confusion about the source, use, and legitimacy of power and identity in the Arabian world. The hidden source of power, found like oil beneath the desert's featureless surface, is accessed in darkness and rivals the sultan's legal power exercised by daylight. The sultan's laws, however, as well as his benign instincts are controlled by his hypnotic first minister, Jafar, who in turn can arrest the powerless Aladdin. He wants to exercise power over Aladdin not because Aladdin has broken the law but because Aladdin has access to the power denied Jafar. These relationships are complicated by the princess who intervenes in all the plots—the marriage plot by refusing to marry, the political plot by urging her father to resist Jafar's advice, and, by befriending Aladdin, the plot to acquire the lamp.

Each of these interventions identify the princess's potential power and her actual powerlessness. She can avoid marriage only by escaping in disguise, but in disguise she cannot identify herself to strangers in the marketplace and therefore is powerless to save herself, *as herself*. At the same time, she proves equally powerless when she assumes her official identity before the soldiers arresting Aladdin because, as the soldiers inform her, their orders come from Jafar.

As the episode in the marketplace—which nearly leaves her dismembered—makes clear, the search for her own identity outside of her father's specific marriage law makes her subject to the unspecific laws of the marketplace, which are also the laws of her father. Only by representing herself as someone else, someone who cannot recognize the true sultan, can she escape. By misrecognizing the sultan she can be misrecognized as insane, which allows her not to be recognized as princess. This symbiosis of misrecognitions serves to disguise with feigned insanity the true insanity of her trying to assert her identity by escaping it, that is, by trying to escape the law of the father to find a power outside the circulation of authority within the film's Middle Eastern iconography.[19] Power does not reside in the princess, whose authority is supplemented by the sultan, nor in the sultan, whose authority is supplemented by Jafar, nor in Jafar, who seeks the supplementary assistance of Aladdin, who is also the most disempowered of all the characters; nor does it reside in the genie, who is by definition potential slave to any and all of the others. The elsewhere that empowers her desire is the West. Her desirability as the exoticized Eastern princess is valorized by her desire to cast off Eastern ritual, law, and custom. The attempted escape is not merely from the palace but from its authority as the site of Eastern power, sexualized by the princess, politicized by Jafar. From the film's perspective, as the princess's plight makes clear, the only appropriate desire is to be empowered as the colonized subject of Western discourse.

Inside the film's Arabia, therefore, overt and covert power, recognition and misrecognition, deceiving friends and deceiving enemies all function—as they did in the multiple plots of the Iran-Contra/Iraq-gate episodes—as interchangeable sets. One could argue, in fact, that far from reflecting the informing narratives of those political episodes, the shifting sands of Middle Eastern identity within Western discourse made the narratives possible. Only by harboring the sense that the Muslim Middle East is the site of confused identity, unstable power, and nomadic allegiances could U.S. intelligence, government, media, or popular opinion shift principals and narratives over the past decade with the ease and alacrity of a reader leafing through *One Thousand and One Arabian Nights*.

Unleashing Arabia's hidden power as represented by the genie in the lamp, moreover, does not resolve *Aladdin*'s confusions over identity and legitimacy. Instead it increases them exponentially, for the genie—whose characterizations draw extensively on Robin Williams's vast array of improvised personae—is a veritable explosion of unstable identities, changing in split seconds. Despite his freedom of form, however, and the limitless array of potential it signifies for others, the genie cannot escape the role of slave, just as Aladdin cannot avoid being a street rat and the princess cannot avoid being royalty. Restricted to the palace, the streets, the lamp, each suffers from a sense of confinement for which the other promises the possibility of release. For Aladdin and Jasmine, the restrictions are the function of their state and culture. The caste system and the sultan's laws divide and confine them equally, so that when the police surprise Aladdin and Jasmine, both respond in exactly the same way, seeing themselves equally in violation of the law. And they are, of course, equally correct. Their confinement, in other words, is inextricably connected to their identity as members of the Arab world, making Westernization the implicit resolution, a point made explicit by the genie when he explains in song to Aladdin that "You Never Had a Friend Like Me!" The song in distinctly Western tones delineates an almost exclusively American set of accents, images, and analogues, the ways in which the genie can end Aladdin's confinement, if not his own.

This ostensive solution to Aladdin's problems depends on the genie's continued confinement, as slave to the lamp and to its owner, a necessary condition—or safety measure, of sorts—given the genie's extraordinary power and instability. A clue to the nature of this immense, unstable power comes from the genie himself, who dubs it a "phenomenal cosmic power in an itty-bitty living space." It is, in other words, atomic power, that product, like the genie's idiom and imagery, of Western technology, now available in the East as a by-product of the wealth that emanates from the wondrous riches beneath the surface of Arabia. Dating to the early days of the Atomic Age, according to Stephen Hilgartner, Richard C. Bell, and Rory O'Conner, "one of the favorite clichés for describing the ambiguous promise of nuclear energy was the *genie in the bottle* taken from the story of the fisherman and the genie in the *Arabian Nights*."[20] Disney productions, in fact, used the image for its 1956 educational film *Our Friend the ATOM*, which turns a hostile and threatening genie into a friendly and beneficent one through the containment powers of the bottle. That Disney production also solves the problem of controlling the *"the atomic genie"* through the controlled release by means of the nuclear reactor.[21]

## Nuclear Proliferation and the New World Order

Although this wondrous technology promises the prosperity that will solve Aladdin's problems by making him a prince, in effect it doubles those problems, just as it doubles his identity, giving Jafar two separate reasons for wanting to kill him, as Aladdin and as Prince Ali, even before Jafar realizes they are one and the same. Nor does it improve his relationship with Jasmine, for in becoming eligible in the eyes of the law he becomes undesirable in the eyes of the princess who wishes to escape confinement within the legal boundaries of her world. Aladdin thus wins her affection not by becoming an Arabian prince but by showing her a "Whole New World" because Jasmine is less interested in the roles that confine Aladdin than in escaping Arabian culture. The "Whole New World," as the song makes clear, is "a new fantastic point of view," "a dazzling place I [Jasmine] never knew." This world provides Jasmine with "100,000 things to see" and makes her realize that she "can't go back to where [she] used to be."

The global perspective of the "Whole New World" provided to Jasmine and Aladdin courtesy of the genie's "phenomenal cosmic power" and the wonders hidden deep beneath the desert floor also has its dark side. The power to liberate can also be the power to enslave, as Jafar illustrates when he gains control of the lamp. Using his first wish to usurp the sultan's throne and his second to become the most powerful sorcerer on Earth, Jafar can create with the lamp what he calls "a new order." The "Whole New World" thus complements the "new order." Taken together they comprise a Whole New World Order: the liberating and enslaving, "good" and "bad" uses of the genie's power, what has been called "the dual nature" of the nuclear fuel, under a plan now almost half a century in the making that still cannot decide to what extent individual nations should be left free to do what they want with the atom. As a result, we have indeed a Whole New World Order underwritten by the terrible power implicit in the atom's potential, a point graphically suggested as Jafar swells to an apex of dark energy surrounded by the halo of an atomic insignia (Figure 1). With his bad motives, Jafar suggests equally the dangers of nuclear monopoly and nuclear proliferation. As the genie at one point says, "I work for Senior Psychopath now."

The genie is thus a slave in a world put at risk by the shifting identities and rampant dissimulation of Muslim Middle Eastern masters. But their instability glosses the potential danger of any world leader in control of phenomenal cosmic power, a point underscored when Jafar at the peak of his tyranny says "read my lips," identifying him simultaneously with President Bush, the erstwhile leader or the New World Order, and with his "evil" Muslim counterpart. The problem, in terms of the film's narrative, is that even if the lamp is made accessible only to "one who is worthy," the worthy can be used by the unworthy. Since in the film, moreover, both the worthy and the unworthy are dishonest, they are hard to distinguish from each other. In global terms, this constitutes an intelligence problem for which even smart bombs provide no solution.

In this regard, Disney succeeds where the U.S. government has failed. If mastery over the genie always entails danger, the Disney solution—

echoing the solution in *Our Friend the ATOM*— is to switch the master and slave, so that the threat of uncontrollable destruction passes when Jafar is tricked into trading places with the genie and thus is safely contained within the lamp, demonstrating the genie's mastery over Jafar and allowing the genie to be set free. As Aladdin says about Jafar's ascent, "It's my own fault. I should have freed the genie long ago."

Since the film thus valorizes the genie's mastery, we need to look more closely at the genie, who in fifteen minutes of screen time assumes over fifty recognizable roles. Although these rapid changes in form and reference are often very funny, it would be hard to call them parodic, because the constant juxtaposition of images, mixing of metaphors, and changing of contexts that comprise the gene's discourse make it impossible to fix a stable referent. *Aladdin*'s Arabia is alternately a metaphor for American culture, a critique of the Muslim Middle East, or the nominal setting for an American stage musical. It is the source of dissimulation and/or the object of it, the origin of misrepresentation and/or the victim, the world to be escaped or to be redeemed. Instead of parody, which requires an object and its deformed version, we have a variety show, an entertainment center, a pastiche. Reduced to media

Figure 1. Jafar swells to an apex of dark energy surrounded by the halo of an atomic insignia.

images, President Bush's New World Order, with uniformed generals hosting video performances of aerial bombings,[22] occupies the same two-dimensional space as the Nintendo game played on the same TV monitor, prior to the evening news, or as the MTV musical special viewed after it. As Bresheeth notes about the Gulf War, "technology supplied both the means of destruction and the means of marketing it for millions of consumers who became, by viewing, innocent onlookers of the greatest media show on earth; what it lacked in realism, it padded with rehearsed dramatic creation, in the best Hollywood tradition."[23] So, too, *Aladdin*'s Arabia contains—and is an extension of—the pastiche of American entertainment.

In this light, it is not surprising that nearly a third of the genie's roles represent him as some form of host or master of ceremonies. His first incarnation after emerging from the lamp establishes this motif as he turns his tail into a microphone and adopts the persona of a nightclub host. He subsequently becomes a game show host, an airline hostess, a maitre d', a chargé d'affaires, a ringmaster, and Macy's parade hosts (male and female), to name a few. He also mimes specific television hosts including William F. Buckley, Arsenio Hall, Ed Sullivan, and Groucho Marx. It is clearly a Western show, moreover, that this consummate master of ceremonies hosts, almost all of his allusions, images, and accents coming from American popular culture. The genie draws heavily, for example, on black and Jewish American idiom, and on characterizations created by American film actors such as Walter Brennan, Jack Nicholson, Peter Lorre, Rodney Dangerfield, and Robert DeNiro (Figure 2). He is also a drum major, a juggler, and an impresario.

## The Disney World Order

The last vision that the genie produces in his introductory song is particularly helpful in contextualizing his performance. The song ends with a musical spectacle on a multitiered stage featuring a chorus line, dancing women, a singer, and in the background fireworks (Figure 3). The kind of entertainment one might find at a theme park like Disney World, it bears in fact some resemblance to the Spectromagic Parade in Disney World's Magic Kingdom. Much of the imagery in fact suggests that *Aladdin*'s Arabia, like everything in the wide Disney World, is a Disney product. From the Pinnochio face that the genie assumes and the Goofy hat that he wears at the end, to Prince Ali's march down Main Street (which is in fact replicated daily in Disney World),[24] the film advertises Disney. It also employs perhaps the most pervasive of classic Disney animated film motifs—the sequestered lady[25]—and even alludes visually to the Disney logo. The fireworks exploding at the end of the "Whole

Figure 2. The genie as Jack Nicholson.

Figure 3. The genie's song ends with a musical spectacle on a multitiered stage.

Figures 4 and 5: The sultan's palace looks uncannily like the new Disney logo.

New World" number suggest the old logo for the Disney television show, while the sultan's palace looks uncannily like the new Disney logo (Figures 4 and 5). Repeatedly the visuals, vocals, and narratives remind us that the story is a product not of the Muslim Middle Eastern world but of Disney's world. In that extradiegetic world, we find the power that animates the princess's desire.

When considered in terms of Disney World, the genie seems much more the host of the super vacation resort than of mythical Arabia, for which his examples of largesse seem like singing advertisements. One Disney World brochure, sounding much like the genie, begins: "What's the most fun vacation in the world? Whatever your answer, you'll find it in our 43–square miles of theme parks, water parks, resorts, fun, fantasy and spectacular nighttime entertainment," and like the descriptions of the various theme parks in *Birnbaum's Walt Disney World* (the official guide), the genie's song sorts pleasures under the rubrics of food, entertainment, and rides.[26]

If, in the postmodern period, as Fredric Jameson astutely pointed out, pastiche replaces parody, then Disney World—particularly in its absence of parody, its rejection of irony, its undermining of referentiality—is a vivid example of postmodernism, in its Orientalist extreme.[27] Perhaps no part of Disney World exemplifies this more than Epcot Center. As *Birnbaum's* explains about the World Showcase, which comprises half of Epcot:

> It is . . . a group of pavilions . . . to demonstrate Disney conceptions about participating countries in remarkably realistic, consistently entertaining styles. You won't find the real Germany here; rather, the country's essence, much as a traveller returning from a visit might remember what he or she saw. Shops, restaurants, and an occasional special attraction are all housed in a group of structures that is an artful pastiche of all the elements that give that nation's countryside and towns their distinctive flavor. Although occasional liberties have been taken when scale and proportion required, careful research governed the design of every nook and cranny.[28]

In this world order, "realism" never conflicts with "entertainment" or surface with essence. "Careful research" is the governing power, and the exercise of liberty serves the interest of proportion. As *Birnbaum's* states elsewhere, "the nations of the Earth are portrayed in all their variety, with extraordinary devotion to detail."[29]

All that variety—in the interest of proportion—is represented by eleven pavilions, five of which are devoted to European nations (United Kingdom, France, Germany, Italy, Norway), three to North American (Canada, Mexico, "The American Adventure"), and two to Asian (China, Japan). The rest of the world, the places where darker-skinned people reside—Africa, the Middle East, the Asian subcontinent, the West Indies, South America—has one representative, Morocco (which is where the *Aladdin* mementoes are sold). All these pavilions organized along one path roughly half a mile long, encircling an artificial lake, create a tour of shops and restaurants that pass for nations, pass so effectively within the Disney World Order, that these simulacra under the auspices of "Disney University Seminars" are the focus of a special course for young people (ten to fifteen years old), "Passport: A Secret Mission to Other Lands." The course, *Birnbaum's* explains,

> brings to life the traditions, art, culture, and history of Epcot's World Showcase. As students travel from country to country [sic], they have the chance to talk with international cast members, study unique architectural styles, learn how to communicate in other languages, decipher ancient hieroglyphics, and uncover secrets "behind" world-famous landmarks. Participants will experience over 3,000 years of history—all in one day.[30]

This is a passport made possible by nations represented in an organization devoid of ethnic conflicts, national rivalries, trade wars, or border disputes, devoid, in other words, of their historical specificity, of their nationality. Instead they form fixed sites on a closed circle, wherein the (primarily Caucasian) world is displayed for tourist consumption, as advertised in "You Never Had a Friend Like Me."

The route into this stable yet consumable world is the other half of Epcot, Future World, where the path of the World Showcase begins and ends. Nor is it any surprise that Future World allows us access to the World Showcase, for Future World is like the genie, himself, the cosmic power of limitless technology, the technological hegemony that allows the New Disney World Order. It is, in other words, the reason that the future is a safe place. Thus one can circle the world and come safely, in the words of another popular film, back to the future. Although the history of the last decade has seen the U.S. policy of "containment" dissolve into one of nonproliferation, the violations of which proliferate exponentially in the East, Epcot Center can still serve as a safe container. Resembling a geodesic version of a nuclear containment dome, it projects the future under a Western roof, situated in a Disney World that has safely substituted for the human world anthropomorphic simulacra, and replaced foreigners with "international cast members."

This is what *Aladdin's* genie promises. Once the potential slave of any master, good or evil, now set free, he can realize his desired potential, to be the quintessential American tourist (Figure 6). As such, he can indeed lead us—as his Goofy hat suggests—from the confinement that typifies Eastern culture in the film to its preferable substitution as a form of Western representation. He can convince us that the world is not only safe but also a terrific tourist attraction, exotic in its look but Western in its conventions and values; in short, a great place to visit, even if you wouldn't be allowed to live there.

Of course, one wouldn't think of living there, any more than one would think of living in the India of *Gunga Din*. Like all tourist attractions, Gunga Din's India is uninhabitable not because it is foreign but because it is entertainment. The foreign locale merely flavors a set of

Figure 6. The genie becomes the quintessential American tourist.

familiar, safe, and ultimately predictable narratives to make them di-
verting, tasty, and consumable. The double remove, then, is only ostensibly effected by the nineteenth-century British regimental unit (or
the Disney theme park), which makes legible the general way in which
the foreign place itself serves as a double remove. The foreign place
itself becomes the medium that allows American cultural narratives—
projected out onto the world as foreign policy, clothing styles, and social codes—to return, blessed by an imaginary Other, as a form of
narcissistic confirmation.

## Notes

1. John McClure, *Late Imperial Romance* (New York: Verso, 1995), looks at
   the ways turn-of-the-century British writers and contemporary American
   writers adopt the romance genre to mediate their anxiety and ambivalence
   about their nation's imperialist activities.
2. See Alan Nadel, "God's Law and the Wide Screen: *The Ten Commandments*
   as Cold War 'Epic,'" *PMLA* (May 1993): 415–430.
3. One could easily construct a bibliographical note longer than this entire
   essay on sources relating the West to the political history of Iraq and Iran,

individually, in relation to each other, and/or in the context of other Muslim Middle Eastern nations. In addition to those I cite elsewhere, some works of interest include discussions of: the Gulf War (Phyllis Bennis and Michael Moushabeck, eds., *Beyond the Storm: A Gulf Crisis Reader* [New York: Olive Branch, 1991]; Haim Bresheeth and Nira Yuval-Davis, eds. *The Gulf War and the New World Order* [New Jersey: Zed, 1991]; Theodore Draper, "The Gulf War Reconsidered," *New York Review of Books*, 16 January 1992, 46–53; and Draper, "The History of the Gulf War," *New York Review of Books*, 30 January 1992, 38–44); the Iran-Iraq War (Anthony Cordsman, *The Iran-Iraq War and Western Security, 1984–87: Strategic Implications and Policy Options* [New York: Jane's, 1987]; "Iraq-gate" (Bruce W. Jentleson, *With Friends Like These: Reagan, Bush, and Saddam, 1982–90* [New York: Norton, 1992]; Alan Friedman, *Spider's Web: The Secret History of How the White House Illegally Armed Iraq* [New York: Bantam, 1993]); and Iran during and after the reign of the shah, who in many ways was a cornerstone of U.S. Middle Eastern policy during the Cold War (Amin Saikal, *The Rise and Fall of the Shah* [Princeton: Princeton University Press, 1980]; Shireen T. Hunter, *Iran and the World: Continuity in a Revolutionary Decade* [Bloomington: Indiana University Press, 1990]; David H. Albert, ed., *Tell the American People: Perspectives on the Iranian Revolution*. [Philadelphia: Movement for a New Society, 1980]; and Anoushiravan Ekteshami and Manshour Varasteh, eds., *Iran and the International Community* [London: Routledge, 1991]). A very detailed chronology can be found in Trevor Moysten, *Major Political Events in Iran, Iraq, and the Arabian Peninsula, 1945–1990* (New York: Facts on File, 1991). This useful book demonstrates numerous ways in which the Muslim Middle East is not only a conflicted area replete with realignments and reorganizations of power, but also one embedded in chronic crises of Western intervention around which many of its conflicts are implicitly or explicitly defined.

4. As Louise L'estranger Fawcett points out in her perceptive analysis of Iran's role in the earliest days of the Cold War, *Iran and the Cold War: The Azerbeijan Crisis of 1946* (Cambridge: Cambridge University Press, 1992), the shah was as early as 1946 an important figure in the Cold War chess game. Cold War discourse and strategy, even in those early years, constructed the conditions that created the shah's reign: "America's initially ambivalent attitude towards Muhammad Massadiq during the latter's premiership from 1951 to 1953, showed how the US administration was not totally convinced that the Shah was the only alternative. However, the fear of communism that coloured US attitudes towards any Iranian leader who was not unequivocally anti-Soviet, prompted the final evaluation that Massadiq, like Qavam, was not the best vehicle for the advancement of US interests in the country. In scenes reminiscent of 1946, when Britain and the USA discussed with the shah the possibility of overthrowing Ahmad Qavam, the two Western powers in 1953 together orchestrated the coup which overthrew the nationalist prime minister" (177).

5. Gary Sick, who examines the misconceptions that led to and surrounded the hostage crisis in *All Fall Down: America's Encounter with Iran* (New

York: Random House, 1985), states that "no one had it right, and the system itself inhibited the flow of accurate information and hampered judgment" (5).

6. James Piscatari, "Foreword" to Ekteshami and Varasteh, *Iran and the International Community*, ix–x.

7. Noam Chomsky, "The US and the Gulf Crisis," in Bresheeth and Yuval-Davis, *The Gulf War and the New World Order*, 14.

8. The "nature" of Iran as a national identity that blurred and distorted issues of geography, ethnicity, and religion is insightfully analyzed by Mostafa Vazari in *Iran as Imagined Nation: The Construction of National Identity* (New York: Paragon, 1993); he concludes that the means by which Iran acquired an "identity" in terms of Western ideology and discourse demonstrates "how Western Orientalism misrepresented a historical reconstruction and interpretation along national and racial lines. The dilemma has not involved misrepresentation alone but also its disgraceful progeny: anti-Semitism, racism, and national prejudices" (214). Cameron R. Hume, *The United Nations, Iran, and Iraq: How Peacemaking Changed* (Bloomington: Indiana University Press, 1994), documents extensively the competitiveness of Iraq and Iran and their shifting relationship to the world order, as represented by the UN.

9. Haim Bresheeth, "The New World Order," in Bresheeth, and Yuval-Davis, *The Gulf War and the New World Order*, 251–252.

10. Department of State, *Policy at the Crossroads, General Foreign Policy Series 3* (Washington, D.C.: United States Government Printing Office, 1948), v.

11. Geoff Simons, *Iraq: From Sumer to Saddam* (London: MacMillian, 1994), provides a concise summary of Kuwaiti terror after the war (19–24). Herbert Kronsky's book-length study *Deadly Business—Legal Deals and Illegal Weapons: The Arming of Iran and Iraq, 1975 to the Present* (New York: Four Walls Eight Windows Press, 1993) provides a detailed account of the fears, dangers, and the West's frustrated attempts to check the development of nuclear and other weapons of mass destruction in the Muslim Middle East.

12. Rob Ben-Yishai et al., "Who Else Will Have the Bomb?" *Time*, 16 December 1991, 40–48.

13. Ibid., 42.

14. Ibid., 47.

15. Tom Post et al., "An Ultimatum for Saddam," *Newsweek*, 3 August 1992, 39.

16. See Kronsky, *Deadly Business*.

17. There are actually two more versions, a 1961 French-Italian version starring Steve Reeves, and a 1978 made-for-TV version starring Peter Ustinov as the caliph of Bagdad who is trying to marry off his daughter, Yasmine. Although it is not apparent what, if anything, *Aladdin* draws from the Steve Reeves version, the name Princess Jasmine and her rebellious character seem in part derived from the Ustinov version.

18. Seeing the sultan as a puppet loosely identifies him with the shah of Iran, who was widely viewed as a U.S. puppet.

19. Although the development of a Lacanian reading of the film is beyond the

scope of this essay, it is worth noting that such a reading might fruitfully investigate the issues of female desire problematized here: that it is a problem of subjectivity, that it is constructed by a gaze that can normalize it as insanity, that it is circumscribed always by the law of the father, that that law disguises a vacancy, and that the desire therefore relies on a promise of a power that always resides elsewhere. I suggest it here merely to note the crucial roles that East and West play in *Aladdin*'s allegorizing of these Lacanian themes.

20. Stephen Hilgartner et al., *Nukespeak: Nuclear Language, Visions, and Mindset* (San Francisco: Sierra Club Books, 1982), 39.
21. Ibid.
22. Some of the very peculiar God's-view shots in *Aladdin* uncannily suggest the perspective created in the widely-viewed Desert Storm bombing raid videos.
23. Bresheeth, "The New World Order," 253.
24. As Birnbaum's "official guide" to Disney World notes: "Inspired by the animated film *Aladdin*, a daily procession of Aladdin's Royal Caravan depicts Prince Ali's grand entrance into the city of Agrabah. Moviegoers will remember that Aladdin is transformed into Prince Ali using one of his wishes granted by the genie. A brass band leads the way down Hollywood Boulevard, followed by the genie, who has transformed himself into a 32-foot giant." (Wendy Lefkon, ed., *Birnbaum's Walt Disney World* [New York: Hearst Business Publishing, 1994], 177.)
25. By "classic Disney," I mean the animated features produced during Disney's lifetime, which the recent successes of *The Little Mermaid* and *Beauty and the Beast* (both focused on sequestered women) echo as a return to the classic Disney style of other sequestered woman films, such as *Snow White*, *Cinderella*, *Sleeping Beauty*, *Lady and the Tramp*, and, in a manner of speaking, *Alice in Wonderland*.
26. Lefkon, *Birnbaum's Walt Disney World*.
27. Fredric Jameson, *Postmodernism or, the Cultural Logic of Late Capitalism* (Durham: Duke University Press, 1991), 16–19. I am not equating postmodernism with Orientalism, but merely noting that some aspects of postmodernism—particularly its implicit valorization of simulacra— facilitate forms of Orientalism. The aspects of postmodernism, on the other hand, that undermine the authority of the frame, that question the hierarchical qualities of foregrounding, or that challenge the colonialist implications of "naming" the Other facilitate powerful critiques of Orientalism.
28. Lefkon, *Birnbaum's Walt Disney World*, 147.
29. Ibid., 125.
30. Ibid., 200.

# PART TWO
# NATIONAL CINEMAS

Charles O'Brien

# The "Cinéma colonial" of 1930s France: Film Narration as Spatial Practice

Reconfiguring visions of empire disseminated through popular novels, the national mass media, public schools, and official spectacles such as the Colonial Exposition of 1931, the *cinéma colonial* of 1930s France provides a complex illustration of an attempt to affirm national identity against a constructed non-Western Otherness. The production of films set in the colonies coincided with what has been identified as the apotheosis of French colonialism.[1] Although known today primarily through the poetic realist classic *Pépé le Moko* (Julien Duvivier, 1936), the cinéma colonial encompassed diverse films with narratives set in the colonies. These included not only poetic realist films—which, in fact, constituted a relatively small subgenre—but patriotic epics such as *Légions d'honneur* (Maurice Gleize, 1938), military comedies such as *Un de la légion* (Christian-Jaque, 1936), melodramas like *Les Hommes nouveaux* (Marcel L'Herbier, 1936), and musicals such as *Princess Tam Tam* (Edmond Gréville, 1935).[2] In addition to Jean Gabin's "Oedipus in a cloth cap," one must include among the protagonists of the colonial film Charles Vanel's lieutenant, Fernandel's legionnaire, Harry Baur's *colon*, and Josephine Baker's Tunisian shepherdess.

Nevertheless, despite the impressive diversity of films, the cinéma colonial has been construed as a relatively unified corpus.[3] The most systematic accounts, informed by structuralist semiology, note that the narratives of the films are typically structured according to a contrast between the representation of a modern metropolitan France and that of a "primitive" Africa or Orient.[4] Among recent examples is the brief commentary published in the brochure for the film and lecture series *Maghreb et Afrique noire au regard du cinéma colonial*, held in Paris during February 1994. Stressing the "profoundly manichean" codes of the genre, the piece enumerates binarisms that commonly structure the films' representation of the colonial world, such as "the unified and the dispersed, the clothed and the naked, [ . . . ] high and low, faciality and dorsality."[5]

Although the relevance of such oppositions can be taken as axiomatic, analyses of the genre that locate the films' Orient exclusively at the level of representation may miss a distinguishing feature of the cinéma colonial. That is, rather than the product of symmetrical differences within an economy of representation, the particular status of the colonies in many French films may derive from the invocation of realities that defy official languages of representation. While it is clear that assertions of difference between West and East can be found in the cinéma colonial, less acknowledged have been ways in which the films work to complicate such assertions. For instance, the journeys of the films' narratives often coincide with border crossings at the level of style and mode of address, in which encounters with alterity are signaled through transformations of filmic space. It seems that in attempting to narrate an allegedly non-Western reality, the films must ultimately transgress the kind of relation between viewer and spectacle that the classical French cinema had inherited from the traditional arts.[6]

## Travel Stories

Like the travel stories analyzed by Michel de Certeau, the colonial films are narratives in the most basic sense. That is, they not only feature a journey—of, for instance, a French doctor, novelist, or legionnaire into colonial Africa—but develop this journey in the form of what de Certeau refers to as a "spatial practice."[7] Essential to such a practice is a narration that involves movement between a homogenous "place" (*lieu*) abstract from the activity of a perceiving subject, and a "space" (*espace*) inscribed with the perspective of an embodied perceiver.[8]

Among de Certeau's examples of a place is the modern map, which is distinguished by the lack of iconic representations (e.g., the symbol of a ship at sea superimposed over a depiction of the ocean) that would suggest events such as voyages, wars, and political and commercial agreements that had made possible the map's production. Like the modern map, or the road sign that indicates miles or kilometers rather than the time required for the journey, a place implies a visual field untroubled by an observer's desires and preoccupations.

A space, in contrast, is "anthropological," indissociable from a subject's "direction of existence." Whereas a place is timeless, a space exists only through the temporality implicit in the activities of a culturally situated subject. Such a subject acts in prereflective anticipation of a future defined with reference to a past of which the subject's disposition to act in particular ways is itself the product. A space, de Certeau proposes, is a place that has been "practiced," in the way in which the street conceived by urban planning is "appropriated" through the movements of pedestrians who "blindly" (that is, without an overarching visual mastery) respond to the contingencies of traffic flow by altering their pace, darting right or left, and so forth. As in the phenomenology of Maurice Merleau-Ponty, a principal source for de Certeau, a space implies a primordial form of experience anterior to the differentiation between perceiver and world essential to conscious intellection. If a place suggests a refined, rationalist gaze, then a space connotes the ontologically primary perspective of the incarnated glance.[9]

The relevance to the cinéma colonial of the spatial transformations that de Certeau describes is suggested by the opening scene of *Pépé le Moko*. The scene occurs in the police station in the French zone of Algiers and features a conversation about master thief Pépé, played by Jean Gabin, who eludes the French police by hiding in the Casbah. The action begins with a shot that frames a map of the city. The camera then pulls back to provide an establishing shot whose balanced framing reveals an interior illuminated by sunlight that enters through large windows. The rationalist conception of space provided by the map's aerial view of the city thus informs the very manner in which the scene is staged. It also anticipates the style of the editing, which functions in classical fashion to anticipate the reactions of individual characters to narratively relevant dialogue.

The narration begins to change, however, when the police chief tells a colleague from Paris about the challenge that the Casbah poses to police surveillance and intervention. As the chief begins to speak, he turns to look at the map, which motivates the camera to reframe so that the map again fills the screen (Figure 1). The image then dissolves into a moving aerial view of the Casbah (Figure 2), and the chief's voice, which has lost the spatial characteristics of the police station, becomes a voice-over commentary like that of a documentary film. In marked contrast to the representation of the police station, the Casbah is presented through an eclectic montage in which handheld camerawork, abrupt changes in the tonality of the cinematography, the appearance of nonprofessional actors, and an unstable combination of location and studio images provide a visual parallel to what the voice-over identifies as the Casbah's indeterminate geography and mixture of national,

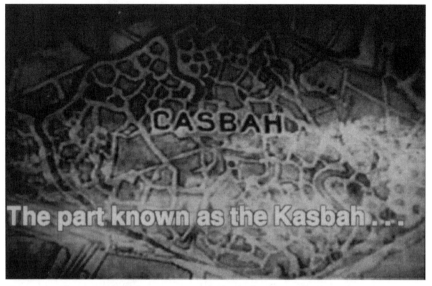

Figure 1. The image of the map in *Pépé le Moko* (Duvivier, 1937) promises to locate the viewer in a position of mastery.

racial, and ethnic types. The Otherness of the Casbah is further established by the emphasis placed on the presence of its female inhabitants. Pushing to excess a familiar trope in which the Orient becomes coterminous with highly conventional notions of femininity, the film forces a distinction between the Caucasian men who congregate in the police station and the "women of all countries, of all shapes and sizes" who inhabit the Casbah.[10]

If, as de Certeau proposes, a "space" is defined by a hero's "direction of existence," then the opening of *Pépé le Moko* suggests a situation in which this hero is none other than the film's viewer. That is, the movement from the neoclassical "place" of the police station to the primordial "space" of the Casbah is also a movement away from classicism's stable distance between beholder and spectacle and toward an indeterminacy in which scientific distance alternates with a kind of tactile convergence. On the one hand, the images of the Casbah are accompanied by a voice-over narration like that of a travel documentary, organizing disparate images into a whole. The diversity of people and locales is all part of "the Casbah." On the other hand, the commentary augments the degree of fragmentation by emphasizing the amorphousness of the Casbah ("there is not one Casbah, but a hundred . . . or a thousand") and by enumerating the multiple nationalities and races. Like-

Figure 2. But the dissolve to the next, moving camera shot initiates a movement into a increasingly indeterminate space.

wise, although close microphone placement eliminates a sense of ambience and thus suggests the transcendent perspective that defines a "place," the commentary evokes bodily sensations such as touch and smell. In fact, the invocation during the description of the Casbah of the full range of sensory experience suggests that the movement from the police station to the Casbah is a shift from one mode of sensory perception to another. The steep stairways descent down to "dank and smelly pits" (gouffres sombres et puants), to "doorways dripping" (porches suintants) with "vermin and humidity." If the police station with its aerial map suggests the disembodied vision that Descartes characterized as the "noblest of the senses," the Casbah is decidedly the realm of the "lower senses" of touch and smell.[11] The difference of the Casbah is further established by the distinctiveness of the musical accompaniment, a rendition of the "oriental" theme composed by Mohammed Iguerbouchen, which contrasts with the "European" theme written by Vincent Scotto that had played during the credits and that will accompany moments featuring Pépé's memories of Paris.[12]

The Algiers of *Pépé le Moko* would seem to exemplify the divided colonial city described by critics from Frantz Fanon to Timothy Mitchell, the "world cut in two" in which the modernity of the French zone is established through the exclusion or deferral of the "primitive" Casbah.[13]

What is intriguing, however, is that the film continues in a way that complicates the very difference that has been asserted. Consider what happens immediately following the documentary sequence, when the scene in the police station concludes with the entry of a new character, Slimane, the "go-between" who will be hired to lure Pépé outside the Casbah and into the French zone. Wearing a combination of Arab and Western dress, and, although a police agent, displaying a bodily disposition that suggests the femininity attributed to the Casbah, Slimane is the very emblem of cultural hybridity. He speaks in a thick accent, and, in describing Pépé as a "son of the devil" (fils du diable) he expands the context of the dialogue to include the supernatural.

Moreover, Slimane's singular presence alters the nature of the space of the police station. Note that the door through which Slimane enters opens and closes without making a sound. Also, whereas other characters had been framed in ways that establish the modified frontality of classical scenography, Slimane faces the camera, directly addressing the film's spectator. In addition, the framing continues to place Slimane within the darkened doorway, which had not appeared in a shot prior to his entrance. The peculiarity of the moment continues with the cut to the next shot, which presents the reaction of the visiting police officer by violating the scene's axis of action. Although the scene continues to unfold in the police station, the latter has acquired a new ambiguity through having taken on a trace of the difference that a moment before had been attributed to the Casbah.

## The Ethnographic Glance

The shifts in narration of a film like *Pépé le Moko* are comparable to certain of the textual practices of modern ethnography, the foundation of whose key institutions in France—from the Institut d'Ethnologie (1925) to the Musée de l'Homme (1937)—coincided with the popularity of the cinéma colonial. Such affinities go beyond the use of ethnographic footage and conventions of the ethnographic film like maps and expository intertitles. According to James Clifford, the new ethnography was constituted on the basis of a distinctive epistemology, which entailed a dialectic in which the stance of the scientific observer alternates with that of a cultural participant.[14] At issue, in effect, was a fusion of roles that hitherto had been separate. Whereas the anthropology of the decades prior to the First World War had rested upon a division of labor that exempted the university scholar from fieldwork, modern ethnography required university-trained specialists to work in non-Western cultures during extended periods. Departing from the nineteenth-century commitment to the notion of a secure division between rational observer and objective representation, modern ethnography assumed a practitioner who functioned not only as a transcendent observer, capable of formulating broad theses concerning the essence of humankind, but as an engaged participant, immersed in the experience of life in a different culture. The emphasis on the observer's presence gave modern ethnography a distinctive authority and at the same time made possible forms of reflexivity that would inspire alternative anthropologies which Clifford links to current suspicion about the very notion of ethnographic science. Clifford locates the effects of the dialectic of participation and observation at the level of literary practice in foundational writings like E. E. Evans-Pritchard's *The Nuer* (1940), whose narration continually tacks back and forth between the "outside" and "inside" of events.

The kind of narration that Clifford describes is comparable to that of colonial films such as *Pépé le Moko*, in which changes in locale entail shifts in the viewer's relation to space. What is intriguing is that such shifts in narration are evident in films that seem to owe nothing to the allegedly countercultural perspective implicit in the pessimistic narratives and expressionistic visual style of *Pépé le Moko* and other Gabin films such as *Quai des brumes* (Marcel Carné, 1936) and *Gueule d'amour* (Jean Grémillon, 1937). In fact, by the late 1930s, ideological conditions ensured that the colonial film would aim to perform an official cultural function analogous to that of the historical spectacle of the preceding decade. It seems clear that the intent behind certain of the films of 1938 and 1939 was to affirm those conceptions of nationhood and citizenship whose authority Marcel Mauss and other French ethnographers during the interwar years had tended to put in question.[15]

Nonetheless, even ideologically conservative films feature moments that suggest a mode of narration at odds with the principles of film classicism. Consider, for instance, Jacques de Baroncelli's *L'Homme du Niger* (1939). *L'Homme du Niger* was among a series of films that coincided with official statements in favor of a military defense of France's African bloc. Identified in its credits as shot on location in the Sudan with the cooperation of colonial authorities and featuring a narrative that alluded to ongoing efforts of the Office of Niger, *L'Homme du Niger* could not be ideologically farther from the film noir of *Pépé le Moko*.[16] Indeed, *L'Homme du Niger* was the kind of film designed to please critics like Emile Vuillermoz, who had condemned *Pépé le Moko* for its "defeatist" portrayal of the ineffectual French colonial police.[17] Instead of the exotic underworlds of films such as *Pépé le Moko* that had repelled Vuillermoz, *L'Homme du Niger* celebrated official heroes and the effort to extend France's "civilizing mission" into the African interior.

The protagonist, Commandant Bréval, aims to build dams near the river-town of Bamako that would improve the health of the population and enable cultivation of the land. A related plotline concerns the efforts of a French doctor to cure leprosy and sleeping sickness.[18]

All the same, *L'Homme du Niger*, despite the deliberate propriety, displays intriguing departures from orthodox narrative form. I refer here to moments when the narration refrains from providing information that would explain a decisive scene. An example is the apparently unmotivated village fire that leads Bréval to rescue Africans from the burning infirmary and thereby to contract leprosy. Was the blaze the result of natural forces, or due to an attack on the village? If the latter is the case, who perpetrated the attack and why? The scene in the hospital that occurs afterward, when Bréval is visited by colleagues, involves considerable dialogue, but none that clarifies the circumstances of the fire. Consider also the climactic scene at the site of the dam, where Bréval, after speaking to a large assembly of insurgent Africans, is suddenly shot and killed by a renegade *sorcier* (sorcerer). The mise-en-scène, which features masses of people and the huge construction at Sansanding, is reminiscent of the historical spectacle, the most official of film genres. In fact, the cinematographer was Léonce-Henri Burel, who had achieved renown for his work on *Napoléon* and other Abel Gance films of the 1920s. In contrast, however, to the historical spectacle, whose narration tends toward the didacticism of the school curriculum, *L'Homme du Niger* entails a narration that works to introduce a degree of opacity concerning the nature of key narrative events. Most notably, Bréval's lengthy address is rendered entirely in native dialect, without subtitles. The only indication of the effect of Bréval's discourse is the succession of reaction shots that feature the faces and comportment of the hundreds of nonprofessional actors assembled at the construction site. As with the eroticized voice that figures in the sixteenth-century travel literature analyzed by de Certeau (and in contrast to the voice-over commentary of *Pépé le Moko*), the language spoken by Bréval impresses the viewer not for what it says—the speech is untranslated—but for its materiality, for what it is and does.[19]

Allusions to realities that escape the representational capacity of visual depiction and linguistic summary are especially pronounced in films less associated with official institutions. Consider an entire scene early in *Cinq Gentlemen maudits* (1931), another film directed by Duvivier.[20] The scene is filmed at an unspecified rural location (perhaps outside the Morrocan city of Moulay Idriss, the next important narrative location?) and features actors who clearly lack theatrical training. The scene appears to show a priest or tribal chief addressing in dialect a group of countrymen, but there is no way of knowing because it is impossible to discern causal relations that would link this scene to any other in the film. To a degree unthinkable in a Hollywood film, basic story questions remain unanswerable: Who are these characters? What are they saying? Where are they? How do they fit into the story of the European vacationers? In failing to provide a framework within which such questions can be answered, *Cinq Gentlemen maudits* gestures toward realities beyond the scope of the causal logic of classical film narration.[21] That the film ends with the revelation that the series of mysterious deaths had been due to a plot engineered by one of the Western men absolves the Africans of the crime while remaining consistent with the tendency, evident in the film's early scenes, to link Africa to occult forces inaccessible to rational explanation.

The emphasis in *Cinq Gentlemen maudits* on ethnographic material is not surprising given that the film had been in production through the summer of 1931, during the peak months of both the Colonial Exposition and the Dakar-Djibouti ethnographic expedition.[22] Moreover, the film's release coincided with the successful exhibition of numerous documentaries on Africa. These included the highly publicized *L'Afrique vous parle* (Paul Hoefler and Walter Hutter, 1931), which was being distributed in France by Marcel Vandal and Charles Delac, the producers of *Cinq Gentlemen maudits*.[23] The complaint that Duvivier had allowed a fascination with ethnographic material to overwhelm the story had been anticipated by Vandal and Delac, who advised publicists to stress that Duvivier had invented "a new film genre" that combined "mysterious intrigue" with "Morrocan ambience."[24] Publicists were asked both to promote the film's surprise ending and to emphasize the rigorously authentic sounds and images, which involved no dubbing or other *trucage* (special effects).[25]

An example of the integration in *Cinq Gentlemen maudits* of ethnographic footage is a crucial sequence that occurs near the film's beginning. The sequence begins shortly after the arrival of the European men in Moulay Idriss, where they have come to witness events surrounding the annual pilgrimage to the Holy City. After meeting at a cliffside location that provides a panoramic view of the city, the men go on a sightseeing tour, visiting locations that remain today part of a tourist's itinerary. As they approach the events of the pilgrimage, the framings become tighter and the space more fragmented. Haïssaouas tribesmen in ceremonial dress perform a tournament, a dance, and a possession ceremony, staging events like those of the famous travel film *La Croisière noire* (Léon Poirier, 1926) or the later ethnographic films of Jean Rouch.[26] Indeed, images such as that of a man staggering with what looks like cracked egg pouring down his head prefigure the depiction of the Hauka cult in Rouch's notorious *Les Maîtres fous* (1954).[27] Another such image, of a man who burns himself with torches (Figure 3), is

Figure 3. The blurred shape of a man's hat in the extreme left foreground of this image from *Cinq Gentlemen maudits* (Duvivier, 1931) suggests an attempt to place the viewer with the scene's space.

Figure 4. This shot from *Cinq Gentlemen maudits* depicts the act that precipitates the curse from the point of view of the European man who breaks the taboo.

Figure 5.  The five gentlemen look offscreen after the sorcerer has cursed them.

among many that are organized in ways that exemplify the anthropological space described by de Certeau. Note the light-colored shape that appears in the extreme foreground. The shape enters the left side of the frame momentarily and then leaves just prior to the cut to the next shot. Close inspection reveals that it is a man's hat, but having no narrative significance, the identity of the object is less relevant than its role in creating the impression of the depth and contingency of a space defined by the perspective of a perceiver proximate to the event.

The climax of the scene occurs when one of the men meets a veiled woman who appears in extreme close-up. The man succumbs to a temptation that will prove fatal when he attempts to remove the woman's veil (Figure 4) and, having violated a taboo, provokes a *sorcier* into cursing the entire party. The action of the sorcier—a nonactor who faces the camera while making the gesticulations of the curse—strikes the men as comical until they look offscreen (Figure 5) and witness what seems to be an animal sacrifice. The latter is presented in a medium shot whose disjunctiveness is accentuated by an abrupt increase in volume of the music track (Figure 6). The sacrifice is rendered in a manner that makes the event nearly indecipherable. It appears that an animal is writhing on the ground, but because of the eccentric, mobile framing and high-contrast cinematography, the type of animal is unclear (a dog? a goat?) as is the precise nature of what has happened. Less a

Figure 6. The shot that represents what the men see is this barely legible
image of the apparent sacrifice of an animal.

sign than a material sensation, the image of the animal seems to function presemiologically, insisting as a raw facticity whose presence ex-
ceeds the intentional structures that ordinarily govern the viewer's
perception. Like an Eisensteinian attraction, the image works to pre-
empt the cognitive processes of classical film viewing and thus directly
to affect the viewer's nervous system. At such moments vision becomes
tactile: our eyes touch the image.

## An Ambivalent Narration

Critics have linked the emergence during the 1930s of new realisms in
colonial cinema and literature with changes in official colonialist culture.[28] Principal among such changes was the abandonment of certain
established distinctions between superior and inferior societies. Extending the principle of the indivisibility of the national territory to the ensemble of the colonial domain, advocates of empire were required to
argue that the colonies be considered not as subordinate territories but
as equal members within a plus grande France. According to Raoul
Girardet, revision of familiar notions of metropolitan superiority had
been enabled both by doubt concerning the morality of technological
progress that had followed the devastation of the First World War and

by the development of a large and relatively precise body of knowledge about the colonies. Such knowledge had been made possible by new technologies of transportation and information, which facilitated the numerous types of exchange that took place after the war, particularly with North Africa. These included a massive increase in trade, a new and steady flow of settlers, air travel enabled by regular flights, tourism fostered by the construction of luxury hotels, and considerable activity in areas of culture such as film production and exhibition.[29] In addition, colonialism stimulated developments in relevant areas within the social and natural sciences. Besides the growth of academic specializations such as Orientalism and Africanism, effects of new scientific effort included increased emphasis in the school curriculum on colonial history and geography, expanded coverage of colonial issues in the press, and new colonial genres in literature and film. An additional indication of general fascination with African cultures was the phenomenal popularity in Paris of African-American performers from Josephine Baker to Duke Ellington.

That colonization introduced conditions that enabled production of the very knowledge that challenged notions of Western supremacy suggests what has been described as a paradox at the center of the postcolonial condition.[30] Just as the bordercrossing of de Certeau's travel story threatens the "law of the place," the drive to expand on the part of imperial nations such as France and Britain produced a destablizing effect on metropolitan preoccupations and authority. In extending the nation's boundaries to include cultures beyond the limits of metropolitan experience, the imperial project challenged dominant modes of consciousness to the degree that monocentric perspectives had begun to become untenable.

Indicative of the waning of faith in a hierarchy of cultures is that the narratives of the colonial films of the 1930s often center on socially marginal protagonists. Unlike the heroic leaders of the historical spectacle—or indeed of earlier colonial films such as *L'Atlantide* (Jacques Feyder, 1921)—the protagonists of the films of the 1930s are typically social outcasts of one sort or another. In some cases, the protagonists are deserters, criminals, and others whose identities are decidedly at odds with bourgeois norms. Often characters are fleeing their urban past, as is the case in *La Bandera* (Duvivier, 1935), *Le Grand Jeu* (Jacques Feyder, 1933), *Gueule d'amour* and *Les Réprouvés* (Jacques Séverac, 1936), films in which the colonies provide the setting for the elaboration of conflicts that had originated in the metropolis. At least one critic has noted similarities between the colonial worlds depicted in French films of the 1930s and the West Africa of Louis-Ferdinand Céline's novel, *Voyage au bout de la nuit* (1932).[31]

As Janice Morgan notes in her essay in this collection, a film such as *Pépé le Moko* likely functioned less as a story about displaced persons in the colonies than as a transposition of desires and repressions integral to social life in metropolitan France. Pursuing a similar line of argument, Christopher Faulkner links the emergence of the cinéma colonial as a major genre to the capacity of the colonial world to redefine emotional, psychological, social, and political horizons at a time when the limits and potentialities of metropolitan identity had come into question as never before.[32] Providing an imaginary space for the transgression of established boundaries of cultural identity, depictions of the colonial world served to organize and represent desire at the limits of bourgeois normality. A telling circumstance is that many of the characters of the cinéma colonial display "affective identities" in which prereflective impulses overwhelm rational cognition. Faulkner notes, for instance, the explosions of rage of the character played by Jean Gabin in *Quai des brumes*, the obsessive desire for distant travel of Marius in the film adaptation (Alexandre Korda, 1931) of Marcel Pagnol's play, the alcohol-induced madness of Pierre in *Le Grand Jeu*, the lesbian passion of Alice in *Club des femmes* (Jacques Deval, 1936), the "nature" assigned to Josephine Baker's character in *Princess Tam Tam*.[33] One might extend the argument to include even the most official of the military films, in which the protagonist's submission to the authority of the military group entails a self-dispossession in conflict with the individualism of bourgeois culture.[34]

Evidence of exploration in the cinéma colonial of alternative identities can be found in the prevalence of forms of narrative closure that suggest attempts to manage or constrain expressions of cultural difference. Consider, for instance, the frequency with which the narratives of the films conclude with scenes featuring either funerals (*La Bandera*, *L'Homme du Niger*) or acts of suicide, both literal (*Pépé le Moko*, *Serati, le terrible*) and metaphorical (*Le Grand Jeu*, *Légions d'honneur*). The issue of the alienation of Europeans in the colonies is elaborated in especially complex ways in melodramas about the experience of the colons, the expatriate settlers and businessmen who populated the major port cites of North Africa and other colonial regions. Prominent examples include *Les Hommes nouveaux* (Marcel L'Herbier, 1936) and *Serati, le terrible* (André Hugon, 1937), both of which star Harry Baur, an actor who specialized in ethnic roles and appeared in numerous colonial films.[35]

In fact, the cultural Other of *Les Hommes nouveaux* is no doubt the colon himself, Bourron, the businessman played by Baur, whose profitable commercial career in Morocco has placed him among the "new men" whose instinctual drive for wealth separates them from the high-cultural traditions of both Europe and Africa. An intriguing feature of the film is the parallel drawn between the rise of Bourron from dockworker to shipping magnate and the "pacification" of Morocco credited to Marshal Hubert Lyautey. The parallel is developed through the juxtaposition of scenes constructed according to conventions of two genres that inform the cinéma colonial: whereas Lyautey's career is presented in a quasi-documentary sequence, Bourron's is configured as melodrama. Bourron's liminal social position is developed through a depiction of his relationship with Christiane, his young French wife. A member of an aristocratic family whose financial failure led to her marriage with Bourron, Christiane eventually gives her affections to a French army officer. The import of the drama is overdetermined by a heavy symbolism. When the officer ultimately dies in the hospital from battle wounds, the moment is presided over by Marshal Lyautey himself, governor general of Morocco and architect of the modernized city of Rabat. Bourron's eccentricity with respect to French identity is underscored at the film's conclusion when Christiane boards a ship to leave forever. An image that shows the elevation of the flag that bears the insignia of Bourron's commercial empire (a B) invites contrast with an earlier moment, the conclusion of the film's documentary prologue, when the raising of the tricolor signaled the treaty of Fes of 1912 and the foundation of Morocco as a French protectorate.

Issues of the hybridity of colonialist identity are explored even in *L'Homme du Niger*, whose eponymous hero is none other than the colonial officer played by Victor Francen. That the "man from Niger" is incarnated by an actor of the Comédie française and star of numerous films with patriotic themes indicates that even in a forthrightly imperialist film differences between French and African identities are remarkably less fixed than certain discussions of the genre would allow.[36] In fact, Francen's character will undergo remarkable metamorphoses. At one point he is diagnosed as afflicted with leprosy, which leads him to adopt the most abject of non-Western identities. Exchanging his white uniform for a black shroud, he vanishes for years into a leper colony, thus performing the sacrifice that allows his young fiancée to marry someone else.

That such instances of hybrid identity reflect official discourses is evident in the parallel between Francen's Bréval and Eugène Bélime, founder in 1932 of the Office of Niger and dubbed in the press as "L'homme du Niger." Recall also designations of Lyautey such as "Lyautey l'Africain" and "Maréchal de l'Islam," which characterize the most famous of the "vrais chefs d'empire" in a manner that likewise implies a mélange of Western and non-Western identities. In fact, an iconographic analysis indicates that Lyautey was often depicted in a manner not unlike that of Slimane of *Pépé le Moko*, in clothing that blends Western and Arab motifs.[37] A rather different construction of the duality of Lyautey's character occurs in *Les Hommes nouveaux*, which features the same actor, Gabriel Signoret, in the roles of both the saintly Lyautey and the worldly Tolly, a colonial administrator and crony of Bourron. In contrast to Signoret's Lyautey, whose heavy makeup and relative silence and immobility seem to place him within a temporality that transcends that of narrative events, his Tolly, all movement and chatter, exists firmly within the present tense. The dual casting is reminiscent of numerous biographies of Lyautey that had appeared during the interwar years, for they presented the marshal as somehow both an aristocrat in temperament, embodying ageless values, and a man of the present, exemplifying the pragmatism essential to modern progress.[38] As the example of *Les Hommes nouveaux* suggests, the colonial film not only explores what Homi Bhabha refers to as the stereotype's role as a "complex, ambivalent, contradictory mode of representation, as anxious as it is assertive," but does so with reference to the most official of Western heroes.[39]

Comparisons between the colonial film and the Hollywood Western (or gangster film, in case of the Gabin vehicles) are suggestive but unfortunately tend to close down an inquiry into the peculiar ambivalence of the French films.[40] The point made by critics such as Michéle Lagny, Pierre Sorlin and Marie-Clair Ropars that the colonial film, unlike the Western, alludes to rather than represents battles is essential because it suggests that in the French films the distinguishing feature of the cultural Other is precisely his or her inaccessibility to official modes of depiction.[41] Such an inaccessibility is often rather literal. For one, Arab characters are often played by Western actors. Moreover, as Lagny, Sorlin, and Ropars note, actors who play Arab characters are frequently unnamed or otherwise marginalized in the posters and credit sequences of the films, regardless of the centrality of the character to the narrative. Thus the credits of *Pépé le Moko* place Lucas Gridoux, the Romanian Jewish actor who played the crucial role of Slimane, among the actors who play members of Pépé's gang. A related phenomenon occurs in films such as *Les Hommes nouveaux*, *L'Homme du Niger*, *La Bandera* and *Le Bled* (Jean Renoir, 1929), whose narratives of colonial history omit reference to events and characters from the histories of the colonized populations.

As in the sixteenth-century travel narratives analyzed by de Certeau, in which the productivity of Western writing is established through difference from the erotic excess of indigenous voices, the presence of the cultural Other in the *cinéma colonial* often seems to be conveyed less through academic imagery and linguistic statement than through extralinguistic sounds and untranslated foreign speech.[42] Consider the battle cries of the invisible rebel forces of *La Bandera* and *Un de la Légion*, the perpetual music of the Casbah that Pépé cannot shut out, or the variety of films that present speech that the Western viewer hears but does not understand. Note also the considerable efforts of film-makers to record "authentic" sounds. For instance, for *Cinq Gentlemen maudits*, one of the first French sound films made on location, Duvivier ordered the construction of a special motorized vehicle, outfitted by Tobis-Klangfilm, to record sound at the actual sites of the Moroccan exteriors.[43] In addition, press reports indicated that Western actors had studied native dialects to ensure "authentic" performances, as was the case for Simone Berriau in *Itto* and Harry Baur in *L'Homme du Niger*. In sum, moments in the French films displaying handheld camerawork, natural lighting, figures outside the camera's range of focus, shots lacking an inscription of a narrative trajectory, absence of blocking for figure movement, abrupt changes in image tonality, conflicting spatial cues, nonprofessional actors, and the lack of subtitles for African speech appear to be essential features of the genre. Rather than simple technical flaws attributable to an undercapitalized national film industry, such stylistic peculiarities are understandable as symptoms of the very project of the cinéma colonial, which endows the colonial world with particular kinds of affect through an association with phenomena that exceed the representational capacities of the official culture. Unlike, say, American films set in North Africa (e.g., Gary Cooper vehicles such as *Morocco* [von Sternberg, 1930]), the distinctiveness of the cinéma colonial resides less in a depiction of the conventionally exotic, however much on display, than in an attempt to provide the viewer with more unsettling forms of experience.[44]

In the case of certain films—an example is *Cinq Gentlemen maudits*—the latter can approach what Julia Kristeva refers to as "abjection," an affective nonconceptualizable contact with an Otherness that the viewer can neither ingest nor expel.[45] A different tendency can be found in the few films whose realism conforms to the liberal progressive vision that had recently been adopted within official colonialist culture. An example is *Itto* (1934), directed by Jean Benoît-Lévy and Marie Epstein. Like *Cinq Gentlemen maudits*, *Itto* was filmed in Morocco with location-recorded sound, but with indigenous Chleuh actors who spoke Berber in principal roles. Whereas *Cinq Gentlemen maudits* tends to construct the indigenous cultures of Morocco as alien, *Itto* employs Griffith-style crosscutting to suggest deliberate parallels between European and African characters. *Itto* is thus a rare example of a film that affirmed the Republican universalism that had come to inform official colonialist rhetoric during the 1930s.

## Cinéma Postcolonial?

An intriguing legacy of the cinema colonial is the work of the first generation of consciously postcolonial filmmakers for whom the colonial
films of the 1930s would seem to have exemplified the representational
paradigm against which they could not but have defined their own
projects.[46] An example is Gillo Pontecorvo's *The Battle of Algiers* (1966),
which elaborates a narrative of the Algerian liberation movement in
terms remarkably congruent with those of *Pépé le Moko*. Like the earlier film, *The Battle of Algiers* begins with a failed police incursion into
the Casbah of Algiers. Moreover, as in *Pépé le Moko*, the Casbah is presented as a labyrinth whose capacity to overwhelm is linked to the presence of its female inhabitants. In contrast, however, to the women of
*Pépé le Moko*, who attract European men into an amorphous Casbah,
the women of *The Battle of Algiers* adopt disguises that allow them to
enter the Western zone, where they set bombs whose explosions constitute an ultimate violation of the boundary that constitutes the colonial city.

Another famous film of the first postcolonial decade in which established codes are both reversed and affirmed is Ousmane Sembene's
*Black Girl* (1966), widely cited as the first feature film of sub-Saharan
Africa. Like *Pépé le Moko*, *Black Girl* features a protagonist who crosses
the boundary that demarcates a seductive exterior. Also like *Pépé le
Moko*, the film begins with a quasi-documentary sequence. After the
woman meets her employer at the dock, he drives her to her new home,
commenting, in the manner of a tour guide, on the sites they pass along
the way. In addition, the narrative ends with a suicide.[47] The protagonist of *Black Girl*, however, is an African woman rather than a European man, and the journey is from Dakar to the French Riviera rather
than from Paris to Algiers. Indeed the film's narrative oddly parallels
that of *Princess Tam Tam*, which likewise features the journey to France
of an African woman under the guidance of a Western sponsor. In *Black
Girl*, though, the narration is organized according to the woman's knowledge of narrative events. An intriguing aspect of the style of *Black Girl*
is the grossly overexposed lighting in the interior scenes in the household in Antibes, where the woman works as a maid. The light that had
clearly illuminated the police station of *Pépé le Moko* is now blindingly
intense, to the point of drawing attention to the very materiality of the
film image. In *Black Girl* what appears to defy available languages of
representation is the reality of postcolonial Europe as experienced by
an immigrant Senegalese woman.

Films such as *Coup de torchon* (Bertrand Tavernier, 1976), in which
Philippe Noiret reprises the role played by Harry Baur in films of the
1930s, indicate the enduring relevance of the conventions of the cin-

ema of the interwar years. That many of the films of the 1930s are now available in home video format in department stores throughout France suggests that their importance in defining the imperial past is unlikely to fade.

Nonetheless, numerous films released during the past decade depart from the cinéma colonial in ways significant enough to suggest the emergence of new genres. Especially notable are films with narratives set during the period just prior to decolonization and featuring female protagonists. Examples include *Indochine* (Régis Wargnier, 1992,) discussed in Marina Heung's essay in this volume, *Chocolat* (Claire Denis, 1988), *Outremer* (Brigitte Rouan, 1990), *Bal de gouveneur* (Marie-France Pisier, 1990), and *L'Amant* (Jean-Jacques Annaud, 1991). In certain of these films the narration is structured as a flashback that presents the personal recollection of a Western woman who at one time lived in a colonial society. That many of the films were written and/or directed by women gives the narratives an autobiographical dimension.

In configuring the borderline of alterity over historical time rather than geographic space, today's colonial films adopt the glossy aestheticization familiar to contemporary advertising—or, for that matter, to the Orientalist literature and painting of the decades before World War I. At issue is perhaps a displacement in which abject realism now figures intertextually, at one remove. Such is the claim made by Francis Ramirez and Christian Rolot, who propose that the inevitable frame of reference for recent films about the colonial past is news coverage of wars, famines, terrorism and political repression in countries in Africa, the Carribean and Southeast Asia. While *Pépé le Moko* connoted regret for an irrecoverable Paris, recent films exhibit nostalgia for an empire that can compare favorably to the "misery and chaos" that televised news continually inputes to the contemporary Third World.[48] Such historical revisionism is manifest in a reversal of the genre's formula. Whereas the melodramas of the 1930s depict outcast men who submit to destinies within colonial hells whose stability goes unquestioned, recent films such as *Indochine* and *L'Amant* present women discovering the most passionate sentiments within exotic edens that exist just prior to social and political collapse. As with the wave of films of the mid-1970s about the Occupation, contemporary colonial films exhibit a nostalgia that indicates what is at issue is less the past than endurance of the past in forms of collective memory.

## Notes

1. On the notion of the 1930s as the apotheosis of France's colonial empire, see Raoul Girardet, *L'idée colonial en France de 1871 à 1962* (Paris: La Table Ronde, 1972), 175–273.

2. For surveys of the colonial genre, see Michèle Lagny et al., "L'Afrique de l'autre," *Générique des années 30* (Paris: Presses Universitaires de Vincennes, 1986), 127–176; Christopher Faulkner, "Affective Identities: French National Cinema and the 1930s," *Canadian Journal of Film Studies* 3, no. 2 (1994): 3–29; François Chevaldonné, "Notes sur le cinéma colonial en Afrique du Nord: naissance et fonctionnement d'un code?" in Sylvie Dallet, ed., *Guerres révolutionaires* (Paris: L'Harmatton, 1984), 100–114; and Pierre Sorlin, "The Fanciful Empire: French Feature Films and the Colonies in the 1930s," *French Cultural Studies* 2, no. 5 (1991): 135–151. Informative but less reliable are Pierre Leprohon, *L'Exotisme et le cinéma* (Paris: Editions J. Susse, 1945); Maurice-Robert Bataille and Claude Veillot, *Caméras sous le soleil: le cinéma en Afrique du nord* (Algiers: Victor Heintz, 1956); Abdelghani Megherbi, *Les Algériens au miroir du cinéma colonial* (Algiers: S.N.E.D., 1982); and Pierre Boulanger, *Le Cinéma colonial: de "l'Atlantide" à "Lawrence d'Arabie"* (Paris: Seghers, 1975). Additional sources are listed in the bibliography at the end of this volume. I should add that my initial investigation was informed by a course packet from a seminar taught by Dudley Andrew at the University of Iowa. The packet included unpublished papers by D. Andrew, James Lastra, Deborah Linderman, Janice Morgan, and David Slavin.

3. The term *cinéma colonial* appears to have become a part of the vocabulary of the film industry in the wake of the commercial success of *L'Atlantide* (Jacques Feyder, 1921). Filmed on location in Algeria, *L'Atlantide* inspired numerous films, a number of which were remade during the sound era, including *L'Atlantide* itself. On early cinéma colonial, see, for instance, Michel Cade, "De la casquette du père Bugeaud aux moustaches du Maréchal Lyautey," *Cahiers de la Cinémathèque* no. 49 (1988): 5–10. Cade lists nine feature films made in 1922 and 1923.

4. Structuralist analyses can be found in Chevaldonné, "Notes sur le cinéma colonial en Afrique du Nord," and especially Lagny, et al., "L'Afrique de l'autre." Although concerned with a different corpus (films made after the Second World War in the Belgian Congo), worth consulting is Francis Ramirez and Christian Rolot, *Histoire du cinéma colonial au Zaïre, au Rwanda, et au Burundi* (Tervuren, Belguim: Musée Royal de l'Afrique Centrale, 1985).

5. In Michel Pastoureau, "Noirs et Blancs en noir et blanc," in *Journal programme: Maghreb et Afrique noire au regard du cinéma colonial* (Paris: Institut du monde Arabe, 1994).

6. I develop an argument on the importance to French film culture of an official classicism in Charles O'Brien, "Rethinking National Cinema: Dreyer's *La passion de Jeanne d'Arc* and the Academic Aesthetic," *Cinema Journal* 35, no. 4 (1996). Issues concerning the classicism of 1930s French cinema are taken up in three new books: Dudley Andrew, *Mists of Regret: Culture and Sensibility in Classic French Film* (Princeton: Princeton University Press, 1995); Pierre Billard, *L'Âge classique du cinéma français: du cinéma parlant à la nouvelle vague* (Paris: Flammarion, 1995); and Colin Crisp, *The French Classical Cinema, 1930–1960* (Bloomington: Indiana University Press, 1994).

7.  In Michel de Certeau, "Spatial Stories," *The Practice of Everyday Life*, trans. S. Rendall (Berkeley and Los Angeles: University of California Press, 1984), 115–130.

8.  De Certeau elaborates this conception of narration with specific reference to ethnography in "Ethno-graphie, l'oralité, ou l'espace de l'autre: Léry," in *L'écriture de l'histoire* (Paris: Gallimard, 1975), 215–248.

9.  One might draw a parallel between de Certeau's distinction between place and space and the distinction between gaze and glance developed by critics from Maurice Merleau-Ponty to Norman Bryson and Gilles Deleuze. The definitive example of the gaze is the Renaissance image theorized by Leon Battista Alberti, which features architectural environments whose lines tend to imply a stable, monocular vantage point. Examples of the glance include certain of the paintings of Paul Cézanne, which offer spaces whose incomplete coherence implicates the body of a painter/viewer who is compelled to adjust his or her comportment.

10.  Among films that anticipate the Orientalism of *Pépé le Moko* is Feyder's *L'Atlantide*, which likewise defines its lost city as a mazelike female space. The link in cinéma colonial between the Orient and femininity is evident at the level of the films' credit sequences and promotional materials (e.g., posters), which emphasize female performers. On this point, see Lagny et al., "L'Afrique de l'autre," 132–133. The general issue of the feminization of the Orient in Western representations has been raised by Edward Said, in, for instance, *Orientalism* (New York: Vintage, 1979). For a survey of film examples, see the essay by Ella Shohat in the present volume.

11.  It is during the 1930s that historian Lucien Febvre, cofounder in 1929 of the journal *Annales*, begins to write a history of the senses that draws attention to the relativity of the Western tendency to privilege disembodied sight. For a survey that situates this work within diverse explorations during the interwar years of alternatives to a Cartesian conception of vision, see Martin Jay, *Downcast Eyes: The Denigration of Vision in Twentieth-Century French Thought* (Berkeley and Los Angeles: University of California Press, 1993), 34ff.

12.  Iguerbouchen had belonged to the team of Algerian filmmakers who had made *Dzaïr* (directed by André Sarrouy and Paul Saffar). A short film about the old quarters of Algiers, *Dzaïr* reportedly inspired the documentary sequence of *Pépé le Moko*. On *Dzaïr*, see Bataille and Veillot, *Caméras sous le soleil*, 63–64. Although virtually all of the documentary sequence of *Pépé le Moko* had been filmed in decors at the Pathé studios at Joinville, Duvivier's success in imitating documentary style led critics to describe the sequence as a representation of the actual Casbah. See, for instance, the review of *Pépé le Moko* in *L'humanité*, 26 February 1937.

13.  See Timothy Mitchell, *Colonizing Egypt* (Berkeley: University of California Press, 1991); and Frantz Fanon, *Les Damnées de la terre* (Paris: Editions de la Découverte, 1985).

14.  In J. Clifford, "On Ethnographic Authority," in *The Predicament of Culture: Twentieth-Century Ethnography, Literature and Art* (Cambridge, Mass.: Harvard University Press, 1988), 21–54. One result of the postwar acceptance within anthropology of relativist notions of culture was a pronounced

attention to effects of choc culturel and déculturation on both Aboriginal peoples and Western anthropologists. On this point, see Girardet, *L'Idée colonial en France*, 228–238.

15. An attention to the subversive implications of Mauss's teaching can be found in Clifford, "On Ethnographic Surrealism," 122–129.

16. In January 1939 President Edouard Daladier made a well-publicized tour of Africa, which coincided with announcements of the production and release of numerous imperialist films. Among the latter was *Unité française*, a film about Daladier's tour which several months later won a Grand Prix du cinéma français. A report on the films can be found in M. Colin-Reval, "Une Nouvelle Vedette: l'empire français," *Cinématographie Française* no. 1063 (17 March 1939): 21.

17. In Emile Vuillermoz, "Un Cas de conscience," *Cinématographie Française* no. 1032 (12 August 1938): 47–48. A translation of this piece can be found in Richard Abel, ed., *French Film Theory and Criticism: A History/Anthology, Volume II, 1929–1939* (Princeton: Princeton University Press, 1988), 250–255. By the time *L'Homme du Niger* went into production in the spring of 1939, differences between the Gabin vehicles and mainstream examples of the genre had become a focus of editorial comment. See, for instance, the satirical invocation of a hypothetical Gabin film, directed by Marcel Carné and with dialogue by Henri Jeanson, that does *not* offer a defeatist view of the empire, in Max Corre, "L'année cinématographique commence bien," *Petit-Journal* (1 January 1939): 6.

18. Although Jacques de Baroncelli reportedly elaborated the film's narrative after arriving in Africa and witnessing the work of French medical personnel, his approach is reminiscent of government-sponsored documentaries such as *Promenade en Afrique equatoriale française* (J.-K. Raymond-Millet, 1931), which likewise depicts both a major construction project (in this case, the building of a trans-Saharan railroad) and the efforts of French doctors to cure sleeping sickness.

19. In de Certeau, "Ethno-graphie, l'oralité, ou l'espace de l'autre: Léry."

20. Given the tendency of the colonial film toward stylistic excess, it is perhaps no surprise that Duvivier, among the French film industry's most eclectic stylists, worked often and definitively in the colonial genre. In addition to *Pépé le Moko* and *Cinq Gentlemen maudits*, Duvivier had directed *Maman Colibri* (1929), *La Bandera* (1935), and *Golgotha* (1935), all filmed in the Maghreb. A different though all the same related film was *Maria Chapdelaine* (1934), whose exteriors were filmed in Quebec and which was reviewed as a film about the lives of French colons in North America. Also, like *Légions d'honneur* and *L'Appel du silence*, *Maria Chapdelaine* won the Grand Prix du cinéma français.

21. One might propose that at issue in *Cinq Gentlemen maudits* is a dual-focus narration that generates meaning less through syntagma that link consecutive scenes than through parallels between alternating scenes that feature opposing characters. In *Cinq Gentlemen maudits*, however, scenes like the one I describe are not the structural equivalent of scenes featuring Western characters, a circumstance indicated by the absence of reference to

these scenes in the otherwise quite thorough plot summary made available by the film's producers. (The plot summary is among publicity materials that comprise a dossier held in the Rondel Collection of the Bibliothèque Nationale in Paris.) A colonial film with an authentic dual-focus structure is *Itto* (1934), directed by Jean Benoît-Lévy and Marie Epstein. On the notion of dual-focus narration, see Rick Altman, *The American Film Musical* (Bloomington and Indianapolis: Indiana University Press, 1987), 28–58.

22. Among landmarks that appear in the film are the Roman ruins at Volubilis, which were featured in a key exhibit of the Colonial Exposition. Concerning the exhibit, see Catherine Hodier and Michel Pierre, *L'Exposition coloniale* (Paris: Editions Complexe, 1991), 46–48.

23. Other documentaries exhibited in 1931 include *Chez de pays du buveurs du sang* (A. Gourgaud, 1930–1931) and *Promenade en Afrique equatoriale française* (J.-K. Raymond-Millet, 1931).

24. At issue was perhaps an implied comparison with the successful earlier version of *Cinq Gentlemen maudits* (Luitz-Morat, 1920), whose ethnographic moments (e.g., the depiction of the preparation of couscous in a Tunisian market) are wholly digressive. Concerning promotion of Duvivier's film, my source is the dossier referred to in note 21, which includes a brochure of *conseils de publicité*.

25. The hybrid nature of the colonial film has been a concern of the critical literature beginning with the work of Pierre Leprohon (1946), who finds the genre flawed owing to an irresolvable tension between documentary and "novelistic" aspects. (In Leprohon, *L'Exotisme et le cinéma*.) An exception that proves the rule is perhaps *Amok* (Fédor Ozep, 1934). Although technically a colonial film (the story is set in Dutch Malaysia), *Amok* was filmed entirely at Joinville (except for the final burial scene at the docks) and often goes unmentioned in studies of the genre.

26. Haïssaous also appear prominently in *La Croisière noire*. Note, for instance, the dance sequence at Zinder that occurs prior to the caravan's climactic arrival at Lake Chad. An analysis of *La Croisière noire* can be found in Dudley Andrew's contribution to this volume.

27. Rouch's *Les Maîtres fous* has attracted controversy since its first screenings. Critics have complained that the film fails to provide information that would enable an adequate understanding of its subject matter, a possession ceremony staged by the Hauka, a religious sect based in Accra, the capital city of Ghana. At issue are shocking scenes that depict animal sacrifices and other rituals of the ceremony, which are accompanied by minimal voice-over commentary. Critics of the film included Marcel Griaule, the ethnographer with whom Rouch had studied, and Ousmane Sembene, who claimed that dissatisfaction with films such as *Les Maîtres fous* had motivated his decision to become a film director. On the reception of *Les Maîtres fous*, see Paul Stoller, *The Cinematic Griot: The Ethnography of Jean Rouch* (Chicago: University of Chicago Press, 1992), 151–160. It should be noted that following *Les Maîtres fous* Rouch's work developed in a very different direction. For instance, *Chronicle of a Summer* (1961) features a

celebrated scene in which a West African student provides an ethnographic commentary on life in Paris.

28. See Girardet, *L'Idée colonial en France*, 225–251.
29. An intriguing and as yet wholly unexplored topic is the reception of Western films by the indigenous populations of colonized countries. An investigation might begin with an examination of the trade journal *Cinématographie Française*, which included regular articles and reports on exhibition in the colonies. The articles provide information on the construction of theaters (which numbered in the hundreds in the Maghreb alone), French films subtitled in Arabic for exhibition in Egypt, special admissions policies in the colonies and other topics.
30. See, for instance, Bill Ashcroft et al., *The Empire Writes Back* (London and New York: Routledge, 1989), 11–12.
31. In Francis Ramirez and Christian Rolot, "D'une Indochine l'autre," *Cinémathèque* no. 2 (November 1992): 40–55.
32. In Faulkner, "Affective Identities: French National Cinema and the 1930s."
33. As these examples suggest, references to the colonies in French films of the 1930s were by no means limited to films with colonial settings.
34. See, for instance, the remarks in Denis Hollier, "L'Adieu aux plumes," *Les Dépossédés* (Paris: Editions de minuit, 1993), 189.
35. "The most slavic of French actors," Baur gave definitive performances in films such as *David Golder* (1930) and *Le Golem* (1935), both directed by Duvivier. In fact, Baur's part as a wealthy colon in *Cinq Gentlemen maudits* prefigures his role in *Les Hommes nouveaux*.
36. Francen had played the roles of patriots and prophets in films such as *Fin du monde* (Abel Gance, 1931), *J'Accuse* (Gance, 1938), *Feu!* (Jacques de Baroncelli, 1935), *L'Aventurier* (Marcel L'Herbier, 1934), and *Veille d'armes* (L'Herbier, 1935).
37. In Daniel Rivet, "Les Batisseurs d'empire," in Pascal Blanchard and Arnelle Chatelier, eds., *Images et colonies* (Paris: Syroc/Association connaissance de l'histoire de l'Afrique contemporaine, 1993), 67–72.
38. In Girardet, *L'Idée colonial en France*, 179–180.
39. In Homi K. Bhabha, "The Other Question: Stereotype, Discrimination and the Discourses of Colonialism," in *The Location of Culture* (London and New York: Routledge, 1994), 70.
40. Comparisons between the cinéma colonial and Hollywood genres can be found in Megherbi, *Les Algériens au miroir du cinéma colonial*, 196, 250–251; Boulanger, *Le Cinéma colonial*, 109, 128–131; Leprohon, *L'exotisme et le cinéma*, 251–255; Bataille and Veillot, *Caméras sous le soleil*, 37, 64–67; and Sorlin, "The Fanciful Empire," 148. Such comparisons date from the 1920s. See, for instance, the excerpts from film reviews in Cade, "De la casquette du père Bugeaud aux moustaches du Maréchal Lyautey," 5–10.
41. In Lagny et al., "L'Afrique de l'autre," 142.
42. See, for instance, the discussion of the figure of the Tupis in the writings of Jean de Léry, in de Certeau, "Ethno-graphie, l'oralité, ou l'espace de l'autre: Léry," 241–246.

43. *Cinq Gentlemen maudits* thus precedes by two years Marcel Pagnol's famous experiments in location filmmaking in *Jofroi* (1933).
44. Hollywood films set in North Africa had been a target of criticism in the French press throughout the interwar period. For an example that focuses on the Gary Cooper films, see Jean Dumas, "Quand dira-t-on enfin au cinéma la vérité sur la légion?" *Cinémonde* 4, no. 117 (1931): 40, 44.
45. My sense of the applicability of the notion of abjection to the cinéma colonial is inspired by conversations with Janette Bayles, who takes up related questions in a dissertation on poetic realist cinema.
46. A topic that lies beyond the scope of this essay is the production of films in the Maghreb by indigenous filmmakers during the interwar years. Tunisia seems to have been a center for such activity. A discussion of key films such as *Aïn-el-ghezal* (Albert Samama, 1924) and *Fou de Kairouan* (J. A. Creuzi, 1939) can be found in Omar Khlifi, *L'Histoire du cinéma en Tunisie* (Tunis: Société Tunisienne de Diffusion, 1970), 52–55, 66–91, and 113–122.
47. Themes of geographical and cultural displacement are suggested more strongly in the film's original title: *La Noire de. . . .*
48. In Ramirez and Rolot, "D'une Indochine l'autre."

Dudley Andrew

# Praying Mantis: Enchantment and Violence in French Cinema of the Exotic

## At One with the Other

The promise of the exotic is among the clearest distinguishing traits of cinema's appeal, the trait that most cleanly separates the medium from theater. And while the exotic can be quickly domesticated into the picturesque, the agreeably tame pet made of a foreign spectacle, there remains a need—feigned or authentic—for the genuinely foreign. Hence the commercial possibilities that tempt every ethnographic filmmaker. Evidently the cinematic eye, that remarkable prosthesis produced by science for science, behaves first like an organ of penetration and then one of ingestion. In this essay, I measure the extent of this peculiar drive as it affected the cinematic culture of interwar France from the right-wing extreme of Léon Poirier's African documentaries to the surrealist "documents" surrounding Luis Buñuel.[1]

Poirier and Buñuel, all of whose films were funded in extraordinary fashion, flank an ample genre of ordinary French films known as the *cinéma colonial*, which staged dramas of penetration and ingestion in quite standard fashion from 1920 to the Second World War. Its tales of alluring women and an ungovernable Africa are familiar in the cinema; they might be said to be a kind of norm, and they are all too easy to read. This is not to say that the cinema set out to deliver a certain Africa to a gullible metropolitan populace; rather cinema used Africa as it used all topics, to further its own expansion as modernity's dominant purveyor of information, attitudes, entertainment, and consensus.

Before anything like an ethnographic film expedition entered Africa, Jacques Feyder had invested the continent with the mythical values every future film would need to deal with. He was the man "who dared" to shoot *L'Atlantide* on location in southern Algeria in 1920. Consuming a year's effort and a fortune, this adaptation of the Pierre Benoit best-seller captured the biggest audience of the time in France and was an international hit of astounding proportions.[2] Its fanciful adventure brought some of France's most popular stars into the desert to the lost city of Atlantis (recreated in Algerian studios, since Feyder insisted on keeping himself and his cast and crew distant from the metropole throughout the lengthy production). Feyder set great store by the location shooting, which he was certain would renew audience fervor for what was in fact a conventional love story, since the cinematography could raise and satisfy another audience need, that of the exotic. This film would be remade often (and notably by G. W. Pabst in 1932); more important its formula would govern a host of films in the 1930s, quintessentially in Julien Duvivier's *La Bandera* (1935). Adapted from a novel by Pierre Mac Orlan,[3] *La Bandera*, like many lesser examples, folded unfamiliar icons and an exciting landscape into a sweet dough of studio work and dramatic artifice, leavened by stars. Unlike the pure ethnographic film, and unlike the hybrid docudramas that gave their geography independent status, the fictions of the cinéma colonial sought to erase the line between the genres so as to produce a homogeneous experience, the experience of classic fiction films.

In fact the Moroccan setting of *La Bandera* is incidental to its psychological plot, and the authenticity of its decor was not really what excited critics. *La Bandera* was praised most for its unity of expression. André Lang writes of the life blood flowing through the six hundred cells of its decoupage.[4] Graham Greene writes of the fluid camera that unites atmosphere with acute moral drama.[5] The film's driving theme is nothing other than integration, a search for personal wholeness through the device of the Conradian double, a search for social fusion in the Foreign Legion, finally achieved only as the brigade is being decimated. *La Bandera* lashes its mesmerized spectator to its hero, as he is tracked by an implacable fatality from Paris to Barcelona into Morocco and deeper still into the Rif Mountains. A common myth of spiritual regeneration in Africa here joins the film's disturbing ideology of brotherhood in the Foreign Legion, where pasts are forgotten and the future belongs to those who give the orders, in this case Francisco Franco.[6]

*La Bandera* (quite like Feyder's *Le Grand Jeu* that preceded it by a year) figures Africa as a lawless, anonymous zone but also as a female body whose contours are veiled; but something larger than law, something like fate, traps those who think to race across its sands or hide in

its unmappable redoubts. In the absence of markers or of distinguishing features, the Foreign Legion cuts roads into the landscape, tattoo-
ing it just as the lovers tattoo themselves to etch visible boundaries of
behavior. This eroticized space, utterly mythological, nevertheless appeared authentic to the French. An article in *Pour Vous* entitled "Le
Visage d'Islam, fidelement refleté par le cinéma français, travesti par
Hollywood," features Annabella from *La Bandera* in her carefully researched berber costume.[7]

But of course it is Annabella, not a berber, playing the courtesan.
She speaks perfect French, learned, she explains, from all the French
men who have passed through her room. When she and her costar,
Jean Gabin, suck each other's blood in a wedding ritual taken from the
Foreign Legion, audiences are not shocked by the mixture. The religious and racial difference coded in Annabella's costume and gestures
depends on and doubles the ordinary power of sexual difference that is
the cornerstone of French and world feature filmmaking. The Otherness of North Africa is after all merely a woman to romance and to
make one's own. The promise of the exotic that these films tender extends, but does not rewrite, the usual promise of an hypnotic experience that fiction films have always advertised.[8] And the African terrain
is nothing other than a double of the flesh of the female star. To die in
the Sahara is to die in a lover's arms, to die deliciously, picturesquely,
and in what must be called cinematographic comfort.

In contrast, the ethnographic enterprise is generally conceived to be
uncomfortable in the extreme; physically uncomfortable for those who
undertake long journeys equipped with few amenities, socially uncomfortable in their rude confrontation with unknown foods and customs,
and spiritually uncomfortable in the discovery of disturbingly opposed
worldviews. Léon Poirier turned to ethnographic cinema because, re-
turning from the Great War, he found the theater far too comfortable
and therefore far too false. Life was larger than the stage, and when
the cinema rose to the challenge of life's grandeur, both profited.
*L'Atlantide* proved him right, and he determined to push Gaumont, the
company over which he governed production, out of the studios and
into places that would be fascinating to look at.

Poirier must be described as a grandiose overreacher in the same
mold as Abel Gance (Figure 1). Romantic and old-fashioned in their
patriotism and heroic aspirations, they nevertheless channeled their
ambitions in ways that gushed through the dams of cinematic conven-
tion and contributed to the future of the art. When the studios began
to appear as mere copies of the hated stage, Poirier went into the mountains with his camera, shooting two films based on Lamartine's *Jocelyn*
(1923). As in his African films a few years later, Poirier's camera ca-

Figure 1.
Léon Poirier
surveying Af-
rica in 1925.

ressed the Alpine terrain, letting the scenery impress itself directly onto the celluloid image. No matter that Lamartine's sinuous verse was muted by the silent screen, Poirier promised to be faithful to the poet's belief in the soul as another form of silent screen on which nature could project its radiance. Under the spell of his title character, he approached the Alps with the longing and respect one gives a woman one admires.[9] His modest, Franciscan style relied on extreme longshots, as though he wanted the pinhole of the camera's iris to gather to it light from every corner of the most extensive possible field of view. His spiritual ambitions were borderless, as was his faith in the power of cinema to provide the oceanic fantasy representing the sublime. How small the camera lens, how vast the light it gathers into focus; just like the human soul, humble yet capable of being majestically filled.

Did the exciting prospects standing before cinema in the early 1920s give to Poirier the inflated sense of the providential that governed his life afterward? He ever associated cinema with expansion: spiritual, geographic, artistic expansion. He was planning immense projects even before he agreed in 1924 to participate in *La Croisière noire*, the trek from Algeria to Madagascar sponsored by Citroën to show off their half-track vehicles. *Jacob's Well* was to have been a tale of Christ set in the rugged hills of Palestine.[10] Poirier lashed his own tortuous moral journey to this script, believing that completion of the film would bring to an end his crippling religious doubts. But the film would not be completed, could not even begin, and the problems in financing and logistics that arose affected his health. Out of a need to relieve his religious anguish, he accepted the unexpected adventure Citroën proposed. He pushed aside his few reservations about the commercialism of the venture, recalling that although Robert Flaherty had been working for the Revillon fur company, the images of *Nanook of the North* (1921) went far beyond the commercial and even the scientific. He had a premonition that Africa would seize him, would lift him onto a plateau above the fog in which he had been dwelling. His devout wife assured him that on the African journey he would find the pure water needed to fill *Jacob's Well*. His mother blessed him on the forehead and ritualistically lit candles as he departed.

*La Croisière noire* (which premiered in 1926) hardly bears witness to the profound spiritual wholeness its director found en route. Like most ethnographic diary films, it lurches from location to location, grabbing extended picture postcards of the people and terrain, and interspersing these with the tale of the trek, anecdotes of dangers or logistical obstacles encountered and somehow overcome (Figure 2). True, Poirier does work to express the physical and spiritual majesty of a native dance by slipping into slow motion. He comes in for extreme close-ups of women with shaped hair or whose facial features had been altered, turning them into sculpture, into bronzes. This is an Africa to be possessed, wrote the young Marcel Carné in reviewing the film as wild and cannibalistic.

But for all the attention he devotes to the mystery of human behavior and religious ritual, it was the dark continent rather than the dark people who cured Poirier's angst. More correctly, it was a sacred light in the darkness that poured over his parched soul. He details an incident early in the journey, when he became separated from his comrades in the mountains of Algeria. Terrified in the utter pitch of a Saharan midnight, he was startled by eerie light emanating from a nearby peak. As it turned out, Poirier was witness to a phosphorescence that the rocks of these mountains sometimes release. The scien-

Figure 2.
Ploughing
through a
continent in
1925.

tific explanation, however, would never account for the power of that
light in his mind. This was his burning bush, and North Africa would
ever after be sacred ground to him. He would associate it with cinema,
with sound and light, this "Appel du silence."[11]

Touched in the mountains, Poirier returned to chronicle the Citroën
expedition with special fervor. He found the native dances and the
esoterica of the shamans to be powerful expressions answering the same
needs he was certain all but the most jaded European also felt. Christianity sublimated into a more blessed form precisely the same human

urges native African peoples dealt with through their rites, including cannibalism. Poirier, who advised André Gide before the famous "Voyage au Congo," felt Gide's patronizing bemusement in the face of native rituals to be obscene. Gide could never put aside his European self-assurance and sink into the sensibility ruling the lands just beyond the banks of the river his boat floated along.[12]

Here lies a tension, even a contradiction, haunting ethnographic cinema, or at least that species of it Poirier represented. The ethnographic cineaste must literally drive deep into the foreign, pushing forward with the might of machinery even though his goal may be to capture an otherness—often a stillness—where machinery and drive are literally out of place. Poirier recognized this as pure difference, not as contradiction:

> The world is a wheel. Those of us in the west are on its outside thrown by a centrifugal force in a ceaseless movement, condemned by an agitation that often vainly conducts us to death without ever giving us time to comprehend why in truth we are agitated. At the center, on the other hand, is the orient whose people, attracted by a centripetal force, tend with all their being toward the immobility of the interior life.[13]

Poirier found himself agitated enough to plow through an entire continent seeking to capture what he knew only stillness could provide. The tension is evident in the way *La Croisière noire* bifurcates its focus between the arduous journey and the strange land journeyed through. This is the tension of colonialism itself, as it was displayed at the Colonial Exposition in Paris in 1931: the pavilions of colonized cultures (lit up by the limitless electrical power pouring into the Bois de Vincennes) encircled a central metropolitan pavilion featuring technologies of progress. Poirier evidently believed that a certain parity could be reached between centrifugal and centripetal cultures. The West's light, created through huge generators, could be projected to illuminate the Orient, while the Orient in turn could serve as a reservoir of spiritual energy for which the phosphorescent Saharan rocks stand as a symbol.

Poirier set out to tap that reservoir in his most famous film, *L'Appel du silence* (1936). One cannot underestimate the significance of this biography of Charles de Foucauld, the legendary Catholic hermit of the Sahara, whom Poirier actually referred to as "a veritable accumulator of spiritual energy."[14] His oriental sanctity attracted attention because it followed upon his earlier life as a dashing military figure and a rake. Penetrating the Sahara as a cavalryman before the turn of the century, he represented the centrifugal West, the West of *La Croisière noire* and of the Dakar-Djibouti expedition, the west of searching rather than becoming. Only later did he find himself seduced by the God that he, anticipating Poirier, found in the stillness of the sands and rugged mountains where he built the little hut that French schoolchildren of the time heard so much about. At the onset of World War I he was murdered by native insurgents, and his fame instantly spread.

The second highest grossing picture of 1936, *L'Appel du silence* outdistanced at the box office all other 124 films made that year, except for Marcel Pagnol's *César*. More than a popular hit, it was from the first a special project that received serious and exceptional attention; it garnered the prestigious Grand Prix du cinéma given out after Christmas. *L'Appel du silence* even today carries a cult value for a fringe of the French right. At a key moment in France's conquest of North Africa, Père de Foucauld was approached by his former military acquaintances, among whom was General Lyautey,[15] to make contacts with the local people so as "to help establish French peace in the region."[16] Inspired by La Patrie and La Foi, *L'Appel du silence* explicitly follows what Poirier called "that French line leading through the Church."[17] It stretches that line out to the larger world beyond French borders where other values must be recognized and "lined up" in an imperial perspective.

In the speech he wrote to raise funds for the film, Poirier didn't shrink from mentioning that he had personally shared his enthusiasm for Charles de Foucauld with General de la Rocque.[18] *L'Appel du silence* was redistributed in 1943 because it was, according to the journal *Le Film*, "a work of art of highest moral and spiritual standards concerning a pioneer of French colonization in North Africa and which takes on special and deep significance given today's circumstances."[19] In describing the 1943 gala, attended by Marechal Petain's cabinet chief, by generals, rectors, and the heads of many religious orders, *Le Film* used the opportunity to praise Charles de Foucauld's closest friend, General de Laperrine, for his heroic penetration of the south Sahara. Poirier had specifically cited his hero for having "accompanied the military in its pursuit of the rezzous, sharing the dangers of combat . . . [during which] he rediscovered one of his old friends just come into this region to write one of the most beautiful pages of the expansion of the genius of our race: Marshal Lyautey."[20]

Let Charles de Foucauld represent the fusion of the military and the religious; he stands for the undying impulse of the West as it invades the unknown in expectation of a revelation unavailable at home. The hybrid nature of such a quest (invasion and absorption) would seem to mock the rhetoric of majestic synthesis that was on the lips of so many officials. A parallel hybridity mocks the promise of films like Poirier's to provide a unified hypnotic experience (absorption) while penetrating new and exotic lands. One imagines that the unfamiliar, by definition, must disturb a movie's forward motion along conventional rails, fracturing its wholeness. This at least would be Buñuel's view and his aesthetic.

In relation to film genres, the ethnographic stands as both foreign and familiar. It comprises a foreign—in fact redundantly foreign—cinematic enterprise that in varying degrees upsets expectations and is designed to do so. But this also is a familiar enterprise, since every genre runs forward on the energy supplied by some measure of novelty and difference. The ethnographic, promising substantial difference, upsets those films that enlist it. In quite distinct ways something like the ethnographic must be said to run through films of serious social scientific intent, through travelogues like *La Croisière noire*, through hybrid melodramas set in exotic locations, and even through pure fiction films (*La Bandera* has been our example), shot primarily in Western studios, that recruit motifs and backdrops from the unknown world to heighten their effect.

This economy announces itself openly in hybrid films, like docudramas, where fiction masks as travelogue, or where scientific research reaches for visual poetry. The hybrid, as its designation suggests, addresses the spectator ambivalently. In the late 1920s and early 1930s a large number of fiction films incorporating African motifs aimed to draw at least two different types of audience.[21] Poirier's 1930 *Caïn* grafts a simple melodrama onto a backdrop of Madagascar with interludes of documentary footage showing untamed animals, bare-breasted native women, and evocative topography. Poirier believed that the power of documentary—of the document—if not directly apprehensible as in *La Croisière noire*, could register its effects on characters in fictionalized situations. The extremity of exotic situations would in turn justify the melodramatic excesses of plot. He expected a spiral to develop whereby the constructed excitement of the fiction would be provoked by the stimulus of the location on which it was set and would in turn open the audience to the phosphorescent luminosity of that location. He aimed at a single transcendent effect all the more powerful for being grounded in the sacred land of Africa. But this effect would always be blunted by the hybrid nature of the genre. Even the fascist critics who fawned over *L'Appel du silence* panned the studio scenes, which were nevertheless required to set up the mystical sequences in the Hoggar Mountains.[22]

Any survey of the uses of the ethnographic in cinema will tell a debilitating story. In fact it is a tale of entropy hardly different at all from the colonialism that spawns it. If the ethnographic film is to take advantage of the fortuitous and the bizarre, if it is to shock us with a temporality far different from our own, we will need to be suspended between our world—what makes sense in life and in movies as we know both—and the world the filmmakers claim to be revealing in its own terms. Yet to the extent that the Otherness of the Orient or of Africa is employed in Western films, either to deliver an experience not available in the West or to fuel tired western fictional genres, the difference between the West and its other must decrease. Pierre Mac Orlan's review of *La Croisière noire* hails the film not for its stunningly novel subject matter but for quite the opposite, for its "singularly nostalgic atmosphere."[23] Nostalgia should hardly be associated with an ethnographic encounter, yet nostalgia may be precisely what Poirier was after in his attempt to provide for thousands of spectators his experience not of the difference of Africans but of cosmic fusion in the Hoggar Mountains.

Poirier next turned to fiction, indeed to the union of a Frenchman and a Malagasy, in *Caïn*, so as to increase the chance of affecting spectators by means of Africa's landscape. His actress, Rama Tahé, although born in Madagascar, had spent all but a few years of her life in Paris. When interviewed by Robert Roy about her role, she was found "at her home in a graceful bourgeois room, seated at an open piano playing an old French song. . . . Delicate and white, she could be taken for a European."[24]

Is the lesson clear? At base even the most rigorous forms of ethnographic cinema in the early years tend to domesticate the mysterious, to make the African woman European, or to make the mystery of Africa serve common European spiritual and erotic longings. This "entropy" where differences are progressively lessened occurs generically as well. The document and fiction are conflated just as are Africa and the female. The land becomes a woman, and achievement of both in a hybrid form becomes a spiritual achievement that has no locality save in the realm of ideology. Thus ethnographic films and standard entertainment fare effectively work in concert, subduing the threat at the outside, or better, as in the exposition of 1931, bringing what is outside inside where it could be appreciated in the proper light and in the relative comfort of a train ride around little lac Daumesnil in the Bois de Vincennes.[25] The cinéma colonial offers just another ersatz journey and one with a conventional terminus: the marriage of Gabin and Annabella, of Caïn and his Malagasy woman. These marriages are equivalent to those of Charles de Foucauld and the Sahara, or of Lyautey and Morocco; all may be taken as variants of a satisfying conquest in which both parties find their fulfillment.

## The Other of the Other

Luis Buñuel, as you might expect, loathed the Colonial Exposition and supported his surrealist friends by staging not just a boycott, but a counterexhibit to display what I call "the Other of the Other." Their protest overtly attacked the patronizing use of colonized cultures; more pertinent to their own agenda, they protested the entropy this exposition signaled and hastened: the lessening of difference, the familiarization with the Other, its aestheticization and consequent banalization.

To maintain or strengthen the spiritual forcefield, the surrealists determined to behave as they thought ethnographers do: they de-aestheticized objects of contemplation and contemplated any object whatever. In *Naissance du cinéma*, written before *La Croisière noire* had been seen, Léon Moussinac already had carved out a specific category of *films documentaires*, although this word would not show up in English until years later.[26] About half the twenty titles he lists are records of journeys into exotic lands, including *Nanook*, but also *Chez les Anthropophages* (1921), *Au coeur de l'Afrique sauvage* (1923), and *En Afrique Equatoriale* (1923). The second subcategory one can pull from his list are documentaries on fascinating natural processes such as *La Germination des plantes* and *La Formation des cristaux*.[27] These two types of documentaries seem specifically concocted to satisfy the taste of surrealists and their associates, those people who in 1929 and 1930 would be reading or contributing to Georges Bataille's scandalous journal aptly named *Documents*, an avant-garde periodical full of bizarre photos and articles.[28]

Surrealist taste is in fact an oxymoron, for the document, as opposed to the art object, fascinates by remaining obtuse, by refusing assimilation to the viewer's tastes and norms. The document can be any object whatever, which, when cut off from its context, appeals to the viewer who, like the ethnographer, has learned to suspend judgment about its function, short-circuiting every attempt to place or rationalize it. In isolation or in unusual contexts, the object is able to release its material power, since it is no longer forced to serve some presumed system to which it is putatively connected, a system that can only limit and discipline it for some questionable higher purpose. This is the power of the scorpion seen in immense close-up at the outset of Buñuel's *L'Age d'or* (1930), the scorpion with the tail broken into five prismatic articulations capped by a final articulation, a vessel holding deadly venom (Figure 3).

The processes of cutting, enlarging, and splicing were part of the explicit formula of the journal *Documents* and of the films of Buñuel. When Jacques Bruinius[29] writes about the latter, he implicitly opposes the surrealist approach to that of Poirier for whom the extreme long shot was the cornerstone of a style that respected natural vision and spatial contiguity. The physical distance Poirier's camera maintains from the amazing and exotic material he goes in search of, not to mention the fictions within which he came to frame this material, serve as pro-

Figure 3. Prelude to *L'Age d'or*, the scorpion's tail.

phylactics against any sensual power that might leap like static electricity from the foreign onto the screen. To use the categories Walter Benjamin would develop in 1936 (and in explicit relation to Poirier's compatriot, Abel Gance), Poirier was a magician, an artist of the old school, standing back in awe of the aura of what lay before him, integrating the spectator while uplifting him via the strange body of life spread out in spectacle. Buñuel, on the other hand, was the surgeon whose camera penetrates the bodies of foreign organisms.[30]

Like Bataille, Michel Leiris, and Roger Caillois, Buñuel was drawn to self-exploration through the study of bizarre rites and foreign peoples. One finds in his films, as one does in the journals *Documents* and *Minotaure*, a reverence for the power of primitive artifacts to confront us with the inexplicable. At the same time he openly aims to outrage those, like Poirier and his spectators, who bask in the comfort of their beliefs and privileged lifestyles. The shock of the very first scene of his first film, the notorious eye slashing of *Un Chien andalou* (1928), deliberately turns the fat stomachs of the bourgeoisie and cuts the threads that make up the delicate web of their precious subjectivity. But at the same time, such violence respects the power of human and inhuman urges. The blood that bursts from Gaston Modot's eye as he swells in sexual passion in *L'Age d'or* serves as an offering to the gods of primitive sexuality, while besmirching the cultured people who sit quietly nearby listening to a performance of Wagner's *Liebestod*.

Wagner may express the force of primitive urges that lie beneath every civilized effort. Recall that in the second part of *L'Age d'or*, the founding of the imperial city by the "Majorcans," an elaborate official ceremony (the laying of the first stone) is interrupted by the bestial copulation of two humans in the mud nearby. Satirized here are films like Flaherty's *Moana* (1926) and Poirier's *Caïn* which discover the primordial force of the universe in the purity of erotic attraction outside the compromises of civilization. Instead of long panorama shots that sing a comforting idyll of nature's fertility, Buñuel's prologue to *L'Age d'or* prepares another, crueler view of nature—including human nature: in graphic close-up the scorpion attacks an unwitting rat.

In the atmosphere of "ethnographic surrealism" prevailing in the avant-garde at the time, Buñuel broke all rules in filming the disturbing *Las Hurdes*, shot in 1932 by Eli Lotar, whose photographs appear throughout *Documents*. The incongruity of this film's narration and its perverse obsession with the ugly facts of existence in the western Spanish highlands mock the humanism at play in virtually all ethnographic films. Buñuel finds nothing beautiful or universal in his subject, certainly no "family of man." Perhaps he wants difference to remain repugnant, lest we ingest and assimilate it; as Jim Lastra has noted, "the Hurdinos are the Big Toe of Spain."[31] Useless, obtuse, they are cut off in the mountains by history, unconnected to other people and, Buñuel hints, to any overriding conception of the human race. By an operation of subtraction the Hurdinos force us to recalculate what it is to be human. Buñuel's most important discovery on this ethnographic adventure is in fact a negative discovery: the Hurdinos have no oral culture, no songs for the sentimental tourist or social scientist to carry back.

It seems hardly remarkable to stand Buñuel once more against the establishment, against bourgeois morality and cinematography. Hardly remarkable, that is, until one looks closer at the alternative that surrealism proposes. We may stand aghast at the clichés of the mysterious dark continent brought to us in standard fiction films like *La Bandera* and in standard ethnographic ones like *La Croisiere noire*, but surrealism for its part propounded a doctrine of *l'amour fou*, of the mysterious woman (*Nadja*, the most famous avatar) lain across urban spaces traversed by shiftless men. Add to this the doctrine of communicating vases which, like l'amour fou, suggests a loss of self through ingestion

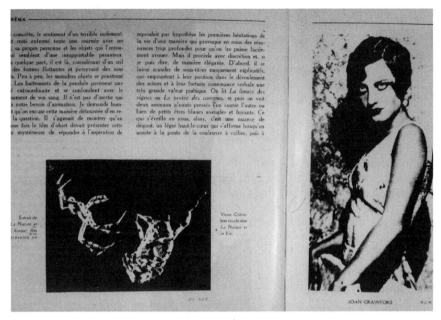

Figure 4. *La Révue du Cinéma* no. 2 (1929): Joan Crawford and erotic predation.

or consumption. One recent article sums up this impulse in its title: "Swallowing Dali"; it is a study of such paintings as *Object Cannibalism, Autumnal Cannibalism,* and *Sacrament of the Last Supper.*[32]

In Benjamin's terms, surrealism served contradictory roles as magician and as surgeon, and it did so in the triple contexts of exploration of the exotic, desire and fear of the female body, and incorporation by eating, being eaten, and spitting out. Even the rather trendy journal *La Révue du Cinéma* showed how far the surrealist and the "documentarist" approach had reached into the culture.[33] In its very first issue and in an article titled "Le Cinéma et l'amour," Jacques Brunius, writing from Dakar, attacked both middle-class love (singing instead about "L'Amour chez les animaux") and the picturesque.[34]

The second issue contains Louis Chavance's strange and emblematic meditation on "Le Symbol du sang."[35] Triggered by an UFA short about the life of minute organisms called "La Nature et l'amour," which he curiously relates to Flaherty's *Moana,* Chavance insists on the untapped emotional power locked within the inhuman (Figure 4). Almost like Bataille, he writes of this film:

Things and beings on the lowest animal level shape themselves to our most secret longings, the longings of our senses. . . . One sees two sticky animals

pressing up against each other. . . . What this awakes in us, is a hint of disgust, that slight rising of the gorge that we feel as we watch a viper lay its
white eggs, then watch enlarged eggs open and tiny black ribbons slither
out, gleaming with slime. . . . The best part is the beginning, the most primitive phase when amoeba and groups of cells take on ambiguous shapes. It
will make some spectators blush, but each of us is free in the interior of our
own souls [to imagine what we please].[36]

Chavance then exposes his interior soul, imagining another film with
an erotic lure much stronger than that of Joan Crawford:

It's the idea of a film in color made completely about blood, about a flood of
blood, jets of blood.[37] I see a man distracted as he crosses the street. Suddenly his glance meets that of a very beautiful woman who is in a car parked
along the sidewalk. He can't take his eyes from hers. An automobile looms
up and runs him down. At that instant, blood is let loose everywhere, in the
slaughterhouses, in the hospitals, on the sidewalks. We are in the room of a
woman giving birth where the whiteness of the clinic dominates. . . . Then
one notices in the corner a pile of laundry soiled with blood.[38]

Chavance's hallucination goes farther than I would have dared by relating the "erotic" attraction of Flaherty's documentaries to the abject
and repulsive associations of a woman's body: the contamination of
the white screen with red—blood in a pile of soiled sheets.

A year later, the same journal ran a remarkable and disturbing lead
article on "The Surgical Film" (Figure 5). In a paratactic staccato, Paul
Sablon observed:

I saw the most terrible operation a woman is made to undergo, a hysterec-
tomy. . . . A mask covering the beard. White coats. The stomach smeared
with iodine. The suffocating odor of ether. And suddenly the operation shroud
kept closed on the sides with pincers, with a slit marking the place where
the scalpel will penetrate. The stomach is opened, the moment of apprehension, the skin pulled back, the interior organs appear with their mysterious
precision. . . . A large steel plate introduced inside the opening to keep the
the lower organs in place. The blood that an assistant washes away with
large tampons has no importance at all. No need to "frame" all this. It's only
at the end of the operation that I had the idea to look at the face of the
young woman lying face down, being given chloroform constantly by a nurse.
A young working girl not very pretty, her nose dilated, her mouth deformed
by the hiccups continually bringing up white phlegm. All my passionate attention is saved for the interior of the black square in the white sheet whose
border little by little reddens with blood.[39]

Sablon, as though speaking in the name of ethnographic surrealism,
finds a perverse poetry in suffering. But who is it that suffers so as to
generate the poetic? A woman, and not a comely one, but a working
girl whose body is being worked over:

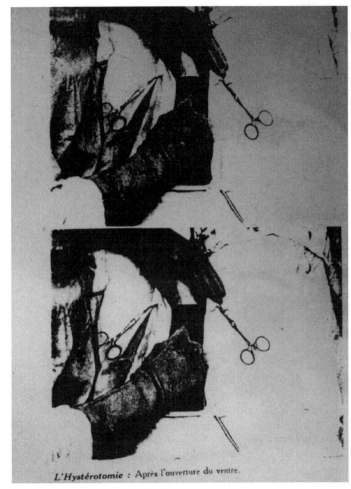

Figure 5.
*La Révue du Cinéma* no. 8
(1930): "The
Surgical
Film."

*L'Hystérotomie* : Après l'ouverture du ventre.

There is no reason that a realist film should not afterwards appear poetic, waking a revolt more irremediable—even more efficacious—than a purely dreamlike film. A certain exactitude often goes deeper than does the imagination. You can reproach such a film for being impoverished, monotonous, empty of properly cinematic inventions. But it can be so laden with suffering and with blood, so close to the earth in the instincts that it calls up, that one should never reproach its realist drive.[40]

This last sentence could have been written by Léon Poirier, for whom even the impoverished ethnographic film provides through its realism the trigger for transcendence and hallucination, a transcendence also sought, though in a different register, by the surrealists. Though opposed

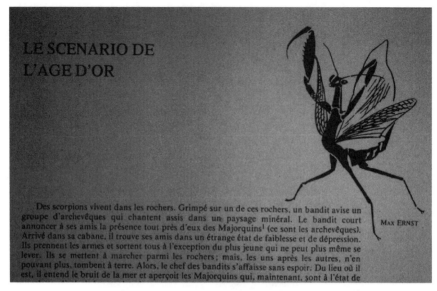

Figure 6. Max Ernst's *Praying Mantis* (1930).

in ideology, aesthetics, and politics, the surrealists and the likes of
Poirier shared a belief in the power of woman, be it the Virgin Mary or
the ugly working girl. Submitting to the spectacle of her engulfing
wholeness or to that of her terrifying fragmentation—her body parts—
the mind of the cinema was in search of the sublime. The fear and the
attraction of Africa, the fears of its attraction, were fears of the feminine that the surrealists were fond of representing in their countless
pictures of "the praying mantis,"[41] the most pertinent version of which
Max Ernst designed for the program of Buñuel's *L'Age d'or* (Figure 6).

The Praying Mantis remains a most vivid image of the Hegelian view
that dominated French thought in the early 1930s. It stands also for
ethnography's peculiarly self-destructive mission, an ultimate loss of
self in something greater: in the communicating vases, in l'Amour fou,
in la Plus Grande France, or in a communion of all races and religions
in some phosphorescent glow. While the surrealists practiced textual
strategies of cutting off the object, cutting it, presenting it enormously
enlarged, unrecognizeable (so to protect themselves from received ideas
of female beauty or from the palatable reception of bizarre, "oriental"
phenomena), such defamiliarization amounts to a fetish. In the milieu
of Dali's *Great Masturbator*, the taste for the fragment constitutes a perverse meditation on the female and the Oriental, where the anxiety produced by difference conjures pictures of kinky violence.[42] Images of the

Foreign Legion in combat and in harems might follow from this, bringing us right back to the cinéma colonial and all that the surrealists claimed to have abhorred.

In this article I have scanned the Parisian cultural landscape from right to left in the interwar years so as to establish the appeal, uniformly and across ideological divisions, of the exotic, particularly as seen in the often linked images of women and of Africa. And I have done so in part to chastise a congenitally self-righteous left wing. One radical figure who understood and later repudiated the presumption of his surrealist interest in Africa was Michel Leiris, the secretary who wrote up the Dakar-Djibouti expedition (as well as his own dream life). Leiris showed himself sensitive to the contradictory ethics of ethnographic surrealism even in its heyday.

To take a case in point, in 1933 he retracted his initially wild discussion of King Vidor's *Hallelujah*, a film championed by the Parisian intellectuals as presenting primitiveness in all its sublimity.[43] After the Colonial Exposition (including the surrealist counterexposition), after the expedition through Africa, and after the growth of a culture industry of Africanisms that followed these events, Leiris found his first reactions to the film self-serving and demeaning. In the second half of the 1930s he showed himself a frequent critic of those who would use "primitive cultures" for their own agendas. Later still, after World War II, Leiris would contribute importantly to a far more sophisticated and morally responsible ethnography.[44] But the enchantment over Otherness that he initially shared not just with his counterculture companions at the Collège de Sociologie, like Georges Bataille and Roger Caillois, but with Europeans from right to left on the political spectrum, reminds us how powerful images can be, how powerful and how oblivious to the consequences those images hold for those who are represented.

Poirier's respect for Africa and its peoples led him to participate directly in a colonial enterprise he believed was in everyone's best interests. On the other extreme, the surrealists, I have argued, together with many utterly anticolonialist fellow travelers, likewise made use of Africans as they did of women. It would take a series of intellectuals—Leiris among them, but also Jean-Paul Sartre, Frantz Fanon, and today Gayatri Spivak, Homi Bhabha, Robert Young, and many more—to expose the cruelties that so often follow what amounts to an essentializing of a people or a gender, no matter what the intention.

Some would charge that the politically correct "homage to difference" that the anticolonialists paraded between the wars masked what was in effect a "homage to violence," since difference leads inevitably to energy expended. As the politics in those prewar days sharpened its focus on the crisis of French identity and the greater crisis of French virility, the consequences of images of "difference" and of "violence" proved increasingly dangerous.[45] World War II would soon alter the terms of difference and would turn up the energy levels until a violence was expended that no one could have imagined, and that remains unimaginable even today.

## Notes

1. This essay was originally prepared for an excellent symposium, "L'Autre et le sacré," held in London in the fall of 1993. The proceedings of that symposium, including a French version of this essay, are gathered in Christopher Thompson, ed., *L'Autre et le sacré* (Paris: L'Harmattan, 1995). This volume contains a number of pieces on Michel Leiris, Georges Bataille, and other figures relevant to my discussion. Some of the paragraphs on *La Bandera* also appear in my *Mists of Regret: Culture and Sensibility in Classic French Film* (Princeton: Princeton University Press, 1995).
2. For details of its production and exhibition, see especially Henri Fescourt, *La Foi et les montagnes* (Paris: Paul Montel, 1959), 271–273.
3. Mac Orlan, a popular literary figure, would also be responsible for *Le Quai des brumes*, which became a film in 1938.
4. André Lang, in *Pour Vous* 357 (19 September 1935): 6.
5. Graham Greene, review of *La Bandera* in *The Spectator*, 6 December 1935.
6. The film was in fact dedicated to Franco, who supplied the production with costumes and extras when the French military refused to do so.
7. *Pour Vous* 494 (4 May 1938): 8–9.
8. For a slightly different view concerning this assertion, see Charles O'Brien's essay in this volume.
9. For a consideration of Poirier's early career, see Fescourt, *La Foi et les montagnes*, 319–326.
10. Poirier discusses his career in the aptly titled *A la récherche d'autre chose* (Brussels: Desclée de Brouner, 1968).
11. Ibid., 247.
12. Léon Poirier, *24 Images à la seconde* (Paris: Mame, 1953), 93–94.
13. Léon Poirier, *Pourquoi et comment je vais réaliser l'Appel du silence* (pamphlet published by the Comité d'Action Ch. De Foucauld, 1935), 16. Consulted at the library of IDHEC (Institut des hautes études cinématographiques) in Paris.
14. Ibid., 25.
15. Lyautey was the colonial general par excellence, having subdued Indochina and then pacified Morocco before World War I. In the 1930s he was honored by being named president of the Colonial Exposition and by having several major biographies written about him, including one by André Maurois.
16. Poirier, *Pourquoi et comment*.

17. *Pour Vous* 423 (31 December 1936).
18. Poirier, *Pourquoi et comment*. General de la Rocque was the famous right-wing leader of French youth groups, modeled, some say, on Hitler Youth.
19. *Le Film* 56 (9 January 1943).
20. Poirier, *Pourquoi et comment*, 27.
21. Hybridity in Hollywood is discussed in detail by Dana Benelli, "Documentary Expressions and Hollywood Filmmaking in the 1930s" (Ph.D. diss., University of Iowa, 1992). His chief and stunning example is the film *Ingagi* (1930), purportedly an ethnographic account of the missing link discovered by scholars studying an African tribe. Independently made, *Ingagi* was peddled in natural history museums and in certain school districts for its scientific interest, while it played in stag theaters elsewhere, promoting its scenes of native women carried off into the jungle by gorillas.
22. François Venneuil, "L'Appel du silence," *Action Français*, 5 August 1936.
23. Pierre Mac Orlan, *L'Intransigeant*, 4 March 1926.
24. Robert Roy, "Rama Tahé jouera Zouzour dans 'Cain'," *Pour Vous* 27 (30 May 1929): 4.
25. Herman Lebovics, *True France* (Ithaca: Cornell University Press, 1992), chap. 2.
26. Léon Moussinac, *Naissance du cinéma* (Paris: J. Povolozky, 1925), 177.
27. These early 1920s films have their roots in the series of scientific short subjects Eclair studios had turned out from 1911 to 1917.
28. As Denis Hollier points out in his introduction to a collection of essays from the journal *Documents*, Bataille used the word at about the same time in a 1922 thesis. See Hollier in *October* 60 (spring 1992): 4.
29. Jacques Brunius, surrealist actor and filmmaker, should be remembered playing the lecher who covorts with the mother in Renior's *A Day in the Country*. His *En Marge du cinéma français* (Paris: Arcane, 1954) is among the best books treating the alternate cinema culture of the interwar years.
30. Walter Benjamin, "The Work of Art in the Age of Mechanical Reproduction," in *Illuminations* (New York: Schocken, 1969), 233–234.
31. James Lastra, "Buñuel's *Las Hurdes* and the ethnographic impulse," unpublished paper delivered at Society for Cinema Studies, Los Angeles, 1991.
32. Carter Ratcliff, "Swallowing Dali," in *Art Forum* 21, no. 1 (1982): 33–39. I thank Tracy Biga for sending me this article.
33. Recall Buñuel's hilarious story about André Breton's loathing for *La Révue du Cinéma* in *My Last Sigh*, trans. Abigail Israel (New York: Vintage, 1983), 108–109.
34. Bernard Brunius, "Le Cinéma et l'amour," *La Révue du Cinéma* 1 (December 1928).
35. Louis Chavance would soon become important as a scriptwriter. In 1933 he authored the script for *Le Corbeau*, although the film would not be made for a decade.
36. Louis Chavance, "Le Symbole du sang," *La Revue du Cinéma* 2 (February 1929): 52.
37. Artaud's playlet "Jet du sang" was published in 1925.
38. Chavance, "Le Symbole du sang," 52.

39. Paul Sablon, "Les Films chirugicaux d'hier et d'aujourd'hui," *La Révue du Cinéma* 8 (March 1930): 12–13.
40. Ibid., 19.
41. David Pressly, "The Praying Mantis in Surrealist Art," *Art Bulletin* 55, no. 4 (1973): 602–615.
42. See Denis Hollier, "The Use-Value of the Impossible," *October* 60 (spring 1992): 21. He speaks of the "unmitigated enthusiasm for fetishism" that runs through *Documents*.
43. See, for example, Georges Ribemont-Dessaignes's review of *Hallelujah* from *Documents* 2, no. 4 (1930) reprinted and translated in *October* 60. He writes that in its treatment of blacks, *Hallelujah* shows us that "the lower regions of the world are stirring," where "each individual is but a part of a crowd governed by a common soul."
44. Michel Leiris, "The Ethnographer Faced with Colonialism," *Les Temps modernes* 6, no. 58 (1950), translated in Leiris, *Brisées: Broken Branches* (San Francisco: North Coast Press, 1989), 112–131.
45. Leiris and the other members of the Collège de Sociologie were acute in their analyses of these crises; some were flagrant in their invocation of violence as a means to break out of the indolence of the Third Republic. See Denis Hollier, *The College of Sociology* (Minneapolis: University of Minnesota Press, 1988).

Janice Morgan

# In the Labyrinth: Masculine Subjectivity, Expatriation, and Colonialism in *Pépé le Moko*

In this essay, I investigate an aspect of French cultural identity by show-ing how the persona of Jean Gabin in the film *Pépé le Moko* (1936) intersects with a number of social issues simmering at the surface of the French national psyche during the 1930s. The list of these concerns is well known to historians of the period: sharp class conflict height-ened by a stagnant, depressed economy, continuing high unemploy-ment, and growing conflict surrounding governmental policy in an increasingly threatening context of rising fascism at home and abroad. National anxieties were further compounded by the combined reali-ties of colonialism, on the one hand, with its attendant necessity of expatriation and confrontation with alternate societal values, and of rising immigration, on the other, with its threat of cultural dissolution and transformation from within. French popular culture participated fully in this sense of national crisis, as the poetic realist films of Julien Duvivier, Jean Renoir, Jean Grémillon, and Marcel Carné reveal. In *Pépé le Moko*, the subjectivity of the Gabin persona is deeply implicated in just such anxieties, ambiguities, and conflicts.

   This film, a stylish, witty thriller from the mid-1930s, brings together a number of important features that bear on our discussion. First, his role as a tough, streetwise, but romantic gangster gave Jean Gabin his first truly international success, establishing him as a bold, new kind

This essay was first published in *The French Review* 67, no. 4 (1994): 637–647. It appears here with the permission of *The French Review*.

of male hero. Second, the film advances a certain realist poetics of the cinema, one that came to be indelibly associated with the specificity of pre-World War II French society and French *milieux*. Third, this playful, irreverent gangster film explores, through the persona of its outlaw hero exiled in North Africa, attitudes toward the self as defined in opposition to racial and cultural difference.

Here, I differ with a number of previous critics, who have insistently denied any political content to the film whatsoever. For example, not long ago, French critic Jean-Pierre Jeancolas insisted that Duvivier's Casbah, "as reconstructed by Jacques Krauss, has the reality of myth, not that of geography."[1] He elaborated this assertion by quoting Barthélemy Amengual to the effect that "colonial Africa, in the film, is scarcely more historical or more realistic than is the Greece of *Phèdre* or the Castille of *Le Cid*."[2] More recently, American critic Henry Garrity has similarly linked Duvivier's *huis clos* vision of "an enclosed modern world in which the hero is inexorably trapped"[3] to the mythology of French classical tragedy à la Racine. I would contend, however, that while such "classical" readings of the film pay homage to the poetic realist aesthetic—as Garrity so evidently does—by attaching it to a canon of tragic masterpieces, they also serve to *detach* that aesthetic from its precise historical and cultural context. In my view, it is possible, and indeed appropriate, to connect an existentialist interpretation of the hero's dilemma to the shaping contingencies of racial, class, and gender difference.

The authors of "L'Afrique de l'Autre" in *Générique des années 30* are among the first to point out that the ambiguous relationship between the European renegade (Gabin) and the Arab police inspector who trails him is, in fact, revealingly emblematic of submerged racial and political tensions in the symbiosis between France and the North African colonies.[4] These writers do not, however, mention gender specificity as a contributing link in the psychopolitical structure revealed by the film's narrative. In particular, they do not show how the masculinity of the hero is played against the feminization of his rival, nor how his European identity is both confirmed and challenged by his association with the two major female characters in the film. Throughout my own analysis it will be significant that Western subjectivity is invested in a *male* hero for, as we shall see, attitudes toward racial and cultural Otherness are implicated *in*—and frequently structured *by*—the specific codes and mythologies of gender difference.

## A New Look at a Male Hero

First of all it is important to recognize how technically audacious this film is. Compared to others, the "look" of this film, as well as the way it compels the viewer to look *at* it, is something entirely new in the French cinema of the 1930s. Much of this audacity is due to director Julien Duvivier's technical virtuosity in borrowing the visual style and pacing of a popular American genre, the gangster film—*Scarface* (1932) by Howard Hawks, is a good example—and placing this style within the exotic context of French colonial Algiers. So successful was the result, that Duvivier and his *équipe* enjoyed the supreme satisfaction of seeing Hollywood, whose production values were generally much higher at the time, not only admire but twice imitate their accomplishment with *Algiers* in 1938 and *Casbah* in 1948.

*Pépé le Moko* features Gabin in a way no other film had done before. Duvivier's camera in *Pépé*, through an extremely conscious use of light and shadow, rapid editing, and use of close-ups, effectively rivets the gaze of the spectator on only *certain* key elements of the mise-en-scène, thereby investing them with greater-than-usual iconic value and psychological interest. The camera lens treats Gabin's body and face in the same intense, iconographical way, making of him not only a visual subject in the film's narrative but the subject of the cinematic "look" itself. Viewers will easily recall how frequently Gabin's persona is figured purely *as* gaze; in several key scenes, the actor's face is presented in close-up, where—against a darkened screen—a narrow band of light features only his eyes. Significantly, however, Pépé/Gabin is also consciously constructed as the desired object of the look, both within the diegesis and beyond it. As Ginette Vincendeau observes, many of the same techniques deployed to eroticize female stars for the viewing audience are here used to display a male star: delayed appearance on the screen, clothing that constructs the body as spectacle (pointed, two-toned shoes, tailored clothing, the jaunty set of a fedora), and finally, the recurrence of fragmented body shots (moving legs, feet, and hands).[5] Furthermore, it is clear that Pépé/Gabin is aware of himself as spectacle, an awareness that fully participates in his charm. Early in the film, while adjusting the angle of his fedora over his forehead, he acknowledges the devastating impact he has on women by remarking to Inspector Slimane: "What do you expect? J'ai du sex appeal."[6]

Vincendeau reads all this simply as the sign of an idealized male ego; by comparing Pépé/Gabin's representation with that of other male figures in the film—and, by extension, linking that identity to the wider context of popular French culture in the 1930s—she manages to integrate these striking visual features into a normative, sociological analysis of Gabin's persona.[7] To my mind, however, Gabin's dual visual construction in the film has much more complex and disruptive implications, for it places an idealized, masculine subjectivity within the framework of a discourse that has typically been reserved for women. Gabin's "to-be-looked-at-ness" seriously displaces what Laura Mulvey calls the "active [male] / passive [female] heterosexual division of labor" where men typically "articulate the look and create the action"[8] while women are objectified, sexualized, and acted upon.

In *Pépé le Moko*, the outlaw hero's visual objectification is paralleled thematically by his confinement to the Casbah, the indigenous Arab quarter of Algiers. His central position of dominance and control ("C'est le caïd des caïds" ["He's the chief of chiefs"]) is therefore limited to a place of exile where—though protected—he is condemned to live under constant police surveillance. In both of these "displacements," then, both visual and thematic, Pépé/Gabin is situated in a position of passivity and potential danger, for his autonomy as a desiring, controlling subject is threatened.

## The Casbah as Spatial and Thematic Metaphor

Far from remaining a mere decor, an exotic backdrop, as the North African setting does in *La Bandera* (1935) or in Jacques Feyder's *Le Grand Jeu* (1934), *Pépé le Moko's* Casbah is an important spatial and thematic determinant (Figure 1). Our first encounter with this alterna-

Figure 1. A dark labyrinth, an impenetrable underworld, the Casbah becomes a powerfully suggestive metaphor for an inner imaginary.

tive city occurs at the commissariat when the French-Algerian police must justify to a visiting Parisian superior their embarrassing lack of success in capturing the wanted outlaw. Projected to the viewer first as a documentary montage from within the dark walls of police headquarters, the Casbah posits a radically Other social order (for the police, a social chaos)—one clearly beyond the capacity of the colonial administration to control or even to understand. Perched high above Algiers, a mosaic of open terraces expanding outward from a long, winding staircase, the Casbah's geography—conveyed by rapid-fire shots of street signs, angled doorways, curving staircases—is figured as an endless succession of thresholds to an alluring but threatening other world.[9] Despite the clipped, matter-of-fact tone of the explanatory voice-over, a distinct note of fascination and fear suffuses this sequence; neither words nor images can adequately describe the Casbah, for there is always much more of a mysterious content that escapes investigation. This is most strongly conveyed by the extremely rapid pace of the montage and the disorienting variety of camera angles, where each image seems to offer much more than the viewer can possibly absorb. The peculiar spatial arrangements of the Casbah effectively foil the rectilinear mechanisms of the law; accordingly, this milieu is inhabited by and protects a strange "fauna"—all those whom the law seeks to confine and control: (a) the multiracial culture of a port city composed of "Kabyles, Chinois, Gitans, Heitmaltlos, Slaves, Maltais, Nègres, Siciliens, Espagnols," (b) both indigenous and illicit European women ("filles de tous les pays et de tous les formats" ["girls from every country and in every format"]), and finally, (c) outlaws.[10] Throughout this explanatory montage, it is important to note how closely the graphic presentation of women's bodies is linked to the dangerous labyrinthine geography of the city.

No less than its connection to an "outside" political and social reality, then, is the Casbah's significance as an inner imaginary. For the Casbah's primary role lies in its relation to the film's hero, for whom it serves as both sheltering home and confining prison. In its likeness to a dark labyrinth, an impenetrable underworld, the Casbah becomes, throughout the film, a powerfully suggestive metaphor for the inner psyche. To live—as Pépé now does—in the world of the Casbah is to live continually in the shadow of the mysterious Other and, across that shadow, to be forced to confront his deepest fantasies and desires. Beyond the apparent simplicity of the film's plot, whose premise is so clearly stated at the beginning ("If Pépé leaves the Casbah, he will be caught"), I believe it is the implications of this dual encounter, both with the Other and with one's own unacknowledged desires, that the poetics of the film attempts to work out.

## A Mise-en-Abyme of Encounters in the Casbah

The dual opposition figured by the Casbah is further elaborated by the presence of two major characters in the film, each of whom, in a different way, serves as a kind of psychic double, or mirror image, for the central protagonist. The first of these is, of course, the ever-present Arab agent, Inspector Slimane; the other is Gaby, the wealthy Parisian tourist who—when unexpectedly detained by Slimane in her hotel—draws Pépé out of his lair and down to the city below to look for her.

As principal member of the shadowy and duplicitous company of informers who pass between the separate worlds of the Casbah and the prefecture of police, Slimane (Lucas Gridoux) is—by far—the most mobile and autonomous character in the film. Yet, however freely he may move across boundaries, he is not fully accepted in either realm; for just as he himself admits to being only "tolerated" in the Casbah, so he is also tolerated by the colonial administration for the special services only he can render as a Westernized native. His very clothing identifies him as such, for though he always appears professionally clothed in a Western suit jacket and tie, he never gives up his flowing pants or his fez, which simultaneously code him as a member of the indigenous culture.[11] His "mixed" identity makes him a disturbing presence, an ambiguous force in the narrative. A cunning mixture of obsequious deferment and stubborn independence, he shows little solidarity with his fellow Arabs, deriding the Arbis and Régis of this world for selling their friends for money. Clearly he possesses his own separate code of honor, his own set of rules, for he is forced by circumstances—like Pépé himself—to invent his own game. Slimane's status as a privileged outsider is similar to that enjoyed by Pépé in the Casbah: both men share the identity of one who has become so deeply complicit with another culture as to be permanently doubled, permanently exiled.

Slimane's mission is to catch his man, the emphasis being placed entirely on *how*, exactly, this will be accomplished. Unlike the quick-fire, conquistador approach of his Western colleagues—which can only fail disastrously in the coiling confines of the Casbah—the Arab inspector, instead, invokes a slower but surer method: "chouia, chouia, à la fatigue" [in mixed Arabic and French, "slowly, slowly, wear him down"]. Like the primitive hunter who, in order to be successful in his quest, must figuratively become one with his prey, Slimane follows Pépé into the very recesses of the other man's fantasy in order to entrap him.

Racial and cultural difference ups the ante considerably in the psychological rapport between the two men. They are each other's strongest adversary but closest friend, their relationship—characterized by a mutual attraction and repulsion, admiration and scorn—giving abun-

Figure 2. The European hero holds either the highest or the most central position within the frame, while the Arab detective Slimane is typically placed at an oblique angle to him.

dant testimony to the West's enduring fascination with the Orient, a fascination strongly infused with eroticism. In effect, to Pépé's strong masculine center, Slimane plays the peripheral, strangely feminized Other. This distinction is plainly revealed in the consistent way the two men are photographed together throughout the film. Whereas in the earlier Duvivier film, *La Bandera*, Gabin and his French detective rival tend to be framed on an equal footing—man-to-man, face-to face—here, Pépé and Slimane are nearly always viewed at an oblique angle to one another, where the Western hero holds either the highest or the most central position (Figure 2). This placement is further reinforced by Slimane's insistent physical proximity to Pépé where certain gestures, like his repeated lighting of the other man's cigarette for him, carry a whole subtext of repressed sexuality. A similar erotic exchange occurs verbally as well, for though the dialogue between the two centers on "shop talk" (police raids, prison sentences, and the like), it is continually laced with mocking, sexualized allusions and epithets. Furthermore, though Pépé's taste runs clearly toward women, this teasing banter gives a sardonic edge to Slimane's repeated warnings: "On t'aime trop, Pépé, les femmes te perdront" ("Women love you too much, Pépé, they'll ruin you").

Figure 3. More than once, Gabin's persona is figured purely as desiring gaze.

It is Slimane who stages the encounter between Pépé and Gaby in the heart of the Casbah. As in a paranoid dream fantasy, Slimane's manipulative use of women in the film exemplifies a kind of *rond infernal* of sexual exploitation where the feminized Other uses sexual difference as an offensive tool against the enemy. Gaby, played by Mireille Balin in what was undoubtedly her first major film role, is just the sort of worldly, self-assured femme fatale that will later become a classic type in Hollywood film noir. Her curiosity fully aroused by Slimane's cleverly disingenuous briefing, this dazzling adventuress is more than ready to behold the prized object of a two-year manhunt. In a series of point-of-view shots highlighting the translucent whiteness of her skin, her sparkling diamond bracelets, and gleaming pearl necklace, Gaby meets the jewel thief's fixed gaze; with Balin, the Jean Gabin persona is confronted by a feminine presence with a "cool" and magnetism to match his own (Figures 3 and 4).

Gaby's relationship to the protagonist is based on a romantic exchange of fantasies, fantasies that begin to link the two characters in a parallel pattern of cross-identification. Whereas between Pépé and Slimane, there is an erotic attraction based on racial and cultural difference, between Pépé and Gaby, the erotic attraction of sexual difference is linked to cultural sameness and affirmation. A major point of

Figure 4. Pépé's first encounter with Gaby in the Casbah: a point-of-view shot highlights the translucent whiteness of her skin, her fur, her gleaming pearl necklace.

connection for the two is a shared city, Paris. Their meeting of minds on this subject finds its metaphorical equivalent in the famous rendez-vous "à la place Blanche" as each dreamily recites, in turn, the name of a favorite street in the French capital. Later during their second meeting, after an especially dizzying twirl across the dance floor, Gaby tells her partner that this reminds her vividly of neighborhood dances on "le quatorze juillet." To their mutual surprise, Pépé and Gaby discover that they both grew up in the same neighborhood near Gobelins and so have in common not only Parisian street slang but a whole world of such childhood memories. In this way, it is implied that they were originally in the same social class; clearly, they both wanted the same things in life and, as their present social situations reveal, took parallel—if different—shortcuts to get them. To Pépé's question "What did you do before?—Before what?—Before the jewels?" Gaby replies simply, "Je les désirais"—a response that speaks volumes about who she is and what she wants. This is just the kind of desiring praxis Pépé can understand, for a similar philosophy undoubtedly explains his own entry into a life of crime. Gaby can only maintain her social status, signified by her costly jewelry, through sexual attachment to a champagne magnate;

Pépé maintains his "prestige" by regularly stealing, among other things, jewelry from pleasure-seeking tourists. Their illicit connection to jewels, then—featured prominently in their relationship from the first moments of a highly eroticized visual encounter—places both characters *outside* the normal, lawful economy of "legitimate" wealth. So despite the exotic decor of the Arab bar that surrounds them, the two are remarkably, *entre pays* (among countrymen).

Yet, within the poetics of Duvivier's film, the Parisian connection between Pépé and Gaby carries a deeper, more particular resonance. Pépé's attraction to a white, European woman takes on its full significance in juxtaposition to scenes with Inès, the Gypsy woman with whom he lives in the Casbah. While Inès (Line Noro) hangs out laundry and stirs couscous on the stove, the exiled Westerner looks out to sea and complains of having not a mere headache (*mal à la tête*) but a "pain in the boat" (*mal au bateau*). Though he denies being bored with her, insisting that it is Algiers he wants to leave, he brushes off Inès's offer to go with him, comparing her companionship to a kind of odious "Casbah portative": "Deux ans de Casbah, deux ans que je suis avec toi! . . . T'es pas une femme, t'es un régime!" ("Two years of the Casbah, two years since I've been with you! . . . You're not a woman, you're a diet!"). He can only reject Inès's furious reminder that for him, Paris is now permanently "blotted out"; Paris, along with Marseille—and, by extension, all of France—no longer exists for him. "Y a plus rien, rien, rien que la Casbah!" ("From now on, there's nothing, nothing, nothing but the Casbah!"). This dialogue, interspersed with the domestic chores of an indigenous household, reminds us that if France is thus blotted out for him, so too is a large part of his past identity as a white European. The very transformation of his name, in fact, already reveals this.

Pépé's desire to escape, then, which becomes more pronounced the more often he meets with Gaby, is at its source based on a compelling need to reconstruct his own identity. Gaby, the other woman, becomes a primary figure of attraction for him precisely because, to Pépé, Gaby *is* Paris; she *is* his past. Gaby's whiteness, her jewels, her perfume are all, as in a Baudelaire poem, treasured means of escape for the male psyche, a mode of transport to the marvelous elsewhere. Only here the elsewhere is back home to Montmartre, and the means of transport is "le métro, en première." Pépé jokingly acknowledges this when, discreetly holding her in his arms, he tells Gaby that despite her fine silks and golden jewelry, all he can think about when he is with her is the métro, French fries, and café-crèmes at the sidewalk cafés (Figure 5).

Just as earlier, in the phantasmagoric police documentary of the Casbah, that city's singular geography became synonymous with the bodies of its women, so now in Pépé's imaginary, Gaby's body has be-

Figure 5. Gaby's whiteness, her jewels, her perfume are all, as in a Baudelaire poem, treasured means of escape. Only here the escape is a psychic return to Paris in pursuit of a lost European identity.

come the privileged site of a lost, but—he would like to believe—recoverable city. Beneath this psychological equation of female bodies and cities lies a profound fear of ego dissolution; in this case, it is not a question of the sexualized dissolution of a male self within a female body but the cultural dissolution of a Western, male self within the feminized geography of an oriental (Arab) city. The difference between the two women, then, embodies a spatial dichotomy (the Casbah/Paris) and a temporal one as well (present/past), both of which impinge directly on the identity of the male protagonist.

Though Gabin dominates the viewer's identifying gaze, it is Slimane who, through his constant surveillance, slowly and carefully weaves the "spider's web" into the which the flawed hero will fall.[12] Indeed, given the strong generic premise of the thriller, it is tempting to view the contest between Pépé and Slimane as an elaborate cat-and-mouse game where the cat (here representing, however ambiguously, the superior forces of law and order) must inevitably win. Yet, I would argue, this reading of the film, where Pépé is reduced to being "merely a toy in Slimane's hands,"[13] does not do justice to the complexity of the existential dilemma confronting him. After all, Pépé is not caught and destroyed out of a mere mechanical error on his part—that is, he failed to perceive the exact nature and extent of the police machinations against him. (Certainly, the extended scenes where the treacherous Régis and Arbi are "flushed" and punished demonstrate that the outlaw is in full control of both his milieu and his métier.) Rather, Pépé is caught because of a more profound failure; a refusal, or an inability, to deal effectively with the contradictions and the ambiguities of his own conflicted identity. In effect, the mise-en-abyme of encounters at the heart of the Casbah has served to trip the switch of an internal fantasy mechanism that was already poised and set to roll.

Nowhere is this more evident than in the film's denouement, when the hero makes his final descent to the city of Algiers. Though ostensibly lured to his arrest by Slimane's clever manipulation of his attachment to Gaby (a maneuver which includes the cruel use of Inès's jealousy to make of her his accomplice), the very way this scene is filmed insists on the deliberate, defiant nature of the hero's choice. In one last, crucial instance of subjective doubling, Pépé's escape from the Casbah is, in fact, a replay of an earlier scene when, in drunken despair at the death of his protégé Pierrot, the outlaw hero ran down the same staircase, nearly throwing himself into the waiting squad car below. This second flight, however, contrasts sharply with the reckless abandon of its preceding version. Calmly composing himself at the height of the winding staircase, Pépé sports his best suit, stopping to adjust the lay of his silk foulard and the exact angle of his fedora. Glancing briefly skyward, the protagonist embarks—not on a reasoned plan of hopeful escape—but, by virtue of its sheer aestheticism—on the deliberate and passionate pursuit of an illusion.

The montage of this sequence bears eloquent testimony to the nature of this fantasy. Filmed, as in the earlier police documentary, from a variety of high- and low-angle shots, the hero's moving body is the center around which the decor of the Casbah—elsewhere so clearly and palpably present in the film—becomes lost in a shapeless blur. As he negotiates the final curves and arcades of the staircase, we view from behind his shoulders what appears to be—quite suddenly—an imaginary seascape. Just as Pierrot, Pépé's surrogate son, was drawn to his death by false news of his ailing mother, so now Pépé's descent to the sea (mer/mère) is an attempt to return to the lost mother country, to the past, to his place of origin. In this way, the elaborate configurations of cross-identification within the narrative pose—as the metaphor of the labyrinth suggests—not so much a contest between characters as an insoluble dilemma *within* the central protagonist himself. Captured by the police before once again meeting Gaby, Pépé covertly takes a weapon to end his own life. In the last moments of the film, the screen is filled with the object of his longing gaze: past the grilled gates of the port of Algiers, a ship with Gaby on it is slowly departing for France.

## Beyond the Casbah

What, then, does this film have to tell us about the issues of working-class masculinity, French prestige, and the complexities of colonial inter-culturalism in 1936? Though some—notably, Deborah Linderman—may argue that *Pépé le Moko*, as an exemplary model of a naive colonialist discourse, purveys a blatant racist and sexist cultural impe-rialism, we would certainly miss much were we to stop at that trans-parent level. We know, for example, that some commentators from the period, notably Emile Vuillermoz in "A Case of Conscience" (1938), were—despite the film's frank assertion of French cultural supremacy—capable of arriving at quite different conclusions about what the nar-rative was really saying. Though admiring the magnetic psychological power of Duvivier's film, Vuillermoz worries publicly about the mes-sage his country might be sending to its European neighbors about its own precarious internal and external affairs. "This portrait of Algiers as depicted by the French is more eloquent than any political essay. France itself admits it is unworthy of possessing and incapable of ad-ministering a colonial empire."[14]

In reading the film carefully from today's critical perspectives, we find it so interesting precisely because there are clearly oppositional strategies at work from within. On the one hand, the film seems to offer an intellectual challenge to colonialist ideology through Slimane's critique as the intercultural outsider/insider consummately able, there-fore, to play the role of the narrative's *meneur du jeu*. On the other hand, the film's emotional energy—like that of its nostalgic hero—flees deci-sively from that critique into an oceanic, all-embracing European he-gemony. Yet, now that the hero himself has become inextricably linked to the colonial culture—in fact, he is dependent on it—his attempt to return to the illusory glory of his European past can only fail.

This profound ambivalence is further exemplified by the film's di-vided viewing structure. Though Slimane's gaze gives him both knowl-edge and power, never during the course of the narrative is he "allowed" to assume the identifying gaze of the viewing public. That role is held from beginning to end by Gabin, as the Western hero. Through an ex-tensive shot-by-shot analysis of key scenes, the *Générique* authors show that "Slimane waits, spies, watches, endlessly hemming in by his pres-ence both Pépé and the two lovers, but not for a single moment does the camera permit [the spectator] to see through his eyes. The camera pretends to do so, but suddenly Slimane moves or looks from the wrong direction; internal focalisation is forbidden to him."[15]

The escapist tendencies of the film are overwhelmingly evident, but is there not also a more culpable strategy at work—that of scapegoating?

By setting this story of a working-class hero-in-revolt in North Africa, is there not also a move to displace—and thereby attempt to quell— French workers' anxieties and frustrations on the homefront? From this perspective, the film is not so much a story of displaced persons in the colonies as it is of displaced desires and oppressions that were actually operating in France. For if the Gabin outlaw hero is trapped within the alien confines of the Casbah, there is also abundant evidence within the film itself to reveal that many individuals, like the ex-cabinetmaker turned thief and the desiring adventuress Gaby, were, in fact, already "caught" in the grip of social and economic oppression at home—whether because of class or gender. Both Pépé and Gaby come, as we observed earlier, from the same working-class neighborhood in Paris, and given the dichotomy between the haves and have-nots in the film—a dichotomy that corresponds quite accurately to the division of wealth in French society of the 1930s—is it not clear why both have chosen to defy the confining strictures of their class identity, and the law, to pursue their desires?

Yet, in the end, both are punished for their transgressions. Moreover, in a mystification with ominous implications, the film's finale seems to "frame" racial and cultural Others as the ultimate oppressors

Figure 6. Inès: the abandoned "other" woman who reluctantly joins forces with Slimane to bring Pépé under arrest.

of the white, working-class male hero.[16] For in the cursory, and truly popular reading of the film's ending, Pépé is destroyed not by a lack of self-knowledge but by the duplicitous machinations of the Arab police inspector and by Inès, a jealous, dark-skinned woman (Figure 6). By the final scenes of the film, the specters of racial, cultural, and sexual difference, which, as we have observed, have been challenged and finessed throughout the film into complex, dialectical patterns of intersubjectivity, are crudely brought back into play with a demonic vengeance.

And who comes out on top? In the end, it is neither Slimane nor Pépé who "wins" but the unempathetic authority figures whose ineptitude and lack of understanding have been so thoroughly exposed and mocked throughout the film: the colonial police, who will almost certainly take credit for Pépé's capture, and the portly champagne magnate M. Klip. As the Gabin hero sinks into the world of shadows, it is the complacent industrialist who sets sail triumphantly for France— his gilded bird, Gaby, in tow along with the rest of his entourage. Through this final scene does the film attempt to pursuade its audience—however regretfully—that what is good for the haves must, of necessity, be good enough for the have-nots as well?

## Notes

This project originated in the context of an NEH Summer Seminar held at the University of Iowa in 1991. The author would like to acknowledge the support of the endowment and to thank all of the participants in this seminar as well as the directors, Professors Dudley Andrew and Steven Ungar, for their stimulating comments, arguments, and suggestions.

1. Jean-Pierre Jeancolas, *15 Ans d'année trente: le cinéma des Français, 1929–1944* (Paris: Stock/Cinéma, 1983), 269. The translation is my own.
2. Ibid., 269.
3. Henry A. Garrity, "Narrative Space in Julien Duvivier's *Pépé le Moko,*" *French Review* 65, no. 4 (1992): 628.
4. Michèle Lagny et al., *Générique des années 30* (Paris: Presses Universitaires de Vincennes, 1986), 161–168.
5. Ginette Vincendeau, "Community, Nostalgia, and the Spectacle of Masculinity," *Screen* 26, no. 6 (1985): 27–28.
6. A full reproduction of the film's scenario can be found in *L'Avant-Scène du Cinéma* 269 (June 1981).
7. In a memorable phrase, Vincendeau states that Gabin represents a "degree zero" of masculinity in such films as *La Belle Equipe* and *Pépé le Moko*; by this, she means he embodies a neutral standard against which the excesses and deficiencies of his male cohorts can be measured. See "Community, Nostalgia, and the Spectacle of Masculinity," 32.

8. Laura Mulvey, "Visual Pleasure and Narrative Cinema" (1975), in *Visual and Other Pleasures* (Bloomington: Indiana University Press, 1989), 20.

9. For a further analysis of French colonial cinema's radically "Other" spaces, see Charles O'Brien's essay in this volume.

10. Deborah Linderman discusses this cultural confrontation in her essay "Pépé and Orientalism," presented at the Society for Cinema Studies conference held 25–28 May 1990, in Washington, D.C. Linderman bases her analysis of the Casbah and its residents on Edward Said's and Homi Bhabha's critique of Western representations of oriental/Arab cultures. From this perspective, *Pépé le Moko* becomes a prime exemplar of Orientalist discourse—that is, a mode of representation whereby the West expresses a "'will to power,' and an intention to control, manipulate, and finally incorporate a world which is manifestly different, alternative, or novel, and which is, as such, implicitly resistant," 3.

11. Ibid., 5.

12. Michèle Lagny et al., *Générique*, 164.

13. Ibid., 164.

14. Emile Vuillermoz, "A Case of Conscience," in *La Cinématographie française* (1938). Translated and annotated by Richard Abel in *French Film Theory and Criticism: A History/Anthology, Volume 2, 1929–1939* (Princeton: Princeton University Press, 1988), 252.

15. Michèle Lagny et al., *Générique*, 167.

16. The film precedes by only a few years the mass deportation of Jews, Gypsies, and other "undesirable foreigners" from French soil under the Vichy government. It is no small irony that Slimane was played by a Jewish Romanian actor, Lucas Gridoux, whose life—like that of so many others—was soon to be in such danger.

Mary Hamer

# Timeless Histories:
# A British Dream of Cleopatra

Can it be chance, one wonders, that the image of the sphinx that fills
the screen at the start of Gabriel Pascal's *Caesar and Cleopatra* (1945)
bears a troubling resemblance to Flora Robson? It is true that Robson,
the British classical actress, who was to end her days as a dame of the
British Empire, does take a part in the film that is about to begin. But
it is an uncharacteristic role that she plays there. In a sort of halfhearted
blackface she takes the role of Ftatateeta, Cleopatra's nurse, a woman
who stabs a man to death before being killed herself in revenge.

It was not a part she enjoyed. For one thing, water pressure in the
studio was so low under the wartime conditions of 1945 that she could
not get off all of her heavy body makeup. She felt she got darker and
darker by the day.[1] The cinema audience, which had registered her as
the dazzling embodiment of Elizabeth I in the 1937 film *Fire over England*, must have found the shift of color weighing heavily on them
too. They could not avoid being intensely aware of it, aware that under
it lay a skin that was European, and they knew that when that familiar
face and features were at home, so to speak, they stood for the most
ambitious of English queens.

Elizabeth I was notorious for claiming, first, in addressing her troops
at Tilbury and again centuries later on-screen—thanks to Robson, who
had persuaded the director that Elizabeth's own words should be used
in the film—that she had "the heart and stomach of a man."[2] When

Robson repeated those words in *Fire over England*, she brought their challenge into a world where they might resonate dangerously, into twentieth-century lives, where the difference between what men and women were equipped to do, particularly in wartime, was not always as clear as it might once have seemed.[3] Can present viewers of *Caesar and Cleopatra* take Elizabeth's words as a cue and ask whether a woman could ever be like a man or deserve the respect that a man gives to other men? The patent falsehood signified by Robson's makeup could be a warning. It is certainly a source of confusion, threatening to mask with a predictable colonialist politics a more challenging question: can young women be rescued from the deforming effects of the gender they have been brought up to practice?

*Caesar and Cleopatra* announces itself as a palimpsest, offering an invitation to careful reading, to make out the different texts jostling for space in this ostensibly familiar story. If this approach seems to suggest an excessive emphasis on words, that strategy is hard to avoid in dealing with a film disparagingly described as "Shaw's mannered dialogue . . . uneasily grafted onto a conventional film treatment."[4] Only the set photography wins a gesture of respect: those images of archaic Egyptian darkness and brilliantly lit classical order offer silent witness to the central problem of the film, the emphasis it lays, like Orientalism, on the question of knowledge.

Orientalism, as Said argued, is in the first place a regime of knowledge.[5] It is the name of an intellectual order created by Westerners out of the study of the languages and customs of non-western peoples. The cultures and civilizations in which Orientalism makes itself expert are ones that are evidently ancient and in their sophistication are able to lay claim to wisdom. They represent an alternative form of knowledge, and it is the paradox of Orientalism that by studying those cultures, obtaining mastery over them, particularly as they exist in textual form, that the Western scholar may undermine their Otherness and their authority. One obvious way is indicated by the grouping implicit in the name Orientalism itself; under this rubric, distinctions such as those between India and Egypt or between the peoples and ways of life that are aggregated under the name of China are subsumed and obliterated.

Instead, a single "oriental character" is substituted, a character based on a premise about political order. In the East, so the story goes, the "mature" political institutions of constitutional monarchy and democracy have not yet come into being. On the notion of the oriental despot—cruel, tyrannical and arbitrary—Said lays particular stress. It is such leadership that produces, according to Orientalist logic, a servile and deceitful populace, corrupt, lethargic, and given to words rather than deeds. In the East ignorance and superstition prevail, particularly among its women, though its men lack the vigor and force of European masculinity, even to the point that oriental societies as a whole are perceived as feminized.

The trouble is, Orientalism is seductive: it offers forms for European pleasure. Luxury is one of these, also cruelty; they meet in the fantasy of the harem, where absolute power can create a space for the play of sexualities—the eunuch, the lesbian, the slave—that are constrained elsewhere. The Orient of these fictions seems to lie beyond the Oedipal organization of desire.

The most effective counter to the fantasies of Orientalism, it has been argued, is to measure them against the historical record. A common complaint against the Orientalist painters of the nineteenth century, for instance, is that they excluded every evidence of the industrial and the modern from their work, to maintain the fiction of a generalized Eastern setting, outside time and by the same token not involved in colonial politics or a party to the operations of world trade.

I have elected to consider here a British dream of the Orient, Pascal's *Caesar and Cleopatra*—a work that is in many ways an exception—is because Egypt and Britain have a substantial past in common. No event in modern Egypt has cast such a lengthy shadow over its history as the British occupation that began in 1882.[6] My choice of topic will enable me to review the historical actuality of Anglo-Egyptian relations and to set up conditions in which the work of both Said and those responsible for creating the film, Shaw and Pascal, can be brought into question. Representing Cleopatra always entails an attempt to bring notions of desire and of political authority into alignment with each other, but the negotiations that take place between them in this film are unusually awkward. It is not clear that Said's formulations are adequate to account for the cultural work that is being done there. Yet, Britain sent an occupying force to Egypt in 1882 and kept one there for the next seventy years; it is impossible not to wonder how that imposition recreates itself in the film.

The story told in *Caesar and Cleopatra* is one that has been around for a long time. It was first recounted on the brink of the Christian era, when Julius Caesar noted in his *Civil War* that on his arrival in Egypt he had found Cleopatra there. He reported that "he had decided that King Ptolemy and Queen Cleopatra should dismiss their armies" and agree to reign jointly.[7]

Since those words were written, the tale of Cleopatra has been repeated many times and told not just for the sake of pleasure.[8] Cleopatra was the last queen of Egypt, and she died rather than give up that title and be known as the captive of Octavian, the future emperor of Rome. In telling her story or making images of her, Europeans have used

Cleopatra as a way of contemplating what authority looks like when it is lodged in a woman's body and of containing the alarm engendered by that prospect, always presented at a distance. The scandal of her authority was usually transposed, so that she became identified not with political power but with a sexuality that was scandalous in itself. Cleopatra's race, until the nineteenth century, remained a secondary matter. With the emergence in the second half of the century of a rhetoric and "science" of "race," however, the fact that Cleopatra was a woman who was born in Egypt became more salient. From then on, stories about Cleopatra also became part of an argument about nation and race.

Pascal's film *Caesar and Cleopatra* was made at the end of the Second World War. Shooting began on 12 June 1944, six days after D-Day, and the film looks forward into a postwar world; it was intended as Britain's challenge to the United States for command of the postwar film audience.[9] Yet it is rooted, word for word, in the past, since it is based on the play of the same name that Shaw wrote almost fifty years earlier in 1898, and follows the original closely. The playwright was still alive when the film was made, though very old. He himself had chosen Gabriel Pascal, an actor turned director born in Hungary, as the man to whom he would entrust his plays for filming. Pascal seems to have admired Shaw's work without reservation and to have functioned as a relay for Shaw's text. His own imagination was not strongly cinematic enough to make him a memorable director in his own right. Shaw was jubilant at the result: "We found that what I had written was a film in the first place," he wrote.[10]

For the viewer at the end of the century, after another fifty years have passed, there is a different cause for wonder. It lies in the complexities of the play's politics, a politics that are amplified by translation into the medium of film. It is in part a question of the divide between conscious reflection and the life of fantasy: the register of fantasy is what is picked up and transmitted by the screen. The effect is to expose the strains between Shaw's wish to dissociate himself from British imperialism and his reliance as a European male on a language of fantasy in which the Orient is an apparently indispensable term.

Shaw was not short of information about Egypt. Self-educated—he claimed to have got his learning in the Reading Room of the British Museum—his intellectual curiosity was acute. He had informed himself thoroughly about Egyptian history and culture, as his stage directions to the play make almost boastfully clear. At the same time he was following what the British were doing in North Africa at the moment, as he was writing his play and publishing his outrage in the press.

In 1898 an Anglo-Egyptian army led by Lord Kitchener had made a successful expedition into the Sudan, the territory immediately south of Egypt. When they retook Khartoum, the capital where General Gordon had been defeated in 1885, they violated the tomb of Gordon's old adversary, the Muslim religious leader known as the Mahdi. The body was seized and mutilated, the trunk cast into the Nile, and the head sent to Cairo. It was further proposed that it might be forwarded to London, where the secretary of the Royal College of Surgeons declared he would be willing to accept it. Following an interview with the Secretary in the issue of 30 September Shaw wrote to the newspaper, the *Morning Leader*.[11]

His letter encapsulates some of the ironies of his position. As an Irishman, he was born in England's oldest colony and in Dublin, a city where nationalist extremists had assassinated the British lord lieutenant in the very year, 1882, that the British were extending their empire overseas by taking on Egypt. Shaw had every reason to be critical of British imperialism and the claims of cultural superiority that supported it. His letter is devoted to exposing those claims, and he is particularly hard on the argument that Muslims are to be treated differently from Christians, since they are "superstitious brutes." Can readers of the newspaper really believe, he asks, that on hearing of the British action the Mahdi's followers will be "so struck with the refinement, humanity, advanced civilisation and deep religious sentiment of the British nation that they will instantly embrace the form of Christianity professed by the Sirdar"?

Shaw sets himself up to arraign British pretension to mastery; meanwhile his own mastery of the arguments from ethnography that were used to legitimate those pretensions is displayed. Shaw's mockery may turn the self-justifying arguments of the colonist against him, but one question remains. The "science" of race that had been developed in the course of the nineteenth century had come to underpin all forms of knowledge. The imagery of the black body had become associated in argument as well as fantasy with intense sexual feeling. Shaw would not be able to free himself from this white person's habit of projecting their own sexuality onto blacks when he came to imagine Egypt for himself.

In 1898, when George Bernard Shaw wrote the original play *Caesar and Cleopatra*, Egypt was standing in a new relation to Europe. Fairly new as far as the British were concerned, that is; in 1882 they had bombarded Alexandria for two days, before defeating the troops of the new nationalist government under Arabi at Tell-al-Kabir. Their army of occupation had been installed since 1882, and a British commander-in-chief had been imposed on the Egyptian army. His title, the "Sirdar," was not a local term, though exotic to British ears; it was Persian, brought from the Urdu-speaking territories in northern India that the British had also taken responsibility for. Egypt was administered by Britain on behalf of its European creditors. The debts, which had given rise to such protest and disturbance inside Egypt that the European powers had intervened, had been incurred in bearing a large proportion of the cost of the Suez Canal. Egypt did not benefit from the tolls, and it was Britain, with its Indian empire, that was the principal beneficiary of the canal.[12] Under the terms of the British "police action," as it was at first styled, the khedive, the Egyptian head of state, and his government continued to rule in appearance while in fact British civil servants advised each minister.

So in 1898 Egypt stood for something relatively new, in British eyes— something no more than sixteen years old, about the age of Cleopatra on Caesar's arrival in fact—as well as for a good deal that was old. Perhaps for Shaw himself it stood for the unexplored territory in which he found himself at that time, too: in 1898, at the age of forty-two, he had just got married for the first time. It was a union that both parties agreed should not be consummated.

We might ask how the Egyptians were thinking of themselves during this period. At the turn of the twentieth century of the Christian era, what were Egyptian voices asking for? Had it changed by the time the film came to be made, in 1945? One thing at least had not altered: in 1945 the British were still stationed in Egypt and still in charge. During the Second World War Egypt had provided the base for the British war effort in the Middle East, and its workforce had supplied the labor to service it. The nationalist voices that were being raised before the British arrived in 1882 had still not secured independence for Egypt in 1945. It is on this historical reality, this tenacious assumption of rights, that the stagey fantasy of *Caesar and Cleopatra* is elaborated.

The film tells the story of Caesar's sojourn in Egypt, where he arrives in pursuit of Pompey, the Roman general with whom he had been struggling for power. What Caesar finds, though, is not his rival, whom the Egyptians have unsportingly killed thinking to please him, but a state in turmoil like the one he left behind in Rome. There, too many good candidates for power, all mature men, squabbled together. The problem in Egypt, though, is that no one is fit to govern: the joint sovereigns, Ptolemy and his sister Cleopatra are hardly more than children and, what is worse, are joined in an incestuous marriage. Caught up in their conflict, Caesar does his best to shape Cleopatra for power: first she must carry herself like a queen; then she must learn the impersonal wisdom of office. It is all in vain. Though she makes her handmaidens cross by reading instead of gossiping (Figure 1), she can never give up her inbred taste for cruelty and intrigue. When Caesar

Figure 1. Cleopatra's companions laugh at her for reading too much. Photo courtesy of the British Film Institute.

departs, however, it is without bitterness; in his wisdom he can accept Cleopatra's limitations and even indulge them. He promises to send Mark Antony, the young man with "fine round arms," to her. Meanwhile, he leaves his lieutenant Rufio behind to govern Egypt on behalf of Rome.

The Cleopatra Shaw was interested in was a young girl, one that Caesar might attempt to train for greatness but who could never move him with the sensuality of a mature woman. That particular force is ruled out of the picture or made to dwindle into the grotesque figure of Ftatateeta. For Shaw, the meeting between Caesar and Cleopatra offered a moment where a wise and skeptical man had a chance to educate an ignorant girl, that is, to transform her by sharing what he himself had learned. There is hope and longing in the attempt, for the man is lonely. He has male comrades, but they are not enough. The attempt turns to tragedy for him, though this is only very indirectly acknowledged, when he realizes that the girl could never learn to be like him.

This story may hint of personal experience, in the wish to keep sexuality literally at arm's length, and it will allow a particular economy of desire to be described. In doing this, however, it will recapitulate some of Orientalism's clichés, and depend on them to structure an argument whose true focus is the artifice of gender. *Caesar and Cleopatra* sets out to show why it is only right that men should be entrusted with power and that it is only in the men of the West, the men of Rome, that genuine masculinity can be located. Women and Orientals, terms which melt into each other as the story is told, reveal themselves to be incapable of the qualities that Caesar embodies and that fit him so eminently for rule. It seems to be a defect built into gender and racial identity, for which no education can compensate. And what are the virtues of the ruler, what are the qualities that no woman or Easterner can hope to match? First, his capacity for penetrative knowledge: his reason, freed from sentiment, affords him an uncanny insight into human behavior; he also works all hours, and his intimacy is reserved for the men he fights with.

The film opens into a world of darkness, where Roman soldiers are laughing together and throwing dice. If there is a trace here of the New Testament world, where soldiers gambled at the foot of the cross, that is perhaps not a coincidence. In the courtyard of the palace at Memphis, one superstition is mapped onto another: the reminiscence of Christianity is complemented, not contradicted, by the huge stone images of animal gods. Out of this archaic world, distant both in time and space, speaks a figure addressed as "the Persian," who is marked out from the Romans by his earring, his curls, and his heartless cunning. The duplicate, in a sense, of Ftatateeta, and like her patently stagey in presentation, the Persian marks the connection between the fiction of femininity and a system of belief understood as archaic and irrational.

In the dark courtyard of the old palace at Memphis, with its huge stone images of cats, where the soldiers are lounging, and in the vast dark halls into which Caesar, a flaming torch in his hand, leads the young Cleopatra a little while later, there is plenty of evidence of the darkness in which Egypt lies enfolded, as it is implied. It seems to be Caesar's role as a man to bring enlightenment there. Before we have even set eyes on him, though, we are shown how unstable this world ruled by superstition can be: at a cry of alarm from a nearly naked black slave, "The sacred white cat is missing," the household, made up of slaves and women, tumbles out of the palace, shrieking.

When we meet Caesar himself, he is composed, even contemplative. The peaceful camp where he is shown standing shares the darkness of the opening sequence and goes in for some of the same tricks with history: as we catch the regular hammering—of armourers perhaps?— we could be forgiven for thinking we were in the same nightstruck camp that Laurence Olivier wandered through in his role as Henry V in the film made the previous year, 1944. The specific register of British patriotism is struck; it puts us in mind, through the image of Henry, of a responsible leader, fighting overseas and burdened with conscious knowledge of how much depends on him, of how much he owes his men. It was an image Olivier had produced for widespread consumption in time of war and involved censoring the text of Shakespeare's play, removing enthusiastic references to rape and pillage, in order to present a British invading force in a favorable light.[13] In recalling the figure of Henry V, Pascal's film invites the cinema viewer to align herself with Caesar, as she did with Henry. By a process of association Caesar has become, if not quite "the very model of a Christian king," as Henry V was known, at least the representative of a just army of occupation: a British commander, for example, on the road for Cairo? In his company we are invited to enter Egypt, sharing his perception of its inveterate superstition and weakness of character.

There is no denying that Egypt is a disappointment to Caesar. He begins with such high hopes. The sphinx itself, for instance, he greets like an old friend: standing alone among the sands of the desert, he looks up at it, the stars behind it, and opens his heart. At last he confides, to what he takes to be an insentient stone figure of unspecified antiquity, he has found an end to his isolation. Or so he tells himself. It is evidently a rather qualified sort of intimacy he is anticipating from the sphinx and he is taken aback to be answered. He is hailed, with unwelcome realism as "Old gentleman." Instead of the silent sympathy of the monument, he is met by a childish little chatterbox, the girl-child Cleopatra (Figure 2).

From the first, Vivien Leigh is made to cut an insistently asexual figure. When she takes Claude Rains, who plays Caesar, by surprise here, the first impression is of their likeness. They are both so white. Classical folds of white fabric dress both bodies, though the woman's is more emphasized, to be sure, for her arms are exposed and the form of her legs can occasionally be made out. Her face, too, is lit to a dazzling whiteness, and the script calls for Rains to draw attention to his own white skin. A common European identity is established for rulers at the very start. Beyond the pair, the camera reveals a desert as bleak as a moonscape; all that is human is concentrated in these white forms. The actors brought with them screen histories of their own that played into this argument about race and mastery. Rains had been usually cast as an urbane and ironic observer, famous for his line in *Casablanca* (1942) "Round up the usual suspects," while the powerful memory of Leigh in *Gone With the Wind* (1939), as Scarlett, placed her again as white and as the appropriate mistress of black slaves.

It is through Cleopatra's voice that Egypt will speak in this film. Yet,

Figure 2.
A girlish
Cleopatra
takes Caesar
by the hand
near the
Sphinx. Photo
courtesy of
the British
Film Institute.

Cleopatra's dependence on teaching is the first feature that is brought to our attention. It leaps out at Caesar, too. In his wonder—perhaps still entertaining some hope that the sphinx was going to offer him a faithful reflection of himself—he had named Cleopatra at first sight as "a divine child" at the sphinx's breast. That glimpse of a lost maternal relation is soon dealt with. Once the Cleopatra that Shaw and Pascal imagined starts to reveal herself in speaking, Caesar revises his opinion. When Cleopatra herself claims to have divine origins and prattles about her ancestor the Nile who had given her such wavy hair, Caesar loses his initial wonder and becomes confident that Cleopatra has got it all wrong. Her sense of her own identity, particularly the femininity she has been schooled in, is clearly, or so we are invited to believe with Caesar, founded on an ignorance and superstition that are lamentable, though touching. Just as baseless is the notion she has of the Romans, whom she believes all have long noses like elephants. Yet we have just seen that Caesar himself has surprising notions about other people's bodies. He uttered solemn words of greeting and recognition to the image of a female body that is part lion, part woman, in the sphinx. If viewers felt that they were picking up a hint of sexual fantasy in the young girl's image of the Roman soldiers she had never met, or even in the Roman's response to the stone sphinx, the film would not offer them any encouragement to do so. Fantasy will be denied from now on, in the special version of a man's world created by the film and in the bright and antiseptic social manner with which Cleopatra greets the Roman who is to take charge of her, Julius Caesar.

It is in the ignorance of Cleopatra that Caesar will find his pleasure. Heterosexual desire is suppressed or absent; for this older man, the promise of Cleopatra lies in the hope that she may be rescued from the culture in which she has been shaped. To his mind, the young girl in white with unbound hair who approaches Caesar with such frank ignorance stands in evident need of his instruction. He intends to set her free from the bondage of a misconceived notion of the feminine, which she has presumably learned from Ftatateeta, to admit her into the larger ways of men. Caesar will be her new teacher. But when pedagogy becomes established as the metaphor that characterizes the relation between Caesar and Cleopatra, Rome and Egypt, colonialist politics are reengaged.

The first lesson is about taking charge. Cleopatra must learn to assume authority as men do, and there is no one, it seems, more important for a man to subjugate than the person who looked after him when he was small and helpless. Ftatateeta stands in the place of the mother; from her first appearance, Caesar makes it clear that Ftatateeta is to be quelled and not trusted. The film itself invites us to realize that we can see through her, by presenting her as an obvious forgery, daubed with the fake tan that was such a labor to Robson. Among the main characters, Ftatateeta's body alone is marked with absurdity in this way.[14] Her name is ridiculous too: Caesar repeatedly mocks and parodies it, as he does the formal language of the Egyptian court. At the end of the film, when Flatateeta is dead and Cleopatra is in mourning for her, Caesar can raise a smile from Cleopatra by a kindly word about "poor Teeta-Tota." It was Ftatateeta who was responsible for instructing Cleopatra in what being a woman meant and about religious observance. Is this what makes her so dangerous and so false?

Sometimes Egypt is an old woman, sometimes a young one, Cleopatra. The audience, if not Caesar, can tell all too soon what she will make of royal power, once she has her hands on it. Even before Cleopatra has put on her robes of state, at the first recognition of her power as queen, she reaches for a whip and a black body—a desiring body?—to beat with it (Figure 3). Though she may seem to be profiting

Figure 3. Caesar enjoying the sight of Cleopatra beating a black slave. Photo
courtesy of the British Film Institute.

from Caesar's instruction, when she agrees to stand firm, in her crown
and regalia, a magic figure before the Roman soldiers, we have been
shown her true nature (Figure 4). We may be compelled by the image
of an ancient authority that is Egyptian, the arms folded on the breast,
the crossed sickle and flail, but the power of that sign is immediately
dissolved as Cleopatra collapses, her head on Caesar's shoulder as he
twinkles and the soldiers smile their approval. Helpless, girlish, yet with
a touch of something vicious in authority, that's Cleopatra—or is it
Egypt?

The pedagogic model is in close sympathy with the way that the British administration claimed Egypt should be tackled at the time when
Shaw set out to tell the story of Cleopatra. This is not to say that the
British increased educational opportunities after their arrival; historians seem to concur that though the British improved the country's finances, expenditure on education was cut back.[15] There was a growing
demand for education, as Leila Ahmed has argued, which the British
met not by increasing the number of schools but by raising tuition fees.

Figure 4. Cleopatra is dressed in her crown and regalia to confront the Roman force. Photo courtesy of the British Film Institute.

Nevertheless, the notion that Egypt needed education had an important place in the rhetoric of its British rulers. And one of the first things that had to be learned from the West was how to bring women out into the world.

Orientalists chose to identify the veiling and seclusion that had become the practice among Islamic women as compelling evidence of the tyranny of their religion and its contempt for women. "The degradation of women in the East is a canker that begins its destructive work early in childhood, and has eaten into the whole system of Islam," wrote Stanley Lane-Poole.[16] It is an assumption that is still hard to challenge today. But the language in which the accusation was leveled, the appeal to the notion of degradation, declares its historical roots. As Lord Cromer, who acted as British agent and consul-general in Egypt from 1883 to 1907, claimed "The position of women in Egypt is a fatal obstacle to the attainment of that elevation of thought and character which should accompany the introduction of European civilisation."[17]

Those give-away images of elevation and decline point directly to the politics that are at stake. The rhetoric is one made familiar through the work of nineteenth-century ethnographers, who made use of developmental scales adopted from the work of philologists.[18] Ethnographers, the first anthropologists, working with the interests of colonialists, had taught that one culture or society could be measured against another. There would be a reliable consistency across their cultural and moral development. The more "advanced" a nation or race, the higher on the developmental scale, the more capable of founding sophisticated political institutions, and the more fitted for government it would be. And the higher the moral qualities its members would demonstrate. So any information about Egyptian society could be used to assess its place on the developmental scale.

Egyptian writings had been the symbol of arcane wisdom in European thought for centuries, but it was still possible to claim that degeneracy, a decline from former greatness, had taken place.[19] Examining the moral character of individual Egyptians in the present and scrutinizing contemporary institutions in Egyptian society would provide evidence on which a diagnosis of the nation as a whole could be based. This explains Cromer's concern to champion Egyptian women. He was so hostile to the advancement of women in his own country that he was a founding member of the Men's League for Opposing Women's Suffrage and had served as its president. The education of Egyptian women figures in Cromer's account only as a means of denoting the backwardness of their country; they are ciphers, ciphers in a colonialist argument designed to prove that Egyptian men are not sufficiently "advanced" to sustain the sophisticated political life of a modern state. Shaw appears to recapitulate that argument by the very form he gives to the relationship between Caesar and Cleopatra. It is because Egyptian culture is primitive and backward, even diseased, that Cleopatra, its queen, is so ignorant and so unfitted for rule. She can only equip herself to govern by learning from the representative of a more developed race and culture, learning from the men of Rome.

The film develops into a demonstration of what real ruling might look like. Early on Caesar had encouraged Cleopatra to put on her robes of state so that she would look like the queen of Egypt; yet she finished with her head on Caesar's shoulder. She may learn to dress like a woman and to claim authority over her nurse, but there is no dignity in her nursery squabbles with Ptolemy. Her brother, the king, has dignity only as he is taken to stand, like a temporary son, beside Caesar; the single lock of hair tied on one side of his head in the fashion of Egypt makes him look both freakish and authentic.[20] Only Roman ways command respect. There is all the difference in the world between the gesture of a Roman general in commandeering an altar for Caesar to use as a seat and the willful blasphemy of Cleopatra when she copies him. Cleopatra has no sense of the sacred.

What is sacred is what goes on between men, what Luce Irigaray calls the hommosexual economy, and the work men do together.[21] Caesar labors at his desk all night, served by Rufio, while Cleopatra, in a scene specially devised for the film, lies in bed asleep.[22] When Caesar goes off to fight, her bid for attention is only a foolish interruption, for his mind is on the men who serve him. When the scene changes to Alexandria, in a sense it moves into a present time that it shares with the film's viewers. For as the troops are introduced to the city they are planning to command, the film invites the audience to recognize that there is a contemporary real-life counterpart to this situation. Caesar jokes about "Peace with honor." In 1898 those words were already a quotation, mocking what Disraeli had said when he gave his account of the Treaty of Berlin. By the time the film was made, that origin was overshadowed by the memory of how Chamberlain, the British Prime Minister, had used the phrase in 1938 on his return from Munich, duped by Hitler. The film, though not the play, gives the words to Caesar; they underline his ironic insight into the world of politics. They even suggest he is looking directly into the experience of the postwar audience. It is this skeptical detachment that supposedly equips him for office and keeps his mind clear so he can profit from observing others.

The priority given to observation and study is quietly enforced in the sets for Egyptian Alexandria. Large areas are left free about white, classical buildings; flights of steps and regular masonry structures stake out a space that is legible, open. The set designer went to some trouble to secure this effect. It is interesting that the only record of significant *cinematic* effort in making the film offered by Marjorie Deans, the script editor who published a book-length account of the filming, concerns the difficulty of photographing the models that were used in creating some of the architectural effects (Figure 5).[23] It is important that the audience should feel that it is being taken into an orderly space which can be reliably known. It is by collecting and ordering knowledge that Orientalism and all institutionalized forms of Western knowledge go about their business.

Yet, the film itself reminds us that there must remain a residue of obscurity, which eludes its own ocular inspection. Near the close of *Caesar and Cleopatra,* that darkness will impose itself in an unexpected form. When the film opened, it did so on a literal darkness, a darkness intended to speak of superstition. That scene in the courtyard at Memphis is recalled toward the end of the film, when Cleopatra entertains her guests on the roof of the palace in the failing light. As the film would have it, she is regressing into the darkness out of which she came,

Figure 5. Architectural models for set photography. Photo courtesy of the British Film Institute.

surrounding herself with the giant stone figures of animals that her people worship. Although the film seems to be simply reproducing the familiar rhetoric that links darkness with superstition and knowledge with light, it is at this very moment that the film chooses to demonstrate how the eye and its ways of knowing fail to deliver the comprehensive account that they seem to claim. Cleopatra has called for the image of her ancestor, Father Nile, to ask a name for the new city Caesar will build her. When she invokes him, the revelation that comes is not a visible one, a sacred ritual to thrill the viewer, while offering the East up yet again for mastery, to be looked into. It is sound, a voice, the cry of a murdered man, that foils any anticipation of a sight. And we are never shown the body of Pothinus, the man who has died. Only his voice, a cry without language, lets the audience know that violence has taken place.

It may be in that moment that the film and the play it follows make their acknowledgment of the violence of the colonial project and show how it is linked with the drive to master by means of knowledge. Until that point the film has been busily engaged in the same work. But it is the emergence of the human voice as a counter to the regime of visibility that takes us back to question the difference between Europe and Egypt. According to Timothy Mitchell, Egyptians noted that the Europeans had a strange addiction to looking, and a poor sense of the risks involved.[24] This observation was one of the ways Egyptians registered their resistance to the habits that Europeans were promoting. Egyptians and Europeans used the senses and powers of the body differently, with Egyptians putting the emphasis on the ear and on the voice. For Egyptians, it was the human voice that transmitted understanding, not the eye. With this attitude went a strong sense of the slipperiness of language; texts needed trained interpreters, words could not safely be left to speak for themselves. The cry at the death of Pothinus in this film is not matched with the sight of the murdered body. The visual, so powerful and so confidently offered as legible evidence up to this point, fails. The wordless cry that is heard stops short of pretending to offer another form of transparency. It simply proposes to the viewer that something has gone terribly wrong, that a violent silencing has taken place.

If analysis of this film has proved disappointing, leading time and again to a dead end, to the banal arrogance of the colonist that was always in view from the beginning, perhaps it is time to try a new tack. What these analyses have lacked is a sense of the object of knowledge as a subject, with its own voice. Leila Ahmed, by lending a careful ear to the Koranic tradition, caught the note of a lost ethical voice that had been almost drowned out in the course of Islam's historical development. It is a voice that is favorable to women, according them equal importance and equal humanity with men.[25]

Tropes that could simply be read as Orientalist have served Shaw's quarrel with the lie of femininity and his impulse to work out its relation to the maternal in this film. It might help to try a different language for thinking about *Caesar and Cleopatra*, to consider it in terms of the relations between men and women, to think even in terms of those relations known as object relations. What has happened to desire in this film? In the end it is the voice of Shaw, as it is echoed by Pascal, that asks for our attention.

When Caesar stands in the sand, at the start of the film, he is unarmed and solitary. A sympathetic listener might register the voice of longing: Caesar's lament for a lost reciprocal intimacy. "Lips that would kiss/form prayers to broken stone" is the way another man wrestling with the Western heritage, the poet T. S. Eliot might have put it. He would go on to imagine the "difficulties of a statesman," like Caesar in his poem "Coriolan."[26] "What shall I cry?" that poem asks, only to answer itself immediately with the words "Mother mother." 

For once Caesar is admitting to a life of feeling and fantasy. He is talking about lack, and though he cannot identify what is missing as a maternal connection, he can allow himself a poetic language, which feels its way gropingly toward understanding. Shaw has put him to stand in a desert to say this: Pascal gives him darkness and space around him as he speaks. Using this language, one much more tentative than is usually endorsed by Shaw, Caesar will admit what he would never utter to another living creature: he feels incomplete; he is missing something that he calls "the lost regions from which his birth exiled him."[27] It is proximity to the sphinx that draws the admission out of him.

Tracking back and forth as he speaks, drawing a contrast between himself and the stone figure, he seems to be re-creating the sense of a dyad, even while he laments his falling out of it. It is an image that the camera creates on its own account: first holding both figures in the frame, then slowly noting the attentiveness of each to the other, focusing backward and forward between them in turn as the creature of flesh speaks. On the one hand stands Caesar, conscious of isolation and conscious also of himself as busy with the tasks of mastery—fighting and understanding. On the other stands the sphinx, with whom he claims kinship. But the sphinx is a reproach to his anxious scurryings: "I wander and you sit still; I conquer and you endure: I work and wonder, you watch and wait." Caesar is the most successful of men, but in the sphinx he finds an image of himself that makes him question masculine effectiveness.

There seems to be an agreement, *pace* Teresa de Lauretis and Laura Mulvey, that the sphinx brings questions rather than answers.[28] What is the world that Caesar is mourning, the world that the sphinx signifies? He calls it a "lost region—the home from which they have both strayed." It is a place where Caesar was once very close to what the sphinx reminds him of. "Have I not been conscious of you and of this place since I was born?" he appeals, wanting to be remembered, recalled.

He has already spoken of it as a place from which he was exiled by his birth. The body of the mother is known to the child both before birth and after it. Philosophers have only recently begun to take the maternal body as a subject for meditation, to question what it teaches the child that it supports. Luce Irigaray, in her recent work *Je, tu, nous*, reflects on the exemplary tolerance of difference manifested by the maternal body when it carries the Other within itself.[29] Teresa Brennan argues that it is only after birth, after being expelled from that enclosure in the mother, that the experience of time can begin, since in the womb there is no lapse felt between the moment of desire and its satisfaction.[30]

But after birth the child is still enveloped in the mother's attention, and it is the memory of this experience that seems to lie behind the sense of an enduring stillness, a mutuality that he once knew which haunts Caesar.[31] It is that way of knowing that shames the strivings for mastery that he has had to practice in order to be called a man. Among men, living under that regime of competition, he could never find mutuality again. It is only to be found with the sphinx, who like him is a "stranger to the race of men."

To the Caesar who acknowledges that this long ago experience has constituted "his Reality," Rome, the enterprise to which he has dedicated himself, is "only a madman's dream." The symbol of Western man's highest ambition and achievement, his accumulated knowledge, civilization itself, is cut loose from its moorings in reason and cast away, while Caesar admits himself to be, like the Sphinx "part brute, part woman, part god." With the Rome Caesar discards so freely at this point, masculinity goes too, apparently cast away as an empty category.

Out of this extraordinary admission, this moment of open repudiation, it is hardly surprising that what emerges is the interrupted dynamic of the film, with its underlying sense of frustration and stasis, its absence of conviction and its failure to convince. What do they say about kitsch? Isn't it the art that lies?

The play of *Caesar and Cleopatra* may represent itself as a celebration of Western ways of knowing, embodied in the authority of Caesar's vision. As a play it does not put that rational, scopic order under pressure. Perhaps only when it comes to be translated into film, a medium that acknowledges the way structures that are unconscious and outside the control of reason are engaged through the eye, does the way open to doubt. What happens to desire in the film, under these circumstances, when it can only be figured under the sign of the sphinx? Perhaps we really were meant to notice something of the sphinx about Flora Robson. (We are told that Pascal was so concerned to get the look of the sphinx's nose right that he modeled it himself in the end, swinging alongside in a painter's cradle.)[32] This woman, carrying a brown stain on her skin and wearing a ludicrous wig, was designed to look ugly and to speak the impossibility of desire through her body. It is a matter of envy, as Melanie Klein might have said, the destruction of what is good in the object.[33] Robson is the one who will tell Cleopatra not to scent or paint herself, not to put on the shows of femininity. Cleopatra must not make herself sexual for that is not something Caesar will respond to. In the contradiction between the maternal body and the masquerade of femininity, Caesar's heterosexual desire is obliterated.

According to the order of colonialism, the many signs of compromised masculinity around the Egyptian court, in the figures of Pothinus,

Theodotus, and Apollodorus, are nothing but degenerate. But if we enter the film anew, on the sphinx's terms, as it were, these men may have something in common with the Caesar who has expressed his doubts about the fiction of masculinity. Certainly he admits some connection with Theodotus, the tutor—"I am an author myself." But it is the casting of Stewart Granger as Apollodorus that prompts the deeper reflection. Granger's body, whether stripped for a swallowdive into the sea, or flaunting itself aloft on a crane, is the most unequivocally eroticized one in the film. His skin is colored with a tan that speaks of pleasures, rather than of race. The clasp of a bangle on his muscular upper arm presents this body as one to be touched, not held at arm's length to be read. The jewelery he wears, from the large single stud earring to the bracelets and choker, suggest the weight of metal on warm skin. His rust-colored off-the-shoulder tunic leaves one nipple just uncovered. Standing beside him in the same scene, the body of Cleopatra extends no such invitation. It is trussed, from the hair bound into pigtails in awkward mimicry of her younger brother's, to the fussy detailing of her tightly done-up bodice. There is a thin glitter of tinsel about her decorations; any resonance of sexuality is suppressed.

Before diving, Apollodorus stands on a high ledge, his skirt swinging as the camera peeps up at him. Caesar is his ungainly copy when he dives; the floundering as he strikes out with Cleopatra clinging to his back, viewed in a muddle of limbs and figures from the air, is the closest the film will come to imaging sexual contact and the position adopted is *a tergo*, a posture of male same-sex desire.

Apollodorus is a figure of mock-heroic fantasy, with his swordfights and his special relationship with Cleopatra, all flourish and charm but empty of sexual tension. He embodies a kind of token identification with her, teasing and unsatisfactory as the audience knows; Caesar and Rufio are in collusion with him, in this masquerade of masculinity, and they tolerate him because he keeps Cleopatra happy and saves them the trouble of talking to her. What constitutes masculinity here is not the recognition of sexual difference but the recognition of the same: it is a hommosexual economy. Heterosexuality is deferred, for Cleopatra's future with Mark Antony.

If femininity, in the person of Cleopatra, has to be created as transparently false, what happens to Ftatateeta, who has to bear the full weight of the maternal, is yet more extreme. She actually executes the murder that Cleopatra only urges her toward. The men stand and watch a criminal complicity between them: when Cleopatra kisses the murderer and hangs her with her own jewels, the identity they share as women is confirmed. The intimacy between them takes on a strongly sexualized tone and is seen to be founded on the wish to destroy men.

There does not seem to be much scope here for resistance. Yet it is open to the viewer to identify with Cleopatra, too. First we must discard the assumption, structured into the presentation, that she is undeserving of trust, worthless. How does the film look then? A promising elderly friend, who offered to make a queen of her, first disappoints her by favoring her brother when they are fighting between themselves. Though Cleopatra starts by wanting to be Caesar's companion, he makes it clear that he doesn't want her with him in his active life. His instruction, rather than helping to strengthen her power, seems to be putting her rule in danger. It becomes essential to hide from him the steps she needs to take to protect herself, to lie. When she asks for reassurance, he crushes her. When Caesar gives up in the end and leaves, she is a little sad to see him go, since she was fond of him, but the last thing she wants is for him to come back. She wants to rule without his admonitions in the company of a young man who will be a sexual partner for her.

Read from the point of view of Cleopatra, the film seems to offer a narrative about difference and the way a man's theories of how to live might force his daughter out of true, make her choose between independence and lying.[34] With that notion of singleness in authority, we are returned to the question of knowledge. But the film itself has suggested that there is more than one way to read Caesar and Cleopatra and how they treat each other. This is the moment when we might be ready to put the film's different ways of knowing together. You can make it into a classical Oedipal narrative: Caesar orders young Cleopatra's sexuality for her: he alone of men won't let her seduce him; he is not to be treated like other men, as the maternal Ftatateeta tells her, but he promises to send her a young man she will be permitted to love in the body. You can make it an Oedipal narrative, and not disturb or add to the stories Western culture tells about how life has to be organized, or you can ask to resist yet again and see it as a story about the girl's loss of the mother. That might be a compulsory part of Western civilization too.

Caesar comes between the two women on his arrival, takes Cleopatra away from the primeval darkness of Memphis to educate her himself in the open light of Alexandria. Envy makes him observe her lingering intimacy with Ftatateeta critically, as evidence of how dangerous both women are and how untrustworthy. The murder of Ftatateeta is represented as an act of justice. For her last appearance in the film, Cleopatra cuts a different figure. She appears with her head covered by a dark cloak, to match her costume. Her person speaks of mourning, whatever words her mouth may utter. It is Irigaray who has theorized mourning as the experience of young women.[35] She names an underlying mourning that girls cannot come to the end of, which manifests itself in depression. They are left stranded with this grief, she claims, because in Western culture, at the psychological level, a separation is enjoined between mother and daughter. Irigaray is not talking about violence but about the way the individual situates herself in the culture: she merely observes that few stories, certainly not enough, are told to mark the relation between mothers and daughters in the West. It is a matter of absence and silence to which Irigaray draws attention and to which, in its way, Pascal's film bears witness.

A new print of *Caesar and Cleopatra* was screened at the London Film Festival in 1992. As the lights went up, viewers where I was sitting glanced uneasily at each other, then concentrated on looking for their gloves. I don't know if it was really shame that we were feeling. Was it such a failure, to have come hoping for pleasure? It seemed to have left us face-to-face with disappointment. Perhaps that disappointment originates in the disappointment of Shaw himself. When desire finds its way into the film, at moments, it is like Caesar and Cleopatra entering the darkened palace at Memphis, in haste and without a word.

## Notes

1. Janet Dunbar, *Flora Robson* (London, Harrap, 1960), 226.
2. Ibid, 196.
3. See Antonia Lant, *Blackout: Reinventing Women for Wartime British Cinema* (Princeton: Princeton University Press, 1991).
4. Liz-Anne Bawden, ed. *Oxford Companion to Film* (Oxford: Oxford University Press, 1976), 103.
5. Edward Said, *Orientalism* (New York: Vintage, 1979), 38.
6. L. C. Wright, *United States Policy toward Egypt 1930–1914* (New York: Exposition Press, 1969), 161. See also Leila Ahmed, *Women and Gender in Islam: Historical Roots of a Modern Debate* (New Haven: Yale University Press, 1992).
7. Caesar, trans. Jane F. Mitchell, *The Civil War* (London: Harmondsworth, 1967) Book 3, chap.107 .
8. See Mary Hamer, *Signs of Cleopatra: History, Politics, Representation* (London and New York: Routledge, 1992).
9. Marjorie Deans, *Meeting at the Sphinx: Gabriel Pascal's Production of Bernard Shaw's Caesar and Cleopatra* (London: 1946), 89, 94–95.
10. Ibid. Shaw's Introductory Note.
11. Quoted in Dan H. Laurence and James Rambeau, eds., *Bernard Shaw Agitations: Letters to the Press 1875–1950* (New York: Frederick Ungar, 1985) 49–51.
12. Wright, *United States Policy*, 84–94.
13. Jack J. Jorgens, *Shakespeare on Film* (Bloomington: Indiana University Press, 1977), 125.
14. Street Egyptians, though not members of the court, are also dyed brown; color marks class as well as race.

15. See Wright, *United States Policy*, 226, and Ahmed, *Women and Gender*, 137–138.
16. Quoted in Ahmed, *Women and Gender*, 152.
17. Ibid., 153.
18. Said, *Orientalism*, 131, 133
19. See M. Bernal, *Black Athena: the Afro-Asiatic Roots of Classical Civilization*, (New Brunswick: Rutgers University Press, 1987).
20. The sidelock of youth or childhood is found in Egyptian representation from the Old Kingdom to the Ptolemaic period. Because it is idiosyncratic and the fashion appeared to remain unchanged over a long historical period, it could seem to offer a casual shorthand for reminding viewers that Egypt might be both exotic and irredeemably backward.
21. Margaret Whitford, *Luce Irigaray: Philosophy in the Feminine* (London: Routledge, 1991), 104.
22. Deans, *Meeting at the Sphinx* , 50.
23. Ibid., 112–113.
24. Timothy Mitchell, *Colonising Egypt* (Cambridge: Cambridge University Press, 1988), 2–3; for the importance of the voice in the transmission of meaning, see 82–84, 92, 132–137.
25. Ahmed, *Women and Gender*, 66.
26. T. S. Eliot, *Collected Poems 1909–1962* (London: Faber, 1963) 142.
27. Bernard Shaw, *Caesar and Cleopatra* (New York: Brentano, 1906), 100. Subsequent quotations from this speech are taken from this edition, 100–101.
28. Teresa de Lauretis, *Technologies of Gender* (Basingstoke: Macmillan, 1989), and Laura Mulvey, *Visual and Other Pleasures* (Basingstoke: Macmillan, 1989). See also Jean-Joseph Goux, *Oedipus, Philosopher*, (Stanford: Stanford University Press, 1994 ) for further explorations of the Sphinx and the problem of knowledge.
29. Luce Irigaray, trans. Alison Martin, *Je, tu, nous: Toward a Culture of Difference* (New York and London: Routledge, 1993), 37–44.
30. Teresa Brennan, *History after Lacan* (New York: Routledge,1993), 105.
31. The work of Colwyn Trevarthen on early interaction between mothers and infants is suggestive here. See particularly "Sharing makes sense: Intersubjectivity and the Making of an Infant's Meanings," in R. Steele and T. Threadgold, eds., *Language Topics: Essays in Honour of Michael Halliday* (Amsterdam and Philadelphia: John Benjamin, 1987), 177–201.
32. Deans, *Meeting at the Sphinx*, 89.
33. See Melanie Klein, *Envy and Gratitude and Other Works: 1946–1963* (London: Virago, 1988).
34. The imposition of this choice has been identified and explored in the work of both Joan Rivière and Carol Gilligan. See Joan Rivière, "Womanliness as Masquerade," in Victor Burgin et al., eds., *Formations of Fantasy* (London: Methuen, 1986), 35–44; and Lynn Mikel Brown and Carol Gilligan, *Meeting at the Crossroads: Women's Psychology and Girls' Development* (Cambridge, Mass.: Harvard University Press, 1992).
35. For a helpful introduction to Irigaray's thought, see Whitford, *Luce Irigaray: Philosophy in the Feminine*, especially 76–89 on the relationship between mothers and daughters.

Phebe Shih Chao

# Reading *The Letter* in a Postcolonial World

"The Letter" is one of six stories by Somerset Maugham in a collection called *The Casuarina Tree* (1926). All the stories are set in the Federated Malay States. Maugham wrote in the preface: "The casuarina tree which grows along the shores of tropical lands as if to protect the land from storms, suggests the planters and administrators who . . . have after all brought to the peoples among whom they dwell tranquility, justice, and welfare."[1] Such a statement does not do justice to his stories, which show more ambivalence and less smugness toward the colonial experience.

In his analysis of colonialism, Frantz Fanon, taking the point of view of the colonized, noted that there are three stages to the process: first, the native peoples imitate, adapt to, and assimilate with the colonials; second, there is a moment of hesitation, a slow awakening and realization that not everything the colonial does has a positive effect for the native, or in Fanon's own words, "the native is disturbed; he decides to remember what he is" and desires to return to the time and place and traditional culture that existed before the arrival of the colonials; third, there is active resistance to the outside power, or "the fighting phase," when the native "turns himself into an awakener of the people."[2] We could extend Fanon to note an analogous process for the white colonial: first, there is both an unquestioning attitude and a near-total acceptance of imperialism; second, the thoughtful moment of guilt in terms of what colonialism has done (can do) to the colonial master—look at the awful thing it has done to me; and finally, usually too late to "rescue" the system, the realization of what it has done to the native peoples and, occasionally, a need to make amends. Each of the two processes, Other and white, goes its own way in its own time. They do not necessarily coincide.

In his work, Maugham reaches the equivalent of what I just labeled the second stage of white (colonial) development. Though he is sensitive to the colonial resonance in all phases of life in Asia, he is not particularly self-conscious about the damage that has been done to the native by British imperialism; his real concern is for the pain and suffering of the white colonial that is the direct result of his relationship with the Other.[3] Very like William Faulkner's guilt over the institution of slavery and his alarm concerning the damage it had done to the whites,[4] Maugham takes a similarly dark view of the British ruling class in Southeast Asia. However, he uses an urbane ironic tone. The protagonist of "The Letter" is (we are led to believe) a heretofore honest lawyer, Howard Joyce, upholder of the authority of the Crown. For his crisis-stricken friends, a "rubber-planter" and his wife, Joyce pays money to acquire and suppress evidence that would damage his client, the wife, in court. The woman, at the end, gets away with murder. So much for white justice, Maugham seems to say.

From the beginning, Maugham's irony is subtle but evident. He contrasts the hot streets crowded with "men of all colours, black Tamils, yellow Chinks, brown Malays, Armenians, Jews and Bengalis" with the "pleasantly cool," "dark," "agreeably quiet" interior of the British law firm, where Howard Joyce is sitting "in his private room . . . with an electric fan turned full on him."[5] Observant of the difference, Maugham clearly prefers the way of life of Empire to an Other alternative; although one could ask, who would prefer the fierce sun beating down, there is nonetheless no identification/sympathy apparent for the Others and, beyond the cataloging, no real differentiation among Them. The capacity to put himself in the shoes of the Other is absent. The multicultural natives are object and never subject. Maugham sees the ludicrous aspect of the native that he wouldn't see in himself. He is not alone; few, if any, in the subject position of white colonialism see themselves as laughable.[6]

In Maugham it is the natives who are laughable; only the lawyer's dilemma has claim toward the high moral plain of the tragic. There is pathos to the white man, no matter how stupid, and at least one, Robert Crosbie, the husband, is called "a stupid man" (208) by his own lawyer. There is also pathos in Leslie Crosbie, Robert's wife, described by Joyce as "a fragile creature . . . graceful rather than pretty . . . [whose]

wrists and ankles were very delicate" (188). Leslie is in jail, after confessing to the murder of Geoff Hammond, a brave ("a D.S.O. and an M.C.") and handsome friend whose only fault, according to gossip, seems to have been "that he was too fond of the girls" (190). Leslie claims that Hammond had come to her house, drunk, to rape her. The lawyer does not understand why she had to pump six bullets into the alleged interloper, and he cannot reconcile the "savagery" of the action with this "most respectable of women" (194). But, a few pages later, Maugham gives us a hint as to what could have motivated Leslie and why she will ultimately be forgiven by her society: "That was one of the things which had turned public opinion most vehemently against Hammond. It came to be known that for several months he had had a Chinese woman living in his house" (196). Still later, to make sure we see, he explains again: "The fact, which was discovered after his death, that [Hammond] had been living with a Chinese woman . . . robbed him of any sympathy which might have been felt for him" (202). If Maugham is ultimately ironic here in his treatment of Joyce's limited point of view, he gives us no internal evidence within the story that the possibility of any response other than disgust could exist to Hammond's choice of a native woman.

It would be appropriate at this point to see the significantly nameless Chinese woman through the lawyer's eyes: "She was a stoutish person, not very young, with a broad, phlegmatic face. She was powdered and rouged and her eyebrows were a thin black line, but she gave you the impression of a woman of character. . . . She walked slowly, with the air of a woman sure of herself, but with a certain heaviness of tread" (211). One could argue that character and confidence might be attractive traits, but it is clear that these male colonials prefer Leslie's thinness and paleness and small bones. As long as Leslie is a "lady," she will be defended; as long as she is able to maintain the appearance of being a "lady," she will be defendable in court. The Law of society is there to prevent her from breaking out of being a "lady," from crossing into desirous transgression against the social code of her own kind. She learns that lesson well. Considerable emphasis is placed on Leslie's good breeding, repeatedly mentioned by the lawyer, "You had only to look at her to know what sort of people she had and what kind of surroundings she had lived in. Her fragility gave her a singular refinement" (198); her refined taste is evident even in jail, where "she was as ever neatly and simply dressed" (197). This, in turn, is contrasted with her Chinese rival. Maugham focuses on the Other's display, "heavy gold chain . . . gold bangles . . . gold ear-rings . . . gold pins in her black hair" (211).

As Leslie is confronted with a native rival for Hammond's affection,

Howard Joyce is also confronted with a native counterpart, Ong Chi Seng, his Chinese clerk. Ong speaks "beautiful English" (184). Yet he has "difficulty with the letter r," which Maugham explains many pages later (205) after the clerk had tripped time and again over *fliend* and the phrase *more better*. This is Maugham seeing the joke of the Other. Mockery is a strategy for keeping Them in check. Ong tells the lawyer of the existence of a letter, written by Leslie to Hammond, imploring him to come to her house while her husband is out of town. This letter must be bought if the lawyer wants to win the case. The letter ruins Leslie's claim to be a lady, and could hang her besides. The lawyer confronts Leslie, who, after coolly denying it, appropriately faints (verifying a white woman's weakness), before she finally admits to having written it. Joyce is too far gone, too committed to winning, too compromised morally by the East ("he had lived in the East a long time, and his . . . honor was not perhaps so acute as it had been . . . " [204]). He persuades Leslie's husband to come up with the ten thousand dollars, and the two men, Joyce and Crosbie, go to the Chinese quarters to pay Hammond's Chinese woman for the incriminating letter. Maugham's "The Letter" ends with Leslie's acquittal and putative freedom, her full admission to the lawyer that Hammond had "been my lover for years" (214). Her husband now knows, and Maugham implies that husband and wife will continue bound together in their own prisonhouse, the gracious estate of the rubber-planter.

In William Wyler's film version of *The Letter* (1940), a significant change takes place.[7] When one compares it to the Maugham story on which it is based, Wyler creates, visually and through subtle changes in the narrative, a far more active questioning of the premises of colonialism. Tony Gaudio's camera and Howard Koch's script demystify the colonial situation, lay bare its problems, and make them accessible to the spectator.

One might well ask why Wyler was more sensitive to the evils of colonialism and the problems of Otherness than Maugham. Maugham took his Britishness with him everywhere, even in his "exile." On the other hand, though Wyler came to the United States from Mulhouse (Alsace-Lorraine), and often returned to Europe before Hitler's rise, he was a Jew of the diaspora. He had to adapt in ways Maugham didn't even dream of. He was an internationalist, like many of the Hollywood crowd, and part of a German colony whose list "grew forever longer as Nazism chased Germany's best minds into exile."[8] These artists experienced firsthand what it was to be an Outsider in the United States. These theatrical gypsies had less in common with the plantation class than they did with the "Armenians, Jews, and Bengalis" who were viewed with disdain by Maugham.

However much can be attributed to the director's personal loss of the comfortable culture of the Old World and the necessity of struggle in the brash new one, the fact of the matter is that Wyler showed that he understood the relationship between the dominant culture and the Other. He went beyond Maugham. He comprehended and empathized with the nonwhite population, the oppressed. Like a later expatriate to Hollywood, Douglas Sirk, Wyler communicated meaning through the use of a deliberate against-the-grain ambiguity.

In the first image of the film, the opening sequence right after the credits, we see the economic base of colonialism, the sap of the rubber tree. If oil is black gold, rubber excrescence was white gold in the Federated Malay States. Later in the film, a bartender at the Anglo club states explicitly the reason for colonialism: "Too bad rubber won't grow in a civilized climate." The milky sap is like semen and is an objective correlative for the economy of miscegenation (Figure 1). The white woman kills the white man for letting it go to the Asian woman—a convergence of race/ gender/ class. The camera pauses to contemplate the dripping sap/semen; then, the camera pans from the moon in a

Figure 1. The sap of the rubber tree in a shot that points to the economic base of colonialism.

high-angle crane shot to a fenced compound, with fences like the open bamboo squares of a cage or a pen.[9]

Through the camera's long-take examination of space, a layout of great claritiy structured by art director Carl Jules Weyl, Wyler shows the separation of the Chinese from the whites: the garden is the buffer zone, with lush plantings barely under control, threatening to return civilization back to jungle. Whatever is outside the walls or fences is uncontrollable. In one of the few signature deep-focus shots in this film, Wyler foregrounds the greenery and fences but in the depth of the shot allows us to see the front door from which two people are emerging, making it visually clear to the audience that one area impinges on the other. The spatial metaphor demarcating house from wilderness, order from disorder, civilization from barbarism, the colonial ruler from the native, occurs throughout the rest of the film, until at the end the Asian woman wreaks her revenge when Leslie Crosbie steps outside the walls of another compound. In the brilliant conclusion of Maugham's story, the British woman has gotten away with her crime and is only punished by having to spend the rest of her life with the husband whom she does not love but who knows her duplicity and transgressions against society. Because the Hays Production Code insisted on the criminal's punishment, Wyler added the coda, which, ironically (since it is hard to imagine that Maugham's ending could be improved), has the effect of heightening the sense that we are seeing the native's side, the native's revenge against white authority.

Wyler uses the image of the moon in the sky with a tall palm tree angled toward the center of the screen in the credit sequences at both the beginning and the end. There will always be a moon, yes. But the film suggests that it is at once absolute (an eternal verity) and ambiguous (it may/might light up the dark). As if to emphasize the possibility that it might not, clouds pass across the face of the moon. Now moonlight, now clouds. Michael Anderegg posits the introduction of "the moon motif as a way of linking conflicting emotions. A full moon presides as Leslie murders her lover, both a witness to and (in its association with lunacy) an instigator of her crime of passion." He also reminds us that "the pronounced contrast between areas of dark and light reinforces the sharp duality of Leslie's nature."[10] Like the Jacobean poet/playwright George Chapman, Wyler has written his own "Ode to Night" and to the nature of obscurity. The moon, like the camera eye, could see all, but then again, the camera can't see in the dark. What Wyler does is present us with a series of visual statements, from which we perceive that the story, as in film noir, takes place in spiritual darkness, with dark motives, dark doings, dark secrets, dark covering over, dark deals, dark conclusions. Murder on a moonlit night begins the action, and murder on a moonlit night ends it.

The narrative begins at the Crosbies' luxurious compound. The opening sequence, however, shows not the Crosbies but the people of color, native rubber workers and servants, who are crowded into an extended open shed, with their hammocks layered one over the other (Figure 2). They are off-duty, one fingering the flute, another the drum, others playing dominoes; most are napping. We hear shots, one after another, and our first glimpse of the white woman is through the leaves, from the point of view of the open shed. The spectator is positioned in the place of the colonized. We see a man stumbling out of the door onto the veranda, followed by the woman holding a gun. The man falls flat at the bottom of the veranda steps, sprawled on the ground. Head Boy (Tetsu Komai), a middle-aged servant, runs through the garden to the house to find his woman-master, Leslie Crosbie (Bette Davis), holding a smoking gun, standing on the steps looking down on the dead man's body. The corpse of the white man is taken to the Asian (Chinese and Malay) workers' space outside the fence, not only because nothing unpleasant should be inside the (white)man-made Eden, but also, we will find out,

Figure 2. Native rubber workers and servants crowded into a shedlike space.

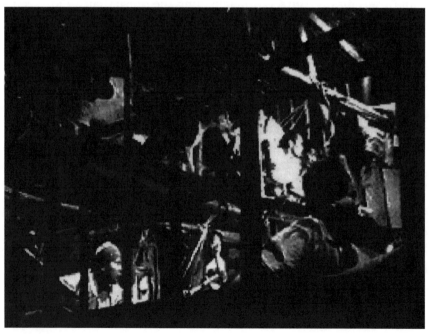

because his trespasses (in the sense of the Lord's Prayer as well) into the native world finally define his identity, his own ethnic bias. A native woman comes to view the body. She is his wife, and therefore, in colonial logic, his transgression. We have noted Maugham's words on the victim's transgression. The film emphasizes it more by adding: "Just produce evidence that Hammond was married to her" and that would be enough evidence of his decadence to win over the all-white jury. By the colonial code, marriage is more reprehensible than concubinage, since a Christian sacrament is being blasphemed. The taboo of miscegenation that Hammond broke is so powerful that he was socially isolated,[11] and now his body needs to be quarantined as if he had had a dread disease. Sexual desire is a "loathsome disease," as Leslie, much later, confessing her desire for the man she killed, names it; sexual desire is intricately tied to the taboo of miscegenation.

Hammond's body is taken to the shed, the space established by the camera as outside exclusively white territory. The Eurasian wife is secretly brought into the compound by Head Boy. As she views the body of her husband, strips of what seem to be rubber, the medium of exchange, the motivation for colonial aspiration, are drying around her (Figure 3). She is speechless and impassive in the moonlight. There's an airless, still, dark quality in the drying shed that contrasts with the end of the film when a "free" Leslie Crosbie ventures out beyond the walls of the safe Eden of residential Singapore. Having been acquitted, Leslie walks away from Mrs. Joyce's celebration victory party in her honor, and from the familiar music of her culture. The camera, once again, in a high-angle shot shows the spatial configuration of colonialism: the Joyces' privileged white compound. The action concludes outside the walls of the compound before the camera pans back to the moon. It is a mirror sequence of the opening shots, or a chiasmus, *ab* beginning and *ba* concluding.

Even though the white residential compounds are in different locales, the effect is the same. In Wyler's coda, Leslie is murdered by the Eurasian wife with a dagger. This satisfies the Hays Production Code by showing that she has been unambiguously punished for her crime. The faintly lit, dark human drama is played out under the inanimate, objective, inscrutable moon, which has been instrumental in what it is we do see. The Asian guard, who encounters the Asian wife and Head Boy, knows instinctively that unauthorized Asians lurking near a compound wall should be apprehended. Again, the Hays Production Code (as well as the need to calm the anxieties of the film's anticipated audience of whites, who might be startled by the spectacle of the colonized taking justice into their own hands) is fulfilled, this time by implying that the wife and Head Boy will not go unpunished, either.[12] What kind of justice these Asians will receive is perhaps a question that only the postcolonial reader of the film will ask, or does Wyler suggest the irony when he pans to the silent moon for an answer? Why would a Western viewer be interested in a continuation of their story? They are not the main characters, and they don't speak English or they don't speak. Ong is the exception that we will come back to.

One could argue that the walled compound is a microcosm of the concessions wrested by the British from the Chinese after the Opium War, large toeholds like Hong Kong and Singapore where the film takes place. The British were not the only imperialistic power. The French concession in Shanghai was the quiet, beautiful, wealthy, and European section of that city. The Germans made Qingtao into a beer-producing cathedral town, capitalism and the church taking over hand in hand. The Opium War is one of the most egregious examples of the West corrupting the East. When Leslie ventures behind Chung Hi's curio shop to buy back the eponymous letter, the proprietor is fouling the air with opium smoke, which can be read against the grain. Admittedly, Wyler

Figure 3. Strips of rubber, the medium of exchange, drying around the Eurasian wife.

does not help the historically uninformed read the scene with an understanding that it was the West, by forcing the opium trade, that was, in fact, ultimately responsible for fouling the air. Maugham, however, commenting on Joyce's declining professional honor, suggests the opposite (in a passage previously alluded to): "[Joyce] had lived in the East a long time, and his sense of professional honor was not perhaps so acute as it had been twenty years before" (204).

Indoors and outdoors are eloquent signifiers, but the real visual focus of meaning in this film is the space between the two, between the inner sanctum of the walled compound where the whites live and the quarters occupied by the natives. The viewer of *The Letter* does not have to know history or geography to understand the significance of the walled compound. It is to keep the races segregated; whites in, dark-skinned natives out. The viewer does not have to be too perceptive either to see that the whites have their own laws and law courts in particular, not to mention their own language and customs in general. A white woman kills a white man and goes to a white court before white-wigged, white lawyers and judges. Asians without much contact with the West would have found the costume and headdress reminiscent of regional opera.

Most of what happens in the film takes place indoors, and mostly connected to British doings: conversation over tea, lunch at the club, a dance party, the interview in prison, the buying of the letter, the courtroom. Very few scenes occur outdoors: the crowded streets of the "native quarter"; the shooting where Leslie has followed Hammond out of the house, emptying the gun as she descends the veranda steps; clearly outdoors, the stabbing of Leslie. Indoors seems to represent civilization and society and its repression, masking, or control of individual feelings and passions. Charles Affron notes that "Davis's face is repeatedly broken by lines of light and shadow and by the light that passes through blinds," and continues, "this use of blinds . . . suggests a 'bar' motif . . . which both points to where Leslie legally deserves to be (in prison) as well as to where she actually is (in the 'prison' formed by her life as a Malayan planter's wife)."[13] Even if Leslie had not transgressed, her gender would have kept her inside the confines of shadow walls. But once again, gender is linked with race. The viewer has seen the "bar" metaphor previously used with the open-work bamboo wall that keeps the natives within their dormitory space. In his essay "White," Richard Dyer speaks specifically of *Jezebel*, the film Wyler made with Bette Davis in 1938. Dyer suggests that Julie, the female protagonist of *Jezebel*, is associated with blackness because of her defiance,[14] "because she does not conform to notions of white womanhood."[15] In a similar configuration, Leslie is associated with the natives not through her actions but in this imprisoning visual image that defines the oppressed place of the Other, whether native or female.

If indoors is civilized order, outdoors is amoral, the realm of nature. As Dyer observes of *Jezebel*, "progressive ideas on race . . . spring from ideas of the closeness of non-European (and even nonmetropolitan) peoples to nature, ideas which were endemic to those processes of European expansion variously termed exploration, nation building and colonialism. . . . Expansion into other lands place the humans encountered there as part of the fauna of those lands, to be construed either as the forces of nature that had to be subjugated or, for liberals, the model of sweet natural Man uncontaminated by civilization."[16] Undoubtedly, Wyler continued to think in those terms for *The Letter*, and his interest in Otherness was obviously whetted by his previous exploration of plantation life in the American South. But by moving the site to Southeast Asia, the Other perforce became Asian instead of African-American. Dyer says that the powerful sense of "life [of the black slaves in *Jezebel*] . . . tends to mean the body, the emotions, sensuality and spirituality; it is usually explicitly counterposed to the mind and the intellect, with the implication that white people's over-investment in the cerebral is cutting them off from life and leading them to crush the life out of others and out of nature itself."[17] But the "natural" aspects of the African cannot be easily transposed to the Asian, whose stereotype is that he is cerebral. In this version of the stereotype, the Asian, unlike the "plantation darkies," is no fun; he can neither dance nor sing. Wyler does, however, keep his "natural" counterparts in the native coolies who have taken the places of the African-American slaves. Like Mrs. Hammond, they are not allowed to speak, but unlike her, they are not of the entrepreneurial class. They must scurry to do the bidding of the white masters; in the first minutes of the film, at Leslie Crosbie's bidding, the door is firmly shut in their faces by Head Boy. These particular natives are signifiers of class as well as of ethnicity. Can we assume that Wyler knowingly constructed these layers of ethnic Others? In any case, Wyler only ambiguously rehabilitated some of the Others, as we will see.

The hatred of the colonized Chinese toward their white oppressors in Singapore is nakedly apparent in the scene where Howard Joyce (James Stephenson)[18] and Leslie (the film's substitution of Leslie for Robert in this scene is considerably more dramatic)[19] are taken by the clerk to the Chinese ghetto to pay the money to Mrs. Hammond. We see and hear the derisive laughter of the woman's agent, Chung Hi (Willie Fung). His was a bit part added by Wyler but, surprisingly, given a name. Chung Hi witnesses the transaction and the enjoyable sight of the humiliation of the white people (Figure 4).

Figure 4. The derisive laughter of the Chinese witnessing the transaction.

Ong (played by the superb Sen Yung), who conducts the negotiation, is an ambivalent character.[20] He subverts his English superior's high principles—that is, he alerts Joyce to the existence of the letter and helps him buy it in order to keep it from becoming a crucial piece of evidence. Has Ong been corrupted by the West, or is his ability to corrupt innately Other? There is no more brilliant depiction in classic Hollywood cinema of the colonized personality metamorphosing from the first stage of Fanon's three-step process (acceptance of colonialism) to the second (awakening), and verging on the third (active resistance). Ong is fawning and obsequious when we first see him; it suits his strategy. Then he takes charge, managing his superior's appointments, engagements, even game plan (for the Crosbies' defense), performing a more natural—that is, independent, precolonized—role. Finally, in the courtroom, his unsmiling face shows that his perfect assimilation of the niceties of the British legal system have led to his realization that the system can be bent to suit the needs of the very people it was designed to crush, or rather, be made to turn itself back on the very whites it was designed to privilege and thus expose their corruptibility to the light of the moon. He leaves assassination and its perils, the violence implicit in the third stage, to Mrs. Hammond and Head Boy.

The half-Chinese woman (a change by Wyler chiefly due to casting considerations), now wife, is played by a non-Chinese, Gale Sondergaard.[21] She also sends a double message: she is a Dragon Lady, tough and scary, dressed in dark material overlaid in gold, a heavy Chinese brocade lit to seem as impenetrable, and as stiff, as armor, while the Bette Davis character is in soft, misty white, romantic and vulnerable. The lacy mantilla on her head is associated with her gentlewoman's hobby of lacemaking. The Chinese woman's eyes are dark slits of hatred; the camera focuses on the Englishwoman's eyes, lit like bright jewels. The unknowable East has emerged briefly to exotic tinkling. That is the only sound at the beginning of the transaction, a striking change before the return to Max Steiner's insistent musical score that parallels and reinforces the emotional excess of the melodrama throughout the film. The Eurasian woman comes through the beaded curtain to stand two steps higher than the white "lady" (Figure 5). She may look frightening, but she is in the right, and after she demands that Leslie come closer (over the objections of the lawyer) so that she can

Figure 5. The Chinese woman standing two steps higher than the white "lady."

get a full view of her husband's murderer, she flings the letter contemp-tuously on the floor for Leslie to pick up. The gesture is so challenging and is meant to be such a loss of face for the white person who would pick it up that the Chinese in the room (and in the theater) fully enjoy the pleasure. It is almost worth the sale (the price to save her from execution) to see her brought down to the ground. Wyler is too wise to bring her to her knees, an image not only too overt but one that would subordinate the story to the message.

Leslie herself sends a double message. The Eurasian woman is on the higher level, but she is frozen there. That moral pedestal is, in its own way, confining, as corseted as her fitted garment. Despite her de-basement, the white lady has the greater mobility. She steadily meets the gaze of her rival, impressing us that she dare peer into the glare of the dragon, without a flicker. She gracefully stoops to retrieve the scrap of paper; the gentility of the improbable "thank you" she murmurs is quietly assertive. She takes the lead in making eye contact with the lawyer to signal that it is time to make their retreat and leaves with dignity. Though the incriminating document to Hammond may reveal the hysterical crack in her deportment that nearly proved fatal, her con-duct here is almost regal in its aplomb. She has taken charge, if not of the unmanageable Asians, then at least of her own emotion, of her law-yer, and most of all, of the system of colonial justice that he represents. The ambivalence in the representation of the women leads to the viewer reading with and against the grain, at once impressed and appalled, not clearly in either the white colonial position or the native colonized one.

Edward Said states: "The Orient was Orientalized not only because it was discovered to be 'Oriental' in all those ways considered com-monplace by an average nineteenth-century European, but also because it *could be*—that is, submitted to being—*made* Oriental." His example of Orientalization, "Flaubert's encounter with an Egyptian courtesan produced a widely influential model of the Oriental woman," ends with the point that it was Flaubert, "*He* spoke for and represented her."[22] Maugham certainly spoke for Hammond's mistress. She never speaks for herself. Wyler, in calling attention to Maugham's orientalizing, both participates in it and counters it. That is, except for a few barely heard monosyllables of some native tongue—Cantonese? Hakka? Malay?—during the letter-exchange scene, the oriental woman in this film does not speak either. However, she *looks*, looking on, looking furiously, as we do. Again, we are in the position of the colonized.

Said convinced the West of what the East already knew, that the Ori-ent is a Western invention. For Said, Orientalism is the form imperial-ism takes in the "Orient": "Once we begin to think of Orientalism as a kind of Western projection onto and will to govern over the Orient, we will encounter few surprises."²³ What constitutes the superior West (modernity, scientific advances, technical advantages) and what constitutes the inferior "Orient" (superstition, adherence to "tradition," spirituality as wisdom) have a strong foundation in the colonialist quest for wealth and profit. In an inextricable way, the conceptual attitudes of Orientalism/imperialism and the practical, powerful economic sphere of colonialism go hand in hand. The film keeps these issues, linked as they are with skin color, before us.

Though some of us realize that the Chinese themselves were and are colonial masters (today, consider Tibet), the film does not consider the problem. The Chinese were not native to rubber-producing Singapore and the Malay peninsula and Sumatra. They came to these places as economic imperialists, to exploit the natural resources and native labor force, as the Europeans would do later. When Robert Crosbie (Herbert Marshall) speaks of buying a plantation in Sumatra from a Chinese, there is little difference between them except that the Chinese plantation owner is living in a series of plantation houses, explicitly built as separate residences for each of his wives. In one culture polygamy is institutionalized; in the other, there is a need to mask the quest for erotic variety with the puritanical rejection of illicit affairs. Leslie's personal hypocrisy is part of the larger hypocrisy of the West.

The film's racial stance derives from the old epithet that the Chinese were "the Jews of the Orient." Here again, Wyler has some personal stake in this. *Jews* and *Orient* are loaded words. What is meant is that as the Jew was in Europe, so the Chinese was in Asia—shopkeeper, businessman, middleman, the bourgeoisie, the money power base. That is the role of Ong Chi Seng, as Sen Yung plays him, a lesson in how to keep cultural authenticity and charm while flirting with stereotype and caricature. Though Ong is the chief law clerk in a British firm, he arranges the deal, he makes money, he wields surreptitious power. He is the connection to the Chinese world as shown in the exchange of the letter in yet another version of the seedy, dark and lurid, narrow, crooked, and cramped, native quarters. Leslie and her lawyer enter a curio shop selling jeweled daggers that fronts for a backroom where opium is smoked and shady deals are transacted. This is a place where morals can run amok.

It is the partnership of James Stephenson's Howard Joyce and Sen Yung's Ong Chi Seng that steals attention away from the star couple (Bette Davis and Herbert Marshall), especially when the discussion is a political reading of the text. Ong is at the heart of the complexity of the colonial paradigm. Though Maugham concedes that Ong "spoke beautiful English" (184) ". . . had studied law at Gray's Inn" (185), he undercuts the ambitious young man by giving us the white man's condescending point of view: "The elaborate accuracy with which the clerk expressed himself always faintly amused Mr. Joyce" (194), and "he continued to look at Ong Chi Seng with the smile of faint amusement with which he generally talked to him" (195). Wyler lets us root for this Asian version of what makes Sammy run.

In the film, in the words of his white master—employer, if you wish—Ong is "the perfect confidential clerk," but obviously not the perfect partner. "Trouble is, after he's left my business, he'll set up his own office in opposition." Though unstated, it is clear that at some point in the near future, they will not be able to continue to work together. Ong outthinks the white man. He is unfailingly ahead: "I've cancelled the appointment;" "I took the liberty to make a luncheon date for you at the Club." He claims "a mutual friend" persuaded the Eurasian Mrs. Hammond to sell the incriminating letter in order to save his master "a great deal of trouble." When his master asks, "Ong Chi Seng, what are you getting out of this?" he responds disarmingly, "Two thousand dollars and the great satisfaction of being of service to you and our client." Buying the letter suits Ong not merely because of "the great satisfaction of being of service" to his white mentor and that mentor's white client, but also to garner the greater satisfaction of observing the spectacle of white moral superiority crumbling in private and public places, in particular before his majesty's law bench.

Ong is a key character to the way we read the film. To Joyce, he is a very "clever fellow." Remember the old phrase and sometime punch line to jokes, "damned clever these Chinese"? He is pragmatic as the Chinese are reputed to be. The white lawyer, quibbling with his client about whether to buy the letter or not, must say for his own sake as well as that of the white audience, "I'm an honest man" unwilling to "suborn a witness." He must say, "A lawyer has a duty to his profession, to himself." Presumably, Ong has no such nice principles. He sees that the only way to save the client is to buy the letter. Even though the Western man is allowed to be agonized, to be torn between his "higher" principles and his need to win, the film undercuts the honor of Howard Joyce. After his high talk, his client Leslie Crosbie muses, "Poor Robert [her husband]. He's never hurt anyone in his life, he's so good, simple, kind, he trusts me so . . . this will ruin his life." She forces the lawyer to choose between race loyalty and loyalty to Western ethics and justice. Will he let the white man down, even though he knows what this white woman is? No, of course not. Keeping a united front for white Western civilization wins out over truth and principles.

That it is the West against the East is evident in the way Joyce refuses to allow Ong to share his thoughts, much less his motives. When he sees Ong waiting for him in the hallway, he pretends the white woman did not write the letter, pretends he doesn't care whether the letter will be turned over to the prosecutor since it must be a "forgery"; his is a mighty bluff in a game with high stakes. Ong is persistent, runs after him, adroitly dodges a column in his path, pursues him up some steps, through a hallway, down more steps, through the parking lot, never allowing the white man to make the error that would lose his case, that would negate all the practical profits that could accrue, but that would allow him to keep his honor intact, to be true to his high principles.

Ong wears the white suit, the uniform of plantation whites. Certainly, in Maugham's story (as in Fanon's analysis of the assimilated colonial) Ong overdoes his imitation of the West. Like Hammond's Eurasian wife, Ong, indulges in glittering display: "As usual . . . [he] was dressed in the height of local fashion. He wore very shiny patent-leather shoes and gay silk socks." And the ostentatious jewelry, the visible signs of prosperity: "pearl and ruby pin . . . diamond ring . . . gold fountain pen and a gold pencil . . . gold wrist watch." (195) There is malice in Maugham's description of Ong's excess and a hint of his bad taste. Ong is co-opted by the West—at least on his glittering surface. But Ong cannot pass for an English gentleman. In Wyler's scene, after Ong has chased Joyce and persuaded his white employer to do as Ong advises, Joyce drives away in his big car. Wyler makes a witty visual joke that could be interpreted in terms of power: Ong cannot "afford" the noble sentiments indulged in by the wealthy Joyce. The action also pokes fun at the difference: Ong's little car cannot be seen parked between the big cars of white men, but it does come tootling out cheerfully and efficiently. It gets him where he wants to go.

A brief shot at the trial shows Ong looking at Joyce without smiling. He has played the obsequious clerk long enough; he has smiled until his cheeks cracked. He becomes the enigma of the nonsmiling colonial. Now that the white lawyer has betrayed his profession, has committed a criminal offense for which he could be disbarred, what is Ong thinking? At a crucial juncture of his summation before the jury, Joyce falters, pausing an uncomfortably long moment before continuing. When the trial is over, Ong says unctiously to Joyce, "Permit me to congratulate you, sir" (Figure 6). This time, Howard Joyce is unable to reply.

Wyler shows that the white oppressor habitually condescends to the natives he oppresses and often reacts to them with deep aversion. When Crosbie wants to buy an estate in Sumatra from "a Malaccan Chinese in financial difficulty," Joyce advises him, "These Chinese estates are never any good; you know how careless and haphazard they are," to

Figure 6. "Permit me to congratulate you, sir."

which Crosbie replies, "He's very progressive; he's had an European manager." When Joyce is in the Chinese inner sanctum, where he has gone to purchase the letter, he wrinkles up his nose when he says, "The air is very bad. Would you mind opening a window?" The supercilious distaste is barely kept under wraps and reflects the white man's smug self-regard in terms of his own moral superiority. Undoubtedly Joyce disapproved of opium, but it was people like Joyce who made sure that Chinese acquired the drug habit. The unspoken distaste is for the native mise-en scène as well, shimmering bead curtains that tinkle when the dragon lady appears, to sell the letter. Leslie, at the end still jealous and hating her image, bursts out, "That, that native woman. I can't believe it. I wouldn't believe it. With those hideous spangles . . . that chalky painted face, those eyes like a cobra's eyes." She's overdecorated for Leslie's taste, and she is the snake who tempted, and won, the white man Leslie loved.

Wyler's *The Letter* is far from a simple story. Outwardly prim but inwardly passionate, Leslie is a complex source of energy. One could interpret Leslie's obsessive lacework which she finds "soothing," as a sublimation of her sexual energy. When it is not kept in check, it erupts in periodic bouts of erotic straying and even murderous frustration. From the Chinese perspective, they've given Leslie a chance to redeem her honor by suicide. They have carefully placed the dagger outside her bedroom door that leads to the garden. (Though she doesn't see him, there is an interesting shot of the shadow of Head Boy passing by in the reflection of her dressing table mirror.) She could have chosen to kill herself, but instead, she instantly recoils from the weapon at her feet, in a visual echo of Mrs. Hammond recoiling as Leslie stoops to retrieve the letter. Each wishes to avoid the contamination of the Other. When Leslie checks the doorsill a second time, the weapon has vanished, and she seems to have a premonition of her fate as she walks outside the walls. The stuffy, dark interior, the inviting, airy, moonlit outdoors that beckons her but is not her territory, that sheds light on what she wants hidden, are other cues for what will happen. Colonial power, embodied in Leslie Crosbie and Howard Joyce, moves toward self-destruction as the white ruling class slowly loses its sense of values. The walls that the whites erected to keep out the people of color will tumble down, because the walls were not their moral right to make. It was never their country; no wonder they could not trust the Asians, not Ong, not Head Boy, not Mrs. Hammond. They may have seemed complicit, but resistance can spring to life at any moment.

Dyer comments on the "scientific difference between black and white [that he had been taught in primary school] . . . a fascinating paradox. Black, which, because you had to add it to paper to make a picture, I had always thought of as a colour, was, it turned out, nothingness, the absence of all colour; whereas white, which looked just like empty space (or blank paper), was, apparently, all the colours there were put together." He is on the same wavelength with Herman Melville's *Moby Dick* in the chapter "The Whiteness of the Whale": the terror of the blank, the absence, the emptiness of white challenges the mind to fill it with meaning. Dyer's comments also converge with Ralph Ellison's *The Invisible Man*—the black man's work in the paint factory mixing white paint, trying to get the whitest white by dumping in more colors. Though not referring to Melville or Ellison, Dyer is struck by "how the explanations manage to touch on the construction of the ethnic categories of black and white in dominant representation . . . . white is no colour because it is all colours."[24] And therefore "only non-whiteness can give whiteness any substance."[25] This is the crux of Wyler's film: the encounter with the dark Other defines the dark colors that make up the white Self.

Segregation, the setting up of white and/against Other, is part of an early stage in Fanon's analysis of colonialism. But in its counterpart, in the development of the white man's consciousness, integration, the ultimate form of which is miscegenation, is a late phase. The trouble is, this late stage is out of sync, too little too late for the colonized. In the context of Howard Joyce's anxiety about Ong Chi Seng ("Trouble is, after he's left my business, he'll set up his own office in opposition"), Fanon's "fighting phase" has taken on a new dynamic of independence: the threat that the Asian will set up his own economy in opposition to the white has already turned into reality. Today, Singapore, the setting of *The Letter*, is one of the minidragons exemplifying the Pacific Rim economic miracle. Although Wyler showed the colonized as powerless, the film clearly suggests the potential of the oppressed in the colonial paradigm for rebelling against the white man's order and his system of injustice.

## Notes

1. As quoted in Stanley Archer, *W. Somerset Maugham: A Study of the Short Fiction* (New York: Twayne Publishers, 1993), 28.
2. Frantz Fanon, *The Wretched of the Earth* (New York: Grove Press, 1963), 222–223.
3. This is precisely the moment George Orwell so brilliantly captures in his essay "Shooting an Elephant," written in 1936.
4. Complex as history is, still for Faulkner, it was the institution of slavery that brought about the precipitous fall of U.S. civilization, the North completely implicated in the descent, sliding with the South toward decay and corruption.
5. Somerset Maugham, "The Letter," *The Complete Stories* 1 (Garden City, N.Y.: Doubleday, 1953), 184. All other citations are from this edition. Page numbers will be indicated in the text.
6. To be fair, neither Fanon nor Said would laugh at themselves, either; Orwell, though, could see himself as the object of native derision.
7. There is a previous film, *The Letter* (1929), directed by Jean de Limur with Jeanne Eagels as star, whose performance was much admired by Bette Davis, Wyler's star. Like Wyler, Jean de Limur was an expatriate, one of the "French crowd" until he returned to France to make films in 1931. See Axel Madsen, *William Wyler: The Authorized Biography* (New York: Crowell, 1973), 200–201. In the opinion of Michael A. Anderegg, *William Wyler* (Boston: Twayne Publishers, 1979), "De Limur's direction is no better than pedestrian," (95).
8. Among film directors, Ernst Lubitsch, for example. Madsen quotes Wyler as saying, "The Sundays at his [Lubitsch's] house were marvelous. Just being there was a tremendous thing . . . Those people were all older than I . . . I was not a friend, I was invited as a young fellow," and quotes S. N. Behrman that the German colony gathered at Lubitsch's was "like a crowd in Renaissance Florence." Madsen continues: "and most of them, even Bertolt Brecht, ended up in greater Los Angeles. The 'intellectuals' included

Thomas and Heinrich Mann, Lion and Martha Feuchtwanger, Otto Klemp-
erer, Bruno Walter, the Franz Werfels. Actors included occasionally Greta
Garbo . . . Pola Negri, Conrad Veidt, Paul Leni, Paul Stein, Vilma Banky,
and her husband, Rod La Roque, Victor Varconi, and Marlene Dietrich . . .
screenwriters, designers . . . the French crowd." (Madsen, *William Wyler*,
100–101.)

9. Wyler's words, as quoted in Madsen, *William Wyler*, are revealing: "We had
a nice set. The day before we started, I laid out the shot. The camera started
in the jungle, went on to the natives sleeping, showed the rubber trees
dripping and ended on a parrot awakened by the [gun]shot and flying away;
all in one camera movement that took more than two minutes. [It looks
like one long take, but in fact it has been cut in two.] This was the first day
of shooting and since none of this really was in the script, we would end
up with a quarter of a page in the can. You were supposed to do three or
four pages a day. On the first day of shooting, I had one quarter of a page.
Jesus, the whole studio was in an uproar, but it became a famous opening
scene" (203). Anderegg, in his *William Wyler*, tells us that "the average shot-
length for *The Letter* has been calculated at eighteen seconds, as compared
to nine to ten seconds for Wyler's previous films" (98). The overall effect is
leisurely, but edgy, too, since the question of justice is held in suspense,
suggesting the way that natives regarded colonialism.

10. Anderegg, *William Wyler*, 96–97.

11. That the wife is Eurasian is invented by Wyler to accommodate his non-
Chinese actress. Ultimately, it works well, as she is herself, then, a product
of miscegenation.

12. Mrs. Hammond and Head Boy seem to be part of a close-knit unit in the
film, suggesting kinship ties between them. Ong might be peripherally related, too, though he had no part in the killing. Yet, the Hollywood casting
mix, the white actress Gale Sondergaard, the Japanese actor Tetsu Komai,
and the Chinese actor Sen Yung, results in subliminal color blindness.

13. Quoted in Anderegg, *William Wyler*, 97. "No one who has seen [de Limur's
1929] film can ever forget the final scene of Leslie's [Eagels's] verbal attack
on her husband and the plantation life he has condemned her to: the sense
of boredon, frustration, and hatred she brings to the four-times-
repeated word 'rubber' is in itself a lesson in great acting . . . The script . . .
places Leslie Crosbie in a far more sympathetic light" (ibid., 95–96) than
she is shown in Maugham's original or in Howard Koch's script for Wyler.

14. Richard Dyer, *The Matter of Images: Essays on Representations* (London
and New York: Routledge, 1993), 145.

15. Ibid., 157.

16. Ibid., 152.

17. Ibid., 153.

18. James Stephenson, who gave a brilliant performance in this film, died nine
months later of a heart attack (see Madsen, *William Wyler*, 202), which
explains why we are puzzled and disappointed not to remember seeing
him in other roles.

19. It must be noted, however, that it was de Limur who "had the Chinese

woman stipulate that Leslie, herself, must come and barter for the letter" (ibid., 203). Koch was following de Limur's lead.

20. Before *The Letter*, Sen Yung was stereotyped in the role of "Number One Son to Sidney Toler's Charlie Chan," then afterward, he was stereotyped once more "in middle age as cook Hop Sing in the long-running television series 'Bonanza'." See Whitney Stine, *Mother Goddam: The Story of the Career of Bette Davis (With a Running Commentary by Bette Davis)* (New York: Hawthorn Books, 1974), 135.

21. Wyler recalls in the "authorized biography" (he took out a copyright with Madsen): "Gale Sondergaard was very good . . . Today, you would take a Chinese girl, but there weren't any then. Anna May Wong was the only Oriental actress I could have used and she was kind of a sex kitten and too young." (Madsen, *William Wyler*, 203). In 1973, Wyler was aware of the political implications of nonethnic casting.

22. Edward Said, *Orientalism* (New York: Vintage, 1979), 5–6.

23. Ibid., 95.

24. Dyer, *The Matter of Images*, 142.

25. Ibid., 144.

Compiled by Matthew Bernstein

# Orientalism in Film:
# A Select Bibliography

Note: The literature on Orientalism in film is considerable and often overlaps with theories and analyses of colonialism and postcolonialism, race, gender, and ethnicity. The following list comprises English-language books and essays whose primary emphasis is on Orientalism and the question of Orientalism in film. The titles were compiled from bibliographies submitted by contributors to this volume, the *Film/Literature Index* and the "Professional Notes" column in *Cinema Journal* since 1985. For further readings, please consult the end notes to each essay.

## On Orientalism

Ahmed, Leila. *Women and Gender in Islam: Historical Roots of a Modern Debate*. New Haven: Yale University Press, 1992.

Alloula, Malek. *The Colonial Harem*, trans. Myrna Godzich and Wlad Godzich. Minneapolis: University of Minnesota Press, 1986.

Clifford, James. "On Orientalism." In *The Predicament of Culture: Twentieth Century Ethnography, Literature, and Art*. Cambridge, Mass.: Harvard University Press, 1988, 255–276.

Garafola, Lynn. *Art and Enterprise in Diaghilev's Ballets Russes*. New York: Oxford University Press, 1989.

Graham-Brown, Sarah. *Images of Women: The Portrayal of Women in Photography of the Middle East, 1860–1950*. New York: Columbia University Press, 1988.

Kabbani, Rana. *Europe's Myths of Orient*. Bloomington: Indiana University Press, 1986.

Lewis, Reina. *Gendering Orientalism: Race, Femininity, and Representation*. New York: Routledge, 1996.

Lowe, Lisa. *Critical Terrains: French and British Orientalisms*. Ithaca: Cornell University Press, 1991.

MacKenzie, John M. *Orientalism: History, Theory, and the Arts*. New York: Manchester University Press, 1995.

Mani, Lata, and Ruth Frankenberg. "The Challenge of Orientalism." *Economy and Society* 14, no. 2 (1995): 174–192.

Mitchell, Timothy. *Colonizing Egypt*. Cambridge: Cambridge University Press, 1988.

Nochlin, Linda. "The Imaginary Orient." *Art in America* 71, no. 5 (1983): 118–131, 186–191.

Pratt, Louise. *Imperial Eyes: Travel Writing and Transculturation*. New York: Routledge, 1992.

Richardson, Michael. "Enough Said: Reflections on Orientalism." *Anthropology Today* 6, no. 4 (1990): 16–19.

Said, Edward. *Orientalism*. New York: Vintage, 1979.

———. *Covering Islam*. New York: Random House, 1981.

———. "Orientalism Reconsidered." *Cultural Critique* (fall 1985): 89–107. Also in *Race and Class* 27, no. 2 (1985): 1–16.

Sharpe, Jenny. *Allegories of Empire: the Figure of Woman in the Colonial Text*. Minneapolis: University of Minnesota Press, 1993.

Spurr, David. *The Rhetoric of Empire: Colonial Discourse in Journalism, Travel Writing, and Imperial Administration*. Durham: Duke University Press, 1993.

Wollen, Peter. "Fashion/Orientalism/The Body." *New Formations* 6 (spring 1987): 5–33.

## On Orientalism in Film

American Arab Anti-Discrimination Committee. *The Arab in American Cinema: A Century of Otherness*. Washington, D.C. (1989). A supplement to *Cineaste* 17, no. 1.

Bhabha, Homi K. "The Other Question: The Stereotype and Colonial Discourse." *Screen* 24, no. 6 (1983): 18–36.

Browne, Nick. "Orientalism as an Ideological Form: American Film Theory in the Silent Period." *Wide Angle* 11, no. 4 (1989): 23–31.

Dagle, Joan. "Effacing Race: The discourse on gender in 'Diva.'" *PostScript* 10, no. 2 (1991): 26–35.

Donaldson, Laura. "*The King and I* in Uncle Tom's Cabin, or on the Border of the Women's Room." *Cinema Journal* 29, no. 3 (1990): 53–68.

Garrity, Henry A. "Narrative Space in Julien Duvivier's *Pépé le Moko*." *French Review* 65, no. 4 (1992): 623–628.

Griffin, Sean. "The Illusion of 'Identity': Gender and Racial Representation in *Aladdin*." *Animation Journal* 3, no. 4 (1994): 64–73.

Holmlund, Christine Anne. "Displacing Limits of Difference: Gender, Race, and Colonialism in Edward Said and Homi Bhabha's Theoretical Models and Marguerite Duras' Experimental Films." *Quarterly Review of Film and Video* 13, nos. 1–3 (1991): 1–22.

Kahf, Mahja. "The Image of the Muslim Woman in American Cinema: Two Orientalist Fantasy Films." *Cinefocus* 3 (1995): 19–25.

Kaplan, Caren. "'Getting to Know You': Travel, Gender, and the Politics of Representation in *Anna and the King of Siam* and *The King and I*." In Roman De La Campa and E. Ann Kaplan, eds., *Late Imperial Culture*, 33–52. London: Verso, 1995.

Lehman, Peter. "What No Red-Blooded Man Needs Lessons in Doing: Gender and Race in *Tarzan of the Apes*." *Griffithiana* 40–42 (1991): 124–129.

Malkmus, L. "Arabs in Film: Interview with Merzak Allouache." *Framework* 29 (1985): 30–31.

Marchetti, Gina. *Romance and the "Yellow Peril": Race, Sex, and Discursive Strategies in Hollywood Fiction*. Berkeley: University of California Press, 1993.

Michalak, Laurence. *Cruel and Unusual: Negative Images of Arabs in American Popular Culture*. Washington, D.C.: American Arab Anti-Discrimination Committee, n.d.

Naficy, Hamid, and Teshome H. Gabriel, eds. *Otherness and the Media: The Ethnography of the Imagined and the Imaged*. Langhorne, Pa.: Harwood Academic Publishers, 1993. Originally published as *Quarterly Review of Film and Video* 13, nos. 1–3 (1991).

Pike, C. B. "Tales of Empire: The Colonial Film Unit in Africa, 1939–1950." *Afterimage* 17 (summer 1989): 8–9.

Seiter, Ellen. "*The Black Stallion*: A Boy and His Horse." *Jump Cut* 23 (October 1980): 11, 63.

Shaheen, Jack. *The TV Arab*. Bowling Green, Ohio: Bowling Green State University Popular Culture Press, 1985.

———. "The Hollywood Arab." *Journal of Popular Film and Television* 14, no. 4 (1987): 148–157.

———. "My Turn: The Media's Image of Arabs." *Newsweek*, 29 February 1988, 10.

Shohat, Ella. *Israeli Cinema: East/West and the Politics of Representation*. Austin: University of Texas Press, 1989.

———. "Gender in Hollywood's Orient." *Middle East Report* 152 (January-February 1990): 40, 43.

———. "Imaging Terra Incognita: The Disciplinary Gaze of Empire." *Public Culture* 3, no. 2 (1991): 41–70.

Shohat, Ella, and Robert Stam. "The Cinema after Babel: Language, Difference, Power." *Screen* 26, nos. 3–4 (1985): 35–58

———. *Unthinking Eurocentrism: Multiculturalism and The Media*. New York: Routledge, 1994.

Smith, Jack. "The Perfect Filmic Appositeness of Maria Montez." *Film Culture* 27 (1962–1963): 28–32.

Sorlin, Pierre. "The Fanciful Empire: French Feature Films and the Colonies in the 1930s." *French Cultural Studies* 2, no. 5 (1991): 135–151.

Stam, Robert, and Louise Spence. "Colonialism, Racism, and Cinematic Representation." Reprinted in Bill Nichols, ed., *Movies and Methods*, vol. 2, 632–659. Berkeley: University of California Press, 1985.

Studlar, Gaylyn. "Douglas Fairbanks, Thief of the Ballet Russes." In Ellen Goellner and Jacqueline Shea Murphy, eds., *Bodies of the Text: Dance as Theory, Literature as Dance*, 107–124. New Brunswick: Rutgers University Press, 1995.

Webster, Robert. "Notes on French Cinema, Colonialism, Immigration, and Race Relations." *Contemporary French Civilization* 17, no. 2 (1993): 304–311.

White, Susan. "Male Bonding, Hollywood Orientalism, and the Repression of the Feminine in Kubrick's *Full Metal Jacket.*" *Arizona Quarterly* 44, no. 3 (1988): 204–230.

Zimmerman, Patricia R. "Our Trip to Africa: Home Movies as the Eyes of Empire." *Afterimage* 17, no. 8 (1990) 4–7.

# About the Contributors

**Dudley Andrew** is Angelo Bertocci Professor of Critical Studies at the University of Iowa, where he directs the Institute for Cinema and Culture. His most recent book, *Mists of Regret: Culture and Sensibility in Classic French Film*, was published by Princeton University Press in 1995.

**Matthew Bernstein** teaches film studies at Emory University in Atlanta, Georgia. His *Walter Wanger, Hollywood Independent* (University of California Press, 1994) examines, among other things, that producer's sponsorship of cinematic Orientalism in the American film industry. His essays and film reviews have appeared in *Cinema Journal, Film Criticism, Film Quarterly, Journal of Film and Video*, and *Wide Angle*.

**Phebe Shih Chao** was born in Shanghai, China, and was educated at Harvard. She has been on the faculty of Harvard, Bennington, and Peking Universities, and Babson College; she writes on film and literature.

**Mary Hamer** is a fellow of the W.E.B. Du Bois Institute for Afro-American Research, Harvard, and also teaches in Cambridge, United Kingdom. She is the author of *Signs of Cleopatra: History, Politics, Representation* (Routledge, 1993) and *Writing by Numbers: Trollope's Serial Fiction* (Cambridge University Press, 1987); she is working on a study of sculpture and race.

**Marina Heung** is an assistant professor in the Department of English at Baruch College, City University of New York. Her writings on film and Asian-American literature have appeared in journals such as *Cinema Journal, Feminist Studies, Film Criticism, Film Quarterly*, and the *Michigan Quarterly Review*. Her essay on films and videos by Asian-American/Canadian women was published in the anthology *Feminism, Multiculturalism, and the Media: Global Diversities*, edited by Angharad Valdivia (Sage, 1995).

**Antonia Lant** teaches cinema studies at New York University. She is the author of *Blackout: Reinventing Women for Wartime British Cinema* (Princeton University Press, 1991) and several articles on Egyptomania and cinema. She is currently compiling a sourcebook with Ingrid Periz, *Women's Writings on the Cinema: The First Fifty Years*, to be published by Johns Hopkins University Press in 1997.

**Adrienne L. McLean** received her M.F.A. degree as a Meadows Fellow in dance at Southern Methodist University and her Ph.D. degree in film studies and American studies at Emory University.

**Janice Morgan** is associate professor of French at Murray State University in Kentucky, where she teaches French language, literature, culture, and film. Her articles on French film have appeared in *Cinema Journal, Iris*, and the *French Review*; with Colette T. Hall, she edited a critical anthology entitled *Redefining Autobiography in Twentieth-Century Women's Fiction* (Garland Press, 1991).

**Alan Nadel,** professor of literature at Rensselaer Polytechnic Institute in Troy, New York, is the author of *Invisible Criticism: Ralph Ellison and the American Canon* (University of Iowa Press, 1988) and *Flatlining on the Field of Dreams: Cultural Narratives in the Films of President Reagan's America* (Rutgers University Press, 1997). His essay on *The Ten Commandments* as Cold War epic, which won the William Riley Parker Prize for the best essay to appear in *PMLA*, 1993, is part of his book-length study, *Containment Culture: American Narratives, Postmodernism, and the Atomic Age* (Duke University Press, 1995).

**Charles O'Brien** is a Chateaubriand Fellow and assistant professor of film studies at Carleton University in Ottawa, Canada. He has published articles in *Iris, Cinémathèque,* and *Cinema Journal* and is currently conducting research on film sound in France.

**Ella Shohat** is professor of film, cultural studies, and women's studies at Graduate Center, City University of New York, and the coordinator of the cinema studies program at the College of Staten Island, CUNY. She is the author of *Israeli Cinema: East/West and the Politics of Representation* (University of Texas Press, 1989) and the coauthor (with Robert Stam) of *Unthinking Eurocentrism: Multiculturalism and the Media* (Routledge, 1994). On the editorial committee of *Social Text*, she has contributed essays to numerous film, cultural, feminist, and Middle East–related journals and edited books. Her coedited collection *Post/colonialism, Gender and Nation* is forthcoming from the University of Minnesota Press, and she is currently editing a volume of essays and visuals on multicultural feminism to be published by the New Museum and MIT Press.

**Gaylyn Studlar** is professor of film studies and English at the University of Michigan, Ann Arbor, where she also directs the Program in Film and Video Studies. Her latest book is *This Mad Masquerade: Stardom and Masculinity in the Jazz Age* (Columbia University Press, 1996).

# Index